DUTCH ART AND SCOTLAND · A REFLECTION OF TASTE · SPONSORED BY SCOTTISH EQUITABLE

JULIA LLOYD WILLIAMS

Dutch Art and Scotland *A Reflection of Taste*

NATIONAL GALLERY OF SCOTLAND
1992

Published by the Trustees of the National Galleries of Scotland
for the exhibition *Dutch Art and Scotland: A Reflection of Taste*
at the National Gallery of Scotland, 13 August to 18 October 1992

ISBN 0 903598 23 X

Designed and typeset in Adobe Garamond by Dalrymple
Printed in The Netherlands by Lecturis bv

Preface

Our major exhibition in the National Gallery this summer is doubly worthy of note. First of all, it offers our visitors a splendid selection of Dutch paintings by Rembrandt and his contemporaries. Secondly, it chronicles the Scots' collecting of such pictures and makes a major contribution to our national cultural history. In the year in which Britain assumes the Presidency of the European Economic Community it is particularly appropriate that our links with another member nation should be celebrated in this manner. We are deeply grateful that the opening of the exhibition will be graced by the presence of Her Majesty, Queen Beatrix of the Netherlands.

Our gratitude extends, of course, to those whose generosity has made this exhibition possible. Many of the greatest private collections in Scotland have allowed us to borrow some of their incomparable masterpieces, as have the directors and curators of public institutions in Europe and America. We are greatly indebted to them all.

The exhibition has been devised and organised by Julia Lloyd Williams, Assistant Keeper at the National Gallery of Scotland. She has worked with great energy and dedication to bring this ambitious project to its successful conclusion. The accompanying catalogue, most of which has been written by Miss Lloyd Williams, also benefits greatly from the inclusion of distinguished essays from Professor Christopher Smout, Dr Deborah Howard and Dr Lindsay Errington.

Without sponsorship major loan exhibitions such as this one are financially unviable. We readily acknowledge the important contribution of Scottish Equitable in this respect. Their support is all the more appreciated in the present economic climate.

TIMOTHY CLIFFORD *Director, National Galleries of Scotland*

MICHAEL CLARKE *Keeper, National Gallery of Scotland*

Sponsor's Foreword

Scottish Equitable is proud of its origins in Edinburgh and aims to make a positive contribution to the community. This contribution comes primarily from the employment opportunities our success has afforded to so many young people in the Edinburgh area. Support for and sponsorship of the arts is the one other way of demonstrating commitment to the community at large.

Edinburgh has a justifiably worldwide reputation for innovation and quality in the arts and I am therefore delighted that we are able to assist the National Gallery of Scotland in presenting this magnificent exhibition of Dutch Art.

The international theme of this book and the exhibition which it accompanies is particularly relevant and timely. At a time when businesses such as ours are currently looking to extend their international activities, the exhibition reminds us that over the centuries the Scots have always highly prized cultural as well as commercial links with our European neighbours.

I hope you will enjoy the exhibition and the account set out in this book. Scottish Equitable is very proud to be associated with this outstanding cultural event.

C. F. SLEIGH *Chairman, Scottish Equitable*

Acknowledgements

The study of what Sir David Wilkie called 'the splendour of the school of Holland' has placed me in the debt of many:

Marina Aarts, Christopher J. Allan, Lady Ancram, The Duke of Argyll, Dr Pieter Biesboer, Hugh Brigstocke, Brodie of Brodie, Ben Broos, Dr Christopher Brown, The Duke of Buccleuch and Queensberry, Mr F. Carroll, Alan Chong, Sir John and Lady Clerk, Sir William Coats, Mrs T. Cranstoun, Lord Anthony Crichton Stuart, Alex Donald, Carol Dowd, John Drummond, Frederik Duparc, Everett Fahy, Mr A. Fisher, Jacques Foucart, Frances Fowle, Jeroen Giltaij, Ian Gow, Vivien Hamilton, Adrian Le Harivel, Christopher Hartley, Mrs A. Hay, Elspeth Hector, James Holloway, Martin Hopkinson, William Hutton, Raymond Keaveney, Dr Jan Kelch, Fennelies Kiers, Richard Kingszett, Dr J. P. Filedt Kok, Alastair Laing, David Learmont, Dr Walter Liedtke, Louise Lippingcott, Christopher Lloyd, The Marquess of Lothian, Dr Duncan Macmillan, The Earl of Mansfield, Brian McMaster, Dr Jean-Michel Massing, Jennifer Melville, Jos de Meyere, Lynn Ramsay, Chris Riopelle, Joseph Rishell, C. van Rossum, Francis Russell, Peter Schoon, Gary Schwartz, Julian Spalding, Charles Stevenson, Hugh Stevenson, The Duke of Sutherland, Peter C. Sutton, Dr Pieter van Thiel, Dr Duncan Thomson, Julian Treuherz, Professor Richard Verdi, Christiaan Vogelaar, Jean Walsh, Rosemary Watt, Denis Weller, The Earl of Wemyss and March, Arthur Wheelock, Dr Catherine Whistler, Christopher White, Jon Whiteley, Clara Young.

I am deeply grateful to the many public institutions who have lent to the exhibition and also to the private collectors, some of whom wish to remain anonymous, for generously agreeing to part with their paintings for a summer.

I would like to extend my thanks to Professor Christopher Smout, Dr Deborah Howard and Dr Lindsay Errington for their contributions to the catalogue which provide a neccessary and broad context for the collecting of Dutch painting in Scotland. In my research for the catalogue I have benefited from the kindness and help of museum and gallery curators in Europe and America and from the expertise of the staff of the Rijksbureau voor Kunsthistorische Documentatie in The Hague. I also owe a particular vote of thanks to Burton Fredericksen's staff at the Getty Provenance Index in Santa Monica for their help in tracing pictures, especially to Maria Gilbert for her speedy efficiency and helpful information.

Closer to home, the staff of the National Galleries of Scotland have been invaluable. The Keeper, Michael Clarke, has provided unstinted enthusiasm and support as well as advice on demand throughout the long planning of the exhibition; the Registrar's Department (in particular Margaret Mackay) has arranged the transport of the loans and their installation; John Dick and the Conservation department have cleaned some pictures and made condition reports on all; Janis Adams, in collaboration with Lecturis, has organised publication of the catalogue; Deirdre Perth has hunted photographs; Sheila Innes has translated my shaky maths into viable accounts; Peter Fotheringham has overseen the building work; Sheila Scott has expertly typed the essays and, with Sheila MacIntyre, has dealt with the colossal correspondence. The exhibition installation has been efficiently organised by the architects Simpson and Brown.

At Scottish Equitable, who generously decided to sponsor the exhibition, David Berridge and Cheryl Lindsay were unfailingly helpful. I should also like to acknowledge the support of Air UK who have kindly provided the Galleries with flights to Amsterdam and London.

Finally, I am most grateful to the Trustees and Director for providing me with the opportunity to embark on such a project. It has been undertaken with enjoyment.

JULIA LLOYD WILLIAMS *Assistant Keeper*

JULIA LLOYD WILLIAMS

Dutch Art and Scotland

A REFLECTION OF TASTE

In 1893 the Dutch art historian Dr Cornelis Hofstede de Groot made his first visit to Britain, travelling to Scotland in early May. De Groot (1863-1930) had taken up the post of assistant to A. Bredius, director of The Mauritshuis, the Royal Picture Collection at The Hague, in 1861. His journey across the North Sea was undertaken to research entries for a new edition of Baedeker's guidebooks, a series to which he regularly contributed. With the methodical thoroughness for which he was renowned, De Groot visited an astonishing number of places, as well as seeing 24 private collections during his stay in Britain.[1]

A suggestion of De Groot's schedule is given in a letter he wrote in somewhat stilted English to Robert Guy of Pollokshaws, Glasgow, of 7 July 1893:

> *Being back in Holland since nearly 6 weeks, I remember still with great pleasure my trip to Scotland and the kind reception I found there. Having left you on Sunday, May 14th, we saw still that same day Mr Kay's pictures and the Hunterian Museum with its interesting sketch by Rembrandt and its beautiful Ph. de Koning. Next morning Sir John Stirling Maxwell showed us the pictures at Kier and in the afternoon Lord Elgin did the same at Broom Hall. Then we went to Dundee, threw there a look at the few old Dutch pictures in the Museum and visited Rossie Priory. Finally we returned to Edinburgh, from whence Hopetoun House and Gosford Castle were visited … We were very much pleased by all we saw in Scotland: art, nature, towns, bridges and last not least a great many kind people who promoted our own purposes in every way they could. I have written a paper on the Dutch pictures I saw in your country and I will send it to you as soon as printed.*[2]

On 18 September he wrote again to say: 'My article on the Dutch pictures I saw in Scotland is now in the press and the first part will appear in the next number of our own periodical *Oud Holland*'.[3]

The results of Hofstede de Groot's whistle-stop Scottish tour were published in two sections as 'Hollandsche Kunst in Schotland' ('Dutch Art in Scotland'), in *Oud Holland*, the Dutch art history journal. The first section dealt with paintings in public collections and the second with those in private ownership.[4] As well as the collections he had listed in his letter above, De Groot also made notes on paintings in Edinburgh at the Palace of Holyrood House, the National Gallery of Scotland, the Scottish National Portrait Gallery and Arthur Sanderson's collection. In Glasgow he went to the Corporation Art Galleries and saw Arthur Kay's paintings. The other two collections he visited were that of the Duke of Buccleuch at Dalkeith Palace near Edinburgh, and, close by, Newbattle Abbey, then the home of the Marquess of Lothian. De Groot noted which Dutch pictures he thought worthy of mention, listing attributions and his assessment of them.[5]

Other distinguished foreigners had, of course, visited Scottish collections before, the most notable being Gustav Waagen, Director of the Berlin Art Gallery, who published *Art Treasures of Great Britain* in 1854, with a supplement in 1857. However, Hofstede de Groot's articles constituted the first specific survey of Dutch art in Scotland. This was not meant to be comprehensive, but rather a collection of abridged notes prompted by the quantity and quality of Dutch pictures in Scotland and intended for 'those interested in this little-known area'.[6] The collections De Groot visited ranged from those which contained Dutch pictures acquired shortly after they were painted in the seventeenth century, to others which had been formed at the end of the nineteenth century. The lists of Dutch pictures made by De Groot provide an inventory of Scotland's taste for and acquisition of Dutch art.

It was not surprising that Hofstede de Groot should have found so much to interest him on his visit to Scotland. As Professor T. C. Smout shows in his essay on the contact between the Scots and the Dutch, Scotland's trade links with the Low Countries go back well into the Middle Ages. The main contact was initially with the southern Netherlands and it is significant that when the Collegiate Church of the Holy Trinity in Edinburgh wished to commission an altarpiece in the 1470s, it secured the services of one of the most important early Netherlandish masters, Hugo van der Goes (active from *c.*1475-82). *The Trinity Altarpiece* (fig.1) may have been a direct commission from the church's first provost, Edward Bonkil, whose portrait appears on the reverse of the right wing of the altar. In contrast to the rather flat heraldic portraits of James III of Scotland and his queen, Margaret of Denmark, Bonkil's portrait is lively and lifelike. Bonkil's brother, Alexander, was a naturalised citizen of Bruges, where he received James III's ambassador in April 1469. It is possible that Edward may have visited his brother there, perhaps hearing of Van der Goes from him, and he may even have travelled to see Van der Goes to sit for his portrait.[7]

Scottish trade with the Low Countries gradually moved away from the mainly Catholic southern Netherlands under Spanish rule as the cities of Bruges and Antwerp were ousted from their position of supremacy by Amsterdam and Rotterdam. The northern and independent Dutch Republic (the United Provinces) was a more obvious trading partner for Scotland. Both countries' churches ('kirks' and 'kerks' in Scots and Dutch) were predominantly Protestant. The officially recognised and politically favoured religion of the Netherlands was Calvinist Protestantism whose beliefs were shared by the leader of the Reformation in Scotland, John Knox. It was a feature of both countries that this religious outlook was attended by an austere moral tone and a diligent approach to work and commerce. There were also certain similarities in language (particularly lowland Scots) to the extent that when Elizabeth Grant of Rothiemurchus and her family went to Rotterdam (for the express reason that her 'father had always had a passion for Dutch and Flemish paintings, farming, buildings, and politicks'), she remarked that she 'found the low Dutch commonly spoken by no means hard to learn a little of' and was 'very soon able to carry on all of the business of our travelling party so as to be perfectly understood by servants and tradespeople'.[8] Given such cultural common ground and the fact that in fair weather a journey from Dundee or Leith to Rotterdam could take virtually the same time as a trip to London, it is little wonder that goods, people and ideas were ferried backwards and forwards across the North Sea.

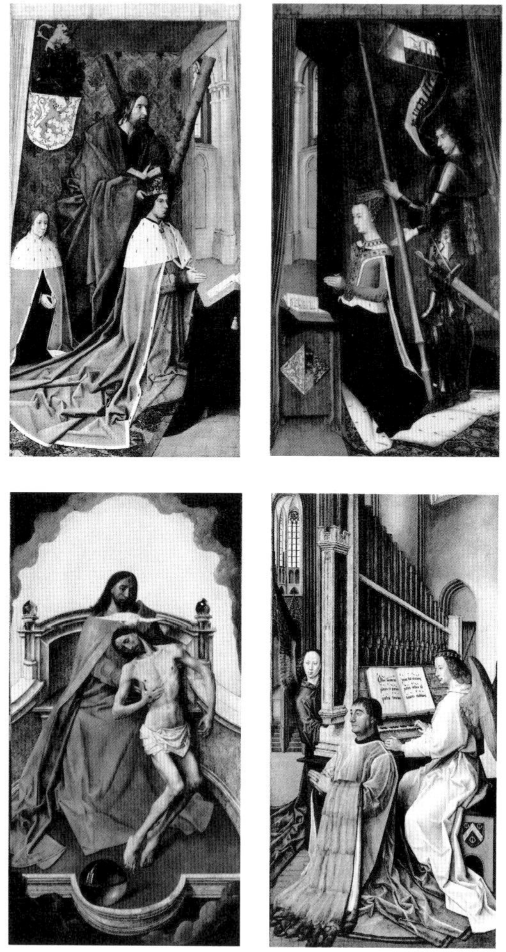

fig.1 *Hugo van der Goes (c.1475-82),* The Trinity Altarpiece. *Left wing: obverse* (above left), *James III, King of Scots, with his son James (?) presented by St Andrew; reverse (below left), the Holy Trinity of the Broken Body. Right wing: obverse (above right), Margaret of Denmark, Queen of Scots, presented by St George (?); reverse* (below right), *Edward Bonkil, with two angels.*
On loan from Her Majesty the Queen to the National Gallery of Scotland since 1931

Some of the first maps of Scotland were published by the Dutch. Timothy Pont, a Scottish minister and an able amateur cartographer, made 36 maps of his country, but had been unable to find a publisher for them. After his death in 1610, his widow sold them to Robert Gordon of Stroloch who later arranged for them to be printed by Johannes Blaeu in Amsterdam in 1654 (fig.23).[9] The 'earliest known view of the Scottish countryside'[10] was also due to a Dutchman, Alexander Keirincx (1500-62), who painted a panel showing *Falkland Palace and the Howe of Fife* (fig.2). The picture was one of a series of ten commissioned by Charles I, recorded in his inventories as 'Two landshapes after ye life being Kings houses of Scotland, done by Carings' and '8 pictures of Kings houses & tounes in Scotland done by Carings', probably painted after 1633, the date of Charles's triumphal entry into Edinburgh.[11] Charles I's court had attracted many Dutch artists to London and, since many Scottish aristocrats divided their time between England and Scotland, the influence of the taste of the English court upon the Scots nobility should not be underestimated. The Duke and Duchess of Lauderdale's 'Green Closet' at Ham House in Richmond (where their grandchildren the 2nd and 3rd Dukes of Argyll grew up) contained over 50 Dutch and Flemish paintings by 1679,[12] while the 1st Duke of Hamilton's position at the English court prompted the commission of his portrait from Daniel Mytens (Catalogue no.37).

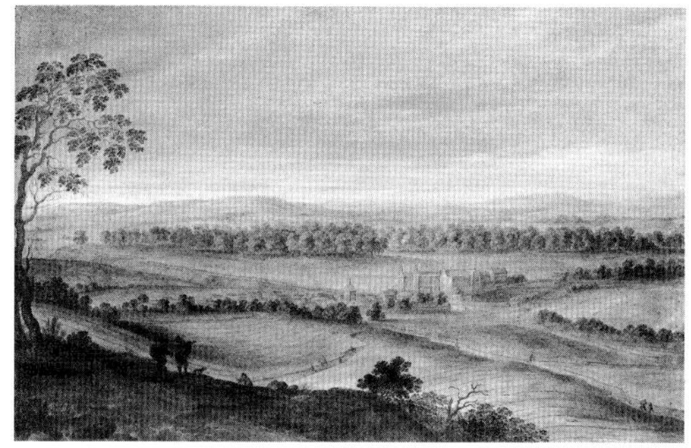

fig.2 *Alexander Keirincx (1500-62)*
Falkland Palace and the Howe of Fife, c.*1633*.
Scottish National Portrait Gallery, Edinburgh

The artists and craftsmen working in Scotland were early intermingled with those whose names sounded far from Scottish. Until the end of the seventeenth century, Scottish portraiture included works by Arnold Bronckhorst, Adrian Vanson and Adam de Colone. De Colone, though born in Scotland, was of Netherlandish parents, and worked in Scotland and England from 1622-8, after which he settled in the Low Countries.[13] Jacob de Wet also came to work in Scotland in conjunction with the architect Sir William Bruce, to decorate the Palace of Holyrood, Glamis Castle and Kellie Castle amongst others (see Catalogue no.73). De Wet knew the carver Jan van Santvoort who arrived in Scotland in 1678 and with whom he worked at Glamis and Kinross. Dutch craftsmen were brought over to work at Thirlestane for the Lauderdales and the Dutch carvers Boyse and Van Nerven were commissioned by the Duke of Queensberry to work at Holyrood.[14] While the Scots painter William Gouw Ferguson left to work in the Netherlands, a Dutch artilleryman, Captain John Slezer, settled in Scotland and was later responsible for a series of engravings of Scotland's main towns in *Theatrum Scotiae* of 1693 (see fig.16).

Scotland's imports not only included Dutch artists but also Dutch art. Some of the earliest information on the shipping of Dutch paintings to Scotland comes from the inventories of the Clerks of Penicuik. John Clerk (1611-74), 1st Laird of Penicuik, was a skilled entrepreneur, running a thriving business shipping goods of almost every conceivable sort from the continent to Scotland. Forming a collection of his own from the 1640s onwards, he fulfilled an undoubted demand in acting as an art dealer (perhaps supplying one of his clients, the Earl of Lothian at Newbattle Abbey). A copy of part of a catalogue of pictures 'sent to Scotland in december-1668' listed 70 works of which at least half were by Dutch or Flemish artists, including paintings by Van Goyen, Abraham Bloemart, Lucas van Leyden, Cornelis van Haarlem, Rembrandt, Cornelis Saftleven, Poelenburgh, Jan Porcellis, Salomon Koninck, Jan Victors, Pieter Codde and Adriaen van Ostade.[15]

Of course, Clerk was not the only person to bring Dutch pictures to Scotland. Research by Professor Smout has found documented instances of paintings sent from the Netherlands between 1669 and 1691 and reveals that the Scottish merchant in Rotterdam, Andrew Russell, certainly exported some pictures to Scotland in 1677 and 1693.[16] One of the most detailed accounts of a Scots commission for Dutch art is in a memorandum for 'Bailie Alexander Brand' from Sir James Dick of Prestonfield House, Edinburgh, which was built in 1687 (fig.3). Dated 30 June 1691, Sir James's letter states:

> *Sir, I doe herewith deliver you Tenn Louidores in Gold to be bestowed upon good hansom Pictures to be bought in flanders or Holland, where you think fittest for hanging of my Staire-Caice of my house at Prestonfield w^h would be in number from Sixteen to Twenty four, as you can have them. Some of them would be large for such particular places on the Staire wch I did lett you see. They would be all without Mullers [frames] for the easy transport Roull them all upon Sticks, least if they be foulded, that may spoile the painting – And after you have bought them, send them in the first ship for Leith, allongst with your owne Goodes, and mark the Box or Case, or matt they are put up in, with D directed for me Lett your choyce runn upon Lively Light coloures and not sadd I remitt the ffancie of ye Pictures to your owne choyce which will oblige.* [17]

Some of the pictures Brand supplied are presumably those which still hang at Prestonfield House. Though Sir James did not specify which artists' work should be purchased, he obviously felt that 'flanders or Holland' pictures were those best suited to adorn his new house built partly in the Dutch style.

The growing tradition of Scottish families such as the Clerks of Penicuik (fig.4), the Lothians of Newbattle Abbey and the Dukes of Argyll sending their young to the Netherlands to study at Dutch universities and to travel there must have encouraged a taste for Dutch paintings, and proof of such a taste can be found in early inventories. Lists of the Duke of Hamilton's paintings [18] show that the newly refurbished apartments at the Palace of Holyrood were hung with a large number of Dutch pictures, including works by Rembrandt (now lost) which were in the collection by 1704. The collections of the Marquess of Lothian and of the Earl of Crawford and Balcarres appear to have contained paintings bought in Holland at an early date, while the Earl of Hopetoun ordered 37 canvases from the Dutch artist Philips Tideman in 1703 to decorate Hopetoun House, newly built for him by Sir William Bruce. These decorative paintings were later accompanied by other Dutch pictures, some inherited from the 2nd Marquess of Annandale.[19] The Dukes of Argyll were also buying Dutch art, the 2nd Duke probably owning Jacob van Ruisdael's *A Wooded Landscape with a Waterfall* (fig.5,

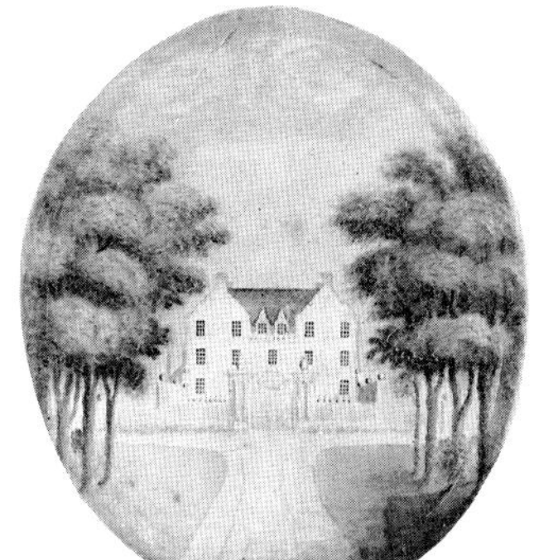

fig.3 Prestonfield House, Edinburgh.
A watercolour of c.*1800 by an anonymous artist, this is the earliest known view of Sir James Dick's house, before the removal of the ornate garden wall and the building of the* porte cochère.
C. Stevenson

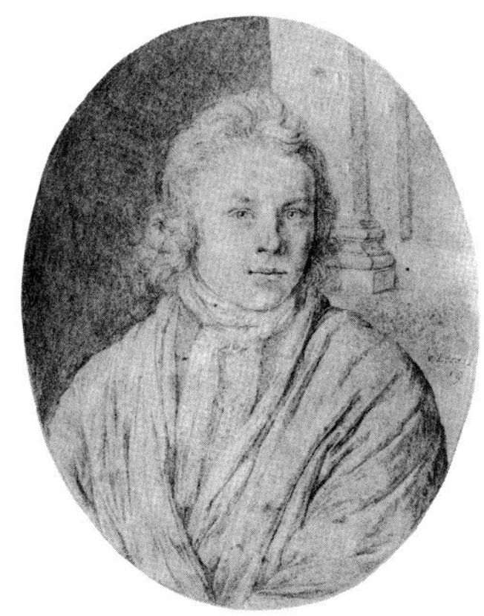

fig.4 *Willem van Mieris (1662-1747)*
John Clerk of Penicuik 3rd Baronet.
This portrait was drawn in 1695 when Sir John Clerk was studying at Leiden University.
The Clerks of Penicuik

later inherited by the Dukes of Buccleuch) at his house at Adderbury. The family also owned Rembrandt's *A Bearded Man in a Cap* (fig.6), which was certainly in the collection before 1781.[20]

By the end of the eighteenth century, Dutch paintings figure on almost every inventory of the major collections in Scotland. This was not a phenomenon peculiar to Scotland, and English collections also reflect such a trend but, interestingly, some of the most outstanding 'English' collections of Dutch art had been formed by Scots, most notably by John, 3rd Earl of Bute (who had gone to Groningen in 1730 and also studied at Leiden University), and by Sir Lawrence Dundas.[21] The demand for works by Rembrandt, Cuyp and Ruisdael was made both north and south of the border, and was catered for by ventures such as that of Lord Kinnaird's partnership to buy the Dutch and Flemish paintings from the collection of the Duke of Orléans, in order to sell them on at a profit in 1793. Whilst Scottish collectors still seem to have acquired Dutch paintings 'at source' from the Netherlands (as, probably, did the 7th Earl of Wemyss, 1725-1808), many pictures were bought in England or found their way to Scottish collections through dynastic alliances (usually involving particularly rich heiresses). Thus the Buccleuch family inherited important Dutch pictures via the daughter of the Duke of Montagu (Catalogue nos 38, 41, 49 and 53). More distant kinships also proved fruitful as when the Marquess of Lothian inherited works from the Gomm collection, and Lady Wantage bequeathed paintings, including Pieter de Hooch's *A Courtyard in Delft* (Catalogue no.25), to the Earl of Crawford and Balcarres.

Scottish collections, like any others, also owe a great deal to serendipity. Dr William Hunter (fig.7) bought the majority of his Dutch pictures, including Rembrandt's *The Entombment of Christ* (Catalogue no.48) and Philips Koninck's *Panoramic Landscape* (fig.8),[22] in London, where he fully intended they should remain in a medical school he wished to found. It was Glasgow's gain that his offer was turned down and his fine collection was bequeathed to the University in 1783. Dutch art also formed the core of the collections of both Glasgow and Edinburgh Universities, the latter bequeathed by Sir James Erskine of Torrie.[23]

Despite the large number of Dutch pictures to be found in Scotland, they were rarely collected in isolation and even collections rich in the Dutch school usually contained fine works by Flemish, Italian, French and British artists, a pattern reflected in the wide range of paintings lent to the first exhibition of Old Masters at the Royal Institution in Edinburgh in 1819.[24] It was also in Edinburgh that Charles Galli decided to auction his Dutch pictures from the Van de Pot collection in 1826, selling Hobbema's *The Avenue at Middelharnis* (fig.9) to James Stuart of Dunearn, who was forced to sell it three years later because of insolvency. (Sir Walter Scott was sent by the Duke of Buccleuch to look at the Hobbema at Stuart's sale in Edinburgh, 9-11 February 1829, but wrote to dissuade the Duke from buying, saying the picture was 'fitter for an artist's studio than a nobleman's collection'.[25] The rate of buying seems to have escalated in Scotland in the early years of the nineteenth century so that by the time of the

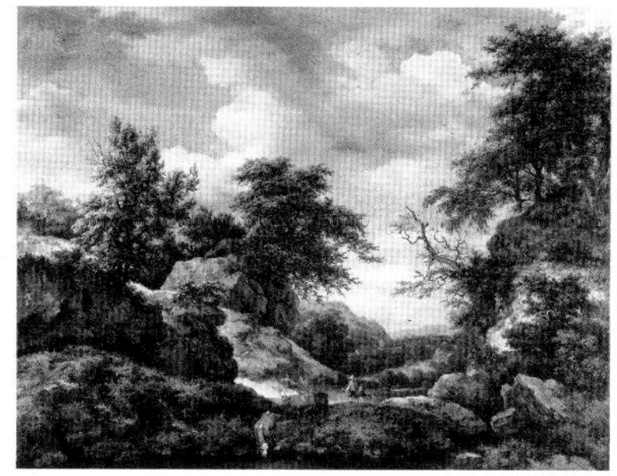

fig.5 *Jacob van Ruisdael (c.1628/29-82),* A Wooded Landscape with a Waterfall, *early 1650s. In the collection of the 2nd Duke of Argyll and inherited by his daughter, mother of the 3rd Duke of Buccleuch. The painting now hangs at Bowhill, near Selkirk, home of the Duke of Buccleuch and Queensberry.*

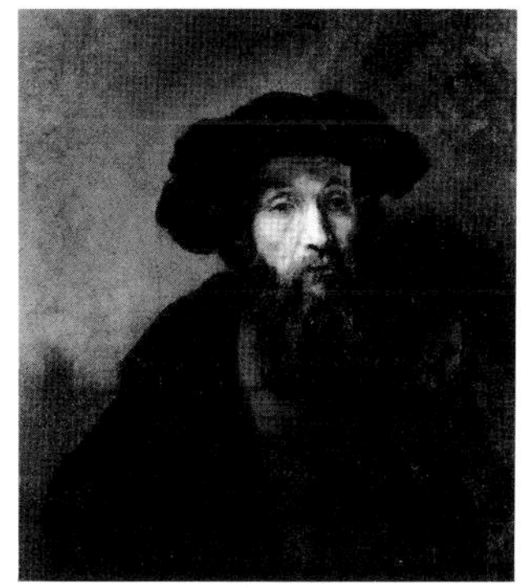

fig.6 *Rembrandt (1606-69),* A Bearded Man in a Cap, *165(7?). Formerly in the collection of the Dukes of Argyll at Inverary Castle, the painting was sold to raise money at auction in 1798.* National Gallery, London

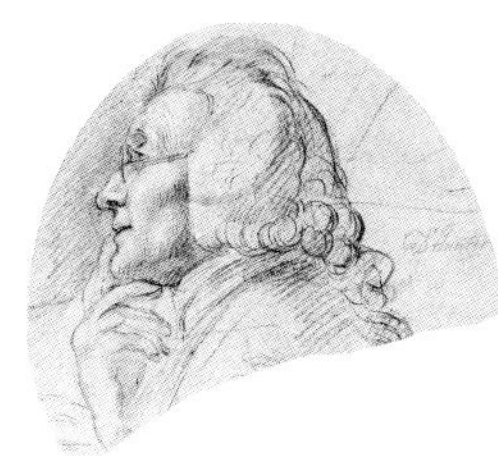

fig.7 *Charles Grignion (1717-1810),* Dr William Hunter, c.*1780. This sketch was made at the Royal Academy, London, when Hunter was sitting for his portrait by Zoffany.* Hunterian Art Gallery, Glasgow

third Royal Institution exhibition in 1826, it was noted that (with a few exceptions): 'the whole of the Fine Works at present exhibited, have been brought to this country so recently as since the establishment of the present Institution' (founded in 1819).[26] By the middle of the century, the cost of Dutch paintings in Britain had risen greatly, driven up by the high prices paid by collectors such as Sir Robert Peel. William Buchanan declared in 1841 that 'they have been run up to a point beyond their *real* value and *must* suffer a depreciation',[27] while in the same year Alexander, Earl of Crawford and Balcarres, remarked that Sir David Wilkie 'in point of moral feeling and purpose was worth the whole broad-bottomed Dutch school lumped together – the Yahoo tribe, I mean, of Teniers, Ostade, Jan Steen etc. – Admirable they are in their way, undoubtedly, but to think of a Lingelbach selling for 5 or 600£ and a Perugino for £200!'.[28]

The Scottish market did not noticeably dwindle as a result of such observations. For those adding to existing collections, and, increasingly towards the end of the nineteenth century, those forming new collections, Dutch painting still had its part to play. Still-lifes, such as the Van de Merck bought for Corehouse in the 1840s (Catalogue no.35), continued to be required for Scottish dining rooms, and Dutch landscapes as well as paintings by Lord Crawford's 'Yahoos' were still acquired and admired. Rembrandt remained the prize of many collections, though with the exception of a very few paintings such as *The Artist in his Studio*, owned by the Earl of Morton at Dalmahoy (fig.10), the Rembrandts collected in Scotland were exclusively portraits. It is significant that the MP and brewer William McEwan regarded the National Gallery of Scotland's collection as incomplete without an example by this artist.[29] Archibald McLellan, John Graham Gilbert and William Euing in Glasgow had earlier set high standards by their gifts to Glasgow Art Gallery, which still contains the largest public collection of Dutch pictures in Scotland, and McEwan presumably decided that the old rivalry between the cities should be honoured, also putting up the money for two portraits by Frans Hals for Edinburgh (Catalogue nos 20 and 21).

The pattern of collecting in Scotland had changed somewhat by the end of the nineteenth century. Scotland's industries were thriving, and Glasgow in particular was full of newly created fortunes and rich businessmen. Perhaps emulating a statement quoted by Sir David Wilkie that 'all collectors begin with Dutch pictures',[30] the industrialists in Scotland who emerged as collectors at this time shared a common interest in the art of the seventeenth-century Netherlands. It is possible that, given the number of Dutch paintings already in Scotland, such art was already partly familiar. It was also, given its everyday realism, comprehensible to someone just starting to buy paintings. However, Dutch art was rarely the sole enthusiasm but was often bought as part of larger collections. Those of Sir William Burrell and W. A. Coats encompassed contemporary art with works by the Hague and the Barbizon schools as well as Scottish painting. It was almost as if Dutch Old Masters provided a revered and respectable base upon which to build, lending weight to the collection of more modern paintings. Often only one or two pictures, preferably by Hals or Rembrandt, were required to

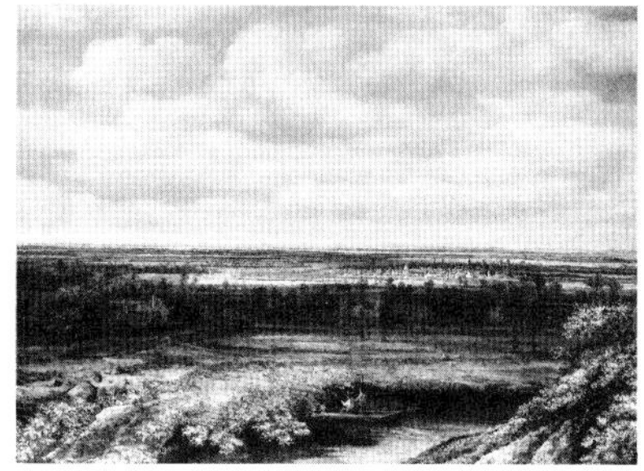

fig.8 *Philips Koninck (1619-88)*
Panoramic Landscape, c.*1665*.
Dr William Hunter bought this painting in 1755, believing it to be by Rembrandt, and though now recognised as the work of Koninck, it remains one of Hunter's most important purchases of Dutch art.
Hunterian Art Gallery, Glasgow

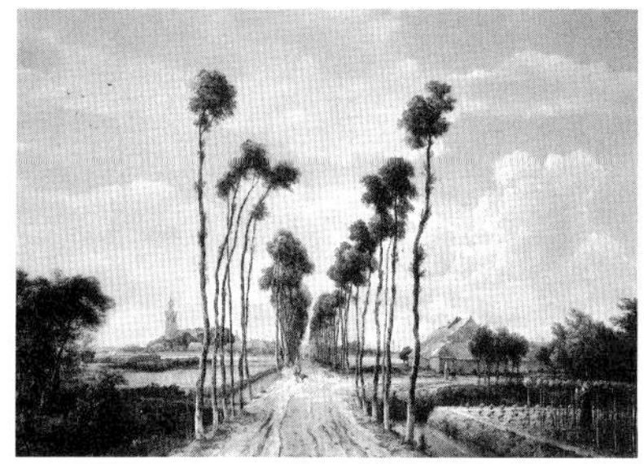

fig.9 *Meindert Hobbema (1638-1709)*
The Avenue at Middelharnis, *1689*.
National Gallery, London

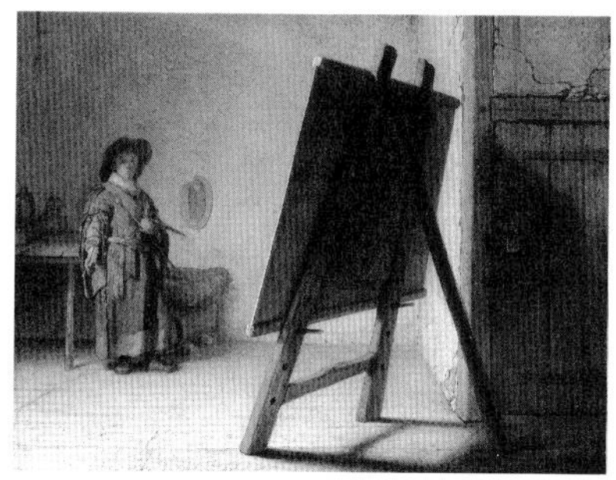

fig.10 *Rembrandt (1606-69),* The Artist in his Studio.
This was bought by the Earl of Morton sometime after January 1773, and remained in his collection at Dalmahoy at Kirknewton, Midlothian, until sold in 1850.
Museum of Fine Arts, Boston

'set the tone', and might be hung, as in the house of Arthur Sanderson (fig.11), in an interior sumptuous with carved wood, Delftware and ornate hangings.

Collections rarely remain static. Though many outstanding Dutch pictures have come to Scotland through centuries of collecting, many have also left. It would be difficult to track down every painting from a particular school to enter a particular country and since Dutch pictures were rarely bought in isolation, such a survey risks misinterpretation. Nevertheless, the great range and high quality of Dutch art that is now or was once in Scotland is undeniable, and it is not unreasonable to suppose that the long-established contact between Scotland and the Netherlands contributed to this. The simplicity of church interiors by Saenredam, or later, Bosboom, so popular in Scotland, might well have appealed to those attending a Scottish kirk. Winter scenes by Avercamp or forested mountains and waterfalls by Ruisdael could have struck a chord of recognition for a Scottish connoisseur. And was the Rembrandt *Self-portrait* (fig.12), found in a Glasgow attic in the 1950s, [31] perhaps one of the many now lost 'Rembrandt heads' to be listed in early Scottish inventories of the Clerk, Hamilton or Argyll collections, brought to Scotland in the seventeenth century?

In conclusion, it may be said that the artistic and cultural links between Scotland and the Netherlands were many and of long standing. Some of them are even rather surprising. The subject of one of the best-loved Scottish pictures, Raeburn's *Reverend Robert Walker Skating on Duddingston Loch* (fig.13), wrote treatises on *Kolf, a Dutch Game*, and *Observations on the National Character of the Dutch* in 1794. Moreover, he had acquired his balletic expertise on ice not on a large pond just outside Edinburgh but on the frozen canals of Holland, where he lived as a child when his father was Minister of the Scots Church at Rotterdam.

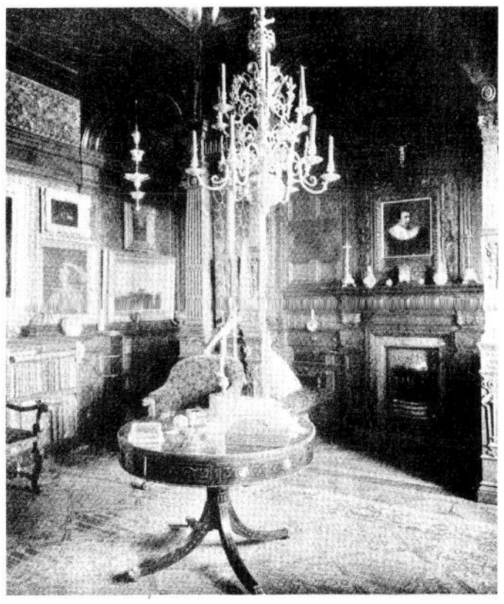

fig.11 25 Learmonth Terrace, Edinburgh.
The library of Arthur Sanderson who owned a Frans Hals now in the Taft Museum, Cincinnati. The library was hung with embossed leather, such as that popular in the Netherlands and Scotland in the seventeenth century. Reprinted from photograph in *The Art Journal*, 1897, p.258

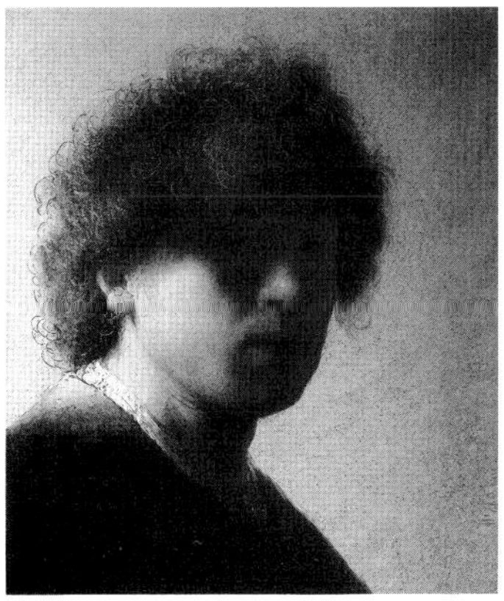

fig.12 *Rembrandt (1606-69),* Self-portrait, *c.1629.*
This belonged to James E. Mackay in Glasgow and was later found in the attic of his granddaughter Mary Winter, wife of a schoolmaster in Bearsden. It had previously been in the collection of Dr Alexander Patterson, a Glasgow surgeon, but its provenance before this is unknown. Rijksmuseum, Amsterdam

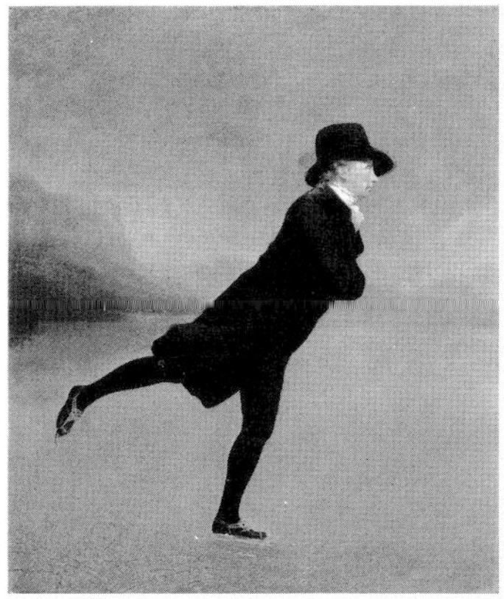

fig.13 *Sir Henry Raeburn (1756-1823)*
The Reverend Robert Walker Skating on Duddingston Loch. *Robert Walker (1755-1808) joined the Skating Society in 1780, and was appointed minister of the Canongate Kirk, Edinburgh, in 1784.* National Gallery of Scotland

1 H. E. van Gelder, 'Dr C. Hofstede de Groot (1863-1930)', *Dutch Drawings from the Collection of Dr C. Hofstede de Groot*, exhibition catalogue (at Groningen Museum), Utrecht, 1967, p.22.

2 Letter no.3105a in National Gallery of Scotland archive.

3 Letter no.3105b in National Gallery of Scotland archive. Robert Guy escorted Hofstede de Groot round Pollok House in Glasgow (in the absence of the owner), as well as showing De Groot his own small collection. When De Groot's sister and brother-in-law, Dr and Mrs W. Postumus Meyes, visited Scotland in July 1893, De Groot (unsuccessfully) tried to organise for them to meet Robert Guy.

4 C. Hofstede de Groot, 'Hollandsche Kunst in Schotland', *Oud Holland*, 1893, XI, 3 (Part 1), pp.129-48, and 4 (Part 2), pp.211-28: quoted throughout catalogue as *HdG 1893*.

5 De Groot also included some early Netherlandish and Flemish works in his survey of Dutch painting, while this exhibition concentrates upon Dutch seventeenth-century painting.

6 *HdG 1893*, p.130: ' … zag ik aldaar zoovele fraaie en interessante schilderijen van onze Hollandsche meesters, dat het mij der moeite waard scheen, mijne aanteekeningen in benknopten vorm aangaande dit nog weinig bekende gebied aan belangstellenden aan te bieden'.

7 C. Thompson and L. Campbell, *Hugo van der Goes and the Trinity Panels in Edinburgh*, Edinburgh, 1974, p.51. (For a full discussion of the possible circumstances of the commission and the import of other works of art from the southern Netherlands to Scotland, see pp.49-54). Also see L. Campbell, 'Edward Bonkil: A Scottish Patron of Hugo van der Goes', *The Burlington Magazine*, CXXVI, 1984, pp.265-74. Hofstede de Groot saw the panels when they were on display at Holyrood (*HdG 1893*, p.135).

8 E. Grant, *Memoirs of a Highland Lady: Elizabeth Grant of Rothiemurchus 1797-1885* (1st edn 1898), Canongate reprint, Edinburgh, 1988, vol. 2, pp.107 and 112. The Grants arrived in Rotterdam in August 1819, having sailed from Leith in a 'common trading vessel, a tub, but with moderate accommodation, the Van Egmont'.

9 *Agnews*, pp.8-9, no.1, from *Joannis Blaeu Theatrum Orbis Terrarum, sive Atlas Novus-Pars Quinta. Amstelaedami Apud Ioannem Blaeu MDCLIV*. For other maps of Scotland published by J. Blaeu, G. Mercator, C. Allard and F. de Wit, see nos 2, 3, 4, 5 and 6.

10 *Dynasty: The Royal House of Stewart*, exhibition catalogue, Scottish National Portrait Gallery and National Museum of Scotland, Edinburgh, 1990, pp.66-7.

11 O. Millar, 'The Inventories and Valuations of the Kings Goods 1649-1651', *The Walpole Society*, vol.XLIII, 1970-2, p.278. Although the inventory states that two were 'from the life', it has been suggested that Keirincx may have painted the landscapes from drawings by Stalbemt, perhaps remaining in London (information from J. Holloway).

12 G. Jackson-Stops, 'The Country House Collector', *Three Eyes*, exhibition at Heim, London, June 1990, p.8.

13 *Dynasty, op. cit.*, p.62. See figs 47, 48, 49, 52 and 70 for examples by Bronckhorst, Vanson and De Colone.

14 J. Cornforth, 'Was there a Scottish Baroque?', *Country Life*, 15 June 1989, pp.185-6.

15 Scottish Record Office, Edinburgh, no.GD18/4653.

16 T. C. Smout, 'The Trade in Dutch Pictures in Post-Restoration Scotland', forthcoming article.

17 Sir Alexander Dick, *Curiosities of a Scots Charta Chest, 1600-1800* (ed. the Hon. Mrs Atholl Forbes), Edinburgh, 1897, p.41. Alexander Brand is the same man mentioned by D. Howard who started the Scottish manufacture of embossed 'Spanish' leather hangings popular in the Netherlands. Prestonfield still has a room of genuine Cordova leather, made in 1676 and brought from Dick's former house in the Lawnmarket, Edinburgh.

18 See Collectors Index.

19 *Ibid.*

20 *Ibid.*

21 *Ibid.*

22 The *Panoramic Landscape* was bought from W. (?) Blackwood in London, who also owned Rembrandt's *A Woman Bathing* (National Gallery, London, no.54). See F. Simpson, 'Dutch Paintings in England before 1760', *The Burlington Magazine*, vol.XCV, February 1953, p.40.

23 See Collectors Index.

24 *Institution for the Encouragement of the Fine Arts in Scotland, First Exhibition of Ancient Pictures*, Edinburgh, 1819. Directors included the Duke of Argyll, the Earls of Wemyss and March, Elgin, Hopetoun, Haddington, Tweedale and Fife and also Sir James Erskine and Sir George Clerk of Penicuik.

25 Scott also remarked that the Duke might 'be reconciled to it' by the presence of a 'shooter and a Spanish pointer who are coming down the road in quest of waterfowl … It is the last thing I would buy from my own taste, yet they seem to think it capital'. Quoted in *Dutch Masters of Landscape*, no.47, p.354.

26 *Royal Institution for the Encouragement of the Fine Arts in Scotland, Third Exhibition of Ancient Pictures*, Edinburgh, 1826, p.6. Further members of the Institution included the Earl of Dalhousie, Lord Eldin, William Brodie of Brodie, Sir Archibald Campbell, Sir Richard Dick of Prestonfield, Thomas Sivright, James Stuart of Dunearn and Francis Grant, as well as the Dukes of Queensberry, Hamilton and Argyll (p.4).

27 H. Brigstocke, *William Buchanan and the Nineteenth-Century Art Trade*, private publication for the Paul Mellon Centre for Studies in British Art, 1982, p.33.

28 *Barker*, p.109. The comments were provoked by the poor prices raised at the sale of Italian paintings in the Lucca Gallery in 1841.

29 For a brief survey of Dutch art in the National Gallery of Scotland, see C. Wright, 'The History of the Dutch and Flemish Collection in the National Gallery of Scotland', *Catalogue of Dutch and Flemish XVIIth Century Old Master Paintings*, Alan Jacobs Gallery, London, 1984.

30 A. Cunningham, *The Life of Sir David Wilkie*, London, 1843, vol.3, p.286. The statement was originally made by Woodburn in Italy.

31 The picture was sold at Sotheby's, London, 27 May 1959. A local newspaper report written two weeks later (clipping in Rijksmuseum file) noted that they 'tried to sell it once before in Scotland but "nobody liked it". For years it hung in the loft, referred to as a Rembrandt by the Winter family "as a joke"'. The family lived in Greenhead Road, Bearsden, Glasgow.

T. C. SMOUT

Scottish-Dutch Contact 1600–1800

Scottish connections with the Low Countries go back deep into the Middle Ages; many of the settlers in Scottish burghs were Flemings, and adventuring feudal families like the Freskins, ancestors of the powerful Murrays, arrived from Flanders in the reign of David I to enjoy grants of land from the Crown.[1] The principal destination of Scottish trade in the thirteenth, fourteenth and fifteenth centuries was Flanders, and the main export was unprocessed wool. The traffic focused on Bruges, where the Scots, alone among European nations, had a quay named for them – the 'Schottendyc'. In a list of 1457, of shipping on the Zwin, the approach to Bruges, some of the biggest vessels were Scottish – the Bishop of St Andrews' great barge, the *Salvator*, 500 tons, another large barge belonging to Robert Barton, 350 tons, yet another barge of 150 tons and a carvel of 140 tons belonging to the Bishop of Aberdeen.[2]

It is clear, however, that the main focus of Scottish contact at this early period was on the southern Low Countries, the area now known as Belgium. A milestone in relations with the northern provinces, the modern Netherlands, was an agreement of 1347 between the merchants of Scotland and the burgesses of Middelburg, in Zealand, to establish a staple in that port: for the next two centuries there was considerable competition between Bruges and Middelburg to secure the Scottish wool trade for themselves, with occasional attempts by Veere (Campheir) and Bergen-op-Zoom to muscle in on the scene. This early contact was not entirely a utilitarian exchange of everyday goods. King James III's aunt had married a son of the Lord of Veere, and in this context Henry van Borselen, in 1474, sent 'a young lion, a royal animal, well tamed', from Veere to the king. In 1497 and 1498 chalices of silver and copper were shipped from Middelburg to St Andrews and Aberdeen.[3] The ledger of Andrew Haliburton, a Scottish merchant settled at Middelburg with the title of 'Conservator of the Scottish privileges in the Low Countries', gives a very vivid picture of the trade of this period, with books, plate, jewels, tombstones, silk, carpets and many apothecary's drugs among the luxury imports.[4]

In 1541 the Scots staple was ultimately fixed at Veere, and thereafter it was the towns of Zealand and Holland rather than those of Flanders that drew Scottish trade.[5] The long Wars of Dutch Independence, the confirmation of the southern Low Countries as Spanish and Catholic but of the north as independent and Protestant, coupled with the decline of Bruges and Antwerp and the rise of Dutch commercial supremacy, quite altered the balance between Belgium and the Netherlands in Scottish eyes. By 1600 it was to the Dutch that Scotland looked in innumerable matters commercial and cultural.

The seventeenth century was a vibrant age in Scottish-Dutch trade. The agreement with Veere declared that certain Scottish exports – principally woollen cloth (raw wool was no longer significant), hides, skins, stockings, salmon and tallow – were to be shipped only to the staple port, where the magistrates agreed to provide a good harbour, with quays and warehouses for the Scots, together with exemption from certain taxes, the right to appoint a Conservator to look after their interests and to build a 'conciergerie', or inn, in the town for their convenience. Veere came to contain a flourishing Scottish community, with its own Scottish kirk, a town well which was donated by the Scots, a Conservator's House and an inn for visiting merchants (fig.14). It remains to this day much as it was in the seventeenth and eighteenth centuries (fig.15). It is interesting to compare it with a late seventeenth-century plate of Dundee, engraved by the Dutch artist John Slezer (fig.16): broadly similar then, with its harbour, warehouses and single dominant tower – vastly different now. In the seventeenth century a boat might sail from Leith or Dundee to Veere, in good winds, in three or four days; in poor weather it could easily take twice the time.

Veere never had anything like a monopoly of Scottish trade. For one thing, the staple regulations were difficult to enforce, and if Scottish merchants thought they could get a better price for their plaiding or sheepskins at another port they were tempted to take them there. For another, coal was never made a staple good; it could be taken anywhere, and coal vessels might easily ship a pack or two of staple goods on the quiet. Middelburg, for one, remained an important destination for the Scots: in one year, from August 1626 to October 1627, out of 66 boats to Zealand, 28 sailed to Veere, but 22 to Middelburg and 16 to Flushing. Particular areas had particular loyalties – all 13 of the Leith boats went to the staple port, but Middelburg and Flushing were serviced that year almost exclusively by boats from Kirkcaldy and Dysart, only one of which went to Veere.[6] The coast of Fife from Culross to Pittenweem was riddled with coal mines supplying fuel to the Netherlands, many of them also associated with salt pans; occasionally the mines were drained or seawater was drawn up to the pans by the Dutch technology of a windmill (fig.17).

In the second half of the seventeenth century the little port of Zierikzee regularly sent its own small ships to Scotland laden with apples and onions, and sold them in the east coast burghs very much as the familiar Bretons did in Edinburgh in the present century.[7] Otherwise Scottish trade to the Netherlands was almost exclusively in Scottish-owned ships. There were few parallels at this period to the great ships listed in 1457, which had been exceptional even then. The average size of a Scottish ship trading to Europe in the later seventeenth century was around 50 tons. Most of them were not built in Scotland but purchased by the Scots in the Netherlands, and resembled the boats shown by Slezer in Dundee in fig.16, or in Van de Cappelle's *Sea Piece: A Calm* (Catalogue no. 12).

From the 1640s onwards it was clear that the harbours of Zealand were all being rapidly eclipsed by the rise of Rotterdam as the main port for Scottish trade. By the 1680s, 85 per cent of boats bound for the Netherlands made for this port. It had many advantages, including accessibility along the waterways of the Maas to the Rhine and the European hinterland, and proximity to the industrial centres of Leiden, Delft and Utrecht. A fast-growing Scottish community persuaded the town council to permit a Scottish kirk to hold services in a warehouse in 1643. It immediately attracted to the congregation not only visiting merchants, skippers and resident factors, but a motley assortment of Scots tradesmen and workmen in

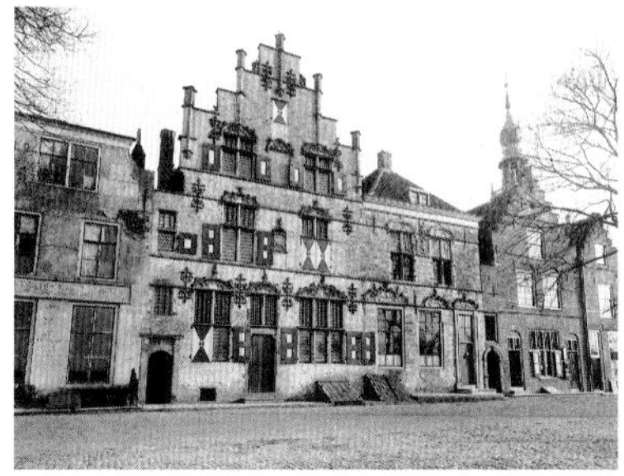

fig. 14 *The Schotse Huis on the quay of the staple port at Veere: the Conservator's House is on the left, the Conciergerie or inn on the right. The carving on the first floor of the latter is thought by some to represent a dodo. The preservation of these houses from destruction was a milestone in the early history of historic building conservation in the Netherlands.*
Rijksdienst v/d Monumentenzorg, the Netherlands

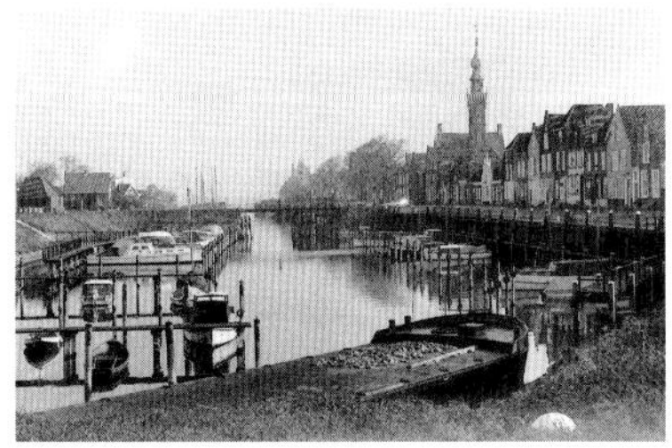

fig. 15 *The harbour at Veere. The tolbooth tower overlooks the 'appointed place within the haven, to loss and to laden the ships' of the Scottish nation.*
Rijksdienst v/d Monumentenzorg, the Netherlands

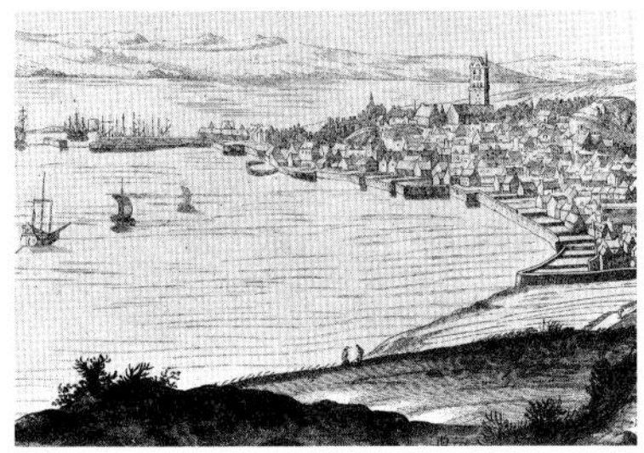

fig. 16 *Dundee engraved by John Slezer in the late seventeenth century. The town crowded round the harbour; the ships were probably Dutch-built, and a good deal of the overseas trade was to the Netherlands. From* Theatrum Scotiae, *London, 1718.* St Andrews University Library

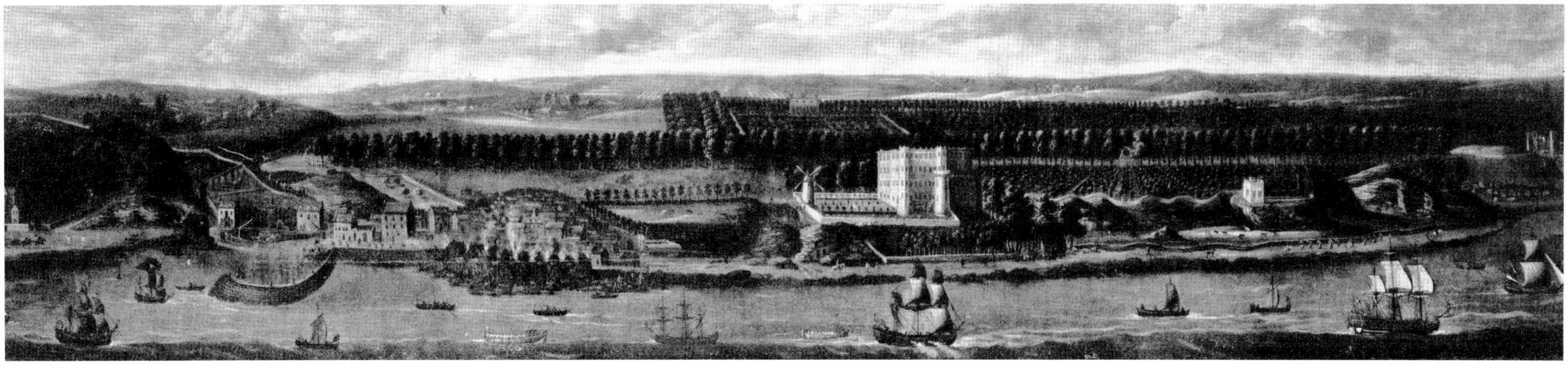

fig. 17 *Jan van Sypen's view of the Fife coast, 1718. This castle was equipped with a windmill pumping water from the coal mines, salt pans and formal plantations – an integrated industrial and domestic project of improvement, very much on the Dutch model.*
Private Collection

breweries, warehouses etc, drawn by high Dutch wages, soldiers serving the Dutch government as mercenaries and sailors working in the Dutch navy and merchant marine. Many thousands of soldiers fought in the 'Scots brigade' in the late sixteenth and the seventeenth century: it had been formed in 1572 during the Dutch struggle against Spain, and was not disbanded as part of the Dutch military establishment until 1782. Many of the sailors, noted the kirk authorities, left for the Greenland whaling in April, 'and when they return in August many of the same persones go to the Southward before the last Sunday of October'.[8] Communion services had to be fixed to accommodate this flow of migrant labour.

By the end of the century, the congregation had moved first to a small church that it shared initially with French Protestants, then in 1697 to a fine purpose-built church provided largely at the city's expense, though built with great quantities of stone provided by boats coming from the Firth of Forth: those of Queensferry, for example, brought the six large stones for the steps, and those of Elie and Pittenweem four stones 'designed for the basements under the pillars'.[9] By this time the congregation had more than 1000 members.[10] The building was blown to smithereens by Nazi bombs in May 1940, but the archives survived and are housed in the strongroom of the present kirk.

We are fortunate to have in the Scottish Record Office in Edinburgh many thousands of letters to one of the leading merchants who was a pillar of this congregation and who also acted as factor for Scottish trade in Rotterdam in the second half of the seventeenth century.[11] Andrew Russell was the son of a merchant burgess of Stirling, and left for Rotterdam after the conclusion of the Second Dutch War in 1668. Though he was back in Scotland during the Third Dutch War (1672-4), he returned immediately afterwards and remained in Rotterdam until 1695; he died in Scotland in 1698. These wars brought trade to a standstill and involved skirmishes between Dutch and Scottish ships, but they were of short duration and involved little long-term ill-feeling between the Dutch and Scots, who were, after all, drawn unwillingly into the conflicts at England's heels.

Russell's letters provide a remarkable insight into the trade between Holland and Scotland.

He had scores of correspondents from right across the Central Belt of Scotland, including many from Ayr and Glasgow who traded out of Bo'ness. From them he received plaiding, stockings, skins and coal, and sent in return an infinite variety of consumer goods and necessities varying from garden seeds and black hats to drugs, linen cloth, whalebone, linseed, industrial equipment and building materials. He traded on his own account and with Dutch and Scottish partners to places as far apart as Boston in New England, Surinam in the West Indies and Sweden. Among his Edinburgh customers was Thomas Robertson, brewer and building speculator,[12] to whom he sent copper vats, pantiles, and grey and black marble building stones – perhaps the same marble that he imported from Öland in Sweden. To the nieces of James McLurg, Dean of Gild, he sent 100 lbs (about 50 kg) of 'caffie berrie' for their coffee house; to the Earl of Leven, Governor of Edinburgh Castle, 10, 000 hawthorn plants, 20 young peach trees and 20 pear trees on a ship for Kirkcaldy. To Robert Douglas, sugar boiler in Leith, he sent equipment and was asked to look out for a skilled Dutch workman to come to Scotland; he was also to seek advice for Robert Mylne, the King's Mason, about suitable Dutch building material (including clinker brick) for making a flat roof. Dr Blackadder wrote to Mrs Russell from Edinburgh speaking with satisfaction of the 'alteration of my state of lyfe' and asking her help in purchasing 'household plenishing which cannot be had in this place; its green and whyte floured droggit of the newest and most fashionable works; its made commonly in Flanders, I suppose in Gaunt: they say that in Rotterdam its understood by the name of Legaturem: my wyfe says she will need four score Scots ells' – about 25 metres.

Russell was involved in the shipment of pictures on a few occasions which occur regularly, though infrequently, in records of seventeenth- and early eighteenth-century trade. A specimen form produced by the customs service to illustrate the new duties imposed on Dutch trade by the Union of 1707, for example, lists in a typical cargo of an imaginary ship 'one Box containing ten Pictures valued at £20' among the linen, silk, whale fins, chocolate, spices, seeds and beer also characteristically imported from Rotterdam.

Compared to Rotterdam and the ports of Zealand, Amsterdam and other northern ports hardly figure at all in commercial records. There is, however, one significant exception, in the shipments of lead from Leith to roof buildings in Amsterdam, and the even more numerous cargoes of lead ore made available for the Delftware factories of northern Holland. The lead came from the Hope mines at Leadhills. It was taken by cart to Biggar, transhipped to other carts for Leith, and the ore then ground in a large windmill constructed by Robert Mylne in 1686 – this mill, long bereft of sails and known since the eighteenth century as the 'Signal Tower', remains a landmark on the Shore of Leith (fig.18). Leadhills ore was used in the Netherlands mixed with tin oxide as the base for the famous 'tin glaze' of the Delftware tiles: in the early eighteenth century, 400 tons a year were being sent under contract to a consortium of Rotterdam merchants.[13]

The Hope connection with the Netherlands was a very personal one, since Sir James

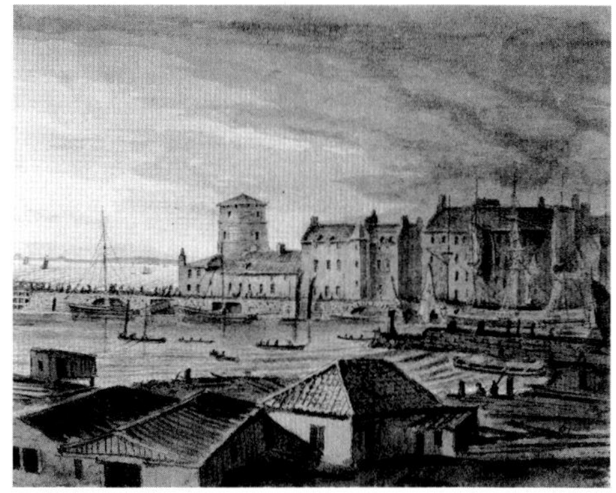

fig.18 *The Shore of Leith, as seen by John Clerk of Eldin in the later eighteenth century. The tower on the left was formerly the windmill used to grind lead ore from Leadhills before shipment to Holland for use in Delftware factories in the glazing process.*
National Gallery of Scotland

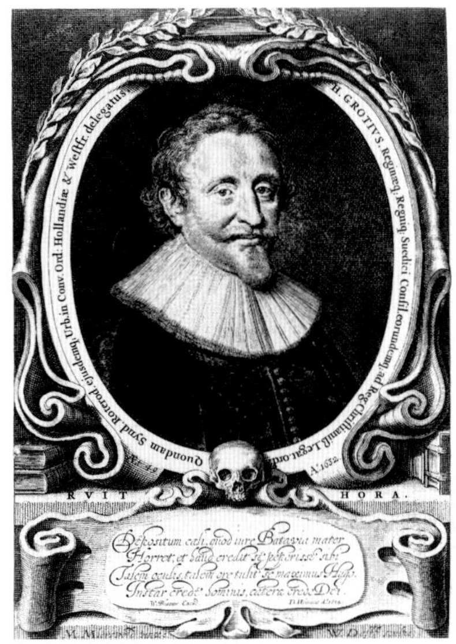

fig.19 *Hugo Grotius (1583-1645), humanist, theologian and lawyer, whose writings had a profound effect on Scottish intellectual life in the seventeenth and eighteenth centuries.*
Bodleian Library, Oxford (fol. B.S. 129 opp. p.1)

Hope, lawyer and politician, who developed Leadhills and whose descendants became Earls of Hopetoun, was a nephew of Henry Hope, who himself had settled in Amsterdam early in the seventeenth century and who also laid the foundation of a famous personal fortune. The family was descended from the Hopes of Craighall in Fife. James visited his business associates across the North Sea, but died in 1661 after catching the 'Flanders fever' on a trip to the Netherlands to look after his lead interests. The Amsterdam Hopes became probably the greatest bankers of the eighteenth-century Netherlands, accumulating incalculable wealth by switching investment from trade to foreign loans, not least the British National Debt. John Hope built himself a splendid house outside Haarlem and filled it with rare pictures: he was part of the court circle of rich financiers, and when the Patriot uprising against the Prince of Orange broke out in 1788 the Hopes were expected to pay for its suppression. On the French invasion of 1795 the family left Holland with the Prince, but they were back again by 1802 helping to finance the Louisiana purchase for the American government. Even at that time it was supposed that the House of Hope controlled assets worth 30 million guilders. They remained at least as much British in outlook as Dutch, one of John's three sons, Thomas, staying behind in Regency London and winning a reputation in Byron's circle as a renowned collector and discriminating connoisseur of art.[14]

The intellectual reverberations of Scottish-Dutch contact spread in all directions in the seventeenth and eighteenth centuries. The two Calvinist societies, for example, had much to offer each other in theology and church government. For a time in the early seventeenth century the divinity schools of the Scottish universities were attractive to Dutch students, at least 25 of whom studied at St Andrews between 1594 and 1623, drawn by the reputation of the famous Presbyterian divine, Andrew Melville, and his successors. The most distinguished of these students was Willem Teellinck, who had a profound influence on Dutch and European Protestantism as one of the founders of Reformed pietism. One St Andrews student died in Veere only a few weeks after defending his theses before Andrew Melville, and was movingly commemorated by a slim volume of Latin poems composed by his teachers and friends, including Melville himself.[15]

Both Scottish and Dutch churchmen shared a lively concern with the central Calvinist doctrine of predestination, espoused by the Dutch theologian Franciscus Gomarus and by Andrew Melville (the two corresponded), but opposed by the great humanist from Delft, Hugo Grotius (fig.19). In the short run, at least, Gomarus had the greater influence on Dutch and Scottish orthodoxy, including that of the Scottish congregation at Rotterdam whose members were made to subscribe to the view that 'Jehovah the Father did, from eternity, choose a certain fixed number of lost undone sinners out of the great mass of fallen mankind to eternal life'.[16] But from the later seventeenth century onwards it was the broad-minded and open heritage of Grotius that gained increasing respect among divines in Scotland, preparing the way for the tolerance of the Enlightenment. At Glasgow University in 1724, for instance,

Gershon Carmichael edited Grotius; his successor at the chair of Moral Philosophy, Francis Hutcheson (Adam Smith's teacher), gave special classes on his *De Veritate Religionis Christianae*, a book which went so far as to assert that the laws of reason would remain valid even if no God existed.[17]

In the seventeenth century, however, Scottish kirks would have had nothing of that. They were distinctly more puritanical than Dutch ones, even in the Netherlands, as demonstrated at Veere in 1643 when the kirk session objected to the arms of the deceased landlady of the Scots inn being erected on a memorial within the church: when it was argued by the lady's relatives that this was commonly allowed in Dutch churches, the session replied that local custom was no good model, or it might be absurdly supposed that magistrates had 'power to erect organs in Church for raysing of the psalms', as had recently happened in several towns in Zealand.[18] Church discipline in the Scots kirk at Rotterdam retained, overseas, quintessential Scottish features, like the custom of sending an elder and a deacon to visit the houses of those who were not at church on Sundays and fast-days. For some reason, however, it was less interested in fornication than the average Scottish congregation but much more concerned about drunkenness. Even one of the ministers and a precentor fell foul of the session on these grounds, but more typical was the case of a poor pensioner in 1684: the 'said Jean [was] so drunk that she had [to] sitt some tyme [and] was not able to go to her owne house so that the said Issobell was necessitate to carey her home upon her back'. Jean was barred from the sacrament and had her pension stopped.[19]

The seventeenth-century Netherlands were a magnet to Scottish clergy out of favour with the government at home. John Forbes, Andrew Melville's exiled friend, was allowed to minister to the English Reformed Church at Middelburg from 1610 to 1621 and later at Delft (it was not uncommon for Scots to serve as ministers to the numerous English congregations in the Netherlands).[20] Another student of Melville's of the same name, John Forbes of Corse, studied at Middelburg and elsewhere, and returned to fill the new chair of Divinity at King's College, Aberdeen; he was the most distinguished of the 'Aberdeen Doctors' attempting to reconcile Presbyterianism with Episcopalianism. His *Instructiones Historico-Theologicae* (1645), like so many Latin works by Scottish scholars, was published in Amsterdam, and won wide acclaim in the Netherlands.[21] Much later, in 1701, King's College tried to tempt Thomas Hoog, previously minister of the Scots kirk at Veere and then at Rotterdam, to take the same chair, but he declined on the grounds that he could not, in war time, force 'a tender and timorous family to adventure upon the merciless fury of the French, who do all they please now at sea'.[22]

In the second half of the century, when Charles II held his court at Breda, James Sharpe, minister of Crail and later Archbishop of St Andrews, visited him to help in the negotiations for his Restoration, and took the opportunity to see the sights in the principal Dutch towns.[23] A few years later, it was Presbyterian refugees who fled from the persecution of Charles II and

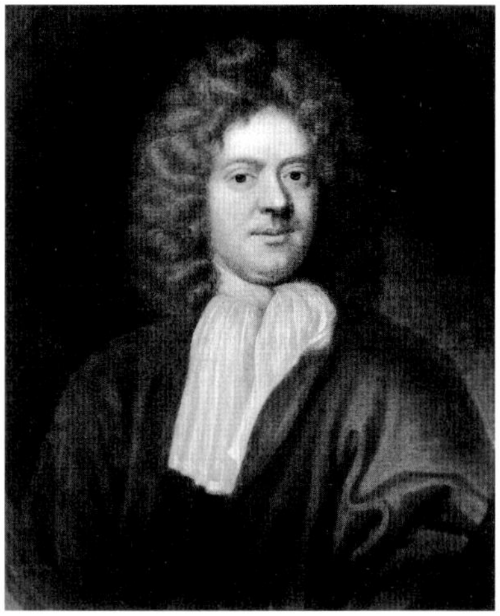

fig.20 *William Carstares (1649-1715), Presbyterian divine, chaplain to William III, architect of the restored Presbyterian kirk and Principal of Edinburgh University, where his academic reforms were partly inspired by Dutch university practice. Artist unknown.*
National Gallery of Scotland

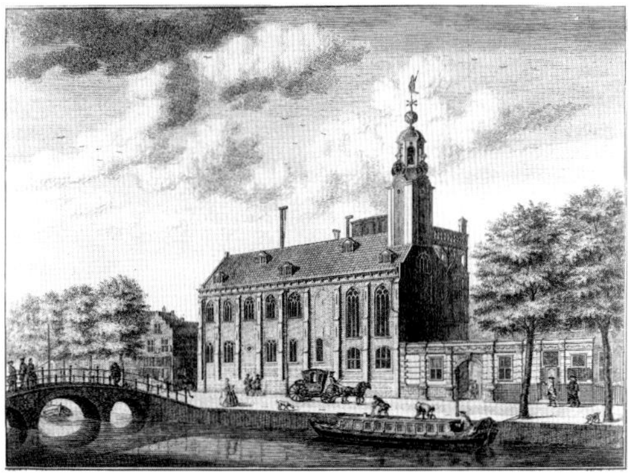

fig.21 *The University of Leiden in the eighteenth century: the Mecca of Scottish students of medicine and law.*
Rijksdienst v/d Monumentenzorg, the Netherlands

his archbishop, escaping to the ever-tolerant Netherlands. One was Richard Cameron, founder of that extreme faction of the Covenanters who refused to be reconciled to the Church of Scotland even after the resumption of Presbyterian rule in 1690. He was ordained in Holland, and one of the officiating clergy was Robert MacWard, the fiery minister of the Scots kirk at Rotterdam at that time. According to tradition, he prophesied as his hands touched Cameron: 'Here is the head of a faithful minister and servant of Jesus Christ who shall lose the same for his Master's interest and it shall be set up before sun and moon, in view of the world'. And so it came to pass. Cameron perished in rebellion at Aird's Moss, and his head was indeed cut off and displayed on spikes in Edinburgh.[24]

A Presbyterian minister of very different stamp was William Carstares (fig.20), the son of another refugee minister, and brother to a substantial merchant in Rotterdam. Carstares was educated as a young man at Leiden, returned to Scotland but was forced to flee back to the Netherlands after being imprisoned and tortured for complicity in the Rye House plot. With Lord Stair the jurist and Andrew Fletcher of Saltoun, he then became one of the group of politicians and intellectuals gathered in exile round the Prince of Orange and his consort, as opposition grew in Scotland to James VII and his Catholic court. Subsequently he refused a call to return to the Netherlands as minister of the Scots kirk at Rotterdam, for he had bigger fish to fry. He became Moderator of the Church of Scotland and architect of that enduring restoration of Presbyterianism that was too moderate for the Cameronians to stomach – too Dutch, perhaps. The same influence of the Netherlands on Carstares could be seen in his rule as Principal of Edinburgh University, when he began a series of reforms in teaching and curricula which aimed to make Edinburgh comparable with leading Dutch universities like Leiden.[25]

The most profound influence of the Netherlands on Scottish intellectual life, however, was found in medicine and in the law. It is impossible to overestimate the importance of the University of Leiden (fig.21) in the history of Scottish medical education.[26] Of the small number of universities in Europe where medical training was available in the seventeenth century, Leiden became by far the most distinguished. Sir Robert Sibbald, the first titular Professor of Physic appointed at Edinburgh in 1685, had studied at Leiden, Paris and Angers; he did not lecture in medicine, but in 1670 he did found the first Edinburgh Botanic Garden after the model of comparable 'physic gardens' in Holland and France. His colleague Archibald Pitcairne was, very briefly, even appointed to a chair of Medicine at Leiden in 1692. The effective foundation of a Faculty of Medicine in Edinburgh University had to wait until 1726, when the first medical school in Britain was established by Alexander Munro and his collaborators with five professors and two extra-mural lecturers, each of whom had matriculated at Leiden between 1718 and 1720 under the illustrious Herman Boerhaave, who taught there between 1701 and 1738 (fig.22). The Edinburgh medical school was a successful organ transplant from Holland. The enthusiasm which George Drummond and the other city

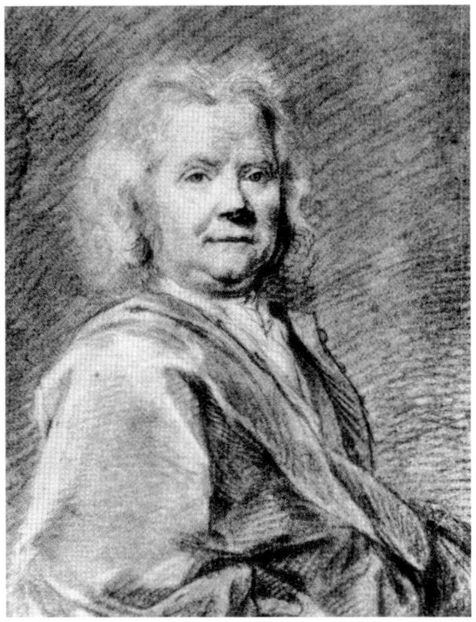

fig.22 *Herman Boerhaave (1668-1738), physician, chemist, botanist and great luminary of the University of Leiden in the early eighteenth century. His students founded the Faculty of Medicine at the University of Edinburgh. Portrait in chalks by Jan Wandelaar.* Medical and Pharmaceutical Museum, Amsterdam

fathers felt for it was based on the belief that it would attract rich students to save Edinburgh from economic decline. The prosperity as well as the learning of Leiden was to be emulated.

The influence of Boerhaave on Scotland was wide and deep. Not only did he teach no fewer than 244 devoted Scottish students at Leiden, but his methods of clinical teaching at St Caecilia's Hospital there were carefully copied for the new Edinburgh Royal Infirmary when it was opened in 1741, and, for many years after his death, his textbooks, the *Institutiones Medicae* and *Aphorismi*, were the standard medical teaching materials in Scotland. And when Edinburgh Botanic Garden fell on hard times, it was pulled together by Charles Alston, who had gone to Leiden to sit at Boerhaave's feet and who was inspired by the master's devotion to the physic garden there. Alston and Boerhaave swapped seeds, the latter writing back in 1720 to his former pupil: 'The agreeable letter which you have sent me demands seeds, but does not specify which kinds you are chiefly anxious to obtain. Ignorant of your wishes, I send a few. I wish they may give satisfaction'.[27] The friendliness of gardeners and the unpompous nature of the Dutch professor speak for themselves.

The life of a Scottish medical student who spent a year at Leiden is illustrated for us by a small packet of letters that passed between Adam Murray in the Netherlands and his brother William at Polmaise in Stirlingshire.[28] He left for Holland in September 1724, and his first letter reports a terrifying voyage from Leith to Rotterdam in a leaky ship that lost its way in a storm and was saved by the chance encounter with a Dutch fishing boat that showed them the way through the shoals off Hellevoetsluis: 'I shall never go to sea again when I can by land'. He made his way to Leiden and to Boerhaave: ' I am now in the most agreeable and I dare say the fittest place in the world for a Student, especially of Physick, our Professor being justly reputed the ablest man alive for such a province'. William suffered from ill health, and next March his brother wrote again saying that he had consulted Boerhaave 'that great oracle in Physick' about his complaints. He enclosed a prescription from the great man, who had recommended ' some other Directions, such as 1. To use the Medicines prescribed for a month. 2. Moderate exercise, but never with a full stomach, that is, let the time for your Exercise be forenoon or Evening, or when you think Dinner pretty well digested. 3. You are to take every day after Dinner 3 or 4 Glasses of good french wine, in order to help on your Digestion. Lastly you are intirely to refrain from chewing of Tobacco ... that vicious Custom'.

Adam then turned to matters more personal to himself. His brother had recommended a marriage with a Scottish heiress, but he preferred his local girl friend: 'My Leiden mistress allows me all freedom, as to turn her o'er, dwell upon her, cast her off, take up with her again, in a word I manage her as I please without the least rebuke; whereas my Heiress, I am affraid, might pout at me sometimes, which my haughty spirit would not brook'. He is honest, but the twentieth century has its own phrase for such a man. In July he wrote for the last time from Leiden. He was intending to come home via Paris, but he summed up his experience in the Netherlands:

I bid adieu to this blessed Land, where I have reap'd so much good. I came as an ignorant into it, and if I know any thing now in Physick I owe it all to a Dutch professor. I had always an inclination to sit with a Book in my hand, but was never taught how to use it. In a word I never read fewer books in a year than I have done this last past, yet have learn'd more these ten months bygone than for 20 years before, the cream of which I have put in writing, and makes six volumes in quart of Annotations upon Mr Boerhaave's two Books … The fatigue as well as the pleasure I have had in my Colleges is inexpressible; but the Toil is now over, and the pleasure lasts.

Could any words have better summarised the appreciation and debt of a student to his *alma mater*?

The number of students studying medicine in the Dutch universities was, however, almost certainly eclipsed by the number studying law. Between 1575 and 1800 no fewer than 1460 Scottish students matriculated at Leiden, of whom 696 (almost half) were law students. The vast majority came between 1650 and 1750, and well over half in the fifty years from 1675 to 1725; and there were also substantial numbers of law students at the universities of Franeker, Groningen and Utrecht. It is remarkable that of the total number of candidates admitted to the Faculty of Advocates between 1660 and 1750, about two-fifths (275 individuals) are known to have studied in the Netherlands.[29] Among these was James Boswell, who went to study law at Utrecht after being advised that its social life was more likely to improve him in culture and manners than that of Leiden.[30] For that manic and bewildered genius, Holland was a mixed experience: initially he fled from Utrecht in a panic of depression back to his friends in Rotterdam, returned and undertook a course of private study which involved hearing only one course of law lectures at the university, fell in and out of love. His friend George Dempster's advice was to 'amuse yourself in acquiring the French, keeping a journal and writing your friends, and debauching a Dutch girl'. The last temptation he largely, and rather uncharacteristically, resisted. But other Dutch habits he acquired:

With same ease that blackguards feed on tripe
Have I, James Boswell, learnt to smoke a pipe:
For I am now a very Dutchman grown
As all at Utrecht cannot fail to own.[31]

The general appeal of the Netherlands to Scottish law students is not hard to explain: Scots law rests substantially on Roman law, and 'as the Dutch were the great masters of Roman law, it was usual for young men preparing for the Scots bar to complete their education in Holland'.[32] The exact influence of Dutch jurists and teachers on Scots law and the legal profession is difficult to delineate. William Welwood, active as an academic in St Andrews in the last quarter of the sixteenth century, published law books in Leiden and Middelburg, partly to avoid the attention of the Scottish Privy Council, as he was at that time a radical Presbyterian and ally of Andrew Melville.[33] He had an interest in maritime law, and as a reply to Grotius' treatise on the freedom of the seas in 1609, he published in 1615-16 an assertion of the British Crown's territorial supremacy over offshore waters, which itself elicited a response from Grotius, and later from Dirck Graswinckel. All were special pleading, of course: Blaeu's map of Shetland (fig.23), published in Amsterdam in 1654 from Scottish surveys, was adorned with pictures of the Dutch herring fleet fishing just off shore, with a Latin inscription explaining that the catch was distributed all over Europe – a decoration that was also a political statement.

The greatest of all Scots jurists, James Dalrymple, Viscount Stair, was in the Netherlands in 1649 and again in 1650 to negotiate with Charles II at Breda; he was obliged to flee to Holland from the same monarch's government in 1682, just after he had finished his *Institutions*. On his third visit he enrolled (with his sons) as a very mature student (aged 63) at the University of Leiden – and then sailed back to Britain in the entourage of William III in 1688. In his codification of Scots law, he was 'strongly influenced in method and arrangement by Roman law', apparently mediated by the Dutch writers, especially Hugo Grotius and Petrus Gudelinus.[34] From Grotius' natural law, he however dissented in fundamentals, maintaining that a rational theory of law cannot be independent of theology, as law was, to Stair, founded primarily on the will of God. It is interesting that the leading Dutch lawyer of the next generation at Leiden, Johannes Voet, had no interest in Stair but was intrigued by the *Jus Feudale* of Sir Thomas Craig of Riccarton, first published in 1655.[35]

Considering the seminal importance of clergy, doctors and lawyers, we may regard Boerhaave and Grotius as founding fathers of the Scottish Enlightenment. Intellectual contacts were not, moreover, restricted to the universities. In commerce, for example, it was commonplace in the late seventeenth and early eighteenth centuries for merchants at home to apprentice their sons to Scottish merchants resident in the Netherlands, like Andrew Russell at Rotterdam, or to send them to one of the Dutch commercial 'schools' at Rotterdam, Amsterdam and Dordrecht, where the skills of cyphering, accounting and languages were taught.[36] Scots also sought technical help in the Netherlands, either by inviting Dutch workers to Scotland to impart their skills (such as the sugar boilers brought to Leith and Glasgow in the 1670s), or by sending workers over to the Low Countries to learn industrial secrets, such as the Meikles of East Lothian who were sent over by Andrew Fletcher of Saltoun to learn more about Dutch milling processes.[37]

By the third quarter of the eighteenth century, the intensity of Scottish-Dutch contact had greatly slackened – partly because Scottish universities had so greatly improved their standing that it was Edinburgh and not Leiden which now proved a model to the rest of Europe in medicine, philosophy and law, and partly because the economic and technological power of Scotland was on the rise as that of the Netherlands waned. The outbreak of the Fourth Dutch War in 1780, civil disturbance, French invasion in 1793 and the ensuing Napoleonic interlude choked off contact between the two countries for a generation.

It would nevertheless be quite wrong to suppose that Scots then totally lost interest in the

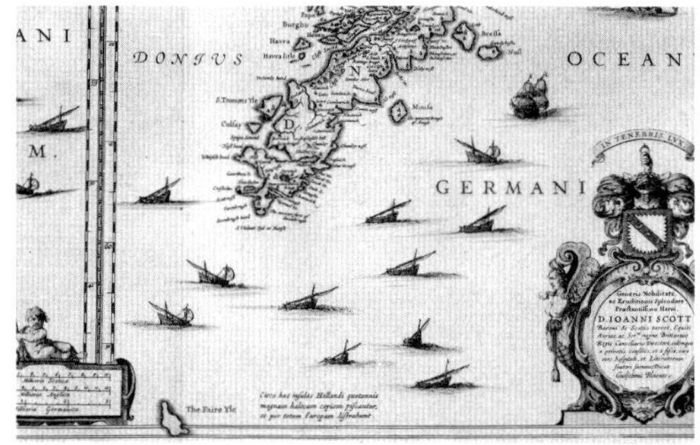

fig.23 *Blaeu's* Atlas of the World *of 1654 contained many maps supplied to him by correspondents in Scotland and worked up in the Netherlands. This plate, dedicated to John Scott of Scotstarvit, humanist and scholar in Fife, shows Shetland with Dutch fishing boats: 'Round these isles the Dutch catch each year great quantities of herring and distribute them throughout the whole of Europe'. From* Theatrum Orbis Terrarum, *Amsterdam, 1649-54.*
St Andrews University Library

Netherlands. Nineteenth-century businessmen, especially shipbuilders, were concerned in Dutch markets, and also were involved in a reverse flow of technology, now assisting the Dutch to establish within the Netherlands the steam and iron shipbuilding pioneered on Clydeside,[38] especially after the invention from 1864 onwards of B. J. Tideman, an expert from the Dutch Ministry of Defence. This resulted in naval vessels being constructed for the Netherlands by Lairds in Birkenhead and Napier in Glasgow: there were also connections with Denny of Dumbarton, and very important ones between the Dutch National Steamship Company trading to Java, SMN, and John Elder and Sons, who built all the vessels for this company between 1870 and 1895. The firm of Elders was also involved, with others, in Dutch dry dock construction. Many Dutch students, too, came over to the Clyde to study their craft. This is a large and little-explored subject, but certainly not without importance in the history of Scottish collection of Dutch pictures. Many of the men in the clubs and drawing rooms of Victorian Glasgow and Edinburgh had, like their great-grandfathers, travelled in the Netherlands and seen in its own setting the art that they coveted.

Finally, there can hardly be any doubt that Scots who found themselves in the Netherlands, whatever the century, found themselves generally in agreeable company. The ties of commerce, religion and academe were strong enough in themselves to ensure that. There was also the mysterious tie of that game called in Scotland 'golf' and in the Netherlands 'kolf' or 'het kolven'.[39] They were not the same, or maybe we should say they were not always the same. Golf is of considerable antiquity in Scotland; the first mention of it is in 1457, and it was clearly a popular sport in the later fifteenth century when, like 'futeball', it was on three occasions forbidden to the king's lieges as a distraction from archery practice; it always seems to have been associated with sandy links and the hitting, with a club, of a small ball stuffed with feathers, into a hole in the ground. 'Kolf', at least as old, was also played with a similar ball and club, but seems to have taken place both on land and on ice. A page from a Flemish book of hours executed in Bruges early in the sixteenth century shows three players (and what looks like a clubhouse) apparently at a putting green, hitting the ball into a hole in the turf with a small club. Other illustrations, notably by Adriaen van de Velde, in a painting of 1668, and on Delft tiles, show kolf being played in a winter landscape, the target being an upright stake driven into the ice, as is also seen in Aert van der Neer's *Moonlight Winter Scene on a Frozen Canal* (Catalogue no. 39)). As there are also seventeenth-century Dutch pictures of kolf on land, it seems a reasonable surmise that in the Netherlands it was played on land in summer and on ice in winter; in Scotland always on the land as the climate was more open in winter. Most eloquent of all the connections between the two games are linguistic terms. A Dutch exponent of 'kolf' drove off from a small heap, 'tuitje' (pronounced 'toytee'); a hole in Dutch is 'put'; and the Dutch for 'it stops me' is 'stuit my' – pronounced 'stytmy', very close to 'stymie'. Can we doubt that when Dutch students came to St Andrews, and the Scottish students went to Leiden, each was fairly familiar with the rules of the game of the other?[40]

1 G. W. S. Barrow, *Kingship and Unity: Scotland 1000-1306*, London, 1981, pp.36, 47, 52-3; W. C. Dickinson, *Scotland from the Earliest Times to 1603*, London, 1961, p.113.

2 A. W. K. Stevenson, *Trade between Scotland and the Low Countries in the Later Middle Ages*, unpublished Ph D thesis, Aberdeen University, 1982.

3 M. P. Rooseboom, *The Scottish Staple in the Netherlands*, The Hague, 1910, pp.20, cvi.

4 C. Innes, ed. , *The Ledger of Andrew Halyburton, 1492-1502*, Edinburgh, 1867.

5 J. Davidson and A. Gray, *The Scottish Staple at Veere*, London, 1909; Rooseboom, *op. cit.* See also E. J. Courthope, ed. , *The Journal of Thomas Cunningham of Campvere*, 1640-1654, Scottish History Society, 1928.

6 Rooseboom, *op. cit.*, pp.190, 193, 224.

7 T. C. Smout, *Scottish Trade on the Eve of Union, 1660-1707*, Edinburgh, 1963, pp.190, 193, 224.

8 J. Morrison, *Scots on the Dijk*, Castle Douglas, 1981, p.7. For the soldiers, see J. Ferguson, ed. , *Papers illustrating the history of the Scots Brigade in the service of the United Netherlands*, 3 vols, Scottish History Society, 1899-1901.

9 Morrison, *op. cit.*, p.29.

10 W. Steven, *The History of the Scottish Church in Rotterdam*, Edinburgh, 1832, p.123.

11 Scottish Record Office, RH15/106 and GD1/885. They are well indexed. See also Smout, *op. cit.*, pp.99-115; D. M. Abbott, 'The family of Andrew Russell', *Scottish Genealogist*, vol. 37, 1990, pp.18-19.

12 H. Armet, '"All the Statelie Buildings of Thomas Robertson", a building speculator of the seventeenth century', and 'Notes on rebuilding Edinburgh in the last quarter of the seventeenth century', *Book of the Old Edinburgh Club*, vols 24 and 29.

13 Many papers in the Hopetoun House archives relate to this trade – see for example the contracts and letters with Van Hoegt and partners, 1641-52. Van Hoegt, a Middelburg man, was personally shown over the mines at Leadhills. The mill's function is incorrectly described in J. Gifford, C. McWilliam and D. Walker, *The Buildings of Scotland: Edinburgh*, London, 1984, p.472, where it is said to be 'for making rape-seed oil' – presumably a mistranscription of 'oil' for 'ore'.

14 *DNB*, vol. 27, London, 1891, pp.315, 325-8; S. Schama, *Patriots and Liberators: Revolution in the Netherlands, 1780-1813*, London, 1977, pp.35, 167, 433, 690; C. Wilson, *Anglo-Dutch Commerce and Finance in the Eighteenth Century*, Cambridge, 1941, pp.66-9.

15 J. K. Cameron, 'Some students from the Netherlands at the University of St. Andrews in the late sixteenth and early seventeenth centuries', in C. G. F. de Jong and J. van Sluis, eds, *Gericht Verleden: Kerkhistorische opstellen aangeboden aan prof. dr. W. Nijenhuls ter gelegenheld van zijn vijfenzevent igste verjaardag*, Leiden, 1991.

16 Morrison, *op. cit.*, p.50.

17 J. Clive, 'The social background of the Scottish Renaissance', in N. T. Phillipson and R. Mitchison, eds, *Scotland in the Age of Improvement*, Edinburgh, 1970, pp.230-3.

18 Davidson and Gray, *op. cit.*, pp.294-5.

19 Records of the Scottish Church at Rotterdam: consistory minutes, 17 February 1684.

20 At Pencaitland Church there is a wall tablet to Katherine Forbes, d. 1639, inscribed 'Daughter to Mr Jo: Forbes Minister to the English Merchant Adventurers at delf'. C. McWilliam, *The Buildings of Scotland: Lothian*, London, 1978, pp.377-8. There is a biography in Dutch – C. G. F. de Jong, *John Forbes (ca. 1568-1634)*, Rijksuniversiteit Groningen: Doctoral Dissertation, 1987.

21 J. K. Cameron, 'The Renaissance Tradition in the Reformed Church of Scotland', in D. Baker, ed. , *Renaissance and Renewal in Christian History, being Studies in Church History*, vol. 14, 1977, pp.260-2.

22 Davidson and Gray, *op. cit.*, p.308. Perhaps Hoog did not like the prospect of academic life anyway, as he later declined the offer of a Dutch chair, and remained in the Scots kirk at Rotterdam until his death in 1723.

23 J. Buckroyd, *Church and State in Scotland, 1660-1681*, Edinburgh, 1980, p.22. Sharpe himself lies in St Andrews in a tomb imported from the Netherlands, with a vivid relief showing his assassination at Magus Muir by covenanting fanatics in 1679.

24 Morrison, *op. cit.*, pp.8-9.

25 A. I. Dunlop, *William Carstares*, Edinburgh, 1967.

26 G. A. Lindeboom, *Herman Boerhaave: the Man and his Work*, London, 1968; E. A. Underwood, *Boerhaave's Men*, Edinburgh, 1977.

27 H. R. Fletcher and W. H. Brown, *The Royal Botanic Garden Edinburgh 1670-1970*, Edinburgh, 1970, p.41.

28 Central Regional Archives GD189/2/44, 44a, 46, 51, 58.

29 R. Feenstra, 'Scottish-Dutch legal relations in the seventeenth and eighteenth centuries', in T. C. Smout, ed. , *Scotland and Europe, 1200-1850*, Edinburgh, 1986, pp.130-3.

30 F. R. Pottle, *James Boswell: the Earlier Years, 1740-1769*, London, 1966, pp.123-45; F. R. Pottle, *Boswell in Holland, 1763-1764*, Yale, 1952.

31 Pottle, *Boswell in Holland*, p.122.

32 *Ibid.* , p.2.

33 D. M. Walker, *The Scottish Jurists*, Edinburgh, 1985, pp.84-6; T. W. Fulton, *The Sovereignty of the Sea*, Edinburgh, 1911, esp. pp.343, 412.

34 Walker, *op. cit.*, p.123.

35 Feenstra, *op. cit.*, p.133.

36 T. M. Devine, 'The Merchant Class of the Larger Scottish Towns in the Seventeenth and Early Eighteenth Centuries', in G. Gordon and B. Dicks, eds, *Scottish Urban History*, Aberdeen, 1983, p.96.

37 J. E. Handley, *Scottish Farming in the Eighteenth Century*, London, 1953, pp.217-8.

38 This paragraph is based on information kindly supplied *in litt.* by Dr J. M. Dirkzwager, who has two publications on the subject: J. M. Dirkzwager, *Dr B. J. Tideman 1834-1883, Grondlegger van de moderne scheepsbouw in Nederland*, Leiden, 1970; J. M. Dirkzwager, 'Om het bestaarsrecht. Over de levensvatbaarheid van de Koninklijke Maatschappij "De Schelde" in de beginjaren van haar bestaan', *Zeeuws Tijdschrift*, 75-1 jaargang, 25, nummer 1. See also M. G. de Boer, *Geschiedenis der Amsterdamsche Stoomvaart*, 1921.

39 G. Campbell, 'The early history of British golf', in B. Darwin et al., *A History of Golf in Britain*, London, 1952, pp.46-50. It is hard to agree, however, with the author's claim that Adriaen van de Velde's picture includes 'two unmistakeable Scots'.

40 I have incurred many debts in writing this essay, but particular thanks must go to Julia Lloyd Williams, Deborah Howard, J. K. Cameron, John Brims and Michael Moss.

DEBORAH HOWARD

Dutch Influence on Scottish Architecture

IN THE SIXTEENTH, SEVENTEENTH AND EARLY EIGHTEENTH CENTURIES

It is exceedingly populous, full of stately houses, and large handsome streets; particularly it has four very good streets, with a large market place in the middle ... The inhabitants here appear like gentlemen, as well as men of business, and yet are real merchants too ... [The town and the harbour] are join'd by a causeway or walk, well pav'd with flat freestone ... and rows of trees are planted on either side of the walk which make it very agreeable. On one part of this walk are very good warehouses for merchandises, especially for heavy goods; and also granaries for corn ... and these being near the harbour are convenient, as well for the housing of goods, when landed, as for the easy shipping off what lies for exportation.

Reading this account by an early eighteenth-century English traveller one is quickly spirited away to a Dutch seaport – Hoorn, for instance, or Haarlem, or Dordrecht. Yet this is no Zuyderzee emporium; the extract is from Daniel Defoe's description of Dundee! (fig.16).[1]

Holland and Scotland might at first sight seem worlds apart. While much of Scotland is rugged and mountainous, Holland's terrain consists of sandy heaths and low-lying polders. Again, the muted colours of Scotland's stony townscapes could hardly be more different from the polychromatic brickwork of Dutch streets: 'houses ... of a brave red brick, the colour of a rose', as R. L. Stevenson remarked in *Catriona*.[2] His hero, David Balfour, felt the excitement of arriving in 'a new world' as he sailed towards the Dutch coast with its 'line of windmills birling in the breeze'.[3]

These are obvious differences; but underneath the superficial contrasts lay a complex network of shared characteristics – political, cultural and religious affinities – which endowed the two countries with a mutual sympathy. Even on a purely physical level there are important points of correspondence. Both countries have a long coastline in proportion to their restricted land area. While Scotland's storm-rent, jagged silhouette is deeply penetrated by firths and sealochs, the serrated coastline of Holland is constantly threatened by invasions from the sea. In their struggle against the elements the two countries became maritime nations, sharing a centrifugal vision and a spirit of enterprising curiosity. As neither nation was richly endowed with natural resources, each relied on overseas trade for its prosperity. Indeed, Holland in the seventeenth century was the richest trading nation in the world.[4]

As well as a self-reliance imposed by their physical disadvantages the two nations shared curiously similar social structures. After the creation of the United Provinces in 1581 Holland became independent of imperial power, and the style of Stadholders of the House of Orange was discreetly subdued in comparison with that of their Hapsburg predecessors. Similarly in Scotland the court had lost much of its former splendour and influence. By the reign of James VI the monarchy had been reduced to financial straits by the feuing of royal lands earlier in the century and the lack of regular taxation; and after 1603 the transference of the king to London left the country without a resident court at all.

Meanwhile the importance of the burgher class in both countries was growing steadily. Soberly dressed in their dark clothes and white collars (see portraits in the exhibition), well educated and diligent, the city dwellers celebrated their modernity by proudly labelling their solid town houses with dates, worthy inscriptions and coats-of-arms. Their Calvinist morality was complex and contradictory: censorious of aberrant practices among their own number yet intellectually open-minded, opposed to conspicuous expenditure yet ascribing to the virtues of family support and hard work.[5] Their aspirations were different from those of the landed gentry who sought to reinforce their ancient roots by clinging to a knightly, castellated architectural style. The urban merchants were Europeans, whose horizons extended far beyond the confines of their own burghs. The respectability and success of their labours were in turn enshrined in the buildings in which they lived, assembled, traded and worshipped.

If we are to investigate the influence of one country's architectural traditions upon another's we must ask what the appeal of that particular source was and how the visual themes were transmitted. First of all, however, we must remind ourselves that other important influences, besides that of the Netherlands, permeated Scotland's architectural traditions in the seventeenth century.

France was an ever-present paradigm in the minds of the Scots; indeed the courtly classicism of the Age of the Sun King made its mark on Dutch architecture too. After 1603 England also offered Scotland a profusion of new architectural ideas, while England, in turn, was at the receiving end of ideas from Italy and France, not to mention Holland. Thus we are faced with a cosmopolitan European picture in which each country, though aware of its own national identity and of the architectural embodiment of this character, borrowed voraciously from neighbouring cultures. To isolate any one line of influence is to take a blinkered view.

With this caveat in mind we can now begin to explore the lines of transmission. First of all, as T. C. Smout has shown, there were resident groups of Scots not only at the staple town of Veere but also in such communities as Middelburg, Rotterdam and Leiden.[6] Scottish merchants sent their sons to Holland to complete their education by learning Dutch and accounting,[7] and the University of Leiden (fig.21) became a popular seat of learning for sons of the landed gentry.[8] Scotland's merchants and shipowners moored often in Netherlandish ports, and many of them used Dutch-built vessels.[9] Although Holland was just one of a range of destinations, extending from Portugal to Scandinavia,[10] the compatibility of Dutch society and its evident material prosperity made it an appealing cultural model.

Thus the tastes and architectural vocabulary of Scots patrons, both merchants and landowners, were informed by the experience of their travels. But ideas from Holland were available even to those who never left Scottish shores through architectural books and treatises.[11] As early as 1560, Hans Vredeman de Vries published his *Variae Architecturae Formae*, the first of his profusely illustrated treatises offering a repertoire of designs in intricate Mannerist classicism. The fidgety strapwork and knobbly protuberance of De Vries's extravagant images had more appeal in the Low Countries than in Scotland, not least because of the cost involved. More relevant was Hendrick de Keyser's *Architectura Moderna* of 1631.[12]

In the introduction the painter-architect Salomon de Bray (Catalogue no. 10) provided a sober analysis of how to adapt Roman classicism to serve contemporary functions, which must have struck a chord in the Scottish consciousness:

> *For that reason all large constructions, like theatres, racecourses or pyramids, have become unfashionable as they are in opposition to the simplicity of Christian teaching and they are also foreign to the frugal industry of our people.*[13]

There followed a stream of books illustrating recent Dutch architecture. Engravings of Van Campen's magisterial Town Hall in Amsterdam were published as early as 1647-8. A lavish illustrated volume of the whole scheme exists in various editions published from 1661 onwards (a copy of the 1664 edition was later to find its way into the library of William Adam).[14] Other engravings and architectural books illustrating the works of Pieter Post and the Vingboons family must also have found their way into Scotland, as well as topographical views of Dutch cities.

Just as many Scottish patrons had first-hand knowledge of the Low Countries, so, too, artists, craftsmen, builders and architects crossed the North Sea. The passport issued to the Scots architect William Bruce in 1658 allowed him to 'returne to Holland', suggesting that he made more than one visit.[15] Bruce was later to employ Dutch carvers at Holyrood Palace and at his own house at Kinross, and he engaged the Dutch painter Jacob de Wet for decorative work at Holyrood and Balcaskie.[16] Some Dutch artists, such as Maximilian Colt, John Nost and Grinling Gibbons' assistant Arnold Quellin, received Scottish commissions when they were already employed in England.[17] Others sent commissioned works directly from the Low Countries, most notably Philip Tidemans, whose cycle of 37 decorative canvases for Hopetoun House was executed in his Amsterdam studio between 1703 and his death in 1705.[18] In 1700 the young James Gibbs left Marischal College in his native Aberdeen and went to stay with an aunt in the Scottish staple town of Veere in the Netherlands, before pursuing his continental travels as far as Italy.[19]

It is in the townscape – above all in the North Sea ports – that we find the strongest architectural links between Scotland and Holland.[20] To the Scots merchant Holland was the most prolific source of luxury goods, derived from all around the globe. Whatever was rare, exotic and expensive could be found in Holland if one had a useful commodity to sell. The eye could be gratified by paintings, oriental textiles, pottery and china; the palette by spices and sweetmeats; and the ear by the peals of carillons. Psychologically the evident prosperity of the Dutch merchant class alone made its towns seem worthy of emulation. But the Dutch themselves used their towns as a medium for celebrating their success in the visual panegyric of townscape paintings, such as Ruisdael's views of *Egmond aan Zee* and *Haarlem* (Catalogue nos 57 and 61), engraved town views, detailed depictions of interiors as well as the food and drink consumed in them, shown in works by Van Beyeren (Catalogue no. 2) and Pieter Claesz. (Catalogue no. 13), and paintings advertising the abundance of the urban market places. This glorification of the town as a work of art in itself must have stimulated the Scots burghs to raise their civic consciousness, especially during the seventeenth century.

Even the ordinary burgher's house became a paragon as a piece in the urban jigsaw. The traditional Dutch town house is timber framed (fig.14). Brick walls between houses, structurally unnecessary, serve as fire insulation.[21] The brick façade is hung from the timber frame, but again is not load bearing. The flexibility of these wooden structures is echoed in the strange inclinations of the walls and plot boundaries. Plots often recede at a sharp angle from the street frontage, with the result that rooms with markedly acute or oblique angled corners are common. One has the curious sensation, especially in parts of Amsterdam, that whole streets have been bent by some colossal force. Even more surprising to a Scots visitor must have been the Dutch practice of making the (non-structural) façade lean forward precariously into the street, as if peering over to see who is passing by in a boat on the canal far below. This incline makes the gables more prominent, and thus more effective as the bearers of inscriptions, dates, coats-of-arms or florid Mannerist ornament. It also allows goods to be lifted into the attic warehouses on pulleys with less danger of damaging the lower part of the façade, and it focuses the reflection of the house more sharply in the water. In the oldest parts of Scotland's towns, by contrast, walls are more likely to lean backward than forward, for greater wind resistance, and plots are normally aligned perpendicular to the street. The disappearance of most of the wooden galleries that once fronted many Edinburgh tenements[22] has removed a precarious element from the townscape that is still visible in Holland, for example on the houses overlooking the Zuiderspui in Enkhuisen.[23] All in all, though, the apparently malleable quality of the Dutch townscape, emphasised by the insubstantiality of shimmering reflections, must have seemed remarkably different from the four-square solidity of the Scots North Sea ports.

Scotland's burghs had been neatly feued in long thin plots of even width, and despite some changes in plot boundaries over the centuries the houses tended to present their narrowest dimension to the street. This meant that the ridge of the roof, as in Dutch towns, would logically run from front to back, with a gable topping the main façade. During the seventeenth century the danger of fire in Scots towns prompted more and more building in stone and the use of slate or tile roofs; and since slates need a steep pitch of at least 45° to prevent them being lifted by the wind, the gables had to be sharply pointed (with an angle of 90° or less at the apex). The resulting zig-zag roofline of the street frontage, emphasised by the vertical rhythm of the tall, narrow houses, characterised the Scots burgh and the Dutch town alike. Gables were crowstepped for ease of building and maintenance,[24] and the stepped profile became a strong element in the identifiable national architectural vocabulary of both countries (figs 14 and 24). However, each retained a distinct local identity. As Dutch roof pitches are even steeper than those of Scotland, each step on the gable end is typically tall and narrow, whereas Scots crowsteps rise in horizontals and verticals of more even length. On a Dutch brick-built

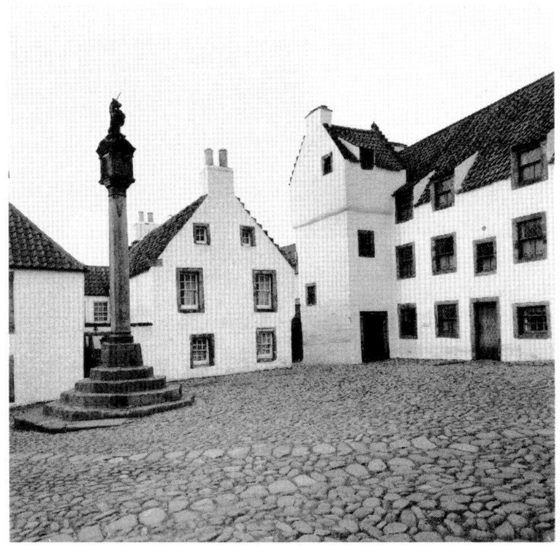

fig.24 *Culross, the Study (1577) from the square: crowsteps, pantiles and half-shuttered windows.* Royal Commission on the Ancient and Historical Monuments of Scotland (RCAHMS)

gable the top of each step is often capped by a little roof of tiles or a stone parapet to prevent water penetration, and the use of this capping as a decorative detail on Dunbar's Tolbooth must have been a conscious recollection of Dutch prototypes (fig.25). Similar gabled crowsteps can be seen on Bruce of Auchenbowie's house in Stirling, and on several old houses in Edinburgh, now destroyed but illustrated in James Drummond's *Views of Old Edinburgh* (1879).

Perhaps the element that is most reminiscent of the Low Countries in Scotland's east coast townscapes is the use of red clay pantiles as a roofing material (fig.24; and see Hobbema's pantiled mill at Deventer, Catalogue no. 24).[25] In 1681 an Act of Parliament, reiterating an act passed 60 years earlier, ordered that houses in Edinburgh, Dundee, Glasgow, Aberdeen and Stirling be roofed with 'lead, sclait, scailzie or tyle'.[26] We do not know what type of 'tyle' was intended, but we do know that pantiles were imported from Holland in large quantities in the seventeenth century. A recent study by John Shaw has dismissed the theory that most of these pantiles were loaded as ballast, although this did happen occasionally.[27] It seems that large quantities of imported pantiles were destined for industrial buildings such as textile mills and salt pans, being cheap and heat resistant, but how many were used in Scottish towns is uncertain. Pantiles were not commonly found on rural domestic buildings before the late eighteenth century.[28] John Clerk of Eldin claimed that William Adam was the first to manufacture Dutch-style pantiles in Scotland,[29] but in fact the Adam works at Abbotshall, opened in 1714, was preceded by that of a Blackness brickmaker, Moses Lawes, who was already making clay tiles in 1709.[30] Pantiles are now widespread on the older houses of the ports of the East Neuk of Fife (sometimes edged with slate at the eaves line for extra resilience), and it would be surprising if imported Dutch pantiles had not been used there domestically before 1700.

Finally we should not forget that building materials were also exported from Scotland to Holland. According to a long-standing tradition, stone from the Longannet Quarry in Fife was sent to Amsterdam for the new Town Hall, completed in 1655.[31] Indeed, James Boswell's father had in his possession a contract between his own grandfather, the 2nd Earl of Kincardine, and the burgomasters of Amsterdam for the supply of stone for the Town Hall.[32] Defoe reports that lead was exported from Scotland to Holland, and documents in the Hopetoun archives confirm that lead was supplied from the Hope family mines for the roof of the mint in Amsterdam.[33]

In seventeenth-century Holland gables became the vehicle for exuberant architectural expression, with flamboyantly curly silhouettes, often composed of several tiers of scrolls, and a little classical pediment at the apex. Curvilinear gables have acquired the generic name of 'Dutch gable', but as Wouter Kuyper has pointed out the most famous early example, Lady Cooke's House in Holborn, drawn by John Smythson in 1619, predates any Dutch examples of this simple scrolled façade.[34] Dutch versions tended to be more restless, many-tiered and ornate. The vernacular examples were probably descended from the undulating gothic

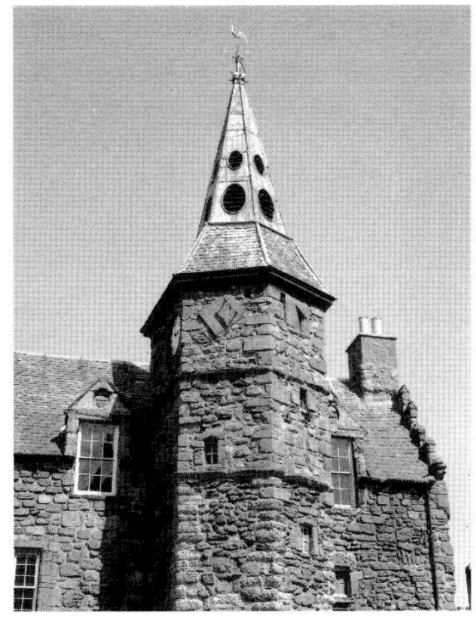

fig.25 *Dunbar Tolbooth (c. 1650): Dutch-style crowsteps and tower.*
RCAHMS

silhouettes of sixteenth-century gables, such as the Beverenburg house of 1556 in Dordrecht (No. 127 Wijnstraat). The most erudite variations were inspired by the florid Mannerism of De Vries, whose impact is seen, for example, in Lieven de Key's façade for Leiden Town Hall of 1593-7.[35]

The simple 'Dutch' gable became very popular in seventeenth-century England, and its appearance in Scotland may have been transmitted via England rather than directly through Holland.[36] North Sea ports where examples may be seen include Banff (fig.26), Portsoy and Pittenweem.[37] Outside the towns the same feature was applied to lairds' houses such as Pitreavie in Fife, and Pilrig House and Prestonfield House, both near Edinburgh.[38] These gables are less steeply pitched than Dutch scrolled gables, as if conceived as a variation on the classical pediment. Significantly they are all topped by chimneys – not a characteristic Dutch solution – and unlike the Dutch curly gables they are structurally separate from, and parallel to, the main eaves line.[39] The curvilinear gable of James Smith's Canongate Kirk in Edinburgh, commissioned by James II and completed in 1690, has often been cited as an example of Dutch influence, but the church is in other respects remarkably Italianate. Since we know that Smith was in Italy and probably visited Vicenza, it is conceivable that he was inspired by the similarly curvaceous façades of Venetian Gothic churches rather than by Dutch prototypes (there is no evidence that he visited Holland).[40]

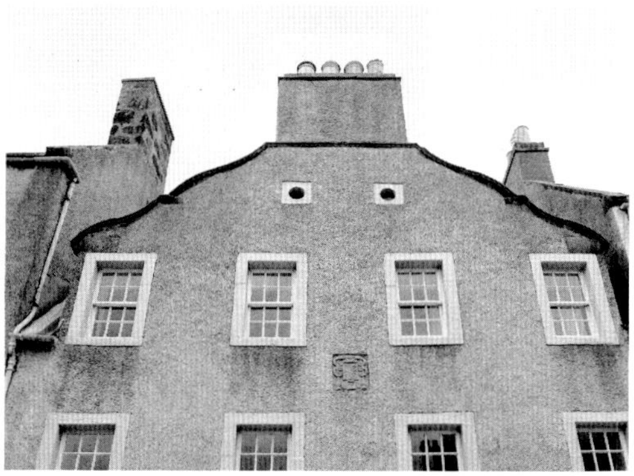

fig.26 *Forbes Lodging, Boyndie Street, Banff (1740): Dutch gable.* RCAHMS

There is a more obvious relationship in the traditional fenestration of Dutch and Scottish town houses, with the lower halves of the windows shuttered and the top halves glazed with fixed leaded lights (figs 14 and 24). This solution made the windows less liable to breakages and loosening of the panes. Moreover, in winter, when it was too cold to open the shutters, the arrangement created the characteristically muted illumination so beloved of Dutch interior painters, with soft daylight falling from above.[41] The more prosperous Dutch houses had inward opening casements inside the lower shutters (as in Jan Steen's *A School for Boys and Girls*, Catalogue no. 68), but this hardly altered the half-shuttered appearance of the exteriors. By the end of the seventeenth century vertically sliding sashes were beginning to replace the traditional half-glazed windows in both countries. The invention is often supposed to have originated in Holland: for example William III had counterbalanced sash windows installed in his palace of Het Loo in 1686. The Duke of Lauderdale, however, had already introduced sash windows into Scotland in the 1670s, and it seems that the real source of this innovation was, in fact, England – yet another illustration of the complexity of the cross-currents of architectural influence.[42]

Dutch domestic interiors, popularised through their own depictions as models of sober, thrifty, god-fearing burghers' homes, exerted a powerful impact on Scotland. Not only did the two societies share ideals and beliefs, but Holland was also the source of many of the contents of a well-to-do Scots home. As well as hardware, textiles (especially the fine linen 'Holland' sheets) and pottery, Dutch furniture was imported and widely imitated, especially the heavy wardrobes, solidly planted on bulbous feet and carved with vigorous Mannerist ornament.[43] Their sheer bulk was enough to epitomise mercantile success and solid respectability. The Dutch and the Scots shared a liking for homely box-beds as well as for more architectural four-posters.[44] Embossed gilt leather hangings, produced in Amsterdam and Malines, were imported to Scotland for wall hangings.[45] Known as 'Spanish leather' because of their origins in Moorish Spain, these hangings became so popular that in 1681 Alexander Brand introduced their manufacture to Edinburgh to satisfy the Scots demand.[46] Blue and white Delft tiles were imported for chimney surrounds, and at Glamis in the withdrawing room off the Great Hall we can even see a florid wooden chimneypiece decorated with both beaten leather and Delft tiles (fig.27).[47]

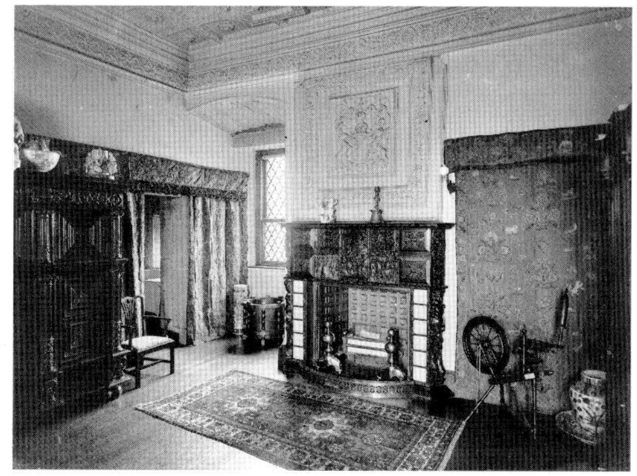

fig.27 *Glamis Castle, King Malcolm's room, chimney piece decorated with Delft tiles and embossed leather (seventeenth or nineteenth century ?).* RCAHMS

In the context of this exhibition we cannot speak of interiors without mentioning the Dutch passion for pictures. Evelyn interpreted this enthusiasm as a form of investment:

> *13 (August 1641) We arived late at Roterdam, where there was at that time their annual Mart or Faire, so furnish'd with pictures (especially Landscips, and Drolleries, as they call those clownish representations) as I was amaz'd: some of these I bought and sent into England. The reason of this store of pictures, and their cheapenesse proceeds from their want of Land, to employ their Stock; so 'tis an ordinary thing to find, a common Farmor lay out two, or 3000 pounds to this Commodity, their houses are full of them ...*[48]

We know from Dutch interior scenes that pictures were hung high and tilted forward (like the façades of old Dutch houses), to give a better viewing angle.[49]

It was customary in Amsterdam and other Dutch ports for merchants to store their merchandise in their attics, raising the cargoes by means of fixed pulleys projecting from the gables. In the Netherlands this was a practical solution wherever heavy goods could be unloaded directly from the quay below, and in any case cellars were prone to dampness. In Scotland, on the other hand, bulk storage in attics was only possible in or near harbours. Surviving examples can be seen at Lamb's House in Leith (fig.28; the pulleys were reinstated by Robert Hurd for The National Trust) and in Pittenweem, at No. 4 Midshore. But warehousing could also be at ground-floor level: beside the entrance to Cor's tenement in Advocate's Close in Edinburgh is a dignified, roll-moulded, stone doorway to the warehouse, decorated with the initials and coat-of-arms of the owner and his wife and the inscription *Spes Altera Vitae* (another hope of life). Many of the imposing purpose-built warehouses erected in Holland by the East India Company in the seventeenth century, with their superimposed tiers of double doors and prominent coats-of-arms, have survived in Dutch ports. It is tempting to suppose that the splendid warehouses which Defoe described in Dundee (quoted at the start of this essay) were of this type, although none of them survived into living memory.[50] They may have resembled the warehouses in the Port of Leith which appear in John Clerk of Eldin's drawing (fig.18).

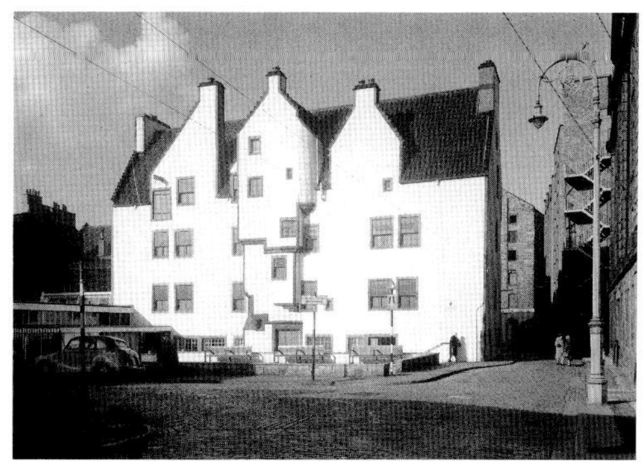

fig.28 *Lamb's House, Leith (early seventeenth century): attic warehouse.* RCAHMS

Intriguingly, one of the first public buildings which openly celebrated Scottish-Dutch commercial links is to be found not in Scotland but in the Netherlands. Beside the parish church at Veere in Flushing stands a public water fountain (actually a cistern) constructed in 1541 on behalf of the Scottish merchants in the city. It was in that very year that the Scottish staple was established in Veere, and it was to remain there for two and a half centuries.[51] The competition from other Netherlandish towns, especially Middelburg and Dordrecht, to take over the staple shows how valuable this arrangement was to the Dutch base as well as to the Scots merchants.[52] Ten years later, in 1551, Veere's fountain was vaulted in a star pattern and covered by an octagonal roof.

The most obvious symbol of burgh power and authority was the town hall, known in Scotland as the tolbooth. Its functions – chiefly to house the council chamber and law courts – were similar in both Scotland and Holland, with or without other possible uses such as the public archive, mint, printing press or prison. The most assertive architectural element was the tower (with its carillon of bells in Holland), and it is not surprising to find Dutch-style belfries on Scottish tolbooths. Slezer's view of Linlithgow, for instance, shows that the original tolbooth tower had the characteristically Dutch combination of a slim pyramidal spire projecting above a broader, square, balustraded parapet. Crail and Dysart tolbooths have stocky towers tapering by gradual stages but remaining solid in appearance, like the one visible in the distance in Ruisdael's *Banks of a River* (Catalogue no. 56). The tower of Musselburgh Tolbooth, compared by Colin McWilliam to 'a slated and static model of a Dutch windmill', is of uncertain date, but we do know that a clock (still in existence) was given to the burgh by the Dutch States in 1496.[53] The Dunbar Tolbooth (fig.25), already mentioned because of its Dutch-style, gabled crowsteps, has an octagonal tower with a leaded spire tapering in two stages, like a dumpy version of the two gates of Sneek in Friesland.[54] Its Dutch air is underlined by the vivid red colour of the masonry, now stripped of its harling and sadly weathered by the North Sea winds that propelled the trade it celebrates. A curious public institution in Edinburgh that was directly inspired by a Dutch prototype was Paul's Work, which stood near the Trinity Church (for which Hugo van der Goes' altarpiece was commissioned, see fig.1). This was a house of correction, with a textile mill operated by offenders, modelled on the famous Spinnhuys in Amsterdam, 'where incorrigible and Lewd Women are kept in Discipline and Labour; but in truth all is so sweet and neate, as there seems nothing less agreable then the persons and the place', as Evelyn observed in 1641.[55] Paul's Work was originally constructed in 1619 as an institution for teaching poor children how to produce woollen cloth, under the tuition of five Dutch weavers brought over from Delft. Two years later, however, a scandal erupted when the 'weavers in Paul's Worke, Englishe and Dutche, set up a high May-pole, with garlands and bells'.[56] The scheme was quickly changed to a house of correction, 'in which there are divers manufactures of linen, wool and silk, where dissolute persons are forced to earn their living with their labour'.[57] Although all traces of Paul's Work disappeared with the construction of Waverley Station, these accounts testify to

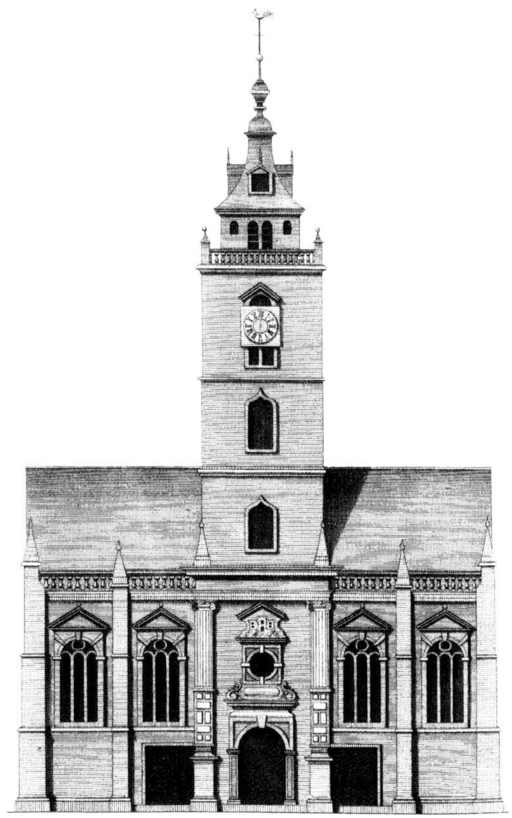

fig.29 *Tron Kirk, Edinburgh, with original tower, by John Mylne the younger (commissioned 1633).* RCAHMS

the rigorously Calvinist preoccupations of seventeenth-century Edinburgh and to Scottish emulation of Dutch public morality.

Public weighhouses in Dutch market towns – characterised by their arcaded lower halls with huge balances suspended from the ceiling – are often grand civic monuments, but in Scotland only that of Edinburgh seems to have been a building of any dignity. Its site was at the corner of West Bow and Castle Hill, and at least four buildings on that site have been recorded. It was rebuilt in 1614, perhaps emulating the newest Dutch Waage such as those of Haarlem (1598) and Hoorn (1609). This weighhouse was destroyed by Cromwell's troops and rebuilt in 1660, but demolished for road-widening in 1822.[58] In other Scottish market towns the public weighbeams, known as 'trons', were more modestly sited in the open-air.

Ironically, one of the remaining buildings that preserves the name 'Tron' is Edinburgh's Tron Kirk, sited near the city's lower weighbeam beyond St Giles (fig.29). Despite its religious use, this is perhaps the civic building of seventeenth-century Scotland that most specifically emulated the Dutch achievement, and the reasons for this will become apparent. The arms of the City of Edinburgh still stand proudly over the main portal. The church was begun in 1637 by the young John Mylne, who in the previous year had succeeded his father as Royal Master Mason at the age of only 25. There is no record of Mylne's having travelled abroad, but when he received the commission in 1633 he evidently consulted Hendrick de Keyser's *Architectura Moderna* for an absolutely up-to-date source (the book was published in 1631). It is significant that a Dutch source book should have been chosen for this burghers' parish church, while at the nearby George Heriot's Hospital, where Mylne was later to succeed William Aytoun as master mason, printed sources from Italy and France were considered more appropriate, the hospital having been endowed by the royal jeweller.[59]

Mylne's approach to De Keyser's work is interesting, for he did not copy any single project. On the façade of the Tron Kirk 'floating' triangular pediments hover above the round-headed windows filled by slim arched lights topped by roundels, an arrangement used by De Keyser on the Westerkerk in Amsterdam.[60] In fact the main façade windows of the Tron Kirk look more like those in the treatise illustration than those of the Westerkerk itself. From De Keyser's Delft Town Hall of 1618-20 (fig.30)[61] Mylne borrowed the fluted Ionic pilasters with Mannerist rusticated detail on the lower sections of the shafts. In both these buildings obelisks with ball finials rise from a cornice which projects over the orders. The relevance of Mylne's choice of a Dutch source book can hardly have gone unnoticed. The courtly allusions to be found in Heriot's Hospital were deliberately avoided in the Tron Kirk, since the whole commission arose from the deeply unpopular decision of Charles I to elevate St Giles to cathedral status, displacing the parish congregation in the process.

The Dutch connection was underlined by the purchase of a 1000-stone (over 6000-kg) load of copper from Amsterdam for the roof of the Tron Kirk. In the end the copper was sold and the church roofed in deal, for even lead and slate had proved too costly.[62] The original

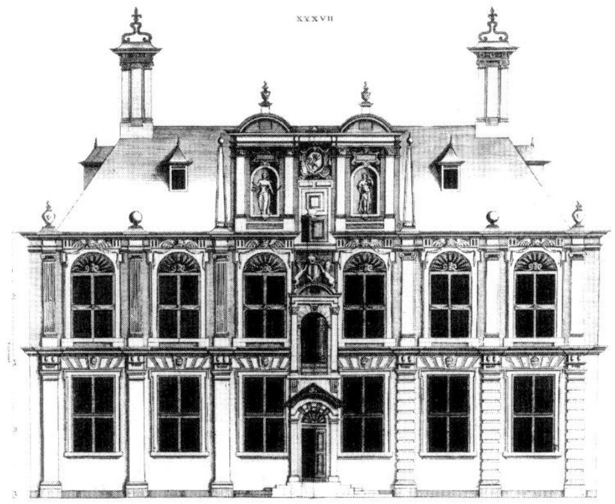

fig.30 Delft Town Hall, *Salomon de Bray and Cornelius Danchertsz, in H. de Keyser,* Architectura Moderna, *Amsterdam, 1631, pl. XXXVII.*
Conway Library, Courtauld Institute of Art, University of London

tower (destroyed by fire in 1824) was also Dutch in style, with an ogee-domed pyramid over a broader, square parapet, like an elaborate version of that of the old Town Hall in Amsterdam.

In Scotland, as in Holland, the new Protestant religion had to invent an architectural form to house the reformed services. The period immediately following the Reformation was a time of experimentation and uncertainty in both countries. Mylne's Tron Kirk was erected on a T-plan, later sadly truncated, but this was just one of a range of possible solutions. The traditional spatial divisions between clergy and laity had disappeared, together with the altar. The focal point of the church interior was now the pulpit, and the divisions became social rather than religious. The enclosed box pews that were introduced into Dutch Gothic churches, such as the Nieuwe Kerk in Amsterdam and St Bavo's in Haarlem (Catalogue no. 65), show the impact of these new concerns.

The most elaborate surviving compartmentalisation of a Scottish church interior is that of Burntisland, where every group in the community had its own pew, from the minister's family to the fleshers and weavers.[63] The T-plan Auld Kirk at Ayr, begun in 1654, has three lofts, one in each arm of the church, for sailors, merchants and traders respectively. Over the sailors' loft hangs a great model of a ship, recalling the two 'modells of Shipps, compleately equipped', which John Evelyn observed suspended in the church at Haarlem, near the west window.[64] In a similar vein, ships and other maritime subjects are painted in the Sailors' Loft at Burntisland, while a model ship still hangs in the kirk in nearby St Monance.[65]

The innovatory, centralised, square plan of Burntisland Kirk, with its pyramidal roof supported on four piers, has long been supposed to reflect Dutch influence. The church was probably begun in 1589 when the town petitioned the Convention of Royal Burghs for 'support to the upbigging of ane kirk within thair ane said burgh'. In 1592 they were granted the right to raise a tax on the timber carried in ships using their harbour. Thus the church had a documented link with North Sea trade. Apart from timber farmhouses, however, no comparable structures can be identified in Holland before 1600. Famous square-planned Dutch churches, such as Van Campen's Nieuwe Kerk in Haarlem of 1649, are too late to have influenced Burntisland.[66] Wouter Kuyper has suggested a plausible alternative source in one of the Huguenot churches in La Rochelle, a port frequently visited by Scots merchants. This square, pyramidally roofed church is visible in a view of La Rochelle of 1620.[67]

The Dutch were suppliers of furnishings and fittings for church interiors as well as for dwellings. The pulpit of Lyne church near Peebles, for example, is said to have been made in Holland, as is the monument to Archbishop Sharpe (d. 1679) in Holy Trinity Church, St Andrews.[68] Above all, the Dutch were the suppliers of Scotland's church bells in the seventeenth century, especially the Burgerhuys family in Middelburg. In 1621 the Edinburgh Gildry paid the huge sum of £1443 14s 0d for three Burgerhuys bells, one for the Netherbow port and two for St Giles.[69] In Crail a new Dutch bell was installed in the church tower in 1613/14 to replace the older one (also Dutch) of 1520, which was transferred to the Tolbooth; both are still in use. The church at Fyvie in Aberdeenshire has a Burgerhuys bell of 1609, while in nearby Midmar the bell of 1642 is from another Dutch workshop, that of Pieter Jansen. At the time of Defoe's visit to Edinburgh in 1726 there was even a Dutch-style carillon at St Giles:

In the great tower of this church they have a set of bells that ... are play'd upon with keys, and by a man's hand like a harpsicord [sic]*; ... and he plays several tunes very musically ... every day, Sunday and fast days excepted, at twelve o'clock.* [70]

There was a close relationship between the burgh councils and the Presbyterian Church in post-Reformation Scotland. The 'luckenbooths' or little lock-up shops that enveloped the north side of St Giles until the nineteenth century, recalling the lean-to shops and houses which can still be seen wrapped around Dutch town churches, would have symbolised the way that the town and its commercial community embraced the church almost literally! It is therefore not surprising to find that church towers with overtly Dutch silhouettes sprouted in seventeenth-century Scottish ports, which eagerly identified with the new Calvinist way of life. On the other hand, country churches, especially in the north-east, were reluctant to relinquish their Episcopalian traditions. Here the local identity was asserted in the region's characteristic little bird-cage belfries, however florid and European the Mannerist ornament of the stonework.

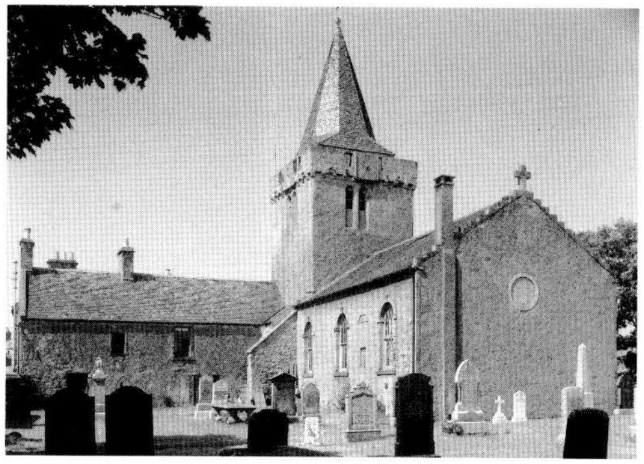

fig.31 *Anstruther Wester, church tower (sixteenth century?).* RCAHMS

In Scotland's towns Dutch recollections can be detected in the bell towers of churches, charitable institutions and civic buildings alike [71] – there was, significantly, little typological difference between them. We have already noted the slim pyramids topping broader, balustraded, square towers, such as those formerly to be seen on Linlithgow Tolbooth and the Tron Kirk. Small octagonal spires over square towers, for instance, those of Anstruther Easter (completed in 1644) and Pittenweem (*c.* 1588), are also reminiscent of Dutch church towers, such as Montfoort. The tower of Hutcheson's Hospital in Glasgow (begun in 1641, now demolished)[72] had boldly projecting corner turrets on its main parapet, recalling the tower, rebuilt in the 1590s, behind the Gothic Town Hall in Veere. Indeed, Glasgow's whole skyline, like that of Amsterdam, was punctuated by numerous, soaring, many – storeyed steeples topped by weathercocks.[73] The slender spire of the church of Anstruther Wester (fig.31) tapers in two stages, pyramidal below and octagonal above, a characteristically Dutch solution that can be seen, for example, in churches at Enschede, Deventer and Hilversum. Even the idiosyncratic west towers of St Machar's Cathedral in Aberdeen, built between 1515 and 1531, show hints of Dutch influence in their tapering tiers and ingenious transition from square to octagonal plan: they recall, for example, the church tower at Winterswijk, completed in 1509. Some Scottish rural church towers, such as the now abandoned churches of Stenton in East Lothian and Fordyce in Banffshire, even emulated the much older type of crowstepped, monopitch-roofed tower that can be seen in Romanesque churches such as Anloo in Holland, as well as in Scandinavia.[74]

By the end of the seventeenth century Scotland's towns, especially the royal burghs with good harbours, were dignified by imposing civic monuments and embellished with stately towers. Yet, they still lacked the copious graphic representations which had made the towns of the Netherlands so well known across Europe. The outstanding exception was James Gordon of Rothiemay's bird's-eye view of Edinburgh of 1647, commissioned by the capital's Town Council and engraved by the Dutch map-makers W. and J. Blaeu. It was in 1693 that the Dutchman, Captain John Slezer, published the first edition of his *Theatrum Scotiae*, a volume of engravings of Scotland's principal towns and buildings (fig.16). In his preface to the reader he wistfully commented:

> *It's a matter worthy of one's enquiry, how a nation, as Scotland, so much addicted to military arts, and so constantly engaged in both foreign and domestick wars, should have been in a capacity to erect such superb edifices as that kingdom abounds with.*

Perhaps an element of flattery was useful, since Slezer went on to petition the Scots Parliament for financial support for his enterprise in 1695! Parliament's initial response was favourable, agreeing to raise a tax on shipping for four to five years to pay Slezer's expenses. This was renewed twice, in 1698 and 1704, but after this, Parliament's enthusiasm began to wane and Slezer complained that he was treated unfairly 'being a foreigner, destitute of any patron to espouse my interest'. No further edition of the *Theatrum Scotiae* appeared until after Slezer's death in 1714.

Although one may question the captain's motives in praising Scotland's architecture, the superb observation and skill of execution in his engravings surely confirm his genuine enthusiasm for the task. He clearly felt that Scotland, too, deserved the kind of visual celebration of the townscape that abounded in Holland. The biography of Slezer in the 1814 edition of the book states that he had been encouraged by Charles II and by James II, then Duke of York, to record Scotland's most remarkable buildings. His main profession, meanwhile, was a military one: in 1690 he was appointed 'Captain of the Artillery Company and Surveyor of his Majesty's Magazines in Scotland', a post which he held until at least 1705. The fact that a shipping tax was used to pay his expenses seems an appropriate recognition of the long-standing commercial links across the North Sea.

After the Glorious Revolution the connotations of the Dutch style were suddenly transformed. No longer simply the idiom of the burgh and the kirk, it acquired aristocratic allusions, as courtiers and government officials sought to pay homage to the House of Orange.[75] Perhaps the Dutch lifestyle itself had already become more flamboyant, if we are to believe the verdict of an English traveller, Sir William Temple, in 1673: 'The old severe and frugal way of living is now almost out of date in Holland'.[76]

In architectural terms the main consequence of this shift in emphasis was to transfer Dutch influence from the burgh to the country estate. By the end of the seventeenth century almost every Scottish country house builder imported materials from Holland,[77] and it would have been surprising if this contact had not extended to architectural borrowings. Sir William

Bruce's visits to Holland have already been mentioned, as well as his employment of Netherlandish craftsmen. He almost certainly used Dutch carvers to embellish the main entrance of his own house at Kinross, with its abundance of fruit and flowers tumbling down over the doorway. John Lowrey has proposed the influence of Philips Vingboons's project for Amsterdam Town Hall on Kinross, seen in the way that the giant pilaster order clasps the corners of the house.[78]

From the time of his early career as Royal Master of Works onwards, however, Bruce's leanings were towards courtly sources. In Holland it was the royal buildings that influenced him most of all. Echoes of Jacob van Campen's Huis ten Bosch of 1628 (fig.32) can be seen in his garden front at Hopetoun of 1698-1703 (fig.33), with its projecting, hipped-roofed side wings, each with a single dormer, framing a pedimented, three-bay centrepiece, and its central hall topped by a little rooftop cupola flanked by weighty chimneys.[79] On the same façade at Hopetoun the flat-topped Ionic portico and splaying staircase seem to allude to the garden entrance of William III's great country villa at Het Loo, of which a description in English was published in 1699.[80]

Bruce's younger contemporary, James Smith, seems never to have visited Holland, but as John Lowrey has shown he was well aware of Dutch architecture from books and engravings.[81] From Vingboons's numerous domestic designs he apparently derived his liking for pediments with their entablatures projecting above the main roofline (once seen in Hamilton Palace, Lanarkshire, begun in 1693, now demolished) as well as his habit of placing staircases off-centre on one side of the entrance hall (as at Newhailes and Raith).[82] Again, Het Loo had its impact, especially on the massing of Smith's remodelling of Dalkeith Palace (1702-10). As was surely intended, the resemblance was recognised at the time: Macky wrote in 1723 that Dalkeith was 'the very Model of King William's Palace at Loo'.[83]

Not only in architecture, but also in the choice of paintings to hang in a stately home, a more Italianate taste began to supersede this Dutch-style classicism after about 1710. The 1723 inventory of the contents of Craigiehall, a house designed by Sir William Bruce for the Marquess of Annandale, reveals that all the state rooms were hung with Italian pictures by that date, apart from the family portraits in the dining room, while all the Dutch pictures were now in store 'locked up in the Library'.[84] In Scotland, however, Dutch elements were kept in play by the career of William Adam who dominated the architectural scene for the next quarter of a century. Adam was brought up in Kirkcaldy, near the Fife seaports that still relied on the Dutch market for their trade, and he is known to have visited Holland, investigating not only pantile manufacture but also barley milling and doubtless architecture too.[85] As well as the book on Amsterdam Town Hall already mentioned he owned a Dutch shipbuilding manual.[86] It seems he must also have known the engravings of Vingboons's work, unless he made such a detailed study of Dutch architecture that he needed no such *aide mémoire*. Adam shared with Vingboons and Van Campen a liking for dangling swags, channelled masonry, pedimented

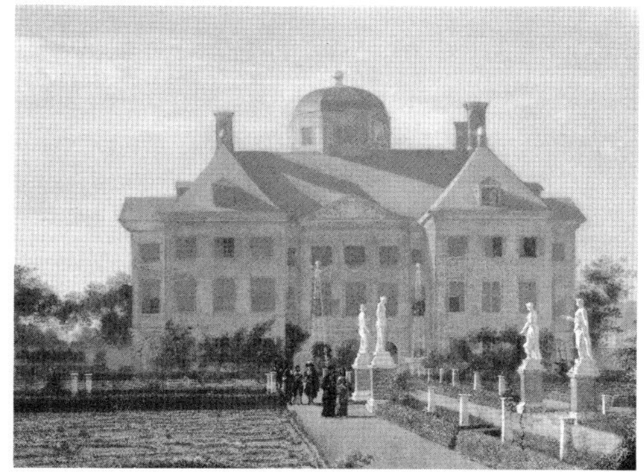

fig.32 *Huis ten Bosch (1628), near The Hague, detail from painting by Jan van der Heyden.*
National Gallery, London

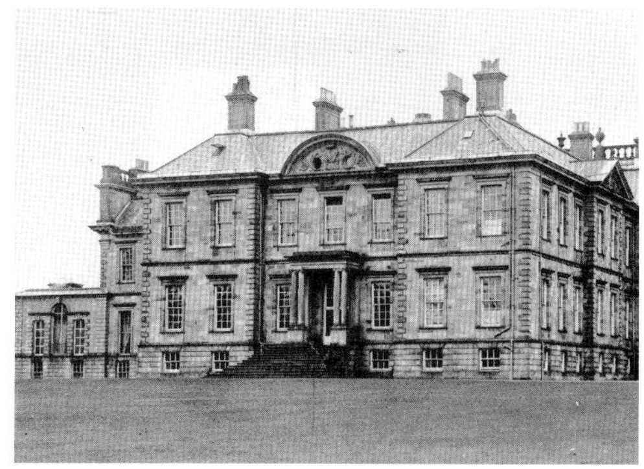

fig.33 *Hopetoun House, garden front (1698-1704), by Sir William Bruce.* RCAHMS

centrepieces, hipped roofs, angle quoins, and robust chimneys with panelling and dignified classical detail. He, too, referred to Het Loo in the chimneys linked by a rooftop balustrade in a design for Mellerstain House.[87] Alastair Rowan has already shown how his interiors were influenced by Amsterdam Town Hall, for example in the panels of trophies that appear in his most flamboyant plasterwork schemes such as the Drum and the House of Dun.[88]

The princely gardens of Holland proved as impressive as the houses. As early as 1617 Fynes Moryson admired the shady tree-lined avenues and parks: in The Hague, for example, he wrote, 'there is a most pleasant grove, with many wild walkes like a maze, and neerer the houses is another very pleasant walke, set roundabout with willows'.[89] In 1641, in the same city, Evelyn enjoyed the gardens of 'the Hoff, or Princes-Court, with the adjoyning Gardens, which were full of ornament, close-Walkes, Statues, Marbles, Grotts, Fountains, and artificiall Musique etc'.[90] At the royal palace of Honselaarsdijk he praised the 'fair Garden and Parke, curiously planted with Limes'.[91]

The dominant influence on the designers of the parks that surrounded Scotland's early classical country houses was probably the French style, with its radiating avenues, *rondpoints* and extensive hunting forests. Although the seventeeth-century Dutch Stadholders, especially Frederik Hendrik (Stadholder from 1625 to 1647), also had leanings towards French taste,[92] their parks nevertheless tended to adhere to more Italianate grid layouts, divided into formal *parterres.*[93] The idealisation of rectilinear planning in Holland's gardens was a natural consequence of the need for systematic drainage channels. Alexander Edwards's design for the gardens at Hamilton, made in 1708, reflects a similar liking for grid planning.[94] Only a few years earlier, in 1701-2, Edwards had been sent on a study tour of the gardens and houses of England, France and the Low Countries, sponsored by several Scottish noblemen.[95]

Holland, like France, was aware of the possibilities of axial vistas in garden planning: poignantly, the main axis of the Stadholder Frederik Hendrik's park at Ter Nieuwburgh was directed towards the monument to William the Silent, his murdered father, in the Nieuwe Kerk in Delft a few kilometres away.[96] William Bruce, too, was to exploit the drama of distant focal points in his garden designs, for example at Balcaskie, Kinross and Hopetoun. But perhaps the Dutch characteristic that was to impinge most of all on Scottish garden design was the glorification of industry (literally as well as figuratively), by the incorporation of utilitarian features into the garden.[97] In the Earl of Mar's park at Alloa, for instance, a Dutch-style lime-tree walk across the park camouflaged the road used by coal waggons.[98] Similarly, power from the great dam opened in 1710 drained the mines and turned the town mills, while the lakes were stocked with fish and fowl. A similar idealisation of economic improvement can be seen in Van Sypen's huge painted view of a major Fife estate illustrated in fig.17.

Setting off from Edinburgh in good weather, a seventeenth- or early eighteenth-century traveller could reach Amsterdam more quickly than London. There he would find a compatible Calvinist society, with a similar respect for education and self-advancement, and a source of almost anything he might wish to buy. In Holland he could purchase enough paintings to furnish his whole house, and he would return with memories of confident, exuberant, yet eminently practical architecture. The Scots were too cosmopolitan and individualistic to become overwhelmed by any one culture, but the Dutch influence, reflected in appropriate and meaningful contexts, had a profound and lasting impact on Scotland's architectural traditions.[99]

1 Daniel Defoe, *A Tour through Great Britain*, 1724-6, eds P. N. Furbank, W. R. Owens and A. J. Coulson, New Haven and London, 1991, p.358.

2 R. L. Stevenson, *Catriona*, 1893, Canongate Classics edn , Edinburgh, 1989, p.193.

3 *Ibid.*, p.189. Windmills were rare but not unknown in Scotland: one appears, for instance, in Slezer's view of Montrose (*Theatrum Scotiae*, London, 1693). For further examples see Ian L. Donnachie and Norma K. Stewart, 'Scottish Windmills – An Outline and Inventory', *Proceedings of the Society of Antiquaries of Scotland*, XCVIII, 1964-6, pp.276-99; and G. Douglas, M. Oglethorpe and J. R. Hume, *Scottish Windmills: A Survey*, Scottish Industrial Archaeology Survey, with *RCAHMS*, 1984. William Adam advised the Earl of Rothes on the design of a wind-powered pump for his mines at Strathore in the 1730s. See W. R. M. Kay, 'What's his Line?Would the real William Adam please stand up? Some Recent Discoveries', in D. Howard (ed.), *William Adam (Architectural Heritage I)*, Edinburgh, 1990, p.55 and fig. 5.

4 J. I. Israel, *Dutch Primacy in World Trade*, 1585-1740, Oxford, 1989.

5 S. Schama, *The Embarrassment of Riches: An Interpretation of Dutch Culture in the Golden Age*, London, 1987; and A. T. van Deursen, *Plain Lives in a Golden Age: Popular culture, religion and society in seventeenth-century Holland, 1978-81*, trans. M. Ultee, Cambridge, 1991. On Scottish religion and society see, for example, T. C. Smout, *A History of the Scottish People 1560-1830*, London, 1969; and J. Wormald, *Court, Kirk, and Community in Scotland 1470-1625*, Edinburgh, 1981.

6 S. G. E. Lythe, *The Economy of Scotland in its European Setting 1550-1625*, Edinburgh, 1960; and T. C. Smout, *Scottish Trade on the Eve of the Union 1660-1707*, Edinburgh, 1963.

7 Smout, *op. cit.*, 1963, pp.77-8.

8 See, for instance, D. Thomson, *A Virtuous and Noble Education*, catalogue of exhibition at the Scottish National Portrait Gallery, Edinburgh, 1971.

9 See, for instance, M. H. B. Sanderson, 'Edinburgh Merchants in Society', in I. B. Cowan and D. Shaw (eds), *The Renaissance and Reformation in Scotland: Essays in Honour of Gordon Donaldson*, Edinburgh, 1983, pp.183-99; and M. Lynch (ed.), *The Early Modern Town in Scotland*, Edinburgh, 1987.

10 M. H. B. Sanderson, 'Walter Morton, shipmaster', in her *Margaret Stewart's People: Life in Mary Stewart's Scotland*, Edinburgh, 1987, pp.120-34.

11 See the useful catalogue of the printed sources in Wouter Kuyper, *Dutch Classicist Architecture*, Delft, 1980, pp.210-28.

12 Kuyper, *op. cit.*, pp.28-33.

13 Translation quoted from E. O. de Bièvre, *The Decoration of Town Halls in the United Provinces: A study in style and iconography*, PhD thesis, Courtauld Institute of Art, University of London, 1986, p.138.

14 A. Rowan, 'William Adam's Library', in D. Howard (ed.), *op. cit.*, 1990, pp.8-33.

15 H. Colvin, *A Biographical Dictionary of British Architects 1600-1840*, London, 1978, p.151.

16 J. Lowrey, 'Dutch Influence on Seventeenth-Century Scottish Architectural and Garden Design', *Scotland and the Low Countries: Sixth Conference of the Scottish Society for Art History*, Edinburgh, 26 October 1992 (proceedings in press).

17 F. Pearson (ed.), *Virtue and Vision: Sculpture in Scotland 1540-1990*, exhibition catalogue, National Gallery of Scotland, Edinburgh, 1991, pp.13 (T. Clifford), and 27-30 (D. Howarth).

18 B. Skinner, 'Philip Tidemans and the Decoration of Hopetoun', *Scotland and the Low Countries, op. cit.*

19 A. Roberts, 'James Smith and James Gibbs: Seminarians and Architects', in D. Howard (ed.), *Scottish Architects Abroad (Architectural Heritage II)*, Edinburgh, 1991, p.50.

20 See the characteristically intelligent discussion of this theme in C. McWilliam, *Scottish Townscape*, London, 1975, pp.72-4.

21 I am grateful to my colleague in Leiden, Wouter Kuyper, for his instructive discussion of these issues. Useful models illustrating traditional Dutch house construction can be seen in Amsterdam's Historisch Museum.

22 McWilliam, *op. cit.*, 1975, pp.55-7.

23 Whistler made etchings of similar galleries in the Jewish quarter in Amsterdam, also drawn by the Scots artist Cameron (J. F. Heijbroek, 'Scottish Etchers in Holland', *Scotland and the Low Countries, op. cit.*

24 McWilliam, *op. cit.*, 1975, p.54.

25 I am grateful to Miles Oglethorpe for discussing this question with me.

26 *Acts of Parliament of Scotland*, VIII, p.357.

27 J. Shaw, 'Dutch – and Scotch – Pantiles. Some Evidence from the Seventeenth and Early Eighteenth Centuries', *Vernacular Building (Scottish Vernacular Buildings Working Group)*, 14, 1990, pp.26-9.

28 R. J. Naismith, *Buildings of the Scottish Countryside*, London, 1985, pp.99-101.

29 J. Gifford, *William Adam 1689-1748: A Life and Times of Scotland's Universal Architect*, Edinburgh, 1989, pp.32, 73-5; and W. R. M. Kay, *op. cit.*, pp.49-61.

30 Shaw, *op. cit.*, p.28.

31 Sir John Sinclair (ed.), *The Statistical Account of Scotland 1791-99*, XI, Wakefield, 1976, pp.620-1. See also D. Beveridge, *Culross and Tulliallan, or Perthshire on Forth: Its History and Antiquities*, 2 vols, Edinburgh and London, 1885, vol. II, p.228.

32 F. A. Pottle (ed.), *Boswell in Holland 1763-1764*, London, New York and Toronto, 1952 edn, p.53. Alexander Bruce, 2nd Earl of Kincardine, married a Dutch heiress in The Hague in 1659 (*ibid.*, note 2). K. Fremantle, in her book *The Baroque Town Hall of Amsterdam*, Utrecht, 1959, pp.37-8 and note 5, claims to have found no trace of Scottish stone in the building, despite the positive documentary evidence mentioned by Boswell's father.

33 Defoe, *op. cit.*, p.34; and B. Skinner, *op. cit.* Members of a branch of the Hope family were bankers in Holland.

34 Kuyper, *op. cit.*, pp.4-5.

35 *Ibid.*, pl. 6; and de Bièvre, *op. cit.*, pp.90 ff.

36 According to R. Noad, 'The Influence of the Low Countries on the Architecture of Scotland', *Quarterly of the Incorporation of Architects in Scotland*, no. 28, Winter 1928, pp.109, William Schaw, the Royal Master Mason and Chamberlain to Queen Anne of Denmark, built a house with a 'Dutch' gable in Dunfermline, now destroyed. Since Schaw died in 1602 this would appear to be its first use in Scotland.

37 The Forbes Lodging, now Boyndie House, at 9 Boyndie Street, Banff, dates from 1740, as does 23-27 High Street, Portsoy. 18 East Shore, Pittenweem, is a house of *c.* 1686.

38 Pitreavie House was built for Sir Henry Wardlaw, Schaw's successor as Chamberlain to Queen Anne, probably in the 1630s. Pilrig House is of 1638 and Prestonfield House was completed in 1689. For illustrations see D. McGibbon and T. Ross, *The Castellated and Domestic Architecture of Scotland*, 5 vols, Edinburgh, 1887-92, vol. II, p.544, and vol. V, p.344; and J. Gifford, C. McWilliam and D. Walker, *The Buildings of Scotland: Edinburgh*, Harmondsworth, 1984, fig.65.

39 McWilliam, *op. cit.*, 1975, p.58.

40 Roberts, *op. cit.*, pp.49-50.

41 Lecture by Mme van de Winckel, 'La baie aux Pays Bas', symposium on *Les Chantiers de la Renaissance*, Centre des Etudes Supérieures de la Renaissance, Tours, 31 May-3 June 1983.

42 H. J. Louw, 'The Origin of the Sash Window', *Architectural History*, 26, 1983, pp.49-72.

43 Examples are illustrated in J. J. M. Timmers, *A History of Dutch Life and Art*, trans. M. F. Hedlund, Amsterdam and Brussels, 1959, p.125.

44 P. Thornton, *Seventeenth-Century Interior Decoration in England, France and Holland*, New Haven and London, 1978, p.159.

45 *Ibid.*, p.118.

46 Lowrey, *op. cit.*

47 I am grateful to Harry Gordon Slade for imparting his views on this interesting piece (letter to the author, 4 February 1992). He believes that this may be a nineteenth-century composite piece, a reassembling of older elements.

48 *The Diary of John Evelyn*, selected and ed. by J. Bowle, Oxford and New York, 1983, pp.18-19.

49 Thornton, *op. cit.*, p.252.

50 Information from Miles Horsey.

51 I am grateful to Wouter Kuyper for bringing this monument to my notice.

52 J. Davidson and A. Gray, *The Scottish Staple at Veere*, London, 1909; and M. P. Rooseboom, *The Scottish Staple in the Netherlands*, The Hague, 1910.

53 C. McWilliam, *Buildings of Scotland: Lothian*, Harmondsworth, 1987, p.335.

54 McWilliam, *op. cit.*, 1975, p.62, comments on the likeness between Dunbar Tolbooth and 'an old building, now destroyed, in Middelburg'. Neil Cameron has pointed out its resemblance to the Dutch town halls of Gennig and s' Heerenberg, which share the centrally placed octagonal tower.

55 *The Diary of John Evelyn, op. cit.*, p.20.

56 J. Grant, *Old and New Edinburgh*, 3 vols, London, 1880-3, vol. I, p.301.

57 J. Slezer, *Theatrum Scotiae*, London, 1693, p.4.

58 *RCAHMS, An Inventory of the … Monuments of the City of Edinburgh*, Edinburgh, 1951, pp.126-7.

59 A useful summary of these sources is given in Rowan, *op. cit.*, pp.9-10.

60 Illustrated in Kuyper, *op. cit.*, pp.340-1, pl. 25-6.

61 Illustrated in Kuyper, *op. cit.*, pp.370-1, pl. 64-5; see also de Bièvre, *op. cit.*, pp.136 ff.

62 R. S. Mylne, *Master Masons to the Crown of Scotland*, Edinburgh, 1893, pp.135-6.

63 G. Hay, *The Architecture of Scottish Post-Reformation Churches 1560-1843*, Oxford, 1957, p.33, fig.6. The Netherlandish influence on pre-Reformation Scottish churches is considered by Richard Fawcett in his article 'Late Gothic Architecture in Scotland; Considerations on the Influence of the Low Countries', *Proceedings of the Society of Antiquaries of Scotland*, CXII, 1982, pp.477-96.

64 *The Diary of John Evelyn, op. cit.*, p.24, 24-9 August 1641. The English visitor, Thomas Pennant, was shocked by the idolatory of the model ship which he saw suspended in a church in Aberdeen (*First Tour of Scotland* in 1769, 3rd edn, Warrington, 1774, modern facsimile edn, Perth, 1979, p.112).

65 J. Gifford, *The Buildings of Scotland: Fife*, Harmondsworth, 1988, p.112.

66 On the experiments with centralised church plans see Kuyper, *op. cit.*, pp.34 ff.

67 Letter to the author, 29 December 1991.

68 D. McGibbon and T. Ross, *The Ecclesiastical Architecture of Scotland*, 3 vols, 1896-7, pp.590-1; and Gifford, *op. cit.*, 1988, p.382.

69 Lythe, *op. cit.*, p.242. The Netherbow's bell, dated 1619, still survives in the Netherbow Arts Centre.

70 Defoe, *op. cit.*, p.313.

71 This subject was first examined by Noad, *op. cit.*

72 Illustrated in A. Gomme and D. Walker, *Architecture of Glasgow*, 1987 edn, p.44.

73 See Slezer's view of Glasgow in his *Theatrum Scotiae*, *op. cit.*, and the spectacular composite engraving by G. van Arkel of the church towers of Amsterdam, illustrated in Kuyper, *op. cit.*, p.402, pl. III.

74 The ruined church at Stenton dated from the sixteenth century (McWilliam, *op. cit.*, 1987, p.440). The belfry of St Talorgan's at Fordyce is dated 1661 (C. McKean, *Banff and Buchan: An Illustrated Architectural Guide*, Edinburgh, 1990, p.49). It incorporates the town prison in the body of the tower.

75 J. Cornforth, 'Was there a Scottish Baroque?', *Country Life*, 15 June 1989, pp.184-7.

76 Quoted in Thornton, *op. cit.*, p.43.

77 Lowrey, *op. cit.*

78 *Ibid.* Vingboons's scheme is illustrated in Kuyper, *op. cit.*, p.429, pl. 158.

79 For the history of the project see A. Rowan, 'The building of Hopetoun', in *Design and Practice in British Architecture: Studies in Architectural History presented to Howard Colvin, Architectural History*, XXVII, 1984, pp.183-209.

80 J. Macaulay, *The Classical Country House in Scotland 1600-1800*, London and Boston, 1987, p.40. On Het Loo, see Kuyper, *op. cit.*, pp.144-7, 181-3 and pls 301-4 and 379.

81 Lowrey, *op. cit.*

82 Illustrations in Macaulay, *op. cit.*, ch. 2. For Vingboons's work see Kuyper, *op. cit.*, many illustrations.

83 J. Macky, *A Journey through Scotland*, London, 1723, p.50.

84 D. Howard, 'Sir William Bruce's Design for Hopetoun House and its forerunners', in I. Gow and A. Rowan (eds), *Views on Scottish Country Houses: Essays in Honour of Kitty Cruft*, Edinburgh (in press). A copy of the Craigiehall inventory is in the Scottish National Portrait Gallery. On the architecture of Craigiehall see J. Dunbar, *Sir William Bruce 1630-1710*, Scottish Arts Council Exhibition, Edinburgh, n. d., pp.17-18, and J. Lowrey, 'Sir William Bruce and his Circle at Craigiehall 1694-1708', in J. Frew and D. Jones (eds), *Aspects of Scottish Classicism: The House and its Formal Setting 1690-1750, St Andrews Studies in the History of Scottish Architecture and Design*, St Andrews, 1988, pp.1-8.

85 Gifford, *op. cit.*, 1989, p.73; Kay, *op. cit.*, p.51.

86 Rowan, *op. cit.*, p.29.

87 Illustrated in Gifford, *op. cit.*, 1989, p.98.

88 Rowan, *op. cit.*, pp.14-19.

89 Fynes Moryson, *An Itinerary*, London, 1617, pp.51-2.

90 *The Diary of John Evelyn, op. cit.*, p.20.

91 *Ibid.*, p.26.

92 Thornton, *op. cit.*, pp.39 ff.

93 See the chapter 'Princely Gardens' in Kuyper, *op. cit.*, pp.139-52.

94 J. Lowrey, 'The Development of the Formal Landscape at Hamilton', in Frew and Jones, *op. cit*, pp.25-32, and pl. 2.

95 *Ibid.*, p.25

96 Kuyper, *op. cit.*, p.141.

97 This point was made by John Lowrey in his lecture cited in note 16.

98 Sir John Sinclair (ed.), *The Statistical Account of Scotland 1791-99*, IX, Wakefield, 1978, pp.659-60; and M. C. H. Stewart, 'Lord Mar's Gardens at Alloa c. 1700-1732', in Frew and Jones, *op. cit.*, pp.33-40.

99 Among those who have helped me in the preparation of this article I must thank especially Wouter Kuyper, Christopher Smout and Neil Cameron for generously sharing their knowledge.

LINDSAY ERRINGTON

Gold and Silver in Shadow

THE DUTCH INFLUENCE ON NINETEENTH-CENTURY SCOTTISH PAINTING

SCOTTISH painters have looked towards and learnt from Dutch artists over a long period of time. In the seventeenth and early eighteenth centuries, before romanticism fostered the idea of a national school of painting that might reflect national history and cultural identity, those Scottish painters who had learnt their skills from Dutch examples produced paintings with little to distinguish them from works produced in Holland. The still-life painter William Gouw Ferguson was a Scot by birth, but it is hard to think of his art as other than Dutch (fig.34), and our present-day categorising of his pictures as 'Scottish School', might well have been a puzzle to him.

In the early nineteenth century, however, Scots began to utilise Dutch examples in a more self-conscious and selective manner, when Scottish artists, led in the first instance by David Wilkie, turned to Holland as another small nation possessing certain cultural and religious affinities with their own. In the seventeenth century the Dutch had created – almost as it seemed, from nothing – a secular school of painting. This was a vivid and sophisticated painting which found its subject matter in the daily life of the people, and therefore might be said to present to the world the image the Dutch had of themselves. A great many of these Dutch paintings were to be seen in private British collections. Prints, etchings and engravings, both original and reproductive, were also in circulation, by which the imagery, if not the painterly technique, of the Dutch old masters could be studied. Edinburgh, at the beginning of the nineteenth century, could offer a young artist several such private print collections, which included numerous examples of Rembrandt's etchings. First Wilkie, and then a number of younger Scots influenced by his example, chose to take Dutch genre paintings and portraits as a starting point for the creation of a distinctively Scottish school of painting. This school borrowed methods, styles and designs from Holland but extracted the Dutch flavour or essence and substituted a Scottish one.

In 1806 David Wilkie, who had recently left Scotland for London, exhibited *Village Politicians* at the Royal Academy, to great acclaim. His extreme success naturally aroused some jealousy among established artists, and prompted one or two spiteful remarks. Northcote, for example, supposed the *Politicians* must have been painted 'in a room filled with the pictures of Teniers',[1] thus implying that Wilkie's picture was no more than a clever pastiche of the seventeenth-century Fleming's art. The following year, whilst Wilkie was completing *The Blind Fiddler* for Sir George Beaumont, his patron lent him a canvas by Teniers to act as a source of stylistic reference and inspiration. However, the immediate results of his kind action did not entirely please Sir George. He began to think that Wilkie's pictorial handling was acquiring unpleasant qualities of a slaty and metallic coldness and hoped that, at the Academy, the picture would not be hung next 'any "Boiled Lobsters": i.e. glaring pictures'.[2] In the event, after the artist and his patron had seen *The Blind Fiddler* exhibited, they were of the opinion that it lacked warmth and richness. Sir George urged Wilkie to turn from the Flemish Teniers and to study instead the Dutch artists Ostade and Rembrandt, from whom he would learn to obtain 'richness of surface and fulness of colour'.[3]

Wilkie was a docile pupil. From now on the words richness, depth, warmth and transparency occur often as standard criteria in his appraisals of pictures old and new. He shared Sir George's belief that the 'golden' picture would always outdo the 'silver' one – i.e. that the painting built up from many layers of scumblings and glazings, with the use of a rich oleaginous medium and 'toned' rather than 'chalky' highlights, was superior to the opaque, sharp pigment and cool greys of masters like Teniers, or the Spanish Velazquez (whom Wilkie likened to Teniers). 'Coldness of tone, and smoothness and dryness of surface, have certainly – what you urge as the surest proof of inferiority – the want of the appearance of a monied value. That they never sell for so much as richly coloured pictures is quite conclusive', Wilkie wrote to Sir George Beaumont in 1823.[4]

For us, in a culture where oblongs of plastic and slips of paper represent wealth, and the coinage is quite devoid of precious metals, such sentiments are possibly hard to understand, particularly at the point where metaphor seems to slip into reality, and the 'golden' in appearance becomes the gold and 'monied' in actuality. The constant allusion to these terms by Wilkie and his contemporaries leaves no doubt, however, that the distinctions between a 'rich' and a 'starved' surface, a warm and a cold colouring, a gold and a silver – or worse a leaden – tone, were of deep importance to them. In John Burnet's half fictitious, half biographical book *The Progress of a Painter in the Nineteenth Century*, Patrick Nasmyth is made to observe that the picture cleaners who removed the scumblings and glazings from old master works were 'robbers of the dead'.[5] In the same book, Wilkie, whilst examining Rembrandt's *Woman taken in Adultery*, noted the 'rich glow of reflected light spread over the half tint: only look at the tone of the upper part of the picture where the Holy of Holies is placed; ... it is a tone of colour which nothing but a combination of gold and silver in shadow can produce'.[6] Burnet was Wilkie's friend as well as his engraver, and notwithstanding the disguise of fiction, he was almost certainly quoting something he had heard Wilkie say.

The Dutch paintings that Wilkie and his contemporaries were adopting as models were old works, with a century and a half of natural discoloration, fading and dirt on their surfaces. Part of their appeal – and their value also – lay in the fact that they not only were, but also looked old. Wilkie and his friends were expressing a preference for what seemed patinated and mellowed by antiquity over what appeared sharp, clean and new. The techniques used by the Dutch contributed to this effect almost as much as natural age. 'The pictures of Ostade are conducted upon a totally different principle from those of Teniers', wrote Burnet in one of his highly popular manuals on art. 'In the one we have all the freshness and touch arising from their being painted at once; in the other, from repeated glazings, often revived with fresh touching into, we have a fulness and richness of effect ... In Teniers, from his sharp and defined edges, everything looks newly purchased. In Ostade's pictures, the various articles introduced have all the bluntness and colour of things long in use, they are also in their proper situations.'[7]

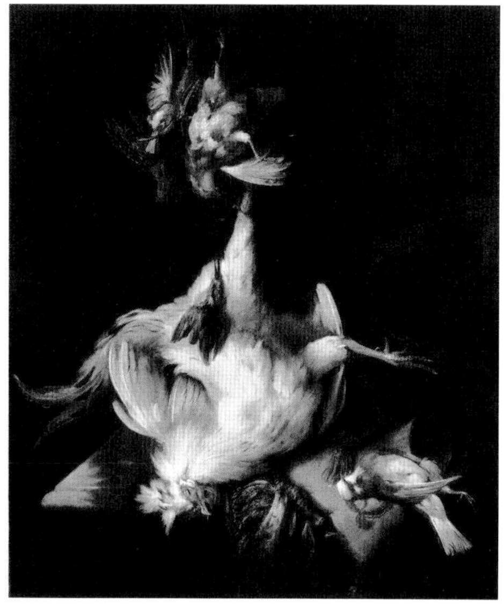

fig.34 *William Gouw Ferguson (b. 1632/3, active till 1695).* Still life: Dead Game. *Ferguson spent many years of his working life at The Hague, and his paintings are indistinguishable from those of the Dutch school. This still-life belonged to the Glasgow collector and dealer, Arthur Kay.* National Gallery of Scotland

If the colours of Teniers were sharp and cold, those of the Dutch masters were, Burnet insisted, often warmed by the tinting of the underlying priming: 'In Potter and Wouverman often of a buff colour; Ostade and Cuyp of a yellow or cane-colour; and in De Hooge and Peter de Laer, dull brown'. The best Dutch painting, he claimed, had a 'liquid touch' and a 'luminous transparency'. The shadows, like the underlying ground, were brown in tint, in Brower [*sic*] and the two Ostades, burnt sienna, in Potter and Wouverman, burnt sienna and black. 'They seem, however', he added, 'all to agree in keeping their darks transparent and thin, while the light portions are opaque and solid.'[8]

Burnet believed that a good picture – like good wine – aged to its own advantage: 'every year becoming more transparent and finished in its effect, from the repeated touching and tints shining through each other', and later, in his essay, he cited, as an example: 'the best works of Brower whose colours seem floating in amber and honey'.[9] This combination of the precious and the sweet was attainable only by using very finely ground colours, repeated glazings and retouchings, and, lastly a suitably mixed vehicle combining drying oil and mastic varnish. The artist who followed these recommendations would, Burnet was convinced, be able to prevent his work from becoming flat, opaque and leaden – qualities the very reverse of those he prized.

In appraising Wilkie, he stated that Wilkie's earlier pictures, *The Blind Fiddler, Rent Day* and *Letter of Introduction* had imitated the precision and sharpness of Teniers and Metzu, but that *Blind Man's Buff, Duncan Gray* and *The Penny Wedding* (fig.35) approached 'the rich tones and glazings of Adrian Ostade'.[10] The last plate in Burnet's etched illustrations to one of his own artistic manuals, *Practical Hints on Composition in Painting* (fig.36), includes three etched copies after respectively, Wilkie's *Blind Fiddler*, Rembrandt's *Salutation of the Virgin* and Ostade's *A Dance* – a further indication of the way in which Burnet bracketed his fellow countryman and contemporary with the Dutch masters of the seventeenth century.

The popularity and many reprintings of Burnet's manuals, his undoubted knowledge and wide visual experience, and the apparent authority with which he advocated certain technical practices as successfully used both by the Dutch in the past and Wilkie in the present, must have acted as a potent and persuasive force upon a number of younger Scottish painters. Sadly, this force was not altogether to the good of Scottish art, for the properties of drying oil and mastic varnish were, in the long run, not quite what Burnet supposed. We shall return to this point in a moment. In the meantime something ought to be said about the relationship between the subject matter of Scottish painting and that of the Dutch old masters.

The use that Wilkie made of the Dutch old masters was twofold. On the one hand it was, as we have seen, technical. He would analyse the methods used to produce specific visual effects, and he would emulate them. This might necessitate a certain choice of pigment, of vehicle and of brushes, or it might consist in the redeployment of a Dutch compositional structure – the connected arrangement of figures within a room, or the balance of lights and darks across the rectangle of the design. These were types of approach to the masterpieces of the past

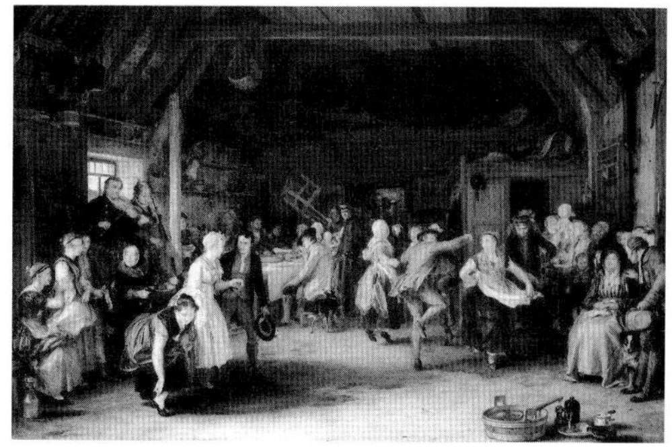

fig.35 *Sir David Wilkie (1785-1841),* The Penny Wedding, *1819. This was painted in the artist's second manner and shows the influence of Adriaen van Ostade.* Reproduced by gracious permission of Her Majesty the Queen

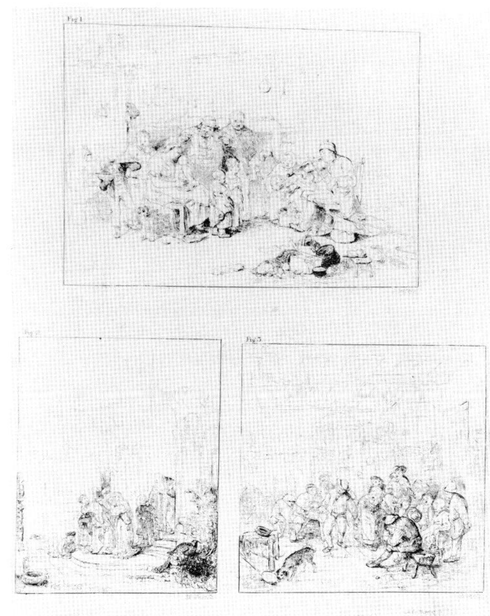

fig.36 *John Burnet (1784-1868),* Practical Hints on Composition in Painting, *London, 1822, pl. 9. Burnet's etching shows (reversed) copies of Wilkie's* Blind Fiddler, *Rembrandt's* Salutation of the Virgin *and* A Dance *by Ostade.* National Gallery of Scotland

that Burnet consistently recommended in his various manuals on art, and Wilkie's *Letter of Introduction* was indeed praised by Burnet for the knowing way in which it borrowed the compositional structure of Ter Borch's *The Messenger* (then in the Hope Collection).[11]

This kind of clever technical recycling was one thing, but it becomes clear, from the way in which Wilkie selected his old master models, that his analysis of them went deeper than mere technique, and that he was sensitive towards the emotional resonance of each master's style and content. It is as if Wilkie understood the various Dutch painters as each occupying some particular psychological territory of his own. For example, he turned to Ostade for the depiction of a charming old folk custom in his *Penny Wedding*, utilising Ostade's ability to give objects the look of old age and much handling – the quality later commented on by Burnet. It was, on the other hand, Rembrandt to whom Wilkie looked when he wished to touch the deepest feelings, especially where he was dealing with religious subjects or those from his own national history. His *Knox Preaching*, his *Cotter's Saturday Night* (fig.37), the unexecuted *Burying of the Scottish Regalia*, and the *John Knox Dispensing the Sacrament* are all examples of this.[12] At least two drawings and an oil sketch for *The Burying of the Scottish Regalia* are known (fig.38). There is a generalised resemblance to such Rembrandt paintings as the *Adoration of the Shepherds*, or the *Entombment of Christ*, or to the etching of *The Presentation of Christ in the Temple.* Wilkie's setting is a gothic church. Deep shadows close about and impinge on the little lamplit group, who reverently lower the sword and golden, jewelled crown into their tomb below the floor. It is as if the light of the nation were going down into darkness and obscurity, to be resurrected in better times. Thus implicitly to compare the emblems of state with Rembrandt's depiction of the dead body of Christ may seem at best inappropriate, at worst sacrilegious, but Wilkie's profoundest feelings for his country were, surely, involved.

A number of artists in Scotland later followed Wilkie's lead, utilising Wilkie's own compositions as well as genuine Dutch paintings as models for the depiction of Scottish folk life, rural customs and history. One of the most important of these later Scots was Sir George Harvey. Harvey's *The Curlers* (fig.39) is a study for a much larger picture. Because of its small size and monochromatic simplicity of tone and colour, it recalls, to a greater degree than the finished work, the little winter scenes of Hendrick Avercamp, particularly the *Winter Landscape* (Catalogue no. 1)which belonged, in 1835 (when *The Curlers* was painted) to one of the directors of the Royal Institution in Edinburgh, and passed a year later to the antiquary David Laing. Although at first glance Avercamp's figure groups occur in seemingly more random and disconnected patches than Harvey's, closer study shows that they too are really arranged along a series of imaginary perspectival diagonals that link the lively dark silhouettes of players, skaters and onlookers across the intervening spaces of pale ice.

The two main alterations that Harvey has made upon his Dutch model – the tightening of the pictorial organisation to produce a single, easily legible and coherent narrative, and the

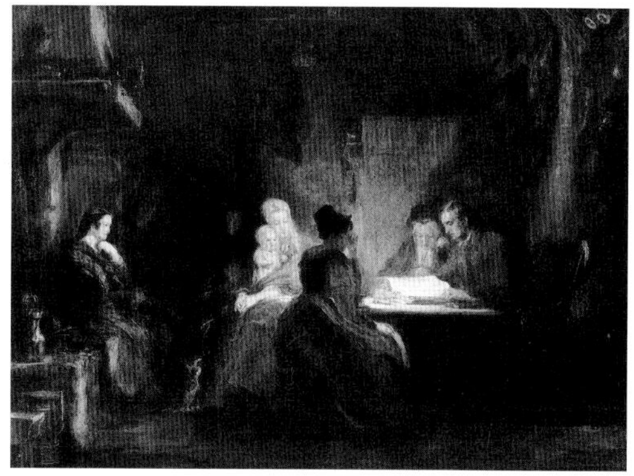

fig.37 *Sir David Wilkie (1785-1841),* The Cotter's Saturday Night, *1837. This is strongly influenced by Rembrandt.* Glasgow Art Gallery and Museum

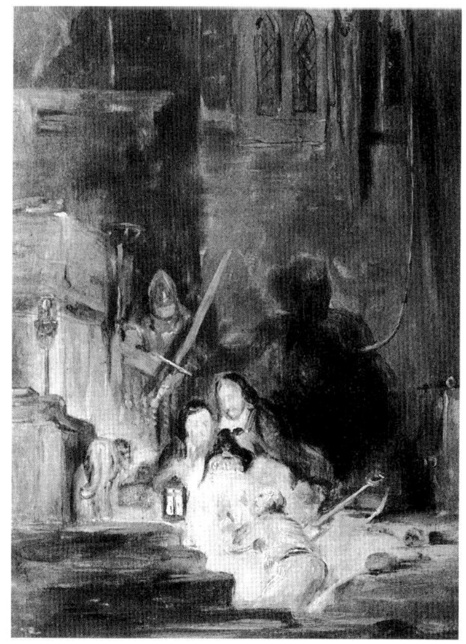

fig.38 *Sir David Wilkie (1785-1841),* The Burying of the Scottish Regalia. *In 1652 the regalia were secretly buried by night, in Kinneff Church, to save them from theft or destruction by the invading English forces. Paintings and etchings by Rembrandt of the* Adoration of the Shepherds *and the* Entombment of Christ *seem to have been Wilkie's sources.*
Mr and Mrs Eugene V. Thaw

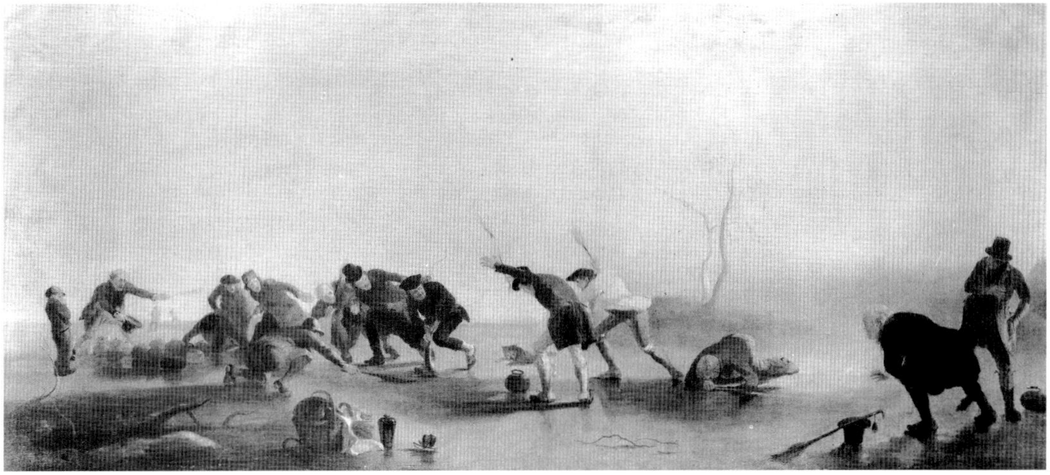

fig.39 *Sir George Harvey (1806-76),* The Curlers, c. *1835. Harvey's rendering of a Scottish national pastime is based on Avercamp's* Winter Landscape *(Catalogue no. 1).* National Gallery of Scotland

fig.40 *Sir George Harvey (1806-76),* A Schule Skailin', *1846. Harvey was possibly following Sir Walter Scott's account of the explosive evening exit of Scottish rural schoolchildren (in the preliminary chapter of* Old Mortality*) but his pictorial sources were seventeenth-century Dutch classroom scenes.* National Gallery of Scotland

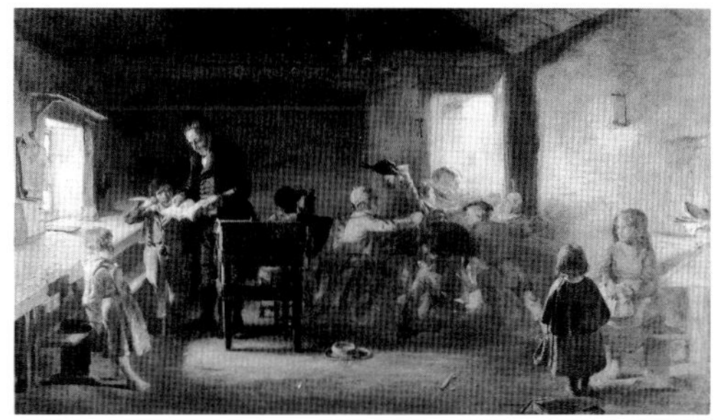

conversion of the subject matter into something still similar to that of the Dutch painter but specifically Scottish – can also be seen in *A Schule Skailin'* (fig.40). Schoolroom scenes abound in Dutch art, but Harvey's title warns us, by its colloquial expression, that he is showing us something characteristic of his own country, the release of rural schoolchildren from the confines of the classroom at the day's end.

In his control of the linked figure groups and carefully disposed light sources and shadows, Harvey may have learnt much from the direct study of Dutch prototypes such as Ostade, Dou and Rembrandt. It is possible, however, that he learnt even more – indirectly – from John Burnet's analyses of their methods in his *Practical Hints on Composition* and *Practical Hints on Light and Shade.* These manuals broke down and exposed the inner workings of many Dutch old master pictures for the benefit of the intelligent art student. The self-conscious juggling with a select number of small entry points for light, and the graded arrangement of wide areas of deep shadow that one finds in *A Schule Skailin'* closely resemble Burnet's analytical approach to the pictorial effects of such old masters as Dou, Steen and Rembrandt.

It was mentioned earlier that Burnet's advocacy of techniques certainly practised by Wilkie, and, as Burnet also supposed, by the Dutch old masters, was not altogether a good thing. Indeed the admiration felt by Wilkie and his Scottish followers for the qualities of depth and transparency found in seventeenth-century Dutch pictures led to incalculable physical damage in their own paintings. The properties Wilkie imitated had, as he recognised, been obtained over a long period of time and as a result of physical changes in the ageing picture surface. His desire to achieve this aged patination instantly and in a new picture led him to employ unsound pigments and vehicles which, drying at different rates, eventually tore his picture surfaces apart.

Burnet described with approval how Wilkie constructed his later paintings in alternate layers of opaque and glazed pigment, and how he dissolved wax with his vehicle. In 1894 Sir J. C. Robinson, the Inspector of the Queen's pictures, published a report on the state of those British paintings that had been executed using the brown pigment bitumen or asphaltum. He singled out as the chief and worst abusers of bitumen, Sir Joshua Reynolds and David Wilkie. 'So completely', he said, was the problem illustrated in their pictures, 'reference need scarcely be made to the productions of any other of our national artists'.[13] In Robinson's opinion, the Dutch masters, especially Ostade and Rembrandt, had also made use of the 'obnoxious' pigment bitumen, but because they mixed it in safer and more suitable vehicles, no bad results had followed. It was the use of the so-called McGilp – a mixture of drying linseed oil and mastic varnish – that was the cause of the trouble in the modern British pictures. This McGilp enabled colours to be applied in 'thick unctuous impasto' that apparently dried quickly. Unfortunately, underneath the surface skin the bitumen still remained in a fluid and mobile state, until eventually cracks, corrugations, fissures, clots and shrivelled, distorted patches of colour appeared over all the darker areas. The process of deterioration was irreversible. Of such pictures, Robinson concluded: 'Although time has conferred upon them certain ripened graces, it has developed more than counterbalancing drawbacks'.[14] Such criticism could be applied not merely to Wilkie, but to his friend William Allan, to George Harvey, and indeed to many Scottish figure painters in the first half of the nineteenth century. Influenced by Wilkie's example, by Burnet's manuals and by Allan's tuition at the Trustees' Academy, a generation succumbed to the enticement of golden brown shadow, and its dire physical consequences.

To Wilkie and his followers Dutch art was that of the seventeenth century, of a deceased set of old masters. Even when travelling in Holland in 1816 he was struck by the 'perfect resemblance' between everything he saw and the pictures of the Dutch old masters with which he was already so familiar. 'It almost seems like as if one had a previous existence'.[15] He showed, on the other hand, no awareness whatever of contemporary Dutch painting. In the last three decades of the nineteenth century this changed dramatically, and it was the new works of living Dutch artists which began to attract the attention of their Scottish colleagues. Whilst the subject matter of these later works – the peasant family groups, the kitchen scenes, and depictions of farm labour – derived, at least in part, from paintings of two centuries earlier, the techniques and colour harmonies used by late nineteenth-century Dutch artists represented a break with their tradition. A similar break in the Scottish tradition occurred wherever Scots fell under the influence of the new continental schools – a break that left a number of older artists and critics extremely unhappy.

The growing awareness, amongst late nineteenth-century Scottish painters and art collectors, of contemporary developments in Dutch painting, particularly at The Hague, has been documented in a number of places. Modern Dutch pictures were lent to the annual shows of the Glasgow Institute, and there was a tendency to claim for the west of Scotland the discovery of this school. For example, a critic writing in *Scottish Art Review* on 'Art in the West of Scotland', described how 'familiarity with the works of Turner, Constable, Corot, Millet, Israels, Mauve, Mesdag, and the brothers Maris revealed to some the comparative narrowness of aim and feebleness of methods identified with what was called the Scotch School'.[16] There is here an implicit, if unstated, criticism of the Edinburgh-based Royal Scottish Academy. In fact, however, awareness of Dutch art seems to have been aroused, more or less simultaneously, in a trinity of areas, centred on Aberdeen, Glasgow and Edinburgh. The painter McTaggart is known to have had direct contacts with the Dutch Artz in 1869,[17] and later with Josef Israels. His friend Chalmers from Montrose, through his friendship with the Aberdonian collector John Forbes White, and Forbes White's protégé, George Reid, also became aware of Israels and his followers. In 1878, when Chalmers' collection was sold following his sudden death, it included a signed etching by Israels and paintings by Mollinger, Artz and Mathew Maris, as well as several paintings by George Reid, whom Forbes White had sent to study under Mollinger.

In 1912 a large loan exhibition held in Dundee freely mingled the oil paintings of Bernard Blommers, Hendrik Willen Mesdag, Josef Israels, Barnard de Hoog, Anton Mauve and Adolphe Artz with those of William McTaggart, George Paul Chalmers, James Lawton Wingate, Sam Bough and Peter Graham. The visual effect of these juxtapositions of Dutch and Scottish was probably coherent and harmonious, similarity of methods being more obvious than differences of nationality.

The critic of the 'Scotch School' mentioned above had placed the aims of the Hague School higher, both imaginatively and technically, than the 'narrowness of aim' and 'feebleness of methods' that had, as he supposed, characterised Scottish art. The East Lothian painter William Darling McKay would have agreed with the first point but demurred at the second. McKay was a thoughtful and articulate artist, whose history of the Scottish school of painting is not only one of the earliest such histories but is still amongst the most useful. 'How different', he wrote in a published lecture,[18] 'is the spirit in which our painters depict the life of the people from that which animated Jan Steen, Ostade, or Terburg, I might even add Wilkie, ... Morally there is no doubt, Israels and Millet, Walker and Mason, and, may I not add, our own painter of *"The Lonely Life"* [Hugh Cameron] address us from a much higher standpoint than the genre painters of Belgium and Holland' (i.e. those of the seventeenth century). This gain in the approach to the presentation of the subject was, however, as McKay believed, counter-balanced by a very serious loss in technical artistry, and that change, 'not of the matter to be expressed, but of the means of expressing it', perturbed him considerably.

McKay saw that the craft of oil painting had grown slowly through the centuries and had been, as he thought, perfected by seventeenth-century Flemish and Dutch artists. Wilkie's debt to these masters for technique as well as subject matter, was as clear to McKay as it had been to Burnet, and he spoke of a small oil sketch for *The Penny Wedding* as being 'evolved from a groundwork of rich transparent umber; and the semi-transparent and more solid pigments were so deftly floated into, or struck over the undertones, as to produce exactly the degree of relief necessary, at the same time preserving that vitality which can only be obtained by variety of surface. And in that small canvas of Wilkie's I could not help feeling at the time that we had the keynote of Scottish painting down to quite recent times, both in its merits and shortcomings'.[19] This is critical language that Burnet, and indeed Wilkie himself, would have understood and approved. What worried and distressed McKay was the new obsessive interest in truth of tonal values to the exclusion of much else, and the wearisome monotony of the new impasted paint surfaces. He felt that Scottish dexterity in handling was being replaced by 'uncouthness, clumsiness, and heaviness of touch'. To McKay there was a vast difference between the mystery, subtlety and delicacy of the Dutch old masters' brown chiaroscuro, and the flatness, mosaic quality, and lack of atmosphere of modern tonal values – the late nineteenth-century substitute for chiaroscuro.

James Guthrie's *A Hind's Daughter* (fig.41) is an excellent example of the type of heavy touch and sticky overall impasto that offended McKay. It is a painting that is often referred to Bastien Lepage for its parentage, but in fact its subject matter, its small size, and its thickly clogged paint surface, together with the proportional relationship between each brushmark and the overall canvas size, suggest a relationship as close, or closer, with the works of Hague School painters (fig.42). The *Hind's Daughter* is essentially a grey painting. Despite the earth colours in Guthrie's palette the overall effect is of a chill grey atmosphere – the colourless, sunless light of winter – and it is a painting that reproduces well in black and white, proving that colour plays little structural part in its make up. This was in accord with Hague School notions. In 1869, for example, Artz had tried unsuccessfully to convince McTaggart that 'tonality' was everything in art.

Shades of grey were highly prized by these new Dutch painters – 'The Grey School' as they were sometimes dubbed. 'These artists ... give precedence to tone above colour', a contemporary Dutch critic commented. 'In that grey atmosphere they find the ideal gradations of tone that they are looking for ... Mauve, Sadée, Israëls, Artz ... all of them patrons of grey painting! With them the reign of grey has begun'.[20] Writing in *Scottish Art Review*, the organ of the Glasgow School, David Croal Thomson quoted Mathew Maris as saying 'that the chief colour he used was black, that he never used any of the umbers [i.e. earth browns], and he showed his palette, with which he was working on a very tender and exquisite landscape, and at the time it contained only black, white, cobalt blue, and a touch of vermilion'.[21] In the preference given to grey tonal values the Dutch were more indebted to their French colleagues' obsession with *valeurs* than to the transparent brown shadows of their own Ostade and Rembrandt. The grey or leaden painters were now valued above the gold.

One might well ask what McKay meant by placing the works of Hugh Cameron and his English contemporaries on a higher moral plane than those of Steen, Ostade, Terburg and

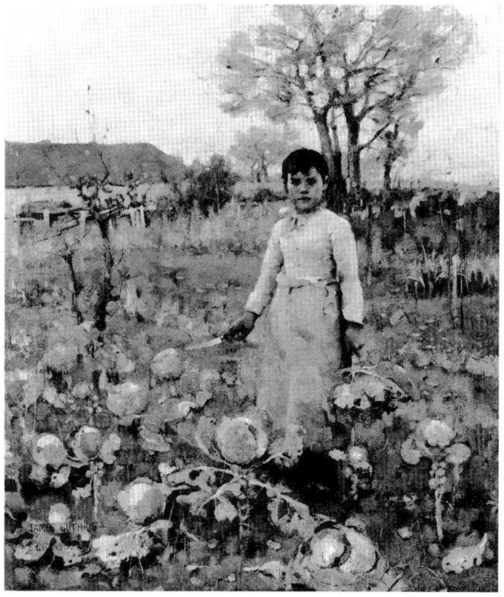

fig.41 *Sir James Guthrie (1859-1930),* A Hind's Daughter, *1883. Guthrie's style, with its sticky impasto, closely resembles that of certain late nineteenth-century Hague School painters.* National Gallery of Scotland

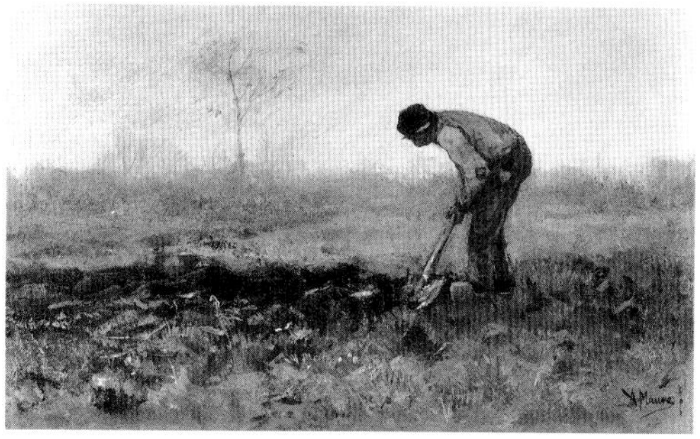

fig.42 *Anton Mauve (1838-88),* Field Labour. *This kind of image of the rural labourer was favoured by late nineteenth-century Scottish collectors of Dutch art, and provides one of Guthrie's sources in works such as* A Hind's Daughter *(fig.41).*
National Gallery of Scotland

Wilkie, especially since he thought that the earlier Scottish and Dutch pictures were much better painted. There are several possible answers to this question. One obvious difference between the two groups of pictures can be found in the humour of Wilkie and the seventeenth-century Dutch, compared with the intense seriousness of their late nineteenth-century successors. Whilst humour is neither moral nor immoral in itself, it may have seemed to McKay inappropriate and, in the last resort, untruthful, when applied to the condition of the old, the poor, the hungry, the bereaved, or those struggling against great odds for existence. Late nineteenth-century perceptions of social relations, of labour and deprivation, were not those of two centuries, or even 70 years, earlier. It was the spirituality and emotional intensity of Israels' *Frugal Meal* that appealed to Van Gogh, and certain Scottish painters, including Hugh Cameron (briefly) and George Paul Chalmers, were searching in their own ways, for a similar intensity of expression. Slight or anecdotal genre themes were now being asked to bear the weight of more profound interpretations of loneliness, poverty, physical toil or old age. Rembrandt, rather than Steen, Ostade, or Ter Borch, was a prime source for both Chalmers and Israels, as indeed he had been for Wilkie in his deeper moments. This was, however, a newly interpreted, perhaps bleaker, Rembrandt, and not the rich dispenser of golden lights and shadows.

Although MacKay had separated out the means of expression (technique) from the matter to be expressed (subject), these two aspects of painting cannot really be so easily disentangled. Any claim made on behalf of late nineteenth-century Scottish painting to have undertaken a more truthful and moral representation of 'the life of the people' can rest as well on the techniques employed as on the subject matter presented. As we have seen, the golden tone denoted, to Wilkie, the more valuable and 'monied' work of art. It had the qualities of an antique, was more collectable, and commanded a better price from wealthy connoisseurs of established and cultivated taste. It might well be argued that such a rich and moneyed style was wrongly applied to subjects of hardship and poverty. On the other hand, the Scottish peasants whom Wilkie, following Rembrandt and Ostade, chose to depict were, though financially poor, culturally rich. It was their rich and antiquated culture – a national antiquity patinated by time and full of the mellow charm of tradition – that Wilkie made the real subject of his *Penny Wedding*. Late nineteenth-century artists like Guthrie, and even those others like MacKay, who attempted to work within modernised versions of the Scottish tradition, cut through the glamour of custom and the charm of folklore to the charmless world of nineteenth-century rural labour. For example, the farming year depicted so often by McKay (fig.43) was not the ancient system of small agricultural holdings or crofts run by their peasant owners, but the newer commercial farming of large units serviced by large itinerant labour gangs.

To some extent the painter who approached the world, and even reinterpreted Rembrandt's chiaroscuro, in shades of grey, was able to eschew the symbolic implications of wealth. *Valeurs*, or values are, paradoxically, negative and abstract in themselves, and devoid of

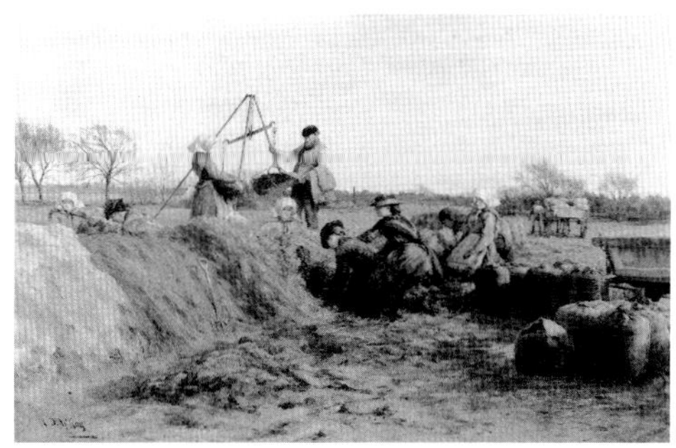

fig.43 *William Darling McKay (1844-1923),* Field Working in Spring: at the Potato Pits, *1878. McKay's picture shows a modified acceptance of contemporary Dutch and French art. He shows the female labourers, known as bondagers, at work on a large commercial East Lothian farm.* National Gallery of Scotland

intrinsic value – a mathematical series of gradations. Their value – in pictorial terms – was seen as being in precise proportion to their truthfulness, and the fineness of discrimination they represented on the part of the artist. This truthfulness and discrimination were just as the artist's brush left the paint lying. Age could not improve, gild or add any jot of value to his marks of that moment. The artist who employed values could no longer lay down his picture like vintage port or a financial investment – to acquire a mellow gold patina in the course of time – nor were there any glazings for a restorer to rob by cleaning them off. The new technique surely represented an intentional honesty of approach in its match of method with subject.

Not all, even amongst the most creative of late nineteenth-century Scottish artists, wished for a complete break with the past. George Paul Chalmers is one example. His unfinished *Legend* spanned many years of his working life, and contains, unresolved, within its four edges, as in a microcosm, the changing history of Scottish figurative art throughout the nineteenth century.[22] Chalmers' transformation of technical and emotive purpose during his many assaults on and reworkings of his design only produced a perhaps ever more insoluble problem. It was much easier to make a clean break with the past, as Guthrie had done, than to try to transmute the golden art of Wilkie's *Penny Wedding* or Harvey's *Schule Skailin'* into the base metal art of the French Barbizon or Dutch Hague schools. There were technical reasons

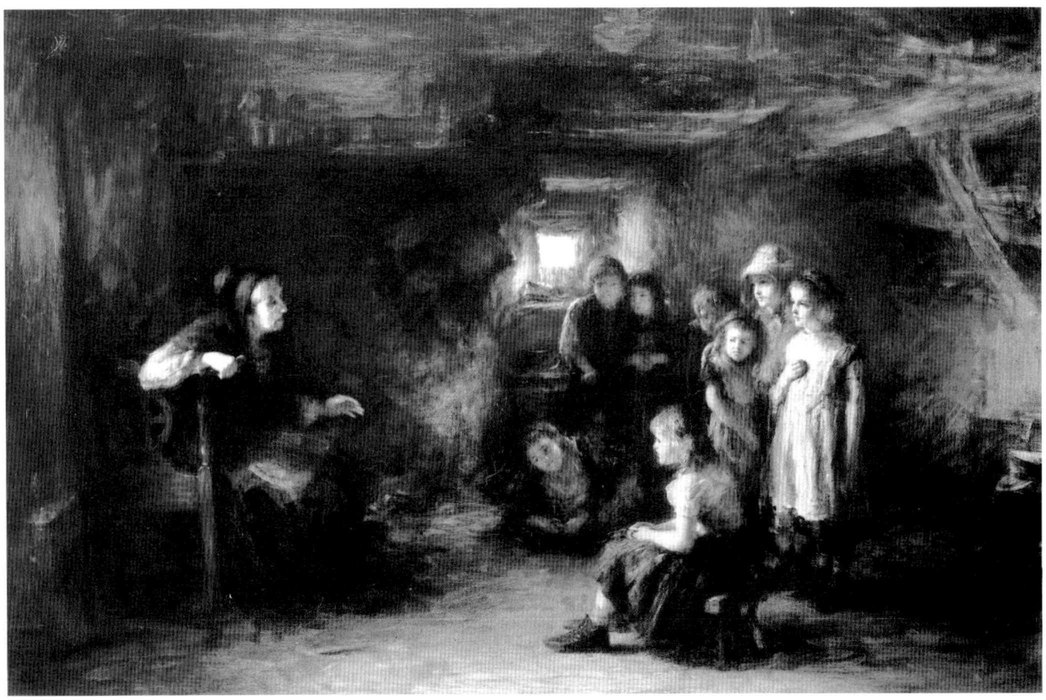

fig.44 *George Paul Chalmers (1833-78),* The Legend *(unfinished). In its technique, as in its thematic contrast of age with childhood, Chalmer's painting comes close to work by the Dutch artist Josef Israels.*
National Gallery of Scotland

for this, well expressed by Peter McOmish Dott in a critique upon McTaggart: 'In technique this group [Scott-Lauder's pupils, including Chalmers] followed the old tradition, "Keep the shadows thin and transparent and the lights solid". Now, as no transparent neutral grey pigment exists, this was practically translated into basing all shadows on transparent brown [a method now generally discarded]. This practice McTaggart has used in lessening degrees till it almost vanishes from his latest works: it, however, leaves on me the impression that his interpretation of transparent shadow is the least successful portion of his technique'.[23]

Chalmers' oil sketch for *The Legend*[24] was entirely prepared in transparent golden brown without the addition of a single other colour. In the large canvas (fig.44) the brown has begun to ebb away. It remains there still, but only as a kind of undertow, with currents of another kind moving above it, and the general impression the viewer may carry off is even of a coolish toned picture. A blue – probably Prussian blue – reappears throughout the shadowed areas, and, where these look most transparent, the effect at close quarters is seen to be an illusion. It is not a paler ground that we glimpse through the shadow, but an opaque scumble of greys and blues lying over the top. Similar effects can be seen in some of Josef Israels' later pictures, and were also employed in landscape by William Darling MacKay. Depth of shadow and mystery or complexity of technique become, in Israels' or Chalmers' paintings, metaphors for an emotional depth or complexity. Both artists were concerned with the inner life of their human sitters, and with the contrasts between the incommunicable experience of being very old, and the unrepeatable one of being very innocent and young. In his last pictures Chalmers was exploring undefined and subtle shadows that form a web or mesh of coloured greys into which his human figures merge, becoming one with the space around them. He had reached a technical position that Israels only attained – in oils at least – in very much later works. When visiting Scotland in 1870, Israels sat to George Reid, George Paul Chalmers and Hugh Cameron who, communally, and presumably in succession, painted his portrait. Israels himself put the final touch of paint on to the canvas.[25] During the session he must have had plenty of opportunity to study the methods of approach used by his Scottish friends. There are portraits painted by Israels many years later in his life – that of Willem Roelofs executed in 1892 is an example[26] – which come very close indeed to heads done by Chalmers in this period of their mutual acquaintance, 20 years before. It is tempting to suggest that it was not only the Scottish artists who learnt from the Dutch, but that influence did also, if rarely, travel the other way.

1 *The Diary of Joseph Farington*, ed. K. Cave, vol. VII, Newhaven and London, 1982, p.2750, entry for Tuesday 6 May 1806.
2 *Ibid.*, vol. VIII, p.3009, entry for Wednesday 8 April 1807.
3 A. Cunningham, *The Life of Sir David Wilkie*, 3 vols, London, 1843, vol. I, p.148. This is endorsed by an entry in *The Diary of Joseph Farington, op. cit.*, vol. III, p.3047, entry for Thursday 21 May 1807, to the effect that Beaumont had said, 'Wilkie might acquire more transparency ... He should not look any longer at the pictures of Teniers's [*sic*] but those of Ostade and Rembrandt'.
4 Cunningham, *op. cit.*, vol. II, p.98.
5 J. Burnet, *The Progress of a Painter in the Nineteenth Century*, London, 1854, p.219.
6 *Ibid.*, pp.53-4.
7 J. Burnet, *The Treatment of Pictures of Fancy Subjects and Familiar Life*, in *Practical Essays on Various Branches of the Fine Arts*, London, 1848, p.98.
8 *Ibid.*, pp.92-3.
9 *Ibid.*, p.114.
10 *Ibid.*, p.93.
11 *Ibid.*, p.115.
12 In the collections, respectively, of The Tate Gallery, London; Glasgow Art Gallery and Museum; Private Collection; and the National Gallery of Scotland.
13 Sir J. C. Robinson, 'Bitumen and Varnish', *The Art Journal*, 1894, pp.326-7. Robinson's original statement appeared in *The Times*, 23 August 1894.
14 *Loc. cit.*
15 A. Cunningham, *op. cit.*, vol. I, p.445.
16 'Art in the West of Scotland', *Scottish Art Review*, vol. I, June 1888-May 1889.
17 MS letter from William McTaggart to George B. Simpson, dated 22 June 1869, in the possession of the artist's family, records a meeting with 'Arts' (*sic*).
18 W. D. McKay, 'Traditional and Modern Methods in Oil Painting', in *Transactions of the National Association for the Advancement of Art and its Application to Industry*, Edinburgh Meeting, London 1890, p.87.
19 *Ibid.*, p.91.
20 J. van Santen Kolff, quoted in English translation from the Dutch original, in the English edition of the exhibition catalogue *The Hague School: Dutch Masters of the 19th Century*, Grand Palais Paris; Royal Academy of Arts, London; Haags Gemeentemuseum, The Hague, 1983, p.83 and note 19, p.88. Kolff's article was published in the periodical *DeBanier* in 1885.
21 D. C. Thomson, 'Corot at Work', in *Scottish Art Review*, vol. I, June 1888-May 1889, p.52.
22 For a more detailed account of the development of Chalmers' picture see the exhibition catalogue *Master Class: Robert Scott Lauder and his Pupils*, National Gallery of Scotland, 1983, nos 69 and 78.
23 P. M. Dott, *Notes Technical and Explanatory on the Art of William McTaggart as displayed in his exhibition of Thirty-two pictures*, Edinburgh, 1901, p.7.
24 Formerly in the Orchar Art Gallery, Broughty Ferry, now in Dundee Art Gallery and Museum.
25 The portrait is in Aberdeen Art Gallery and Museum. The information concerning the joint authorship of the painting is recorded in an inscription on the reverse.
26 This portrait is in the Haags Gemeentemuseum, The Hague.

Index of Lenders

	Her Majesty the Queen: Catalogue no.26
Amsterdam	The Rijksmuseum: Catalogue no.54
	His Grace The Duke of Argyll: Catalogue nos 33, 34
	Brodie Castle, National Trust for Scotland: Catalogue no.72
	His Grace The Duke of Buccleuch and Queensberry KT: Catalogue nos 38, 41
	Colonel Cranstoun of that Ilk: Catalogue no.35
Dublin	The National Gallery of Ireland: Catalogue nos 74, 75
Dundee	Dundee Art Galleries and Museums: Catalogue no.2
Edinburgh	National Gallery of Scotland: Catalogue nos 1, 5, 6, 7, 8, 18, 20, 21, 22, 31, 50, 66, 68, 71
Edinburgh	Scottish National Portrait Gallery: Catalogue no.37
Edinburgh	The Torrie Collection, The University of Edinburgh: Catalogue nos 19, 40, 44, 56, 70
Glasgow	The Burrell Collection: Catalogue no.47
Glasgow	Glasgow Art Gallery and Museum: Catalogue nos 23, 55, 57, 65
Glasgow	The Hunterian Art Gallery: Catalogue no.48
The Hague	The Mauritshuis: Catalogue nos 25, 64
	Kellie Castle, Fife, National Trust for Scotland: Catalogue no.73
London	The National Gallery: Catalogue nos 16, 49
	The Rt Hon. The Marquess of Lothian: Catalogue no.30
	The Rt Hon. The Earl of Mansfield: Catalogue no.28
Oxford	The Ashmolean Museum: Catalogue no.76
	Polesden Lacey, The National Trust: Catalogue no.42
	Private Collection, England: Catalogue no.29
	Private Collection, The Netherlands: Catalogue no.67
	Private Collections, Scotland: Catalogue nos 3, 10, 11, 12, 13, 14, 17, 26, 27, 32, 36, 39, 45, 59, 60, 69,
Rotterdam	The Boymans-van Beuningen Museum: Catalogue no.51
	His Grace The Duke of Sutherland: Catalogue nos 4, 24, 52
Toledo, Ohio	Toledo Museum of Art: Catalogue no.15
Washington	The National Gallery of Art: Catalogue no.53
	The Rt Hon. The Earl of Wemyss and March KT: Catalogue nos 9, 43, 58, 61, 62, 63

Catalogue

Where names of collectors are shown in SMALL CAPITALS, a corresponding entry can be found in the Collectors Index.

The references in the catalogue entries to exhibitions and literature are not comprehensive. Publications which provide more information on exhibitions and bibliographical references are marked ‡.

HENDRICK AVERCAMP

1585-1634. Born in Kampen, a mute, Avercamp may have trained in Amsterdam with the portrait and history painter, Pieter Isacksz., in 1607. He settled in Kampen by January 1613, and specialised in winter scenes, particularly views on the ice.

1 *Winter Landscape*

Oil on copper: 28.6 × 42.2 cm
Signed: *HA* in monogram, bottom centre
PROVENANCE: (?) Cardinal Valenti (1690-1756), Rome; his sale in Amsterdam, 28 September 1763, lot 66.[1] Presumably the picture in the THOMAS SIVRIGHT sale, C. B. Tait's, Edinburgh, 17 February 1836, lot 2840, bought by DAVID LAING (for 7 guineas) by whom bequeathed to the National Gallery of Scotland in 1879 (no.647).

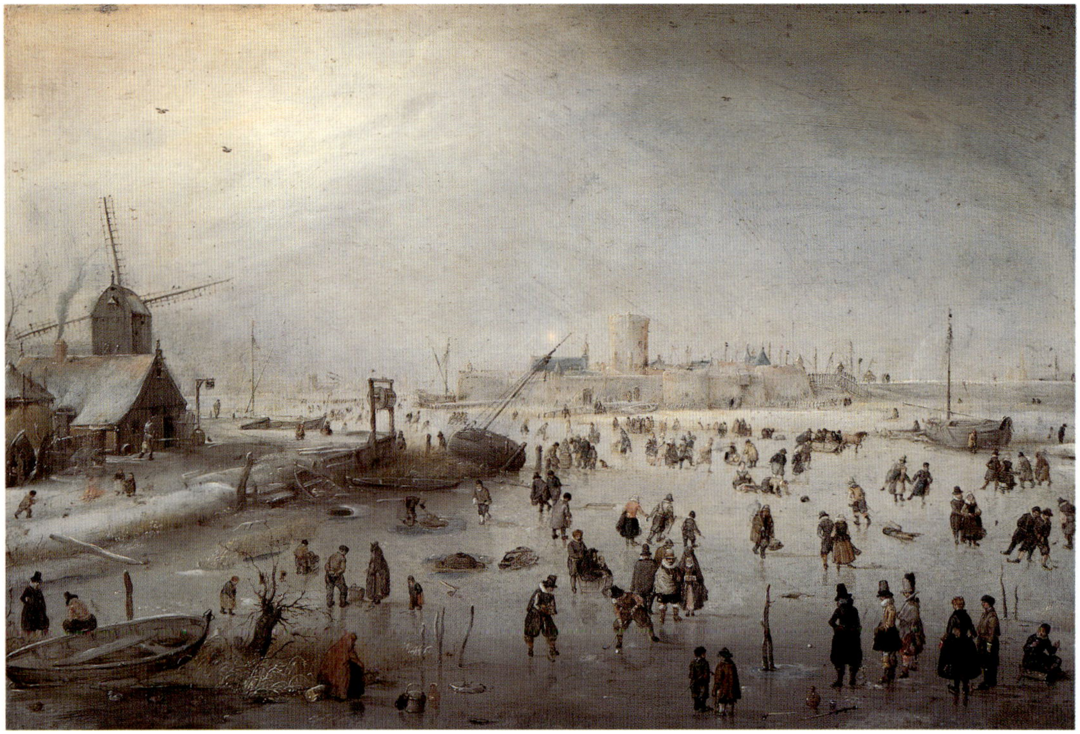

Avercamp was influenced by the winter landscapes of Pieter Breughel the Elder and may have come into contact with his Flemish followers in Amsterdam. Probably painted in the early 1620s, this is a mature work, but includes motifs found in Avercamp's earlier pictures, such as the up-ended boat used as a privy at the left of the composition.[2]

The walled town of Kampen is seen in the background with an inn in the left foreground, which appears in another larger but almost identical composition.[3] The inn sign in the Edinburgh picture shows a white crescent with one gold and one white dot (or star) at each cusp on a blue background. Similar crescents on barrels recur in other works (e.g. no.1346, National Gallery, London) and possibly refer to the Half Moon brewery in Kampen.[4]

Such wintry scenes were popular with Scottish collectors (perhaps the climate seemed familiar). For example, the Duke of Hamilton certainly owned an unattributed 'Winterpiece with men goeing with sketts on the Ice' by 5 October 1704.[5]

LITERATURE: *HdG 1893*, p.130; C. J. Welcker, *Hendrick Avercamp 1585-1634, Barent Avercamp 1612-1679, 'Schilders tot Campen'*, Doornspijk, 1979, S 46, p.210, pl.VII, fig.xx.‡

NATIONAL GALLERY OF SCOTLAND

1 S. Slive, *Simiolus*, 17, 1987, p.185.
2 E.g. *Winter Landscape with Skaters*, c.1608, Rijksmuseum, Amsterdam (no.A1718), exhibited *Masters of Dutch Landscape*, no.5.
3 Photograph in *RKD* files marked 'De Boer Nr.135', oil on panel: 33 × 57 cm; see Welcker, *op. cit.*, S14.4. Barent Avercamp also painted a similar view which omits the windmill and gives the inn the sign of a swan; *ibid.*, B.A. S 5.3.
4 *Ibid.*, S55. Welker claims this is shown in the *Scene on the Ice near a Town* (National Gallery, London, no.1479), which is refuted by *MacLaren and Brown*, vol. 1, no.1479.
5 *Waterhouse Notebooks*, transcriptions of Hamilton inventories in the Getty Archive, Santa Monica, Document 8, no.5. It is listed as hanging in the dining room in the Hamilton appartments at the Palace of Holyrood House.

ABRAHAM VAN BEYEREN

1620/21-90. Born in The Hague, Van Beyeren moved to Delft in 1657, later working again at The Hague, then Amsterdam, Alkmaar and Gouda. He settled in Overschie, near Rotterdam, in 1678, where he died. He painted lavish still-lifes and also sea pieces.

2 *Still-life with Lobster, Fruit, Silver and China Ware*

Oil on canvas: 98.4 × 84.5 cm. Signed: *AB f* in monogram on corner of table below left
PROVENANCE: GEORGE DUNCAN MP, who bequeathed it to Dundee Art Gallery, 1878 (no.29/12).

Van Beyeren was renowned for such elaborate 'banketjes' or banquet pieces. As E. van de Wetering points out in a letter in Dundee's files, the same silver wine-jug with its reflected portrait of the artist and a similar china dish can be found in examples in the Cleveland Museum of Art (no.6080) and in a work in the Ashmolean Museum, Oxford.[1] The composition recurs in Van Beyeren's work many times after about 1655, with certain stock objects used in slightly different arrangements.

George Duncan collected Dutch, Flemish and Scottish pictures and presumably considered these schools as complementary. Paintings in his collection such as Heemskerk's *The Alchemist*[2] and Wilkie's *The Village Politicians*[3] would thus have been regarded as natural counterparts, just as this still-life by Van Beyeren had a Scottish companion in a gamepiece by James Thom (b. 1785-after 1815).[4]

Arthur Kay owned a marine piece by Van Beyeren, as well as two fine still-lifes, one recently exhibited in Vienna (Galerie Sanct Lucas, Winter 1990-1, no.8) and the other now in Cape Town, South Africa (The Old Town House, Michaelis gift). He also had two of Van Beyeren's still-lifes of fish; one now in Cape Town (Michaelis gift) and the other which Kay presented to Glasgow Art Gallery in 1901 (no.935).

EXHIBITED: *RA 1952-3*, no.84; Graves Art Gallery, Sheffield, 1956, no.4; *RA* exhibition 1962, no.84; *Birmingham 1989*, no.121.

LITERATURE: *HdG 1893*, pp.147-8; W. R. Hardie, *Dundee City Art Gallery Catalogue*, 1973, no.29/12.

DUNDEE ART GALLERIES AND MUSEUMS

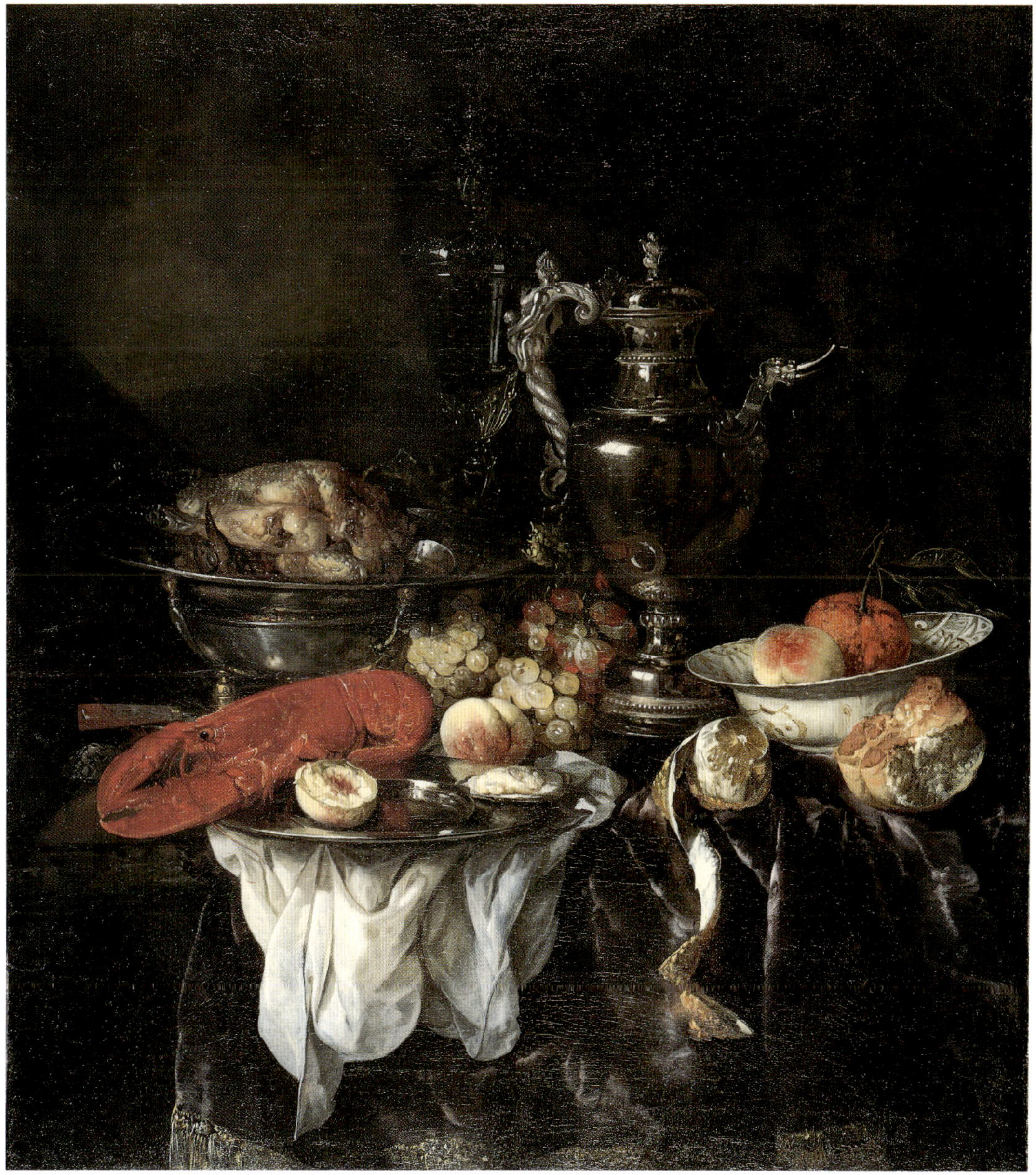

1 *Catalogue of the Collection of Dutch and Flemish Still-life Pictures bequeathed by Daisy Linda Ward*, Ashmolean Museum, Oxford, 1950, no.10.

2 Now given to the studio of Egbert van Heemskerk, Hardie, *op. cit.*, no.1/12.

3 Now ascribed to the artist, *ibid.*, no.20/22.

4 *Ibid.*, p.112, no.28/12.

ABRAHAM BLOEMART

1564-1651. Born at Gorinchem near Dordrecht, Abraham moved with his family to Utrecht, then to Amsterdam where his father, an architect and painter (and Abraham's first master), worked. Abraham was in the studio of Joos de Beer, later moving to Paris but returning to Utrecht in 1583 where he remained, apart from a period in Amsterdam from 1591-3. Like the work of Wtewael, a fellow pupil with De Beer, Bloemart's early work is Mannerist in style, but he later incorporated more naturalistic elements and was influenced by the Utrecht Caravaggists in the 1620s.

3 *St John Preaching*

Oil on panel: 37 × 52 cm
Signed and dated: *A Bloemart fl 1631* at bottom left
PROVENANCE: Duke of Orléans, Paris, by 1727;[1] Louis-Philippe ('Philippe Egalité'), Duke of Orléans, until 1792 when purchased by Thomas Moore Slade on behalf of the 7th LORD KINNAIRD, together with Thomas Hammersley and William Morland and exhibited for sale by private contract at 125 Pall Mall, London, April-June 1793, no.48. Sold at the sale of Francis Dukinfield Astley of Dukinfield Lodge, Cheshire, by Messrs Winstanley and Crole of Liverpool, 21, 22, 25-29 August 1817, lot 47 (as Cornelius Bloemart);[2] Private Collection, Scotland.

It was noted that this was the only painting by Bloemart in the Orléans collection when it was engraved by H. Guttemberg in the *La Galerie du Palais-Royal ...*, Paris, 1786-1808, vol.3, pl.2, see fig.45. There are various different versions of the composition but only one is dated (1618) at Copenhagen Museum.[3] Versions in the Herzog Anton Ulrich-Museum, Braunschweig (1932 catalogue, no.172)[4] and the Musée des Beaux Arts in Nancy (no.61.1.1) are close in style to the 1631 work and so may be of a similar date. No drawing for the whole composition is known but there is a sketch of a figure '*avec un pannier sur la tête*' in the De Grez collection in the Royal Museum of Fine Arts in Brussels, which is presumably a study for the figure at the left of the painting.[5]

The Duke of Hamilton owned 'Ane old man's head of Bloemart' by the early date of 2 April 1698 [6] and also a 'Head of a Man' by Goltzius,[7] but in general there were remarkably few paintings by Dutch Mannerist painters to be found in Scottish collections. The Kinnaird family's *Adoration of the Shepherds* by Wtewael, which was in fact acquired as a Bloemart (Catalogue no.76), formed another notable exception as did the *Liberation of St Peter* (now in Cincinnati Art Museum), in the collection of Sir Archibald Campbell by 1854.[8] Sir James Erskine of Torrie owned a bronze of *Cain and Abel* of 1612 by Adriaen de Vries[9] but this was very much an exception and there were no Dutch Mannerist paintings in his collection.

EXHIBITED: *RA 1938*, no.166; *RA 1952-3*, no.32; *Manchester 1957*, no.101; C. Brown, *Art in Seventeenth Century Holland*, exhibition catalogue, National Gallery, London, 1976, no.8.

LITERATURE: G. Delbanco, *Abraham Bloemart*, Strasbourg, 1927, p.77; *Waterhouse Notebooks*, vol.22, 7 July 1937.

PRIVATE COLLECTION, SCOTLAND

1 Dubois de Saint-Gelais, *Description des Tableaux du Palais Royal...*, Paris, 1727, pp.1-2.
2 Maria Gilbert at the Getty Provenance Index, who provided the sale information, also noted that though the sale catalogue attributes the picture to Cornelius, an original annotated copy of the catalogue in Manchester Public Library has the entry corrected to 'Abrm Bloemart'.
3 I am grateful to Mr H. van Baarle for bringing this to my attention.
4 Repr. *Mercury*, 1986, no.4, p.4, pl.3.
5 *Inventaire des Dessins et Aquarelles Donnés à l'Etat Belge par Madame la douairière de Grez* (unattributed), Brussels, 1913, no.350. I am grateful to Mr H. van Baarle for bringing this to my attention.
6 *Waterhouse Notebooks*, transcriptions of Hamilton inventories in the Getty Archive, Santa Monica. See, too, DUKES OF HAMILTON in Collectors Index. The Bloemart is listed again as at Holyrood House on 5 October 1704, no.7, along with another work by the same artist 'an admirable head by old Bloemart, an original', no.26, as well as a 'length by 'Bloomart', no.107. An inventory of Kinneil Castle made a few days later, on 13 October 1704, lists 'A Woman with a Kercher', no.274, and 'An old man's head with a white beard on a board', no.304, both by 'Bloomart'.
7 *Waterhouse Notebooks*, as above, transcriptions of Hamilton inventories of 8 January 1697 and 10 July 1699. In Holyrood House by 5 October 1704, no.12.
8 *Waagen*, vol.3, p.294 (as Honthorst).
9 *The Torrie Collection*, no.49.

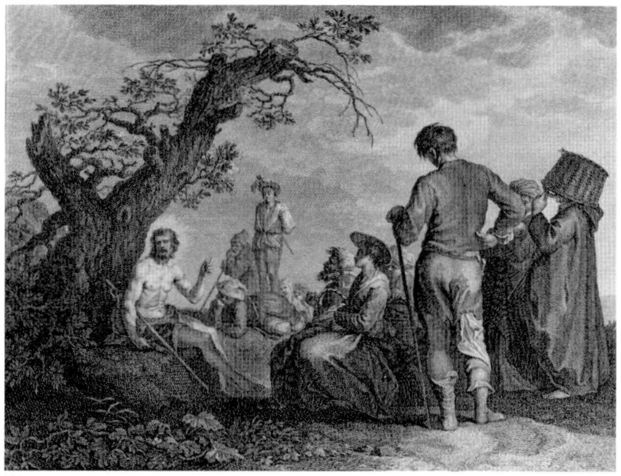

fig.45

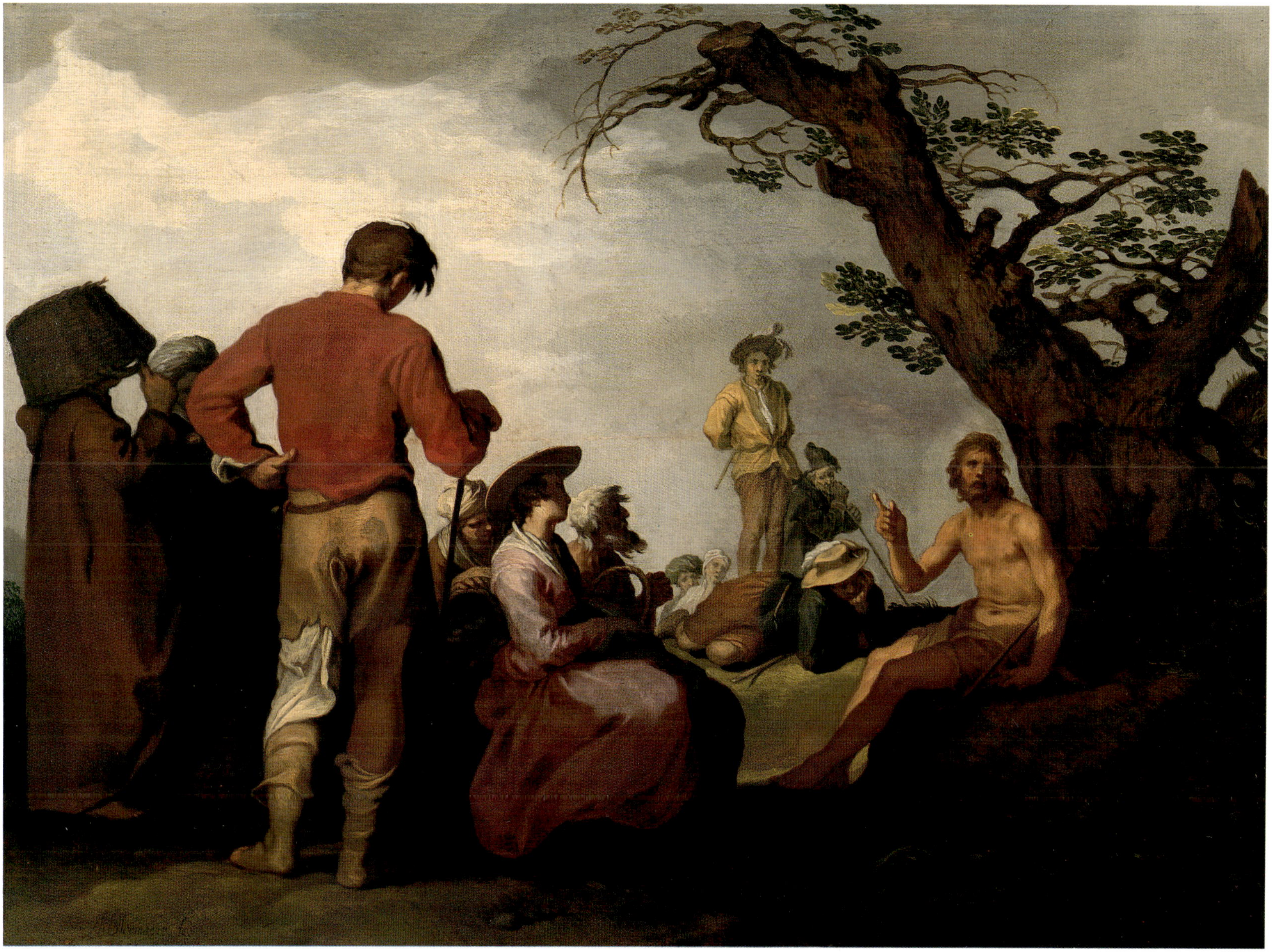

1617-81. Born in Zwolle, his first master was his father, an artist who had been in Italy. He was probably in Amsterdam in 1632, and then became a student of Pieter Molijn in Haarlem in 1634, entering the guild there in 1635 and working the same year with his uncle in England. He may have returned to Zwolle in April the following year but then travelled extensively in Europe. He was in Delft on 22 April 1653, where he witnessed a document for the young Vermeer. He married in Deventer in 1654 and seems to have spent the rest of his life there. He painted genre scenes, developing an independent style in the 1650s, and also some miniatures and small full-length portraits.

4 *A Singing Practice*

Oil on canvas: 73.8 × 79.6 cm
PROVENANCE: A. de la Hante sale, Phillips, London, 2-3 June 1814 , lot 42; sold by Lord Wharncliffe to J. Smith in 1841 from whom bought by Lord Francis Egerton, who became 1st Earl of Ellesmere in 1846 and thence by inheritance to John, 5th Earl of Ellesmere (later 6th DUKE OF SUTHERLAND in 1963), who placed the work on loan at the National Gallery of Scotland in 1946.

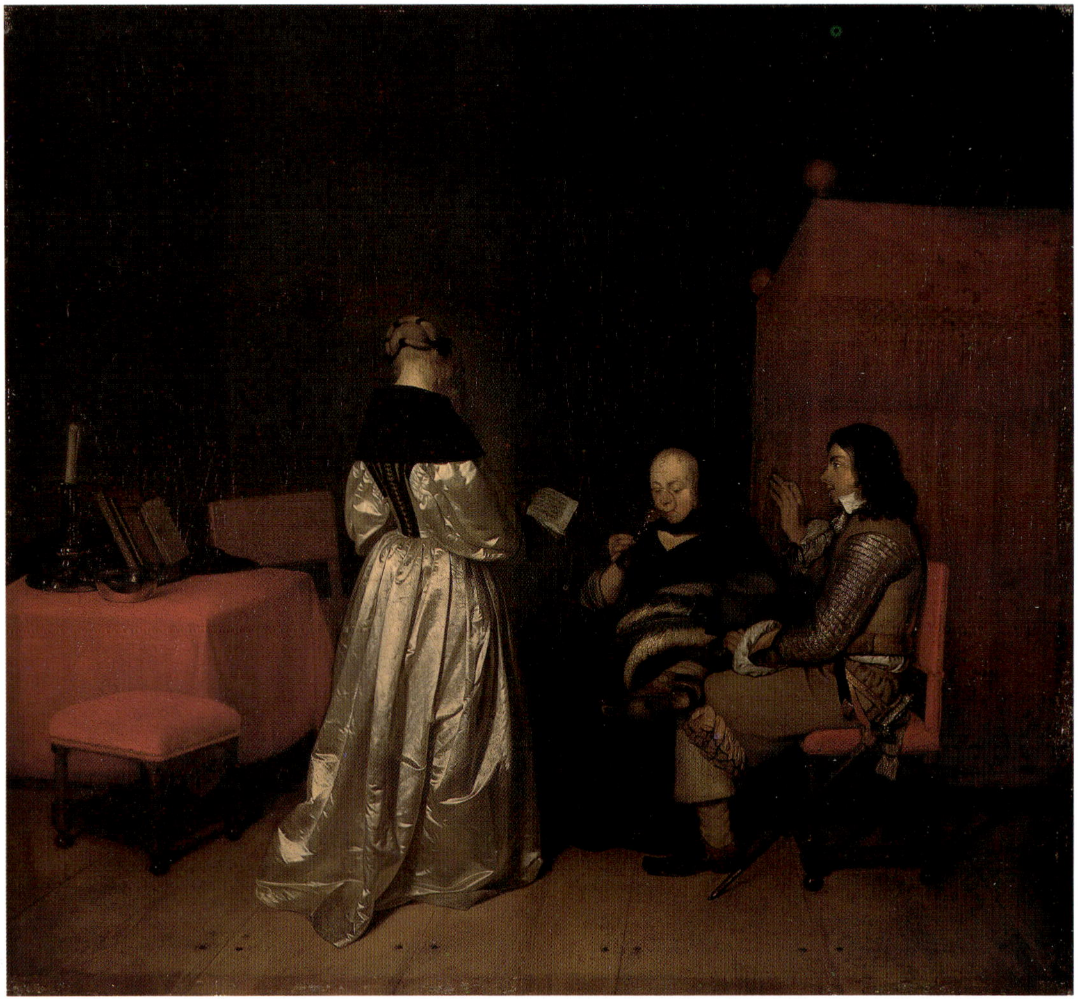

There are two other main versions of this composition: in the Rijkmuseum, Amsterdam (no.A404, painted *c.*1654 and generally regarded as the prime version) and in the Gemäldegalerie, Berlin-Dahlem (no.791, *c.*1655).[1] The Berlin painting was engraved by J. G. Wille in 1765, while the Amsterdam picture was engraved by Vailliant and White under the title of *L'Instruction Paternelle* (which the Bridgewater House Catalogue of 1851 also called the Sutherland painting). The precise subject has long been a cause for debate for it was thought that the coin held by the officer in the Berlin version (and absent in the Amsterdam and Sutherland pictures) pointed to a little polite prostitution. However, Otto Naumann[2] has suggested that the coin held in the Berlin version is perhaps betrothal or marriage money and mentions a 'marriage mirror' in the background. The Sutherland painting is the only one to show the girl holding a sheet of music. It seems that these may not represent straightforward brothel scenes, as was once believed. It remains hard to imagine that the officer is the girl's father though, as he eyes her less with paternal admonition than with the interest of a potential suitor.

EXHIBITED: *Manchester 1857*, no.1049; *Edinburgh 1945*, no.198; *Manchester 1957*, no.114.

LITERATURE: *Smith*, no.4, and addenda to supplement no.30; *Bridgewater House Catalogue 1851*, no.198; HdG, no.188; *Bridgewater House Catalogue 1926*, no.198; S. J. Gudlaugsson, *Katalog der Gemälde Gerard Ter Borchs*, 1960, no.110a.‡

THE DUKE OF SUTHERLAND

1 Exhibited in *Masters of Dutch Genre Painting*, no.9.
2 Letter in picture file (no.791) in Gemäldegalerie, Berlin-Dahlem.

JAN DE BRAY

1626/7-97. Born in Haarlem, Jan probably trained with his father, Salomon (Catalogue no. 10). He occasionally worked in Amsterdam (perhaps from 1686-8), but spent most of his life in Haarlem, where he was a guild officer. Influenced by the classicising style of Cesar van Everdingen and Pieter de Grebber, he painted portraits as well as depicting biblical and historical scenes and also architectural designs. He was declared bankrupt in 1689 in Haarlem, where he died.

5 *A Dutch Man aged 47*

Oil on panel: 23.5 × 17.4 cm
Inscribed and dated: *1662 / out 47 jaer* bottom right

6 *A Dutch Woman aged 47*

Oil on panel: 23.6 × 17.6 cm
Inscribed and dated: *1663 / out 47 jaer* bottom left

7 *A Dutch Boy*

Oil on panel: 21.2 × 15.2 cm
Signed and dated: *J Bray* (*JB* in monogram) *1663 / out 17 jaer* bottom left

8 *A Dutch boy aged 7*

Oil on panel: 21.5 × 15.8 cm
Signed and dated: *J D Bray 1662 / out 11 jaer* bottom right

PROVENANCE of Catalogue nos 5, 6, 7 and 8: Purchased by Mary Nisbet; inherited by her daughter, Lady Mary Bruce (who married R. C. Nisbet Hamilton) who died in 1883; inherited by her daughter MRS NISBET HAMILTON OGILVY OF BIEL, by whom bequeathed in 1921 to the National Gallery of Scotland (Catalogue nos 5, 6, 7, 8 are Gallery nos 1500, 1501, 1502, 1503).

Few groups of family portraits such as this have survived.[1] The paintings are in fine matching seventeenth-century Dutch Lutma frames. The panels were originally rectangular but were reduced to their current oval format, presumably to fit the frames. The backs of the panels are inscribed with the name of Frans Hals (no.1501 has *François Hals*, which suggests a French provenance, perhaps implying that Mary Nisbet purchased the panels while in Paris with her first husband, Lord Elgin). Jan de Bray lived and worked in the same city as Hals,[2] but the restricted palette of subdued colours used here is typical of burgher portraits in Haarlem at this date and does not neccessarily indicate Hals's influence. The attribution of the panels to Frans Hals in the Edinburgh exhibition of 1883 reflects the growing popularity of this artist in Britain at the end of the nineteenth century (see Catalogue nos 20, 21 and 22).

On 29 December 1883, A. Bredius, the renowned Dutch art historian, saw two of the panels then on exhibition in Edinburgh, and wrote: 'the owners possess others of the family like them. They are not Hals's but excellent examples of the eminent portraitist Jan de Bray ... The inscriptions enable us to recognise the known handwriting of the painter as we do his free handling in the execution'.[3]

EXHIBITED: *Edinburgh 1883*, nos 247 and 252 (as Hals); *Birmingham 1989*, nos 56, 57, 58 and 59.

LITERATURE: J. W. von Moltke, *Marburger Jahrbuch für Kunstwissenschaft*, XI / XII, 1938-9, nos 78, 130, 163 and 164, pl.50.

NATIONAL GALLERY OF SCOTLAND

1 Dr Pieter Biesboer of the Frans Halsmuseum (note in Gallery file) believes that the woman is dressed as a matron and is therefore the boys' grandmother, which would probably mean that these portraits are four from a larger set. If this is correct, it is possible that a small rectangular portrait of a woman in the Smith College Museum of Art, Northampton, Mass. (1964:2 TR 1295 attributed to Verspronck), may relate to the group.

2 It seems, however, that Jan's father Salomon collaborated with Hals on the Viscount Boyne's *Family Portrait in a Landscape* (*Slive*, vol.3, no.15) in which he painted a seated child and inscribed his work 'Salomon de Bray 1628'.

3 Quoted in a letter from Gilbert Ogilvy, 5 January 1921, in Gallery bequest files.

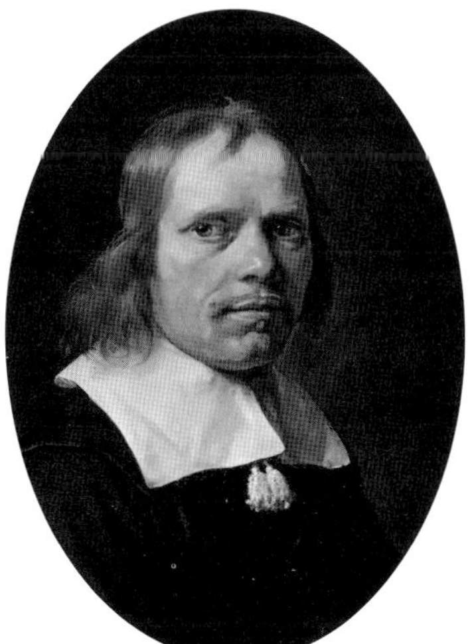

5

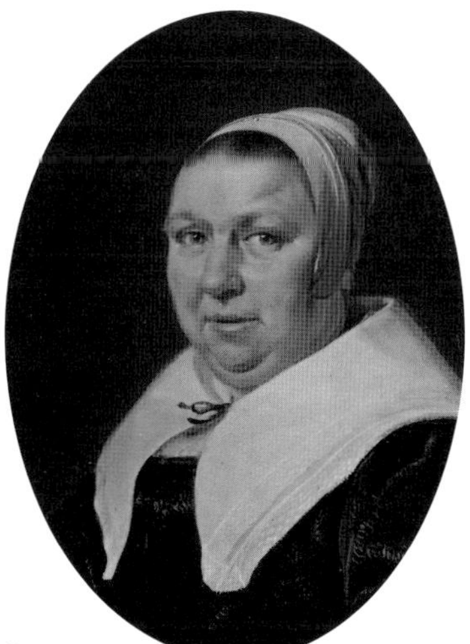

6

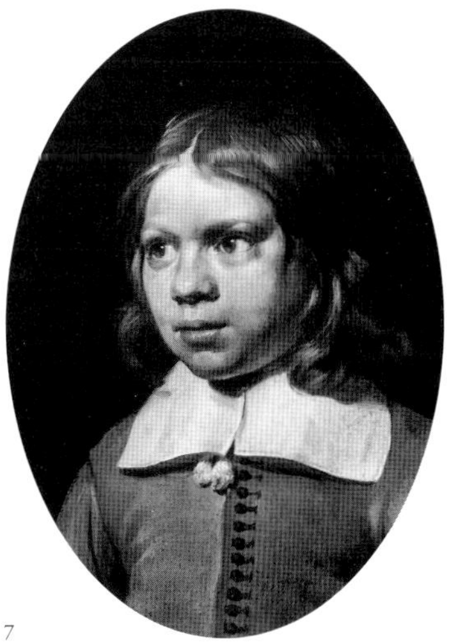

7

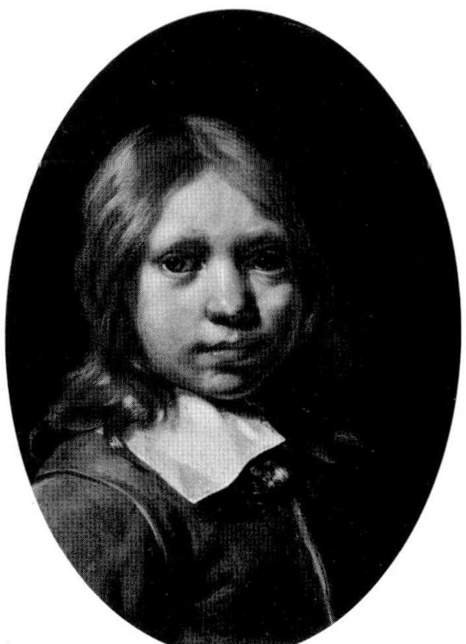

8

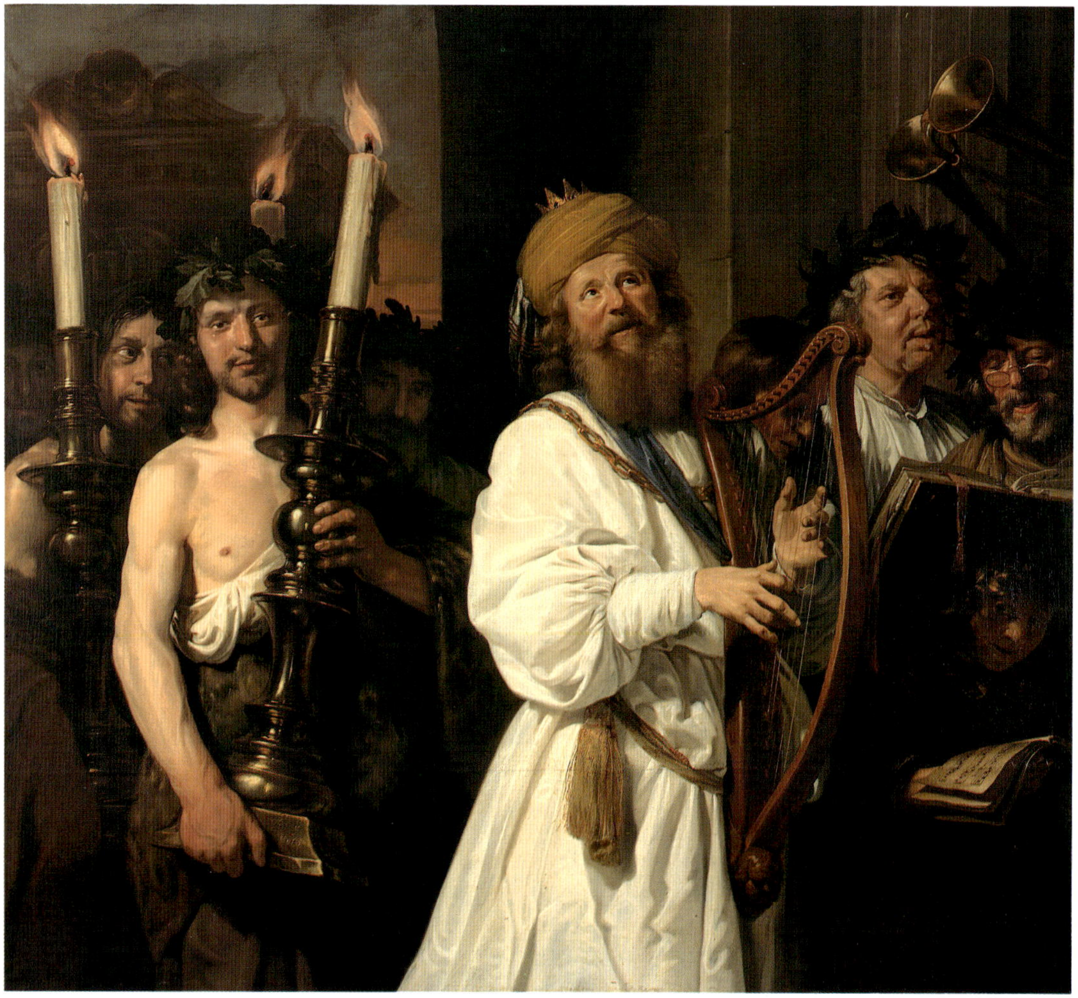

9 *David Playing the Harp*

Oil on canvas: 142 × 154 cm
Signed and dated: *J dBray 1670* (*JdB* in monogram) on the base of the candlestick in the left foreground
PROVENANCE: Possibly the picture by De Bray of this subject in the Taets van Amerongen sale, Amsterdam, 3 July 1805, lot 10, and later in another Amsterdam sale, 23 August 1808. In the collection of the 10th EARL OF WEMYSS AND MARCH in 1914 (but probably purchased before his succession) by descent.[1]

The painting shows King David bringing the Ark of the Covenant to Jerusalem after the defeat of the Philistines.[2] The Ark is visible in the left of the background. The story is taken from 2 *Samuel* 6, v.12-15, a subject which Jan's father, Salomon, had also painted.[3] A later variant of the composition, signed and dated 1674 (on the base of the harp), is in Herzog Anton Ulrich-Museum, Braunschweig (see fig.46). Instead of the main candle bearer at David's left in the Wemyss picture, there is a High Priest who carries a censer and wears a gold breastplate with twelve jewels representing the tribes of Israel.[4] The wreathed figures in both paintings are Levites, the servants of old Israel. De Bray closely follows the biblical text in showing David in his plain white linen robe. Houbraken mentioned a painting by De Bray of this subject which he saw with Arnold van Halen in Amsterdam which he stated was dated 1697.[5]

A larger history painting by De Bray of a subject from Heliodorus's *Aethiopica*, *The First Meeting of Theagenes and Chariclea* (147 × 182.8 cm) is in the Hunterian Museum in Glasgow as part of the SMILLIE gift.

EXHIBITED: *RA 1952-3*, no.637; *Pictures from Gosford House*, no.26.

LITERATURE: J. W. van Moltke, 'Jan de Bray', in *Marburger Jahrbuch für Kunstwissenschaft*, XI / XII, 1938-9, p.465.

THE EARL OF WEMYSS AND MARCH

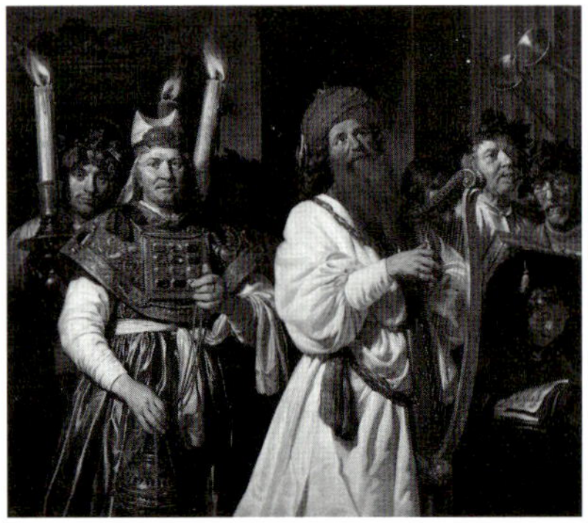

fig.46

1 Suggested by C. Thompson in *Pictures from Gosford*, p.19, presumably on the basis that the 10th Earl's taste was not for this sort of painting.
2 For a discussion of the depiction of this subject in Dutch seventeenth-century painting see *Het Oude Testament in de Schilderkunst van de Gouden Eeuw*, exhibition catalogue, Joods Historisch Museum, Amsterdam, and Israel Museum, Jerusalem, 1991, pp.92-3. The Wemyss painting is cited on p.103, note 40.
3 J. W. van Moltke, 'Salomon de Bray', in *Marburger Jahrbuch für Kunstwissenschaft*, XI / XII, 1938-9, p.381, no.19.
3 T. Döring, *Holländische Historienbilder des 17. Jahrhunderts*, Herzog Anton Ulrich-Museum, Braunschweig, 1990, no.29.
4 R. Klessman, *Die Holländischen Gemälde Kritisches Verzeichnis*, Herzog Anton Ulrich-Museum, 1983, p.35.
5 A. Houbraken, *De Groote Schouburgh der Nederlantsche Konstschilders en Schilderessen*, Amsterdam, 1718, vol.1, fol.176.

1597-1664. De Bray (or Braij) lived and worked in Haarlem, a gifted architect and poet as well as painter. He married in May 1625 and Jan de Bray was his eldest son, whom he seems to have trained. He had at least ten children of whom four died in infancy. He died of the plague in Haarlem which also carried off his wife and four more of his children, leaving only Jan and a brother alive.

10 *The Twins Clara and Aelbert Bray*

Oil on canvas: 82.6 × 64.8 cm
PROVENANCE: Probably the picture exhibited at the British Institution in 1834, no.90, by Sir Charles Bagot.[1] Private Collection, Scotland.

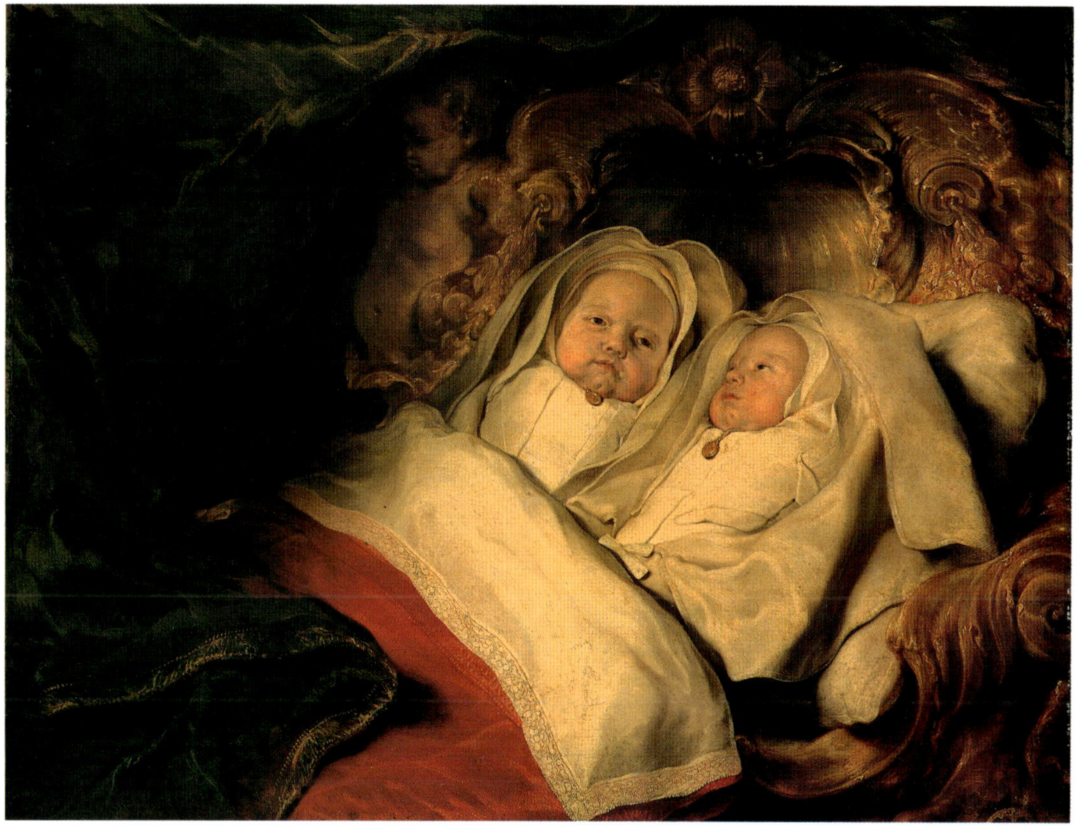

There is a pencil study of these two babies in the Pierpont Morgan Library, New York (fig.47). The drawing is inscribed '*1646 8/12 / Neef Simon de Braÿ Symon / 2 lingen { Clara / en. / Albert*'[2] (presumably Clara on the left and Albert on the right from the format of inscription). The twins were the children of the artist's nephew, Simon, who was a lawyer and the son of Salomon's brother Simon. It has been suggested that this painting is really a funeral picture on the basis that the infants' gaze is rather sombre and the painting is obviously elaborate and formal.[3] However, both twins wear baptismal lockets (*pillegifts* presented by godparents) around their necks, while the baroque shell which forms their cradle may also be symbolic of baptism. It is more likely that the twins' great-uncle wished to celebrate their official membership of the church rather than commemorate their dual demise. The New York drawing must have been made while the infants were sleeping and the artist presumably decided to show them in the painting with eyes open and perhaps souls awakened.

EXHIBITED: *Trésors de l'art belge*, Brussels and Paris, vol.I, 1912, no.CII [240], pl.89.

LITERATURE: J. W. van Moltke, 'Salomon de Bray', in *Marburger Jahrbuch für Kunstwissenschaft*, XI / XII, 1938-9, no.95; discussed by F. Stampfele, *Rubens and Rembrandt in their Century, Flemish and Dutch Drawings of the 17th Century from the Pierpont Morgan Library*, exhibition catalogue, New York, 1979, p.93.

PRIVATE COLLECTION, SCOTLAND

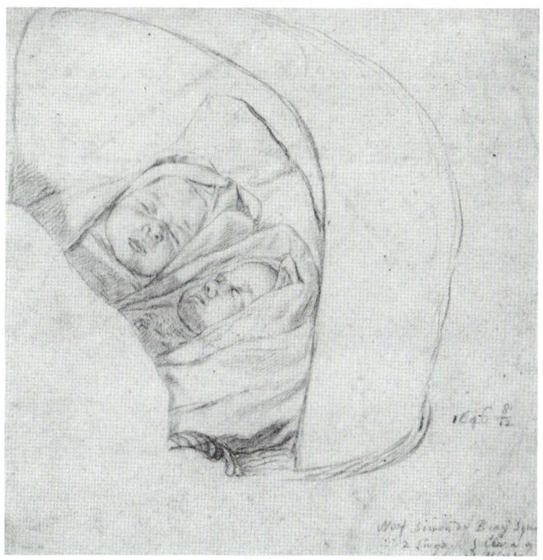

fig.47

1 Moltke, 'Salomon de Bray', *op. cit.*, no.95a. There was probably a smaller (26 × 33.5 cm) painting of the twins which related closely to the Pierpont Morgan sketch: 'Das Bildnis zweier Kinder in der Wiege. Sie liegen friedlich zusammen, gut eingepackt, so dass nur ihre Gesichter zu sehen sind. Beide schlummern.' Judging from the description of 'slumbering children', it would seem that the smaller version showed the twins with their eyes closed as in the sketch. The picture was in the *Arundel Club Portfolio*, 1906, III, no.IX, as by Jordaens (Moltke, 'Salomon de Bray', *op. cit.*, no.95) although Stampfele conflates this with the larger picture in this exhibition.

2 F. Stampfele, *op. cit.*, no.61.

3 *Ibid.*, p.92.

BARTHOLOMEUS BREENBERGH

1598-1657. Born in Deventer, Breenbergh was living in Amsterdam in 1619, during which year he went to Rome. There he was one of the founders, in 1623, of the Schildersbent, the group of Netherlandish artists in Rome, and he knew Cornelis van Poelenburgh and Paul Bril (copying some of the latter's works). Breenbergh returned to Amsterdam probably c.1629 and is twice listed as a merchant in the city before his death there. He painted Italianate landscapes, which he continued to develop after his return from Rome, and also history paintings with religious and mythological subjects.

11 *Joseph Distributing Corn in Egypt*

Oil on canvas: 111.8 × 88.9 cm
Signed and dated: *Bart.^S Breenbergh fecit / A^o. 1654.* bottom left
PROVENANCE: Perhaps Jan Agges sale, Amsterdam, 16 August 1702, lot 22; B. van Cley sale, Amsterdam, 1 April 1756, lot 9, bought by P. Leendert de Neufville; his sale, Amsterdam, 19 June 1765, lot 2, bought by Braamcamp; his sale, Amsterdam, 31 July 1771, lot 27, bought by Fouquet.[1] In the collection of John, 1st MARQUESS OF BUTE by 1800 and thence by descent; Private Collection, Scotland.

The subject first appears in Breenbergh's work in 1644, in a smaller horizontal picture[2] (now destroyed) which the artist himself engraved. He was influenced in his composition by Pieter Lastman's painting of the same subject (after which Rembrandt made a drawing),[3] but in the reworking of the design ten years later Breenbergh altered the format, stressing the vertical with the obelisk and steep steps rising on the left to the high building (based on the church of Santa Maria degli Aracoeli on the Capitoline in Rome). This picture is the only work which Breenbergh is known to have replicated, presumably on commission, and the replica, dated 1655, is now in the Barber Institute of Fine Arts, Birmingham. Though Breenbergh painted fewer works towards the end of his life, his ability did not lessen with age, as attested by *Joseph Distributing Corn in Egypt.*

The picture is in the 1822 catalogue of Luton Hoo and is listed as hanging in the dressing room: 'Joseph and his brothers in Egypt – His touch light and spirited colouring pleasing, taste of the Roman School, and his pictures have force and delicacy – his figures gracefully designed, expression lively simple and natural, his works rare and highly valued'.[4]

Waterhouse noted when he saw the picture at Mount Stuart on 25 July 1949[5] that it was 'very unusual and in excellent condition'.

EXHIBITED: *Bethnal Green 1882-3,* no.24; *Edinburgh 1949,* no.2; M. G. Roethlisberger, *Bartholomeus Breenbergh,* Richard L. Feigen & Co., London, 1991, no.26.‡

LITERATURE: M. G. Roethlisberger, *Bartholomeus Breenbergh, The Paintings,* Berlin, 1981, no.230.

PRIVATE COLLECTION, SCOTLAND

1 Roethlisberger, *op. cit.*, 1991. p.69. However, it is not possible to confirm the early provenance of the work since all of these references could equally describe the Birmingham version rather than the Bute painting as both are the same size.
2 Formerly in Dresden. A copy of the painting is reproduced in Roethlisberger, *op. cit.*, 1981, no.204.
3 A. Tümpel and P. Schatborn, *Pieter Lastman, the Man who taught Rembrandt,* exhibition catalogue, Het Rembrandthuis, Amsterdam, 1991-2: Lastman's *Joseph Distributing Corn in Egypt* (National Gallery of Ireland, Dublin) and Rembrandt's drawing (Albertina, Vienna) are reproduced on p.75.
4 The Duke of Hamilton owned a Breenbergh of a 'Dutch Fair' which was in the Beckford inventory of 13 September 1844, in *Waterhouse Notebooks,* transcriptions of Hamilton inventories in the Getty Archive, Santa Monica.
5 *Waterhouse Notebooks,* vol.30, p.57 as one of the pictures borrowed from the Marquess of Bute for exhibition in Edinburgh that year.

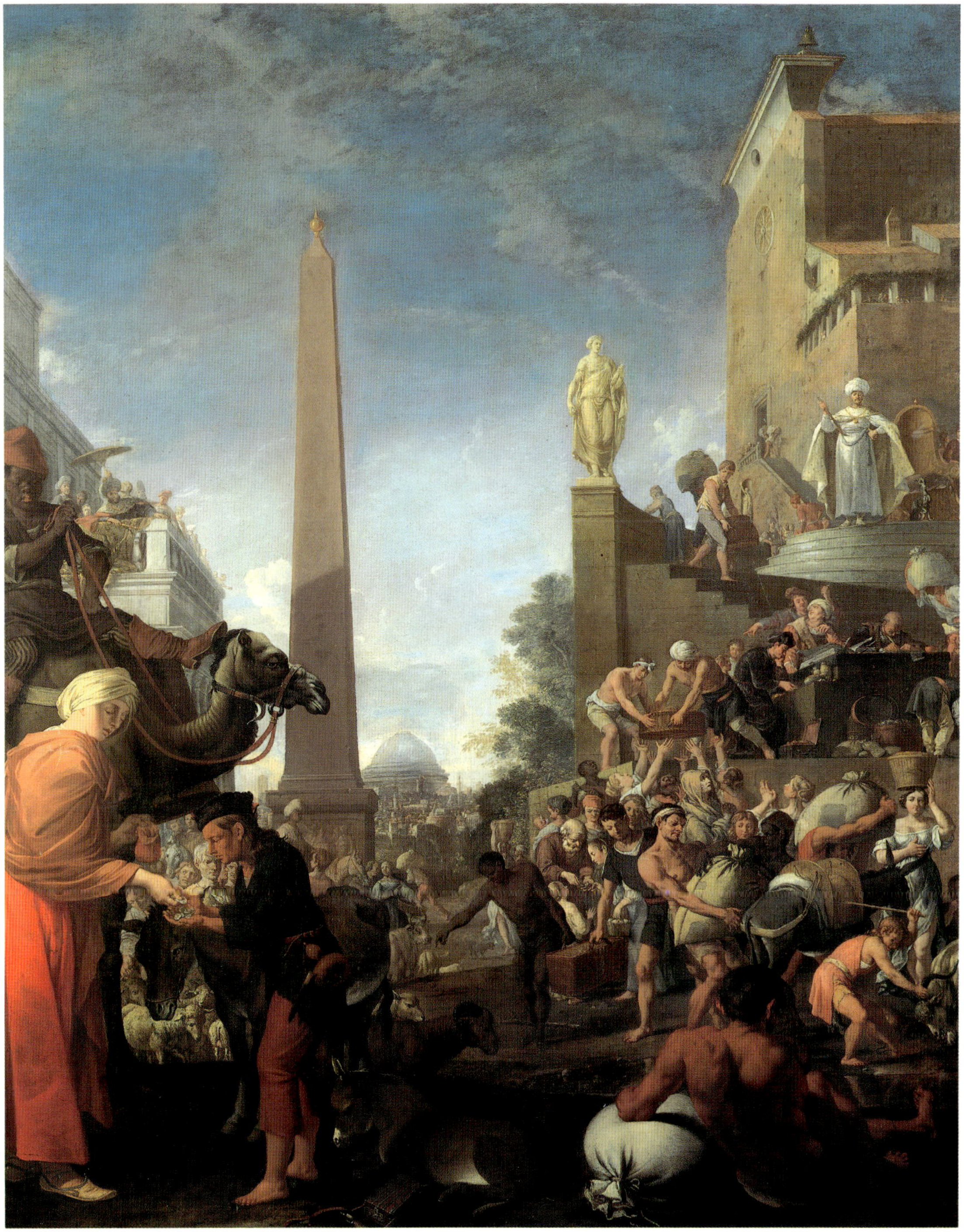

JAN VAN DE CAPPELLE

1626-79. Born in Amsterdam where he married and died, Van de Cappelle was the son of the owner of a dye-works in the city. He may have trained with Simon de Vlieger whose style certainly seems to have influenced his early work in which he specialised in views of rivers and estuaries, although he did paint some winter scenes in the manner of Aert van de Neer. He inherited his father's business and had a large collection of paintings and drawings by his contemporaries, including some 1300 drawings by De Vlieger.

12 *Sea Piece: A Calm*

Oil on canvas: 48.2 × 59.7 cm
Signed and dated: *J V Cappelle 165 (3)* at corner of bottom right
PROVENANCE: Lord Overstone, London, by 1857; his daughter, Lady Wantage, London, by 1883; Private Collection, Scotland and placed on loan at the National Gallery of Scotland in 1988.

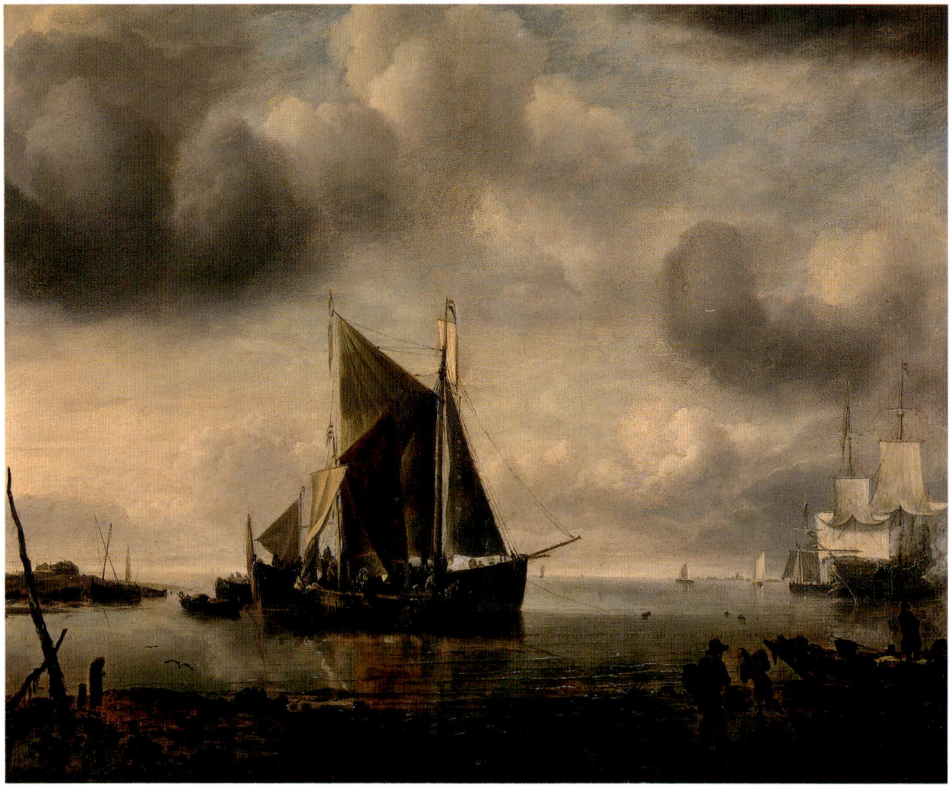

There has been some debate about the reading of the date which is not entirely clear. However, it is generally read as 1653 which is consistent with Van de Cappelle's style of painting at this period. M. Russell also notes that the form of signature found on this work was not used by the artist before 1652 (until which date he spelt his name 'Capelle').[1]

Waagen praised the painting noting that it was 'in all respects – for example, in the reflections on the water – of such delicacy and transparency, and at the same time so picturesquely composed and carefully finished, that it belongs to the best works known to me of the master'. Another outstanding painting by the same artist of *A River Scene* is also illustrated in the *Wantage Catalogue* (no.39). The latter was purchased in 1876 from Albert Levey, but unfortunately there does not seem to be any more information about the acquisition of *Sea Piece: A Calm*.

The types of boat shown in the painting were commonly bought by the Scots from Dutch suppliers in the seventeenth century (as pointed out by T. C. Smout, p.22).

EXHIBITED: Guildhall Gallery, London, 1895, no.118; Slatter Gallery, London, 1949, no.4; *Agnews*, no.28.

LITERATURE: *Waagen 1857*, p.137; *HdG*, no.51; *Wantage Catalogue*, no.40; M. Russell, *Jan van de Cappelle*, Leigh-on-Sea, 1975, no.51, p.25 and p.68.‡

PRIVATE COLLECTION, SCOTLAND

1 Russell, *op. cit.*, and *Agnews*, p.52.

PIETER CLAESZ.

1597/8-1661. Born in Burgsteinfurt in Westphalia, he had married and moved to Haarlem by 1617 where his son, Nicolaes Berchem, was born in 1620. Claesz. only painted still-lifes, of which the earliest is dated 1621. He continued painting until the last year of his life in Haarlem, and he is noted for his monochrome breakfast or banquet scenes which he and Willem Claesz. Heda made famous in Haarlem.

13 *Still-life with Glasses*

Oil on panel: 73.03 × 99.06 cm
Signed and dated: *PCH* (in monogram) and dated *16 (4)1*. Also *492* (Newbattle Abbey number) lower left corner
PROVENANCE: MARQUESS OF LOTHIAN, Newbattle Abbey, by *c.*1788[1] and thence by descent until 1953; Private Collection, Scotland.

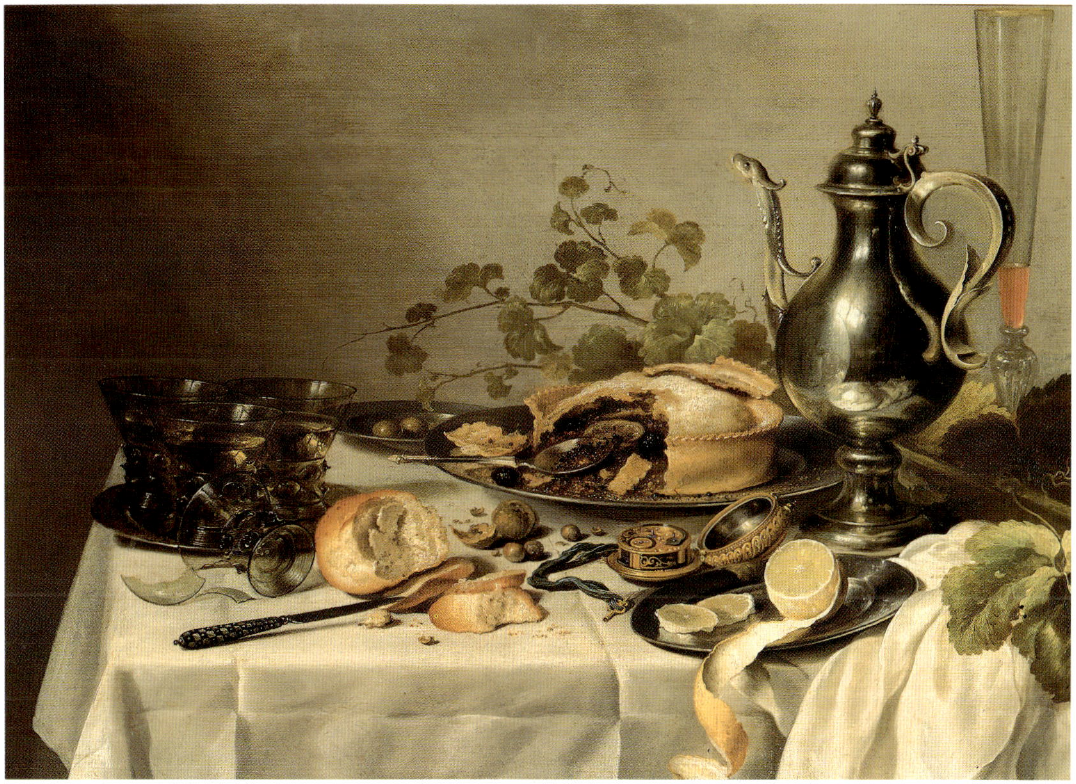

The third digit of the date is somewhat unclear and was once read as '1', but this is inconsistent with the style of the picture and a later date of 1641 seems more likely. The composition relates closely to a *Banketje* in Vassar College Art Gallery, Poughkeepsie (no.40.1.5), which is signed and dated 1641.[2] That composition is a variation of the Lothian painting in reverse, including many of the same elements, such as the silver pitcher with its faint reflection of the artist, which can also be found, for example, in a work of the same date formerly in the collection of E. C. Francis.[3]

The Lothian collection is remarkably well documented but early inventories are often somewhat vague and although the first mention of this painting in the collection is in a list of *c.*1788 as 'Glasses and a Pie',[4] it is not inconceivable that it might have entered the collection somewhat earlier. A list of *c.*1670 describes 'Une vielle piesse su du bois' bought in Leiden for 'Un Guilders'[5] and it is tempting to imagine that this is the Lothian picture, but the paintings acquired at that time cannot be traced with any certainty. However, it is likely that the Claesz. was purchased by Robert, Ist Marquess and 3rd Earl of Lothian (1636-1703), who was responsible for the rebuilding of Newbattle Abbey outside Edinburgh, and the refurbishing of its interior with paintings, books, tapestries and overdoors.[6] It seems that he might also have bought at least 24 such works, including flower and game pieces, two paintings attributed to De Heem and numerous bird pictures.[7]

LITERATURE: *Wenley*, no. 492.

PRIVATE COLLECTION, SCOTLAND

1 Wenley, *op. cit.*
2 I am grateful to Ben Broos for this information. The Vassar picture is reproduced in his entry on the picture in *Dutch Paintings from America 1990*, no.16.
3 *RKD* photograph, exhibited *RA 1952-3*, sold Sotheby's, London, 30 November, 1983, lot 87.
4 Wenley, *op. cit.*
5 *Ibid.*, p.81.
6 *Ibid.*, pp.75-92.
7 *Ibid.*, p.90.

AELBERT CUYP

1620-91. Trained in his home town of Dordrecht with his father, Jacob Gerritz. Cuyp, who was primarily a portrait painter. Aelbert's first landscapes from the late 1630s are influenced by Jan van Goyen, but he later developed a more Italianate style inspired by Utrecht artists such as Jan Both. As well as landscapes and river views, Cuyp painted some biblical subjects and portraits.

14 *The Fleet at Nijmegen*

Oil on canvas: 113.7 × 166.2 cm
Signed: *A Cuyp* on ship at left (on sail to right of mast)
PROVENANCE: Possibly with Anthonetta van Haerlem (or Van Bouthem, the widow of Arent Dichters) where an inventory of 1673 describes a large picture by Aelbert Cuyp of a '*Rendevou*' of a fleet at Nijmegen. The painting also occurs in an inventory of Abraham Lisse at Breda in 1675.[1] Perhaps Sir George Colebrook Sale, London, 1774.[2] The 3rd Duke of Bridgewater by 1802.[3] Private Collection, Scotland.

The seated blue-sashed figure in the rowing boat has traditionally been thought to be Prince Maurits but there is no proof of this, although Prince Frederick Hendrik did visit Nijmegen in 1647.[4] The painting probably dates from the mid 1650s.

It was described in 1818 by William Young Ottley as 'one of the finest works of Cuyp which this country can boast and is in the most perfect state of preservation'. Ottley remarked that 'never was the warm glow of an evening sun more happily expressed than in the sky, or more truly reflected than on the even surface of the calm water'.[5] Waagen saw the picture in 1838 and, writing of it later, simply observed that it was 'as if the painter had dipped his pencil in light' (*Waagen*, vol. 2, pp.72-3).

The picture was certainly at Cleveland House by May 1802, when it was seen by Joseph Farington, who sketched a plan of how it was hung opposite a 'Gaspar'. In a gallery full of Titians, Claudes and Poussins, it was the only work he wrote about in detail, stating he 'was particularly interested by a picture of Cuyp, a Port Scene, Evening, most scientifically arranged and bea[u]tifully coloured'.

Cleaned by De Wild in 1931,[6] a tinted varnish seems to have been added to prevent the Cuyp from outshining uncleaned paintings in the collection. However, the colours Farington praised were recently revealed following restoration by John Dick in 1991.

Early accounts often mistake the background with Dordrecht but in fact it shows Nijmegen from the north-west, effectively from the same point as that found in a work by Jan van Goyen now in the Rijksmuseum, Amsterdam (no.365).[7] Versions of this composition were used with alterations in various pictures (such as *HdG*, no.36c, which was owned by the Duke of Buccleuch in 1872), while a copy was with Leggatt Brothers, London, in 1949 (noted in *RKD* files).

The original composition was etched by John Burnet, the Scots painter and engraver, in his *Essay on the Education of the Eye* [8] (which was popular as a reference manual, with copies in the Royal Scottish Academy and Ferguson's Drawing Academy in Edinburgh). There is a watercolour copy of the painting in the Dowse collection of the Library of the Boston Athenaeum.

EXHIBITED: *Edinburgh 1945*, no.216.

LITERATURE: *Stafford Gallery Catalogue 1808*, no.142; *Stafford Gallery Catalogue 1818*, vol.3, no.37; *Bridgewater House Catalogue 1851*, no.216; *Waagen*, vol.2, p.48; *Bridgewater House Catalogue 1903*, no.84; *HdG*, no.30; *Bridgewater House Catalogue 1926*, no.216; *Reiss*, no.103.

PRIVATE COLLECTION, SCOTLAND

1 This early provenance has kindly been supplied by Alan Chong. The painting was traditionally believed to have been purchased from the artist by his friend and patron, Johan van der Linden van Slingeland and purchased at his sale in Dordrecht (Yver, Delfos), 22 August 1785, lot 69, by the 3rd Duke of Bridgewater (*Bridgewater House Catalogue 1903*, no.84). The Slingeland sale description of lot 69 tallies closely with *The Fleet at Nijmegen* as both Smith and De Groot noticed. However, the entry may well refer to the Waddesdon Manor Cuyp (*Reiss*, no.106) whose pendant (*Reiss*, no.104) is now in the National Gallery of Art, Washington DC.

2 Both Reiss and Chong suggest that the work was probably in the sale of Sir George Colebrook in 1774, where it reached the highest price then ever paid for a picture by this artist – 290 guineas. It was only listed in the Colebrook sale catalogue as 'a view of Nijmegen' but is referred to at greater length in the catalogue of John Bertel's sale in London of 26 April 1780, lot 74, where a picture by Cuyp is described as a 'View on the water near Dort, representing a calm with a multitude of vessels, and boats floating and ferries crossing, equal to a picture of his (a view near Nimwegen) which sold in Sir George Colebrooke's sale for 300 gns'.

3 *Farington*, vol. 5, pp.1774-6, 5 and 8 May 1802.

4 Information kindly given by Alan Chong.

5 *Stafford Gallery Catalogue 1818*, vol.3, no.37.

6 *Waterhouse Notebooks*, 21 December 1931, p.112.

7 For views of the city see *Het Valkhof te Nijmegen*, exhibition catalogue, Nijmegen Museum, 1980. Examples by Cuyp can be seen in the National Gallery of Scotland (no.2314) and in the collection of the Marquis of Tavistock. Both works were painted *c*.1655.

8 London, 1837, fig. 1, pl.1.

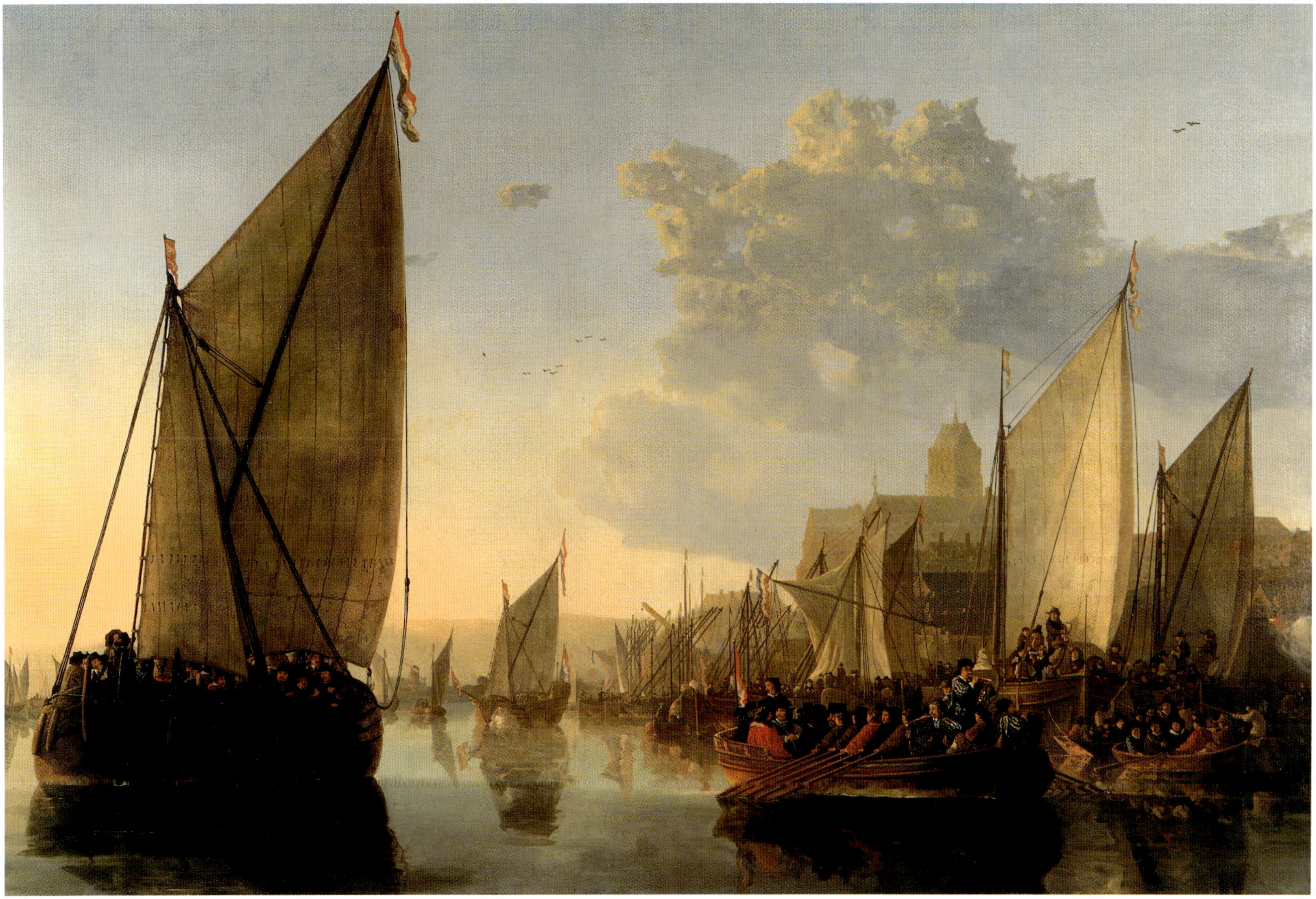

15 *The Riding Lesson*

Oil on canvas: 118.7 × 170.2 cm
Signed: *A. cuyp* at lower right
PROVENANCE: J. van der Linden van Slingeland, Dordrecht, by 1752 (Yver, Delfos, Dordrecht, 22 August 1785, lot 72 – as a pendant to lot 71).[1] Dubois sale with Lebrun, Paris, 20 December, lot 17. The EARLS OF HOPETOUN at Hopetoun House, near Edinburgh, before 1826 and thence by descent certainly until 1886 and perhaps until after 1908.[2] Edouard Rothschild, Ferrières, France, by 1912 and by descent. Seized by Germany in 1941 and in the collection of Hermann Goering, Berlin (inventory no.8), Central Collecting Point, Munich, 1946 (inventory no.5352); returned to France, 1946. André Seligmann, Paris. Rosenberg and Stiebel, from whom purchased in 1960 by Toledo Museum of Art, Ohio, with funds from the Libbey Endowment (no.1960.2).

It is likely that this is the painting referred to by Houbraken in 1718 as a 'Pikeurbaan', a riding school or *manège*, 'where the most picturesque horses were usually brought to be schooled, in order that their value might be realised'.[3] It seems the old title of 'Training Horses' is pertinent, the lesson being for the animal rather than the rider.

Reiss wrote that there 'is no other Cuyp quite like it. It seems as if he is making some deliberate tribute to the older generation of Utrecht painters: Poelenburgh, Breenbergh ...'[4] and certainly the fanciful classical statuary and Italianate buildings are reminiscent of similar elements in these masters' works. The Romanesque church, however, seems to be based on the Mariakerk in Utrecht.[5] Reiss dates this painting to the late 1650s although it may be earlier than this, as proposed by Chong who suggests that it should be dated *c*.1655.

The picture does not appear in the 1817 list of paintings at Hopetoun but was certainly in the collection by 1826 when it was exhibited in Edinburgh. A wedding photograph of the 1870s shows it hanging on the right side of the fireplace in the Red Drawing Room at Hopetoun House near Edinburgh (fig.48) where Hofstede de Groot failed to see it (due to repairs being carried out) on his visit in 1893. Another picture attributed to Cuyp still hangs as an overdoor in the Red Drawing Room (*HdG*, no.197).

EXHIBITED: *Ancient Pictures*, Royal Institution, Edinburgh, 1826, no.60 (as *Training Horses* lent by the Earl of Hopetoun); *RA* Winter Exhibition, 1883, no.238; *Edinburgh 1883*, no.276.

LITERATURE: G. Hoet, *Catalogus of Naamlyst van Schilderyen ...*, The Hague, 1752, vol. 2, p.495; *Smith*, no.11; *Waagen*, vol.3, p.309; *HdG*, nos 448 and 615; W. Hutton, 'Aelbert Cuyp, The Riding Lesson', *Toledo Museum of Art News*, VI, no.4, Autumn 1961, pp.79-85; *Reiss*, no.135.

TOLEDO MUSEUM OF ART
TOLEDO, OHIO

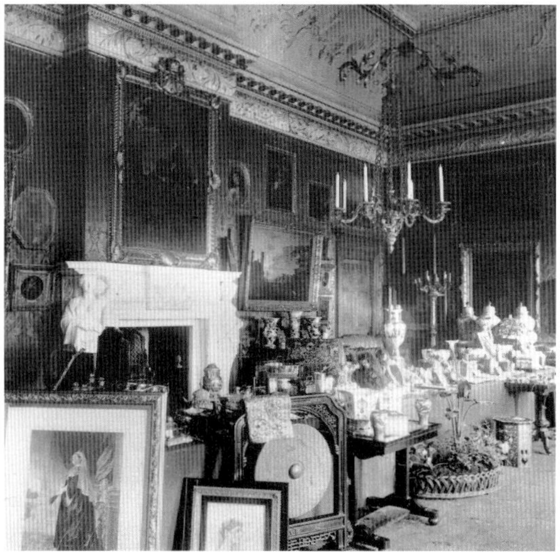

fig.48

1 The listed pendant *River Landscape, Huntsmen and Peasants* is now in the National Gallery of Art, Washington DC (no. 1942.9.16 [612]). Though the compositions of the paintings do not make them 'standard' symmetrical pendants, they are exactly the same size and painted in the same manner. It is surely important (as Chong believes) that they were accepted as pendants in the Slingeland collection, a statement which perhaps reflected the way the paintings were hung, although F. J. du Parc thinks the compositions are simply too different to be regarded as pendants (*Italian Recollections, Dutch Painters of the Golden Age*, Montreal Museum of Fine Arts, 1990, p.110).

2 Alan Chong notes that Hofstede de Groot saw the painting at Ferrières in 1912 and believed it to be in the collection of the Marquess of Linlithgow in 1908 (the Earl of Hopetoun was created Marquess of Linlithgow in 1902).

3 A. Houbraken, *De Groote Schouburgh der Nederlantsche Konstschilders en Schilderessen*, Amsterdam, 1718, vol.1, p.248: 'de Pikeurbaan, daar hij dan de schilderagtiste Paerden die daar gewoonlijk kwamen, in te pas braght, zoo dat men dezelve Kost onderkennen'. I am grateful to Alan Chong for bringing this to my attention.

4 Letter in Toledo files. Reiss also notes that the price for the Hopetoun painting was f.2650, 'a quarter much again as any other painting in the famous Slingeland sale of 1785', the next highest price of f.1920 being for the 'pendant' now in Washington DC.

5 J. de Meyere, *Utrecht op schilderijen: zes eeuw topografische voorstellingen van de stad Utrecht*, Utrecht, 1988, p.20, fig.2. Chong suggests that the church is also close to those at Maastricht and Cologne.

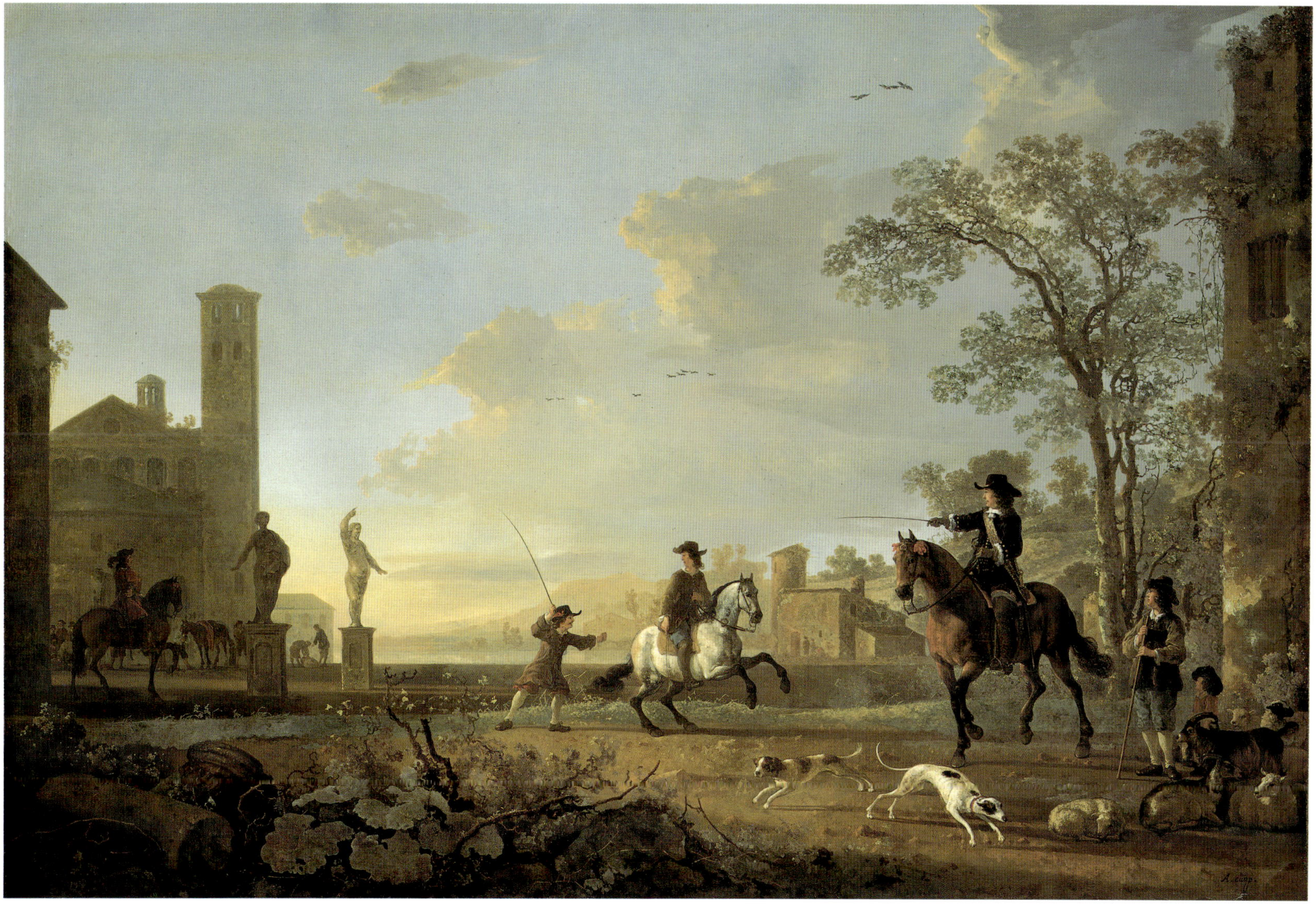

16 *Landscape with Rider and Peasants*

Oil on canvas: 123 × 241 cm
Signed: *A cuijp* at lower right
PROVENANCE: Bought in the United Provinces by Captain William Baillie for John, 3rd Earl of Bute, by 1764; MARQUESS OF BUTE, Luton Hoo and Mount Stuart, Isle of Bute; on loan to the National Museum of Wales, Cardiff, 1975-87; on loan to the National Gallery of Scotland, Edinburgh, 1988-9; purchased by the National Gallery, London, with grants from the NHMF and NACF, 1989 (no.6522).

Painted in the late 1650s, the picture is the largest Cuyp is known to have painted and arguably his masterpiece. It was engraved by William Elliott in 1764 (and inscribed as belonging to the Earl of Bute). As well as giving the name of the artist as 'Adrian Cuyp' (so little known was Cuyp's work in Britain at the time), Elliott also gave the composition a higher sky, leading to the assumption that the canvas had been cut down at some stage after 1764, which, however, is not the case.[1]

Joseph Farington noted on seeing the picture in 1818[2] that Benjamin West told him that it 'was brought to England by the late Captn. Baillie, and was the first picture by that master known in England. Having been seen, pictures by Cuyp were eagerly sought for and many were introduced and sold to advantage'. Though the painting may not have been 'the first' to enter a British collection[3] it was certainly much admired from an early date, praised by John Boydell in 1769 as 'inexpressibly bright, clear and sunny: the choice of scene is elegant and picturesque'.[4] This rural idyll, with its sunlit peasants, would have appealed to the Dutch landed gentry of the mid seventeenth century, a class into which Cuyp had recently married, and it would seem that this same appeal held good for British collectors a century later.

Landscape with Rider and Peasants was recorded as no.118 in a manuscript inventory of the Bute collection in 1790 (although it is not mentioned in a 1799 manuscript), and it may be the painting by Cuyp in an inventory of Luton Hoo made in 1822, listed as hanging in the Little Breakfast Room, no.56, 'Landscape and Figures, A good pencil with broad and free touch, tone of colouring sweet and agreeable, outline correct, great transparence in his water, his cattle well grouped and the particular times of the day expressed with truth and nature'. Waagen saw the picture which he described as a 'chef d'oeuvre' at Luton Hoo, the house which was badly damaged by fire in 1843 and which the family subsequently sold. This painting was eventually moved to Mount Stuart on the Isle of Bute in Scotland (where Waterhouse saw it on 25 July 1949, prior to its exhibition in Edinburgh the following month).[5] Although the finest, this was not the only Cuyp in the Bute collection and Reiss lists three other paintings (*HdG*, nos 19, 349 and 392). All of these were exhibited at the National Gallery of Scotland together with *Landscape with Rider and Peasants* in 1949, nos 5, 6, 7 and 8.

EXHIBITED: British Institution, London, 1818 – no.85, 1819 – no.37, 1847 – no.66; *RA* 1870, no.102; *Bethnal Green 1882-3*, no.202; *Glasgow 1884*, no.38; *Edinburgh 1949*, no.7; *Masters of Dutch Landscape*, no.25.

LITERATURE: 'The Marquis of Bute's Pictures at Bethnal Green' (anonymous review), *The Athenaeum*, 6 January 1883, p.23 (as *Morning Landscape with a River*); *HdG*, no.433 (with wrong size); *Reiss*, p.183, pl.140; *MacLaren and Brown*, supplement to catalogue, no.6522, pp.555-6.‡

NATIONAL GALLERY, LONDON

1 *MacLaren and Brown*, p.555. Inspection shows the canvas edges are unpainted on all four sides. Elliott's motive may have been either whimsy or there may have been an additional strip of canvas at the top of the painting to give it a 'fashionably higher sky'.

2 *Farington*, vol.15, p.5203, 18 May 1818.

3 Chong, in his entry on the picture in *Masters of Dutch Landscape*, notes that a Swiss dealer 'Grand Jean' was meant to have imported Cuyps into the country at an early date (one of which was later purchased by Sir Lawrence Dundas and is now in the National Gallery, London, no.53).

4 J. Boydell, *A Collection of Prints, Engraved after the Most Capital Paintings in England*, London, 1769, pl.12.

5 *Waterhouse Notebooks*, vol.30, p.66. The picture is described as 'a landscape with cows, a rider, sheep, ducks, a sportsman and nearly everything. Signed ... Prevailing silvery golden greenish tone. A very little old flaking on tree tops upper R. Light thickly impast'd but the pigment is not quite as clotty as that in the two small ones. The reflections in the water are enchanting'. The 'small ones' he refers to are catalogue nos 5 and 6 in the Edinburgh exhibition of 1949, together with no.8, *Orpheus Charming the Beasts*, listed as the artist's 'only mythological subject'.

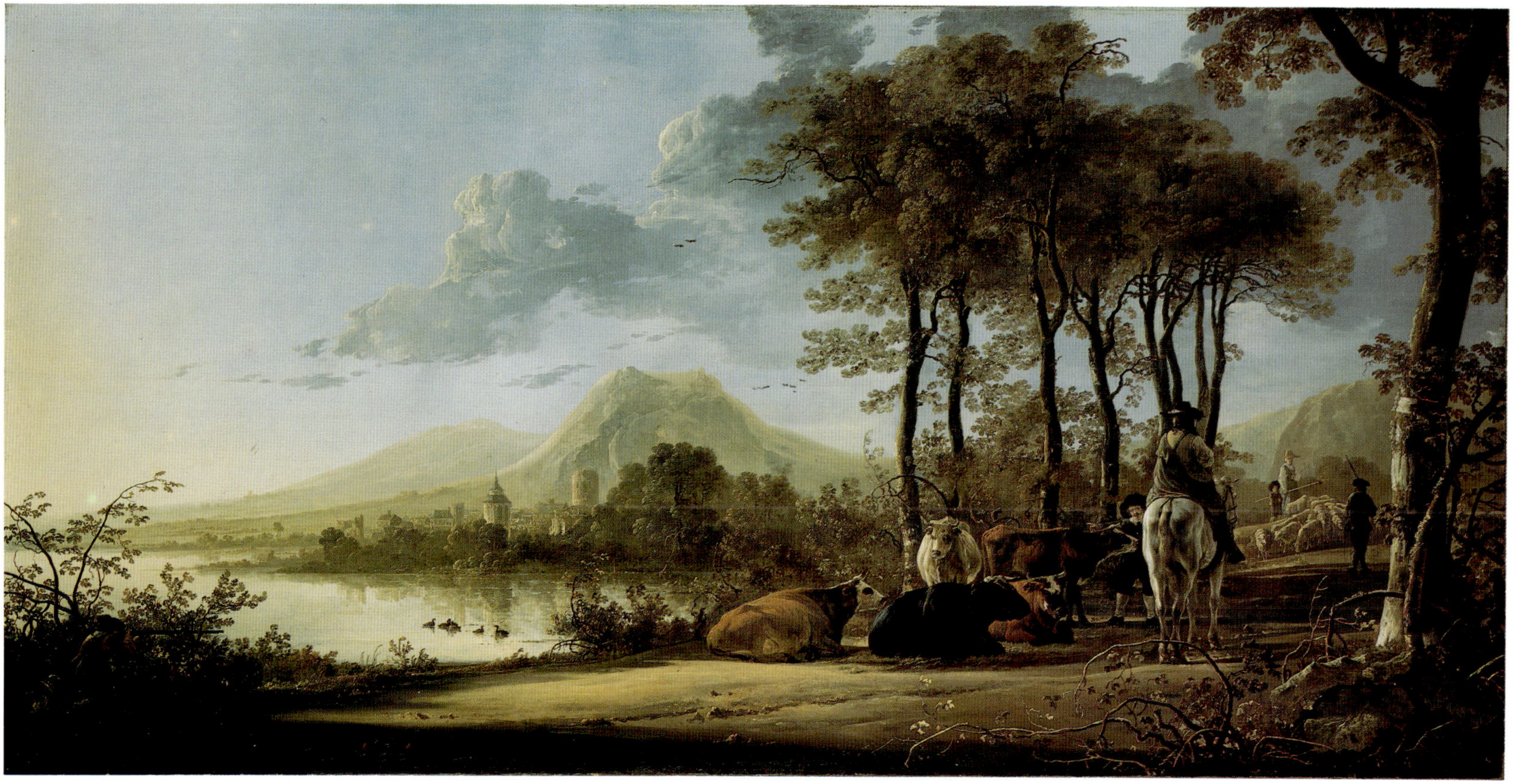

GERARD DOU

1613-75. Born in Leiden, Dou was apprenticed to his father as a glass-engraver. In 1628 he went to study in Rembrandt's workshop until Rembrandt moved to Amsterdam in 1631/2. Dou then began to perfect his painstaking brushwork for which he became famous. He was the first of the school of 'Fijnschilders', or fine painters, in Leiden, and taught pupils including Frans van Mieris and Godfried Schalken.

17 *Self-portrait*

Oil on panel: 17.8 × 15.2 cm
Signed: *GDOV* (*GD* in monogram) on right
PROVENANCE: Purchased in The Hague in 1819 when it was bought by John Smith,[1] from whom purchased by Lord Francis Leveson Gower[2] (before 1846).
Private Collection, Scotland.

This panel relates closely to the painting in the National Gallery, London, no.192, which has also traditionally been believed to be a *Self-portrait* by Dou (fig.49).[3] The paintings are similar in scale but the London composition (which Brown dates *c.*1635-40) is somewhat more elaborate, while this panel does not show the artist's hands (always notoriously difficult in a self-portrait). This has traditionally been believed to show Dou aged 22 which, if true, would indicate a date of 1635. This date would seem compatible with the style of this panel (which perhaps predates the London picture). The paint here is fairly thin and is applied with verve. However, Dou also makes use of precise brushstrokes, particularly for each hair of stubble on his chin and the touches of colour in his otherwise sombre hat. The character and pose are strongly reminiscent of Rembrandt who seems to have influenced his pupil in this composition. Dou's panel recalls Rembrandt's most famous early etched self-portrait of 1631, as well as giving slight presentiments of his more ambitious *Self-portrait Leaning on a Stone Sill* of 1639.[4]

The panel, bevelled at the back on all four sides, is in excellent condition, save slight wear on the signature. It was surface-cleaned by John Dick in 1992.

A copy was in the sale of the Delaroff of St Petersburg collection held in Paris in 1914, as by Rembrandt (14.5 × 12 cm), and was later with Goudstikker in Amsterdam in 1927 (where it was exhibited, catalogue 33, no.31), before going to an American private collection.[5] There was also another Dou self-portrait in the collection of Lord Clerk of Eldin which was sold at his auction in Picardy Place, Edinburgh, 14 March 1833, lot 30. It measured approximately 14 × 11.4 cm and was described as 'his own portrait by candlelight. An exquisite cabinet gem, painted with admirable effect, in his most finished manner'.[6]

LITERATURE: *Bridgewater House Catalogue 1851*, no.124; *HdG*, no.273, *Bridgewater House Catalogue 1926*, no.124.

PRIVATE COLLECTION, SCOTLAND

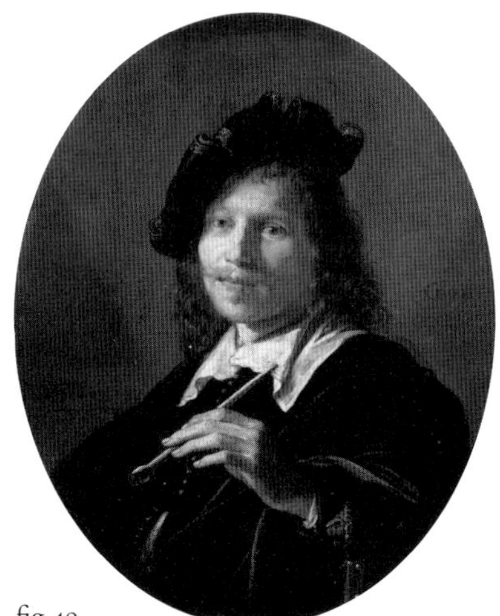

fig.49

1 It was lithographed in reverse as a frontispiece to *Smith* and no.97.
2 *Bridgewater House Catalogue 1903*, no.67.
3 *MacLaren and Brown*, p.106.
4 *Rembrandt 1991, Drawings and Etchings*, fig.12, p.168 and no.13.
5 *RKD* neg. no.2140. It was exhibited in *Rembrandt and his Pupils*, Museum of North Carolina, Raleigh, 1959, no.87.
6 *Catalogue of the Eldin Collection of Pictures, Prints, Drawings, and Objects of Virtu*, Edinburgh, 1833, p.5.

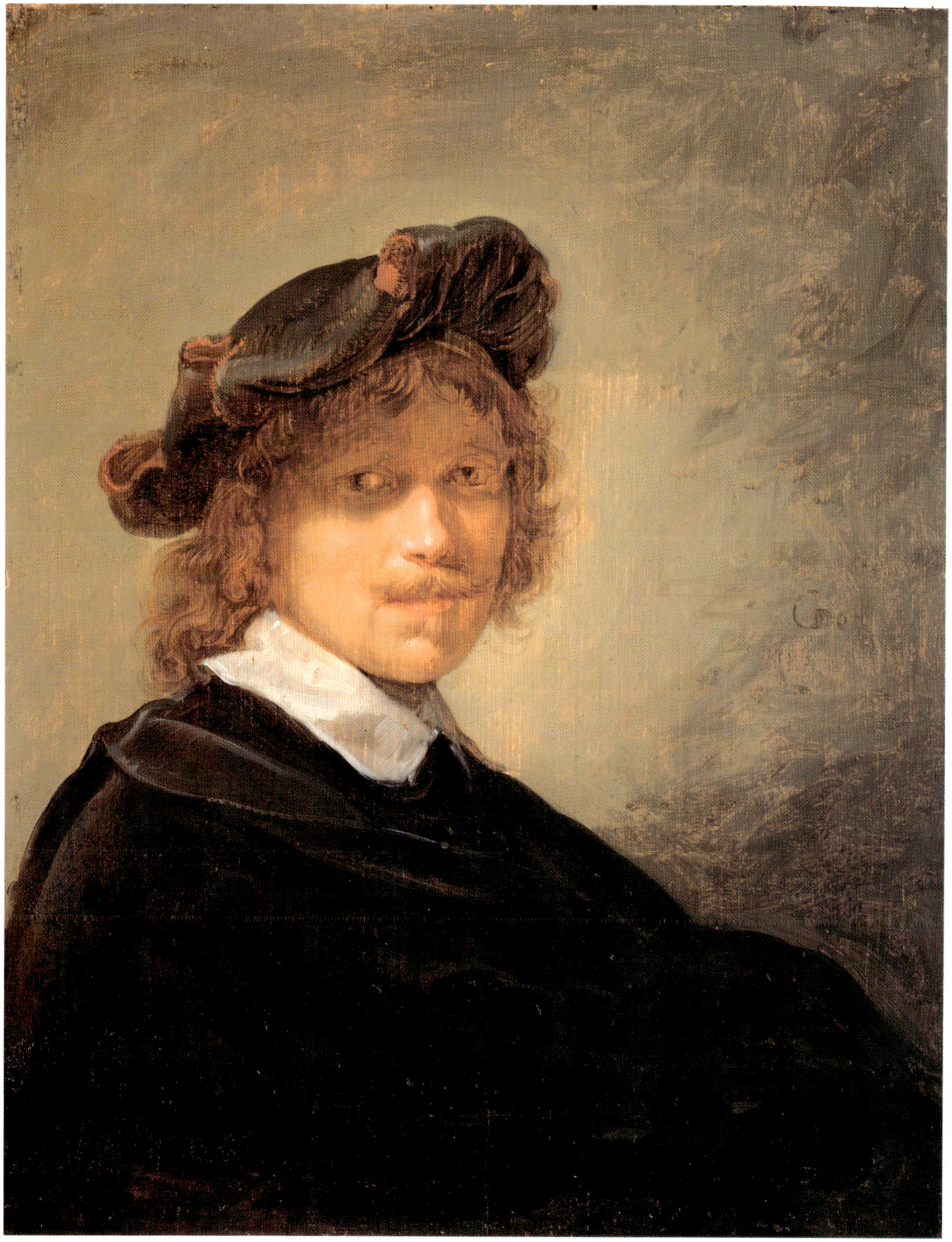

18 *Interior with Violinist*

Oil on panel (arched top): 31 × 23.7 cm
Signed: *G. Dou. 1637* (*GD* in monogram) on lowest stair

PROVENANCE: Possibly given by Pieter Spiering to Queen Christina of Sweden and returned to Spiering by 1652.[1] James Brydges, 1st Duke of Chandos[2] (1674-1744) and in his sale, 6-8 May 1747, lot 170 on 8 May, for 88 guineas;[3] sold Christie's, London, 29 March 1800, lot 91, for 357 guineas (possibly to Ladbroke collection – inscription on verso); 2nd Marquis of Stafford by 1808; thence by descent to John, 5th Earl of Ellesmere (later 6th DUKE OF SUTHERLAND), by whom placed on loan in 1946 to the National Gallery of Scotland; purchased by Private Treaty with a NHMF grant by the National Gallery of Scotland in 1984 (no.2420).

This is the first known signed and dated painting by Dou. It was probably the picture described as '*Un petit tableau où un homme joue du violon selon la tabulature*' in the 1652 inventory of the collection of Queen Christina of Sweden.[4] Against this entry is marked 'De Mr Spiring rendu', indicating that this is likely to be one of the pictures which the Queen's Ambassador to the Netherlands, Pieter Spiering, gave to her. Spiering paid Dou 500 guilders per annum to reserve the exclusive right to purchase his paintings but Spiering's gifts may not have been entirely enthusiastically received since the queen returned the *Interior with Violinist* together with nine other works by Dou in 1652 after Spiering's recall from the Netherlands.[5]

X-rays reveal that Dou's original ideas for the composition were somewhat different. The face of the sitter has been altered as has the position of the book, while there is a different shape by the sitter's right foot, perhaps another book.[6]

There is a watercolour after this painting in the Dowse collection of the Library of the Boston Athenaeum, while a copy in oils is in Cheltenham Art Gallery.[7]

EXHIBITED: *Edinburgh 1945*, no.244; *De Hollandse Fijnschilders: van Gerard Dou tot Adriaen van der Werff*, Rijksmuseum, Amsterdam, 1989, no.3.‡

LITERATURE: *Stafford Gallery Catalogue 1808*, p.131, no.186; *Stafford Gallery Catalogue 1818*, vol. 4, p.101, no.75; *Smith*, no.102; *Bridgewater House Catalogue 1851*, no.244; *Waagen*, vol.2, p.43; *HdG*, no.82; *Bridgewater House Catalogue 1926*, no.244.

NATIONAL GALLERY OF SCOTLAND

1 The picture probably mentioned by Joachim von Sandrart in his *Teutsche Academie* of 1675: 'Lautenschlager an einem Tisch sitzend, der vor ihme Bücher ligen hat, ungefähr einer Spannen gross'.

2 The panel has the Duke's seal on the back, identified by H. Macandrew.

3 G. Vertue, *The Walpole Society*, XXII, 1933/4, p.136. The Duke of Chandos owned five paintings by Dou included in this sale.

4 Cited by O. Granberg, *Svenska Konstsamlingarnas Historia*, Stockholm, 1929, vol.1, no.3.

5 I. Gaskell, 'Gerrit Dou, his Patrons and the Art of Painting', *The Oxford Art Journal*, 5: 1, 1982, pp.15-16.

6 A letter from R. Baer in gallery files notes that Dou's *Hermit* in the National Gallery of Art, Washington DC, also underwent similarly radical change in the positioning of the book.

7 C. White, *Catalogue of Foreign Paintings from the de Ferrières Collection*, Cheltenham Art Gallery and Museums, 1988, p.20.

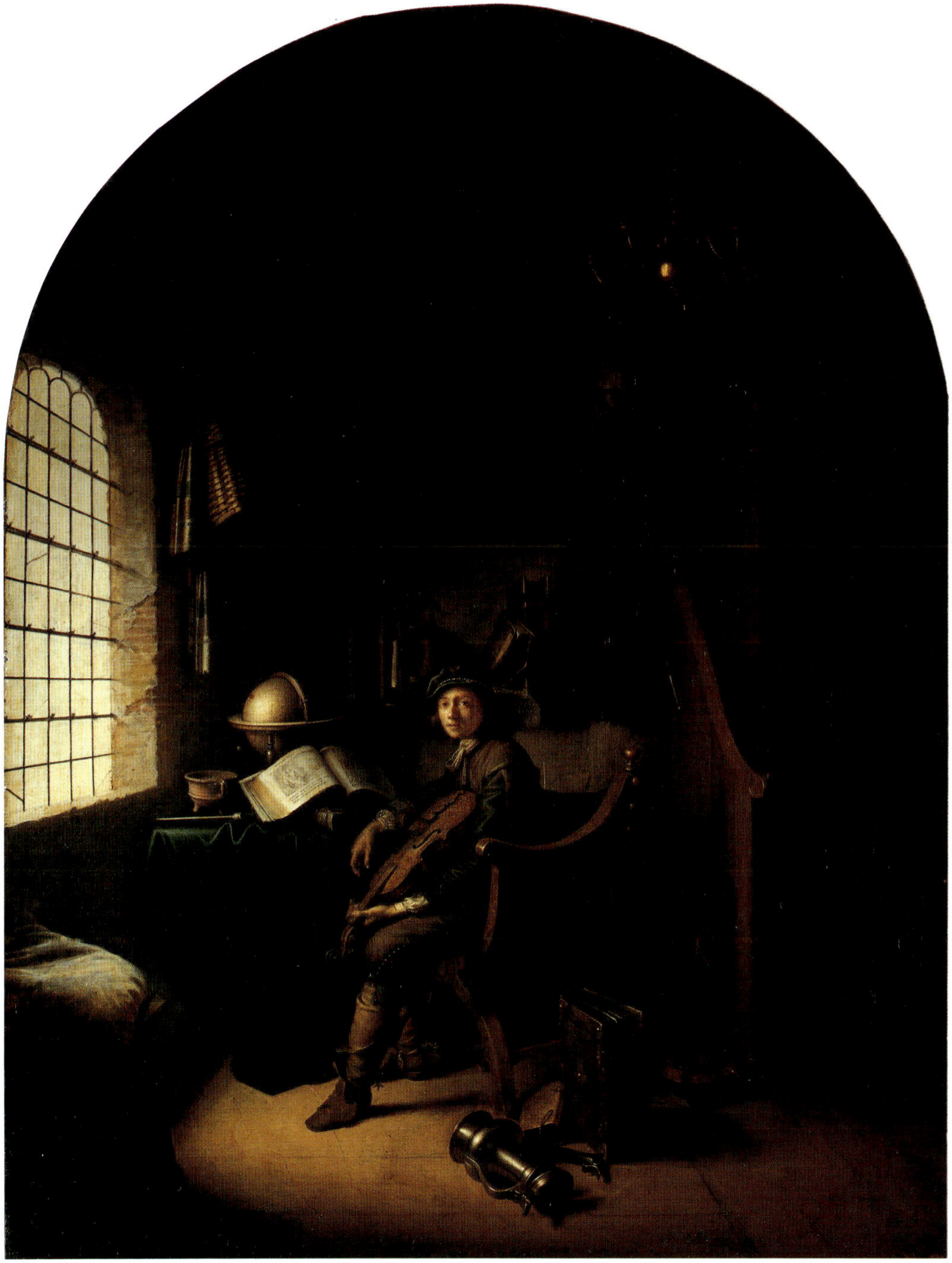

KAREL DUJARDIN

c.1622-78. Probably born in Amsterdam, Dujardin was a pupil of Nicolaes Berchem who was only a couple of years older than him. He may have been in Rome in the late 1640s or late 1650s. He was in Amsterdam in 1652 and was a guild painter in The Hague in 1656. He returned to Amsterdam in 1659 but went to Italy in 1675, moving to Venice in 1678 where he died. His Italianate scenes were much influenced by Berchem and Jan Asselijn, but he also painted portraits and history pictures and made many etchings.

19 *Halt at a Wine House Door*

Oil on canvas: 81 × 89.6 cm
PROVENANCE: SIR JAMES ERSKINE OF TORRIE by 1819 (when exhibited), by whom bequeathed in 1825 to the University of Edinburgh which received the picture in 1836; placed on loan to the Board of Manufactures, Edinburgh, first at the Royal Institution, then at the National Gallery of Scotland for its opening in 1859 until 1983, when returned to the University of Edinburgh.

Cleaned in 1936, this is one of a group of late landscapes painted in Italy, perhaps datable to *c.*1675 or slightly later.

Waagen thought that the tone of the distance in the horizon was 'somewhat too uniformly insipid' though he pronounced it a beautiful picture, whereas Hofstede de Groot was altogether more disparaging, suggesting that it was only a copy of a genuine Dujardin composition. J. Kilian suggests that the picture relates both in composition and theme to a painting currently in Turin, *Extensive Landscape with Travellers Halted for Refreshment at an Inn*[1] by Dujardin which was sold at Sotheby's, London, 15 February 1989, lot 188 (as Hendrick Mommers).

Sir James Erskine acquired this painting sometime before 1819 when he showed it at the inaugural exhibition of the Royal Institution in Edinburgh, where it was listed as as *Woodscene with Boy and Cow.* Sir James seems to have been fond of Dutch Italianate landscapes for he also owned paintings by Berchem, Andries and Jan Both, Lingelbach and Pynacker (Catalogue no.44).[2]

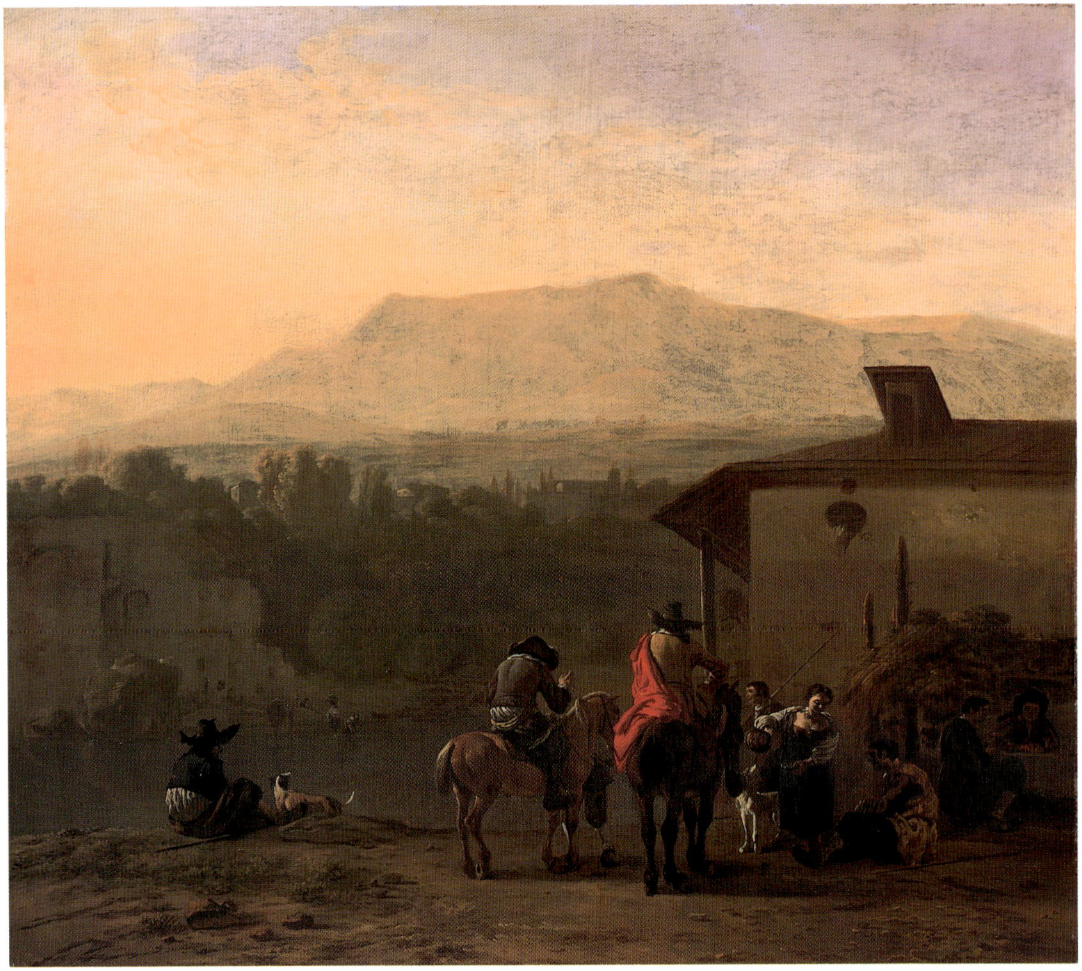

EXHIBITED: Royal *Institution Exhibition of Ancient Pictures*, Edinburgh, 1819, no.20; *Le paysage hollandais au XVIIIième siècle*, Musée de l'Orangerie, Paris, 1950-1, no.23; *Nederlandse 17 Eeuwse Italianiserende Landscapschilders*, Centraal Museum, Utrecht, 1965, no.131; *The Torrie Collection*, no.19.

LITERATURE: *Smith*, supplement no.24; *Waagen*, vol.3, p.272; *HdG 1893*, p.132; E. Brochhagen, *Bulletin des Musées Royaux*, Brussels, 1957, p.236.

THE TORRIE COLLECTION
THE UNIVERSITY OF EDINBURGH

1 I am most grateful to Jennifer M. Kilian for allowing me to see her draft entry for the Torrie painting from her catalogue raisonné. The work mentioned was at the Giorgio Caretto Gallery, Turin (62 × 77.5 cm).

2 *The Torrie Collection*, nos 2, 3, 4, 24 and 30.

FRANS HALS

c. 1580/5-1666. Probably born in Antwerp (though perhaps from Mechelen, from where his parents came), the date of Hals's birth is uncertain. The family was in Haarlem by 1591 where Hals spent most of his life and probably trained with Karel van Mander before 1603. He joined the Haarlem guild in 1610 and painted portraits of the regent class and militia there. He may have visited Antwerp in 1616, the year which saw the start of his unresolved financial problems. Despite continuing commissions, he died impoverished in Haarlem. He is famous for his portraits but also painted some genre scenes and religious works.

20 *A Dutch Gentleman*

Oil on canvas: 115 × 86.1 cm

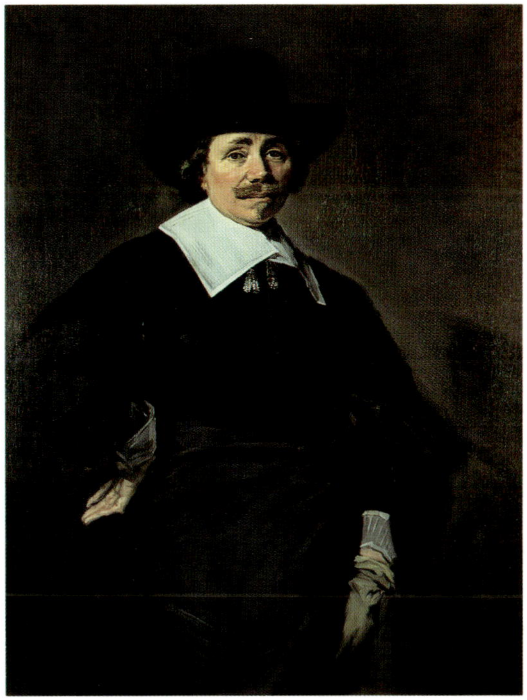

21 *A Dutch Lady*

Oil on canvas: 115 × 85.8 cm

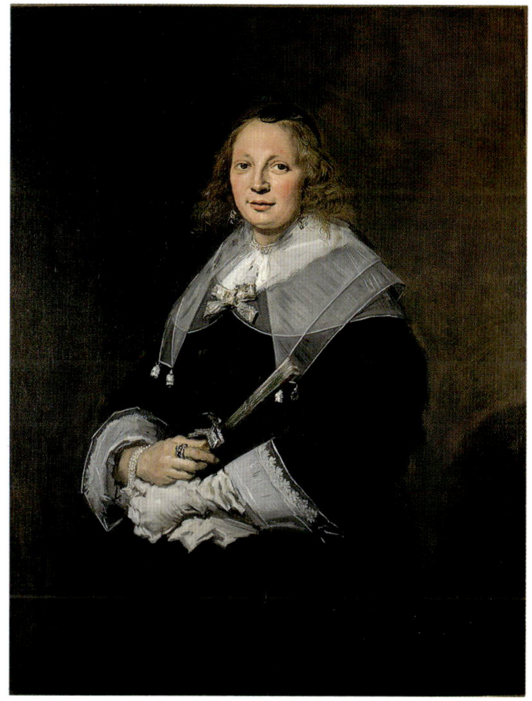

PROVENANCE: Major Jackson of St Andrews, from whom purchased by the RT HON. WILLIAM MCEWAN in 1885 and presented by him in the same year to the National Gallery of Scotland, Edinburgh (nos 691 and 692).

The Duke of Hamilton owned 'A head of Franc Halst' by 2 April 1698[1] but the painter did not become popular in Scotland before the nineteenth century. The wealthy brewer and MP for Edinburgh, William McEwan, was keenly interested in Dutch painting as attested by his own collection, much of which can now be seen at Polesden Lacey, owned by the National Trust (Catalogue no.42). In view of his enthusiasm, McEwan decided that the National Gallery of Scotland should be able to represent two of what he presumably perceived to be the finest Dutch painters and he put up the money for the purchase of Rembrandt's *A Woman in Bed* (Catalogue no.50) in 1892 and later for these two portraits by Hals of the 1640s. None of the three pictures originated from McEwan's own collection but the works by Hals were purchased in Scotland from a Major Jackson of St Andrews in Fife. It is not known from where they came before this, or for how long Major Jackson had owned them, except that he had placed them on loan to the Gallery in 1894, a year before their purchase. It has been suggested that the 'rediscovery' of Hals in the late nineteenth century was partly due to a new appreciation of Hals as a type of proto-Impressionist with his broad sweeping brushstrokes and bravura of handling. Van Gogh admired him as 'a colourist amongst colourists', remarking that Hals had no less than 'twenty-seven different shades of black'.[2] This new enthusiasm for Hals's work was reflected in Scottish collections. Though what was bought was not always genuine, the demand was keen. Hals's *Conradus Viëter* was in the Bute collection when it was exhibited at Glasgow in 1884 (no.69), while Arthur Sanderson had bought the *Portrait of a Man* (now in the Taft Museum in Cincinnati) by 1893. Mrs Broun Lindsay of Colstoun, near Haddington, owned a portrait of *Hendrick Swalmius* until 1934, while Sir William Burrell bought his *Portrait of a Man* in 1948, which can now be seen in Glasgow at the Burrell Collection (no.475). A copy after Hals's *René Descartes* was sold from the Lothian collection at Dowells in Edinburgh, 1 July 1972, lot 170.[3] It is notable in the context of such collecting that the *Young Man Holding a Skull* in the National Gallery, London (no.6458), seems to have been purchased before 1847 by the Scottish painter Andrew Geddes for Sir James Stuart Bt.

EXHIBITED: *RA 1929*, no.114 (*Portrait of a Man* only); *Hals 1989-90*, nos 57 and 58.‡

LITERATURE: *HdG 1893*, p.131; *HdG*, nos 274 and 275 (c.1635-40); *Grimm*, nos 138 and 139 (c.1648); *Slive*, vol.3, nos 156 and 157, p.80, pls 239, 240 and 245.

NATIONAL GALLERY OF SCOTLAND

1 *Waterhouse Notebooks*, transcriptions of Hamilton inventories in the Getty Archive, Santa Monica, Document 7, paintings unnumbered. What is listed as 'another small head by Francis Holst , an originall' (no.28), was in the Duchess of Hamilton's drawing room and a 'Boy's head with a band done by Francisco Holst' (no.137) in the Duke's closet in the Hamilton appartments at Holyrood House, Edinburgh, on 5 October 1704.

2 *The Complete Letters of Vincent van Gogh* (1st edn, London, 1958), 1978 reprint, vol.2, letter 428, p.424.

3 *Slive*, nos 152, 85, 126. The Burrell work is not listed but the Lothian copy is n o.175.

22 *Verdonck*

Oil on panel: 46.7 × 35.6 cm
Signed: *FHF* (the last two letters *HF* in monogram) at centre right
PROVENANCE: Lawrence W. Vaile[1] who sold the work at an anonymous sale at Christie's, London, 13 July 1895, lot 85; Agnews, London, who sold it *c.*1908 to John J. Moubray of Naemoor[2] who presented it in 1916 to the National Gallery of Scotland (no. 1200).

John Moubray was a JP and a lieutenant for the county of Kinross, living at Naemoor near Alloa in Perthshire. He gave the painting to the gallery in memory 'of wet Saturday afternoons spent happily there in his youth'.[3] When Moubray owned the painting it was called *The Toper* (see fig.50) after it had been prettified for the taste of the late nineteenth century.[4] The additions of the beret and wineglass were removed during cleaning in 1928 and the unkempt man brandishing a jawbone was revealed. It was discovered that this was the work painted by Hals in about 1627 which had been engraved by J. van de Velde, together with the verse: ' This is Verdonck, that outspoken fellow whose jawbone attacks everyone. He cares for nobody great or small – that's what brought him to the workhouse'.[5] Verdonck has been identified as the violently argumentative Pieter Verdonck, possibly a Mennonite in Haarlem, who 'destroyed his enemies with his words as Samson did with his jawbone'.[6] A copy is in Cincinnati Museum of Art (1976.432).[7]

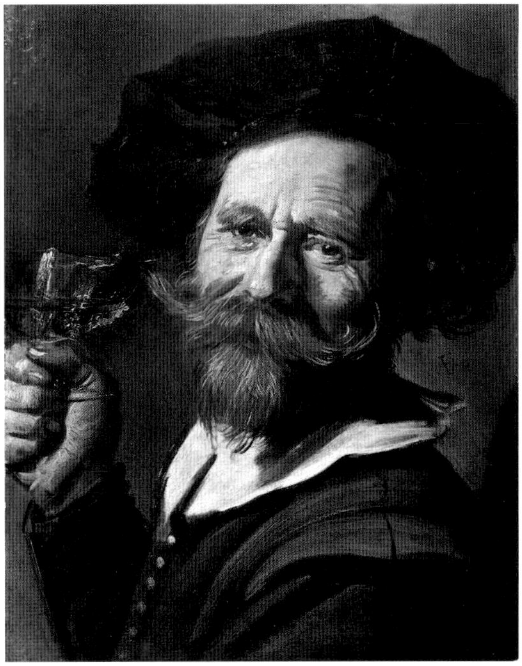

fig.50

EXHIBITED: *Frans Hals. Tentoonstelling ter gelegenheid van het 75-jarig bestaan van het Gemeentelijk Museum te Haarlem,* Frans Halsmuseum, Haarlem, 1937, no.6; *Frans Hals. Exhibition on the Occasion of the Centenary of the Municipal Museum in Haarlem,* Frans Halsmuseum, Haarlem, 1962, no.16; *Hals 1989-90* (exhibited in London and Haarlem), no.24.‡

LITERATURE: *HdG,* no.235 (identical with *HdG,* no.77); *Slive,* vol.I, pp.80-3; *Grimm,* no.37; P.J.J. van Thiel, 'De betekenis van het portret van Verdonck door Frans Hals: de ikonografie van het kakebeen', *Oud Holland,* XCIV, 1980, pp. 112-40.

NATIONAL GALLERY OF SCOTLAND

1 Letter in Gallery files from Vaile's daughter states that her grandfather was given the picture by his stepmother in the 1820s.
2 A letter from the Duchess of Sutherland of 4 January 1982 (also in Gallery files) notes that her aunt, who was the daughter of John Moubray, told her that Moubray had purchased the painting from Agnews in about 1908. It was certainly in his possession by 1914.
3 Quoted in *Pictures for Scotland,* p.85. Moubray apparently told this to James Caw who recalled it in *The Scotsman,* 21 August 1928.
4 A restorer J. L. Naps (b.1853), working at Riga City Art Museum, undertook the repainting in compliance with the wishes of the wife of the collector (presumably Vaile). Letter in Gallery files of 28 December 1930.
5 'Dit is Verdonck, die stoute gast, / Wiens kaekebeen elck een aen tast, / Op niemant, groot, noch kleyn, hÿ past, / Dies raeckte hÿ in t'werckhuis vast.'
6 See Van Thiel, *op. cit.*, p.140 and *Hals 1989-90* , pp.30-1 for discussion of the identity of Verdonck. The jawbone of an ass was a biblical attribute of Samson (although the bone in Hals's picture is that of a cow but the latter was perhaps more easily obtainable for use as a prop for the portrait).
7 M. A. Scott, *Cincinnati Museum of Art Dutch Flemish and German Paintings Catalogue,* Cincinnati, 1987, no.23.

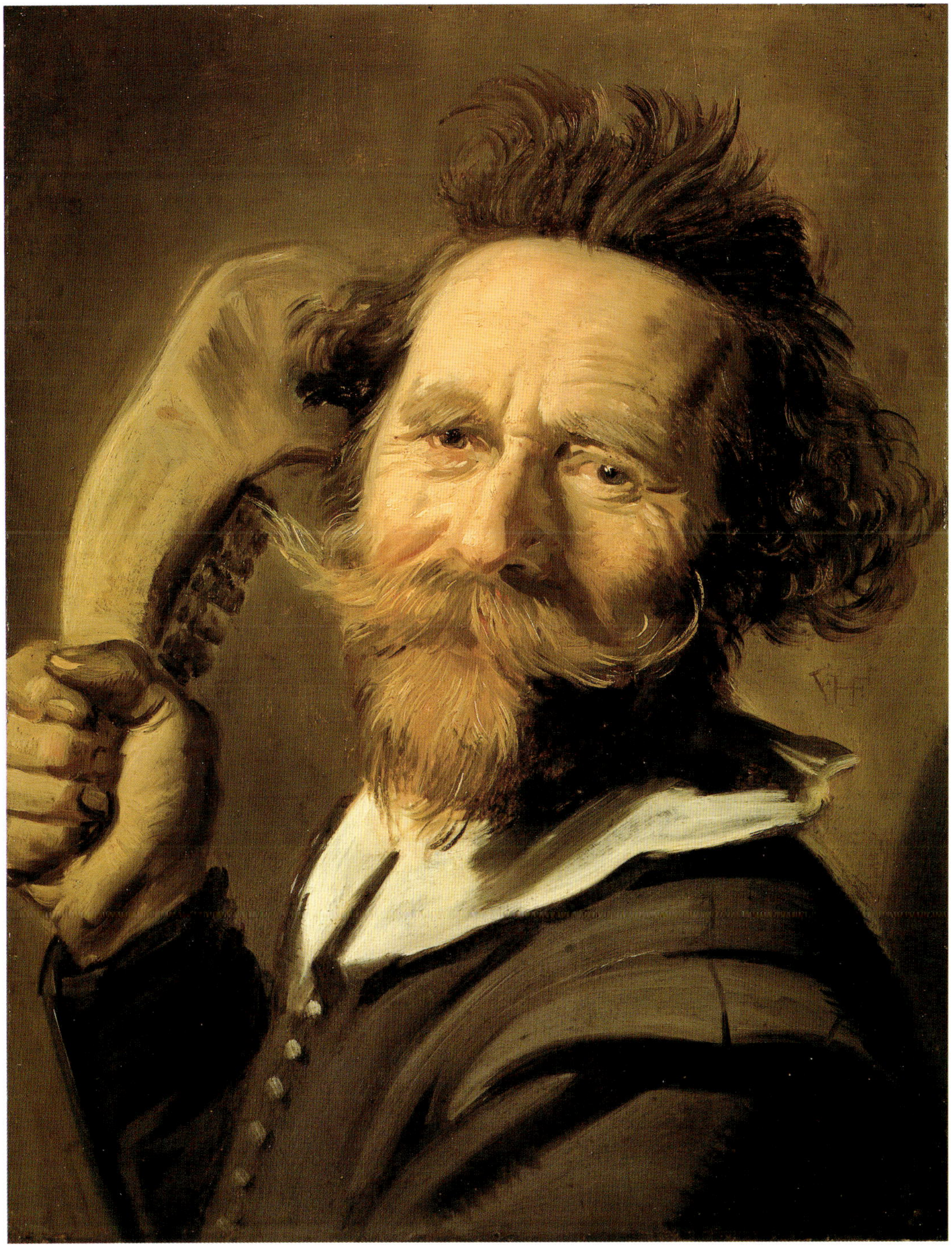

BARTHOLOMEUS VAN DER HELST

1613-70. The son of a Haarlem innkeeper, Van der Helst was probably the pupil of Nicolaes Eliasz. in Amsterdam. He became an immensely successful portrait painter in the city, mainly of guild and militia pieces. He probably used assistants on some of his works as the quality varies widely. He influenced the style not only of his son, Lodewijk, but also of Ferdinand Bol and Govaert Flinck.

23 *A Dutch Rear-Admiral*

Oil on canvas: 113 × 91.4 cm
Signed and dated: *B vander Helst f 1662* at bottom left
PROVENANCE: Martin Colnaghi, London, from whom purchased for £400 by Glasgow Museum and Art Gallery in 1895.

The identity of the sitter has been much debated. The painting was bought from Colnaghi as a portrait of Cornelis de Witt but was also called 'De Ruyter'. However, Arthur Kay (who owned the Van Wijnen, Catalogue no.75) was adamant that he had managed to reveal the name of the sitter in the Glasgow painting. He discovered 'an exact copy' of the picture in Endell Street in Long Acre in London, painted by a Dutch seventeenth-century artist, Christoffel Pierson, which was inscribed 'Admiral Stell de Werff' and dated 1674.[1] Kay's offer to give the Pierson copy to Glasgow was rejected on the grounds that it might have cast doubt on their painting, which Kay rancorously stated was due to ' the mental opacity and lack of vision of the Municipal Galleries Committee'. However, B. W. F. van Riemsdijk, then Director of the Rijksmuseum, disproved the Admiral Augustus Stellingwerf trail,[2] and more recently M. Gehlen has suggested that the sitter is the *schout-bij-nacht* (Rear-admiral) Willem van der Zaen, who was buried in 1669 in the Oude Kerk in Amsterdam, where his tomb medallion can still be seen.[3]

Question of identity aside, the portrait is a fine example of Van der Helst's work. The confident pose and resplendent costume combined with a certain gravity of expression make this painting a successful boast with restraint, a swagger portrait with dignity. Van der Helst's popularity with his patrons is understandable in this context, and it is not surprising that in 1889 this portrait of a naval man should have appealed to the Municipal Galleries Committee of Glasgow, a city of successful and flourishing shipbuilding.

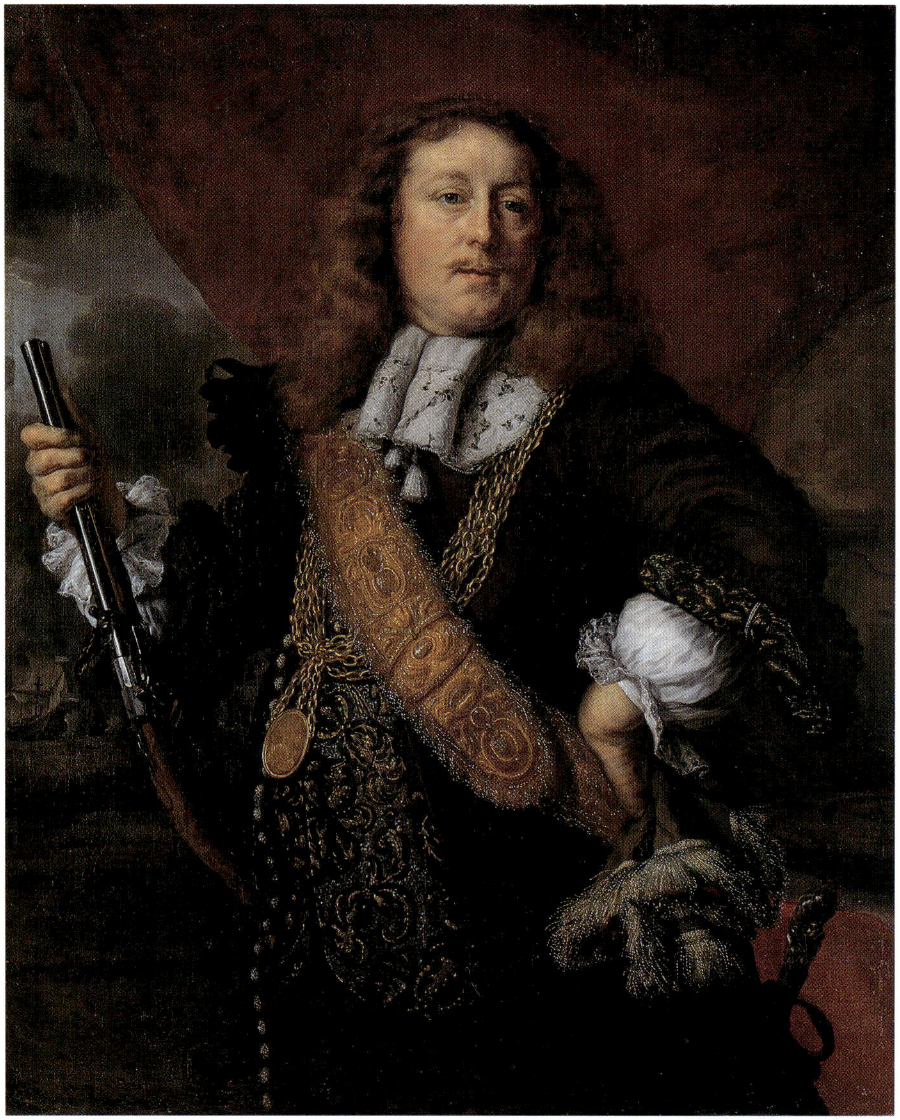

EXHIBITED: *Het Nederlandse Zeeuwen*, The Hague, 1964, no.1664 (with sitter as Witte de With).

LITERATURE: J. J. de Helder, *B. van der Helst*, Rotterdam, 1921, no.201; A. Kay, *Treasure Trove in Art*, Edinburgh and London, 1939, pp.84-5; *Glasgow Catalogue*, vol.1, p.66.

GLASGOW MUSEUM AND ART GALLERY

1 Presumably the picture in the 2nd Hoogendijk sale, Amsterdam, 28 April 1908, lot 105. A larger copy of the Van der Helst was in the collection of the Duke of Portland, see R. Goulding, *Catalogue of the Paintings belonging to His Grace the Duke of Portland*, 1936, no.103.

2 In a letter of 15 November 1906 in *RKD* files.

3 Typescript article in *RKD* library (no.9200440 Ned / Mon / Helst / geh.).

MEINDERT HOBBEMA

1638-1709. Born in Amsterdam, the son of Lubbert Meyndertsz., Meindert adopted the name of 'Hobbema'. In July 1660 Jacob van Ruisdael said that he had been Hobbema's master for some years. Hobbema's early work recalls that of Salomon van Ruysdael, Jacob's uncle, but the influence of Ruisdael himself is apparent c.*1662. Appointed a wine gauger by the city of Amsterdam in 1668, after which his output declined, he continued to paint the wooded landscapes and mill views which he had made his speciality.*

24 *View of the Bergkerk, Deventer*

Oil on panel: 38.6 × 53.8 cm
Signed and dated: *m. Hobbema f. 168?* at bottom right
PROVENANCE: Probably J. van der Marck sale, Amsterdam, 25 August 1773, lot 1271, bought by Fouquet. R. de St Victor, Paris, 26 March 1822; purchased before 1835 by Lord Francis Egerton[1] who became 1st Earl of Ellesmere in 1846 and thence by inheritance to John, 5th Earl of Ellesmere (later 6th DUKE OF SUTHERLAND in 1963), who placed the work on loan at the National Gallery of Scotland in 1946.

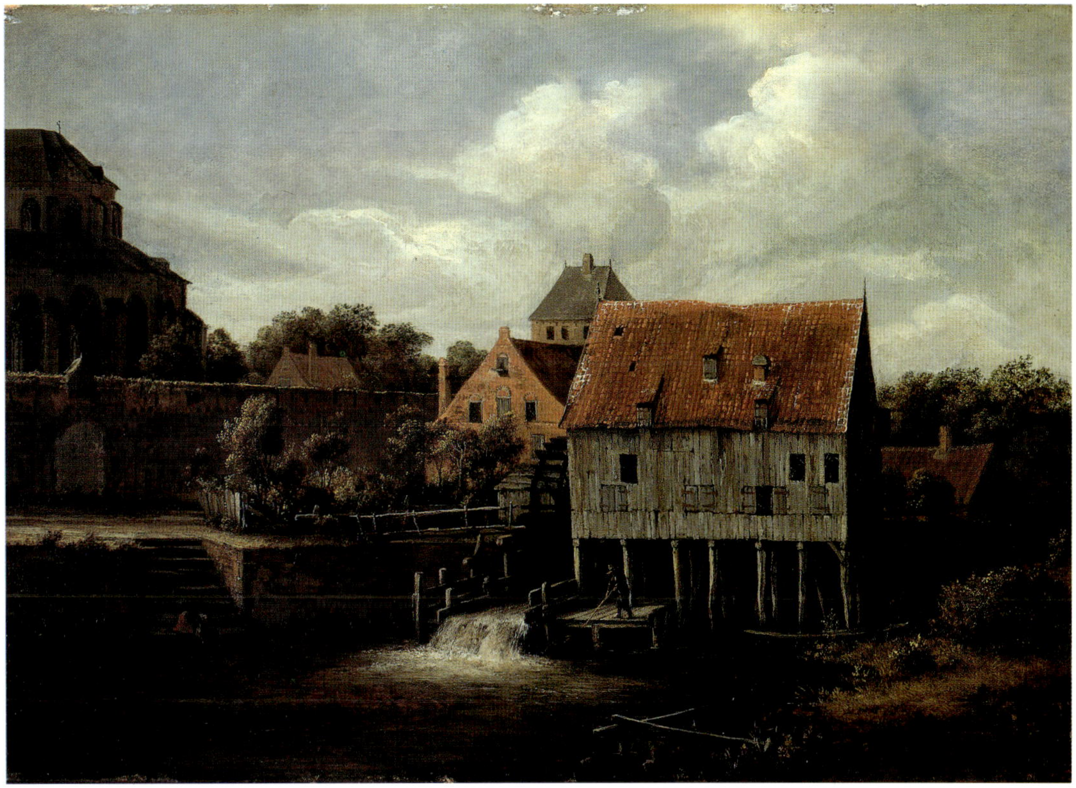

Hobbema was much influenced by Ruisdael particularly in his depiction of watermills in his landscapes – motifs which both artists drew and painted many times in their careers. Hobbema seems to have travelled with Ruisdael to the town of Deventer where both master and pupil made sketches of the mill.[2] Hobbema's drawing (fig.51) now in the Museé du Petit Palais, Paris (no.1052), was probably made in about 1662 or 1663,[3] but a comparison with the Sutherland picture makes it clear that he made virtually no changes when he came to paint the same scene years later. The date on the painting is not entirely legible and has been interpreted as 1681 by Stechow[4] and as 1689 by Broulhiet,[5] the year now generally accepted as the date for the artist's *Avenue at Middelharnis* in the National Gallery, London (fig.9). In addition to the latter work, which was once owned by James Stuart of Dunearn, there were various paintings ascribed to Hobbema in Scotland. Sir James Erskine of Torrie owned at least three pictures then believed to be by the artist,[6] while the National Gallery of Scotland's *Waterfall in a Wood* (no.1506) was in the collection of Mrs Hamilton Nisbet Ferguson by 1826 when lent to the Royal Institution in Edinburgh (no.31). (A photograph of a bad copy of the Sutherland painting is in the files of the *RKD*, neg. 01.057).

EXHIBITED: *Edinburgh 1945*, no.148.

LITERATURE: *HdG*, no.77; *Smith*, no. 51; *Bridgewater House Catalogue 1851* and *1926*, no.148; G. Broulhiet, *M. Hobbema*, Paris, 1938, no.53.

THE DUKE OF SUTHERLAND

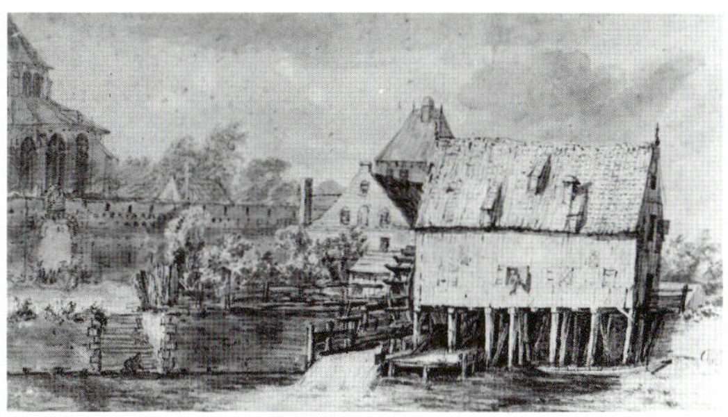

fig.51

1 Listed in the collection of Lord Francis Egerton in 1835 in Smith, *op. cit.*
2 *Walford*, p.125. Ruisdael's drawing is in the British Museum, London (no. 00-11-242).
3 *Ibid.* The date is suggested on the basis of the style of Hobbema's *Wooded Landscape with View of Deventer* in The Mauritshuis, The Hague, no.899.
4 W. Stechow, *Dutch Landscape Painting of the Seventeenth Century*, London, 1966, p.201, note 57.
5 Broulhiet, *op. cit.*
6 *The Torrie Collection* , nos 17 and 18, and Dunimarle catalogue, p.222 – see Collectors Index.

1629-84. Baptised in Rotterdam, at first he used the name De Hooch but was later to spell it d(e) Hoogh. He was probably a pupil, together with Jacob Ochtervelt, of Nicolaes Berchem in Haarlem but is mentioned as living in Delft in August 1652. De Hooch worked as a retainer for Justus de la Grange between 1653 and 1654, and travelled with him. He is also listed as a painter at this period and De la Grange owned eleven of his works. De Hooch lived in Delft until c.*1660 when he moved to Amsterdam. He is most famous for his interiors and subtly constructed courtyard scenes usually showing background views of Delft. His painting became more elaborate but somewhat coarser after his move to Amsterdam.*

25 *A Courtyard in Delft*

Oil on canvas: 78 × 65 cm
PROVENANCE: J. Smith, 1822; bought by William Wells of Redleaf by 1828 and in his sale, 12 May 1848, lot 95, bought by Farrer; Lord Overstone, London, by 1851;[1] his daughter, Lady Wantage, London, by 1888; The EARL OF CRAWFORD AND BALCARRES by 1921 until after 1929 ; Katz Dieren in 1935; Mr and Mrs ten Cate-van Wulfften Palthe of Almelo by 1938 by whom donated to The Mauritshuis, The Hague, in 1947 (no.835).

Waagen praised this work in which De Hooch as 'the painter of sunlight *par excellence*, appears in this beautiful picture in the highest perfection of all his powers'. The picture was probably painted between about 1658 and 1660 and is an authentic replica of a painting now in the National Gallery of Art, Washington DC (*Sutton*, no.36A). The Washington painting differs in having another man sitting at the table holding the tankard also visible in the Crawford picture. However, old photographs in the *RKD* show that this extra figure also originally appeared in the composition of the Crawford painting but was overpainted for some reason by a later hand. Faint traces of the brim of the missing figure's hat can still be seen to the left of the base of the woman's glass.[2]

Lord Crawford also sold a Hobbema (*HdG*, no.86) was which was bought by H. E. ten Cate by 1939. Other Dutch pictures from the Crawford collection also went to Holland, such as Rembrandt's *Titus at his Desk*, now at the Boymans-van Beuningen Museum in Rotterdam (Catalogue no.51).

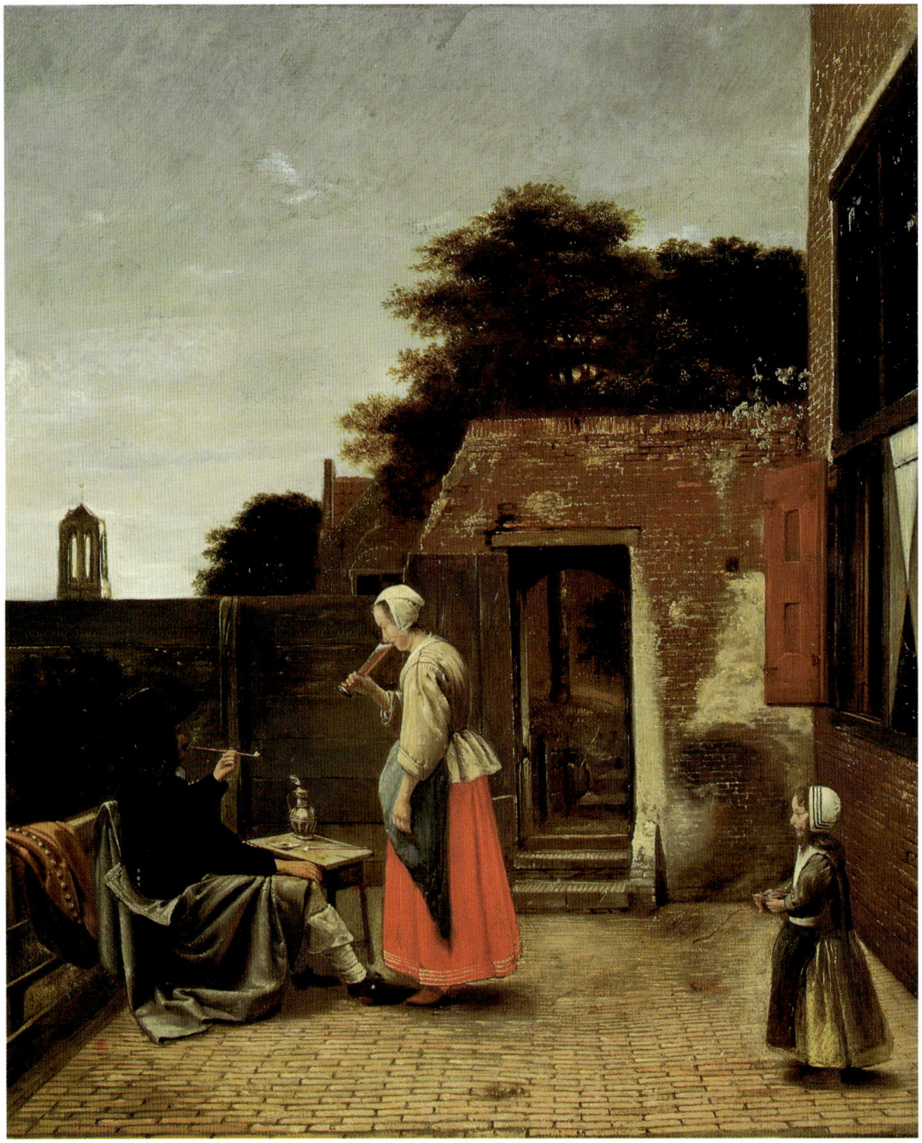

EXHIBITED: British Institution, London, 1828, no.93, and 1851, no.208; *RA*, 1871, no.208; *Exposition Hollandaise*, Musée du Jeu de Paume, Paris, 1921, no.25 (lent by the Earl of Crawford); *RA 1929*, no.319 (lent by the Earl of Crawford); *Vijf en twintig jaar aanwisten*, The Mauritshuis, The Hague, 1970, no.35.

LITERATURE: *Smith*, no.30; *Waagen 1857*, pp.130-1; *HdG*, no.297; *Wantage Catalogue*, no.108; *Sutton*, no.36B, fig.35.‡

THE MAURITSHUIS, THE HAGUE

1 The painting may have been purchased shortly after 1848 by Samuel Jones Loyd, but before he was made Lord Overstone in 1851, as suggested by the *Wantage Catalogue*.

2 A letter of 14 February 1928 from Lord Crawford in Gallery files states that Martin de Wild cleaned ' Both my Rembrandts, the Pieter de Hooghe, Hobbema, Van de Velde and other pictures of first rate importance'.

26 *The Disputed Reckoning*

Oil on canvas: 71 × 63 cm
Signed and dated: *P. D. H. 1658* on piece of furniture to right
PROVENANCE: G. Braamcamp sale, Amsterdam, 31 July 1771, lot 86, bought by Fouquet; 1st MARQUESS OF BUTE by 1800 and thence by descent. Private Collection, Scotland.

The painting was not in the unpublished catalogue of the Bute collection made in 1799 but does appear in that of 1800 (no.291) and is listed in the 1822 catalogue of pictures at Luton Hoo (no.279) as hanging in 'the Best Dressing Room De Hooge Interior – His usual subjects, a conversation in which the draperies are taken from the fashion of the times, his colouring good, natural and strong'. It was described as 'one of the most famous pictures in this collection' when the Bute paintings were exhibited at Bethnal Green Museum, London, in 1882-3.[1] De Hooch dealt with the same subject much later (c.1694) in *An Officer Paying a Woman in a Stable* in the Metropolitan Museum of Art, New York (no.58.144).

Although De Hooch's work is rare in Scotland, some paintings can be traced to Scottish collections. The Rijkmuseum, Amsterdam, has *Two Women at a Linen Chest* (no.C1191), which was in Scotland from *c.*1794 until purchased by J. Smith, while the *Kolf Players*, now at Polesden Lacey, was owned by Sir Hugh Hume Campbell by 1861 and was purchased by William McEwan at Campbell's sale in 1894. H.A.J. Munro (of Novar) may have owned the *Young Couple with a Dog* now in the Metropolitan Museum of Art, New York (no.14.40.613) but in any case he certainly owned two De Hoochs (which appear in his 1865 catalogue, nos 313 and 314. See Collectors Index). The Wallraf-Richartz-Museum, Cologne, has *A Couple with a Parrot* (Dep.239) which was bought at Dowell's Auction Rooms, Edinburgh, by D. M. Koetser at an unspecified date while *A Woman Knitting* (*Sutton,* no.103) was a Montagu picture inherited by the Dukes of Buccleuch but was sold in 1965. *The Box Bed,* now in the National Gallery of Art, Washington DC (no.629), was in the collection of the Duke of Sutherland until 1846.[2]

LITERATURE: *Waagen,* vol.3, p.477; *Richter,* no.84; *HdG,* no.268; *Sutton,* no.27, figs 24 and 25 (detail).‡

EXHIBITED: British Institution, London, 1822 – no.116, 1847 – no.93, 1854 – no.103; *RA* 1870, no.13; *Bethnal Green 1882-3,* no.80; *Glasgow 1884,* no.84; *RA 1929,* no.309; *Edinburgh 1949,* no.17; *RA 1952-3,* no.508; *Agnews,* no.22.

PRIVATE COLLECTION, SCOTLAND

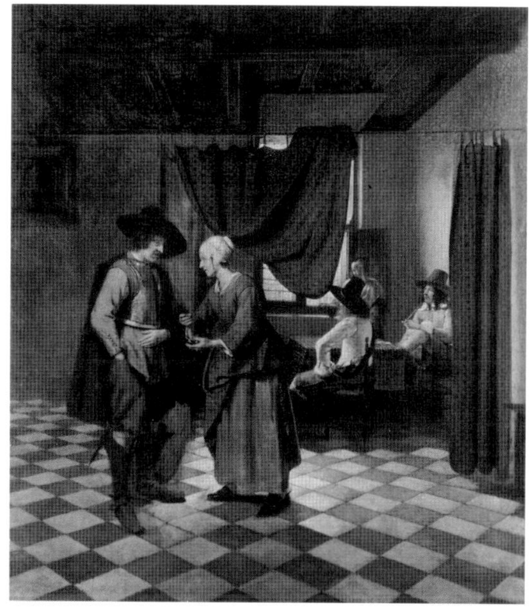

1 'The Marquis of Bute's Pictures at Bethnal Green', (anonymous review) *The Athenaeum,* 6 January 1883, pp.23-4: 'One of the most famous pictures in this collection is the characteristic De Hoogh, called "The Disputed Reckoning." It is dated 1658, the year of the luminous "Courtyard of a Dutch House", No.835 in the National Gallery (Peel Collection), and represents the interior of a large chamber paved with squares of black and white marble; the light of a window is screened by a brown curtain hanging from a rod in the middle of the chamber. The pavement has been painted with rare zeal and zest. Mr. Tadema himself could not do it better. The tone, soft illumination, and homogeneous effect of this picture are in De Hoogh's best style. The figures show his weaknesses in design, and are almost entirely without animation. Some parts remind us of Ver Meer rather than De Hoogh.'

2 Provenances taken from *Sutton.*

PHILIPS KONINCK

1619–88. Born in Amsterdam, Philips trained with his elder brother Jacob in Rotterdam in about 1637. Houbraken states that he then worked in Rembrandt's studio, presumably after Koninck's move to Amsterdam in 1641, and the style of his work in the late 1640s and early 1650s would bear this out. He was a successful artist, today best known for his panoramic landscapes, but he also painted history pieces, portraits and genre scenes. However, he seems to have given up painting some time after 1676, perhaps to concentrate on a shipping line he owned between Rotterdam and Amsterdam.

27 *The Approaching Storm*

Oil on canvas: 130 × 166 cm

PROVENANCE: The Comte de Vence until the end of the eighteenth century.[1] Purchased in Paris in 1838 by Mr Chaplin for Samuel Jones Loyd (created Lord Overstone in 1851), London; his daughter, Lady Wantage, London, by 1883. Private Collection, Scotland, and placed on loan to the National Gallery of Scotland, 1988.

Koninck had started to paint his panoramas by 1647 and the best date from between about 1654 and 1665. The countryside in Gelderland seems to have provided the inspiration for his typically high views over a broad expanse of land.

This picture was believed to be by Rembrandt until it was cleaned by Martin de Wild in 1922. It has been consistently admired. Thoré-Bürger described it as the most extraordinary and beautiful landscape he had ever seen, from any school or country.[2]

Another fine example of Koninck's work is in the Hunterian Art Gallery in Glasgow, which was bought by Dr William Hunter in 1755, also as a Rembrandt. The magnificent *View over Flat Country* now in the Ashmolean Musum, Oxford (no.A 719), was also once in Scotland, where it was owned by the great Glasgow engineer Robert Napier until his death in 1876, and later by John Bell of North Park, Glasgow. Koninck's *Landscape with Figures on Horseback* was exhibited from the Bute collection at the National Gallery of Scotland in 1949 (no.20, and at *Agnews*, no.27) while *A Wooded River Landscape*, formerly in the collection of the 2nd Duke of Sutherland, is now owned by the British Rail Pension Fund and is on loan at the Fitzwilliam Museum, Cambridge. The National Gallery of Scotland purchased *An Extensive Landscape* (no.2434) in 1986.

EXHIBITED: *Manchester 1857*, no.698; *Exhibition of Old Master Painting, RA*, 1870 no.3; *Dutch Paintings*, Guildhall Galleries, London, 1903, no.174 (as by Rembrandt); *Exhibition of Old Masters*, Grafton Galleries, London, 1911, no.75 (as by Rembrandt); *RA*, 1925, no.191; *RA 1929*, no.243; *Nederlandsche Landschapkunst in de 17e eeuw*, Van Abbe Museum, Eindhoven, 1948, no.34; *RA 1952–3*, no.317; Art Gallery of Toronto,1955, no.48.

LITERATURE: *Smith*, no.596; *Waagen 1857*, p.131; E.J.T. Thoré [W. Bürger], *Trésors d'Art en Angleterre*, Brussels, 1860, p.247; *Wantage Catalogue*, no.184, pp.132–3, repr.; H. Gerson, *Philips Koninck; Ein Betrag zur Erforschung der holländischen Malerei des XVII. Jahrhunderts*, Berlin, 1936, no.37; *Sumowski*, vol.3, p.1546 (mentioned in entry for no.1053).

PRIVATE COLLECTION, SCOTLAND

1 The Comte de Vence was the Maréchal de Camp des Armés du Roy. The picture was described (as Rembrandt) while in his collection as 'un beau paysage où les différents plans se trouve séparez [*sic*] par les beaux effets' by J. B. Descamps in *La Vie des Peintres*, Paris, 1754, vol.2, p.96. The painting was etched in 1758 by A. de Marcenay de Guy when in the Vence collection.

2 Thoré-Bürger, *op. cit.* 'Pour moi, c'est la peinture de paysage la plus extraordinaire et la plus belle que j'ai jamais vue, de n'importe quelle école et dans n'importe quel pays'. He goes on to say: 'Je la classe dans l'oeuvre de Rembrandt à côté de ses chefs-d'oeuvre du Musée d'Amsterdam "La Ronde du Nuit" et "Les Syndics". Hobbema et Ruysdael pouvaient venir au monde; Rembrandt avait inventé le paysage qu'ils allaient peindre'.

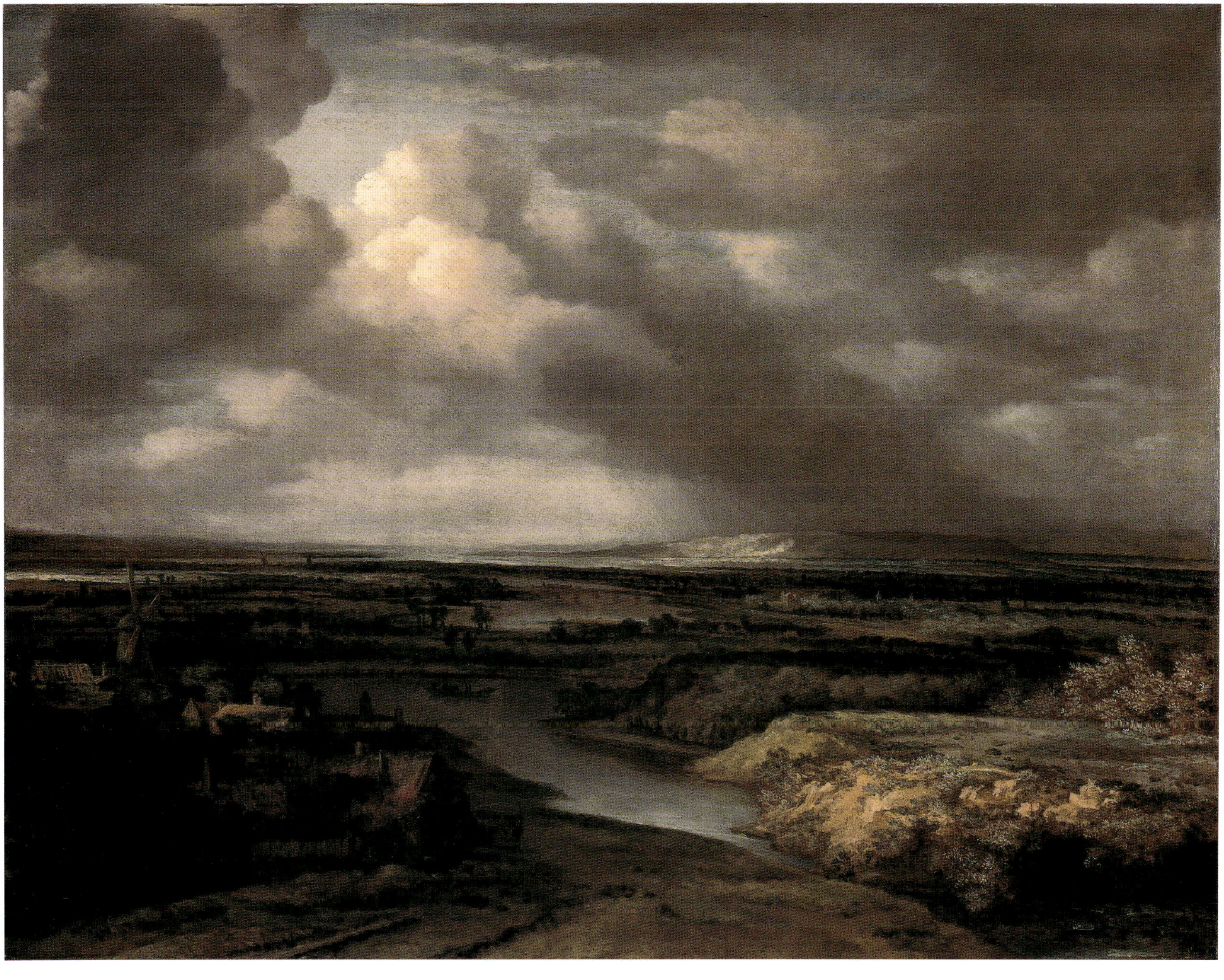

SALOMON DE KONINCK

1609-56. Born in Amsterdam, Salomon was the cousin of Philips Koninck: their fathers were brothers, goldsmiths originally from Antwerp. Salomon may have set the example to become a painter, followed by his younger cousins Jacob and Philips. When he was 12, Salomon was apprenticed to David Colijns and later trained with Nicolaes Moeyaert. He started to paint in a Rembrandtesque style from the 1630s and continued to paint in this manner until his last years. He painted mythological and biblical scenes, genre pieces and portraits.

28 *An Old Man Reading*

Oil on canvas: 146 × 131 cm
PROVENANCE: The EARLS OF MANSFIELD, Scone Palace, Perthshire.

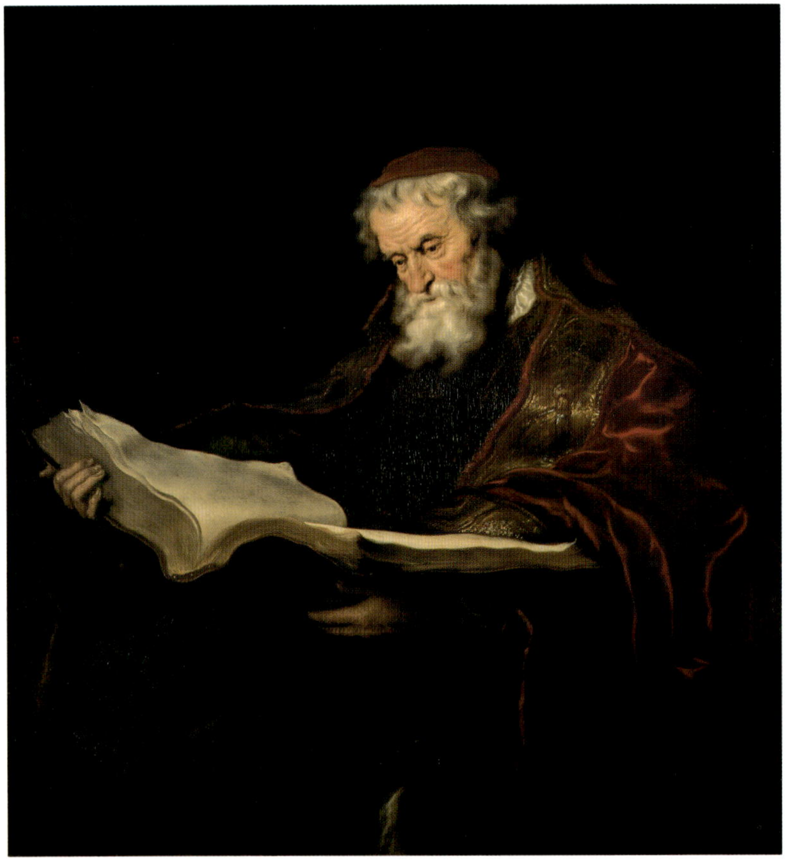

Although traditionally called *The Philosopher*, the old man is in fact wearing religious robes and the edge of his cope clearly shows an embroidered figure with a halo, perhaps that of Christ. This type of old man occurs frequently in Koninck's work and it may be that the same model was used for these paintings, adapted with variations for different compositions. Similar features can be seen in a painting in the Musée des Beaux-Arts in Brussels[1] and in the *Old Bishop* in the Dresden Gemäldegalerie[2] and, indeed, in many other works. The large open book (here presumably the Bible) with its broadly painted rumpled pages can also be found in many of Koninck's pictures of scholars, saints and philosophers, such as a work of 1649 in the Herzog Anton Ulrich-Museum, Braunschweig,[3] or one of 1643 in Dresden.[4]

Waterhouse, on seeing the painting at the Earl of Mansfield's Logie House in Logiealmond in 1951, ascribed it to Salomon Koninck but wrote in brackets 'or Philips Koninck – An old prophetic person reading from an enormous book ... Nearly full length, ... bespectacled(!) Too big for Salomon at his best but it has a faint Rembrandtesque echo and the ancient volume is in Rembrandt's style'.[5] The exact provenance of the painting has been difficult to establish and it is not known whether it was one of the works which decorated the Mansfield's Scottish homes or if it was bought for Kenwood (the London house to which many of the family's pictures were taken from Scotland by the 2nd Earl). The painting was moved from Logie House to Scone after 1951 and now hangs in the dining room accompanied by a large *Denial of St Peter* by Gerard Seghers.

W. A. Coats (Catalogue nos 66 and 71) owned an *Old Woman Weighing Gold* (signed and dated 1649),[6] at Skelmorlie Castle, while *A Portrait of an Old Woman,* previously thought to be by Salomon de Koninck in the collection of the Marquess of Linlithgow at Hopetoun House (in the Yellow Drawing Room), has now been ascribed to S. Kick by Sumowski.[7] A copy of Koninck's *Rabbi* in the Galleria Sabauda, Turin, is in a private collection near Edinburgh.[8]

THE EARL OF MANSFIELD

1 *Sumowski*, vol.3, no.1129.
2 *Ibid.*, no.1117.
3 *Ibid.*, no. 114.
4 *Ibid.*, no. 1108.
5 *Waterhouse Notebooks*, vol.32, p.80, 26 April 1951. The man is not wearing spectacles but has deep folds of skin around his eyes.
6 *Sumowski*, vol.3, no.1110.
7 *Ibid.*, p.1640.
8 *Ibid.*, no.1124.

JAN LIEVENS

1607-74. Born in Leiden, Lievens's father was originally from Ghent. He was apprenticed to Joris van Schooten in 1615 and then to Pieter Lastman in Amsterdam from about 1619 to 1621. He returned to Leiden as an independent artist, later working in close conjunction with Rembrandt, his companion and competitor, from the late 1620s until about 1631. Lievens left for London in 1632 and worked at the court there, then settling in Antwerp by 1635. By 1644 he had moved to Amsterdam though he also spent some time in Leiden, The Hague and Berlin. He painted mythological and biblical subjects as well as portraits, landscapes and some still-lifes.

29 *Portrait of a Capuchin Monk*

Oil on panel: 96.5 × 86.5 cm
Signed and dated: *L / 1629* at lower left and *249* (Newbattle Abbey number) at bottom left
PROVENANCE: Perhaps given to or purchased by Sir Robert Kerr, 1st Earl of Ancram; by descent to the MARQUESS OF LOTHIAN[1] and placed on loan at the National Gallery of Scotland in 1950;[2] Private Collection, England.

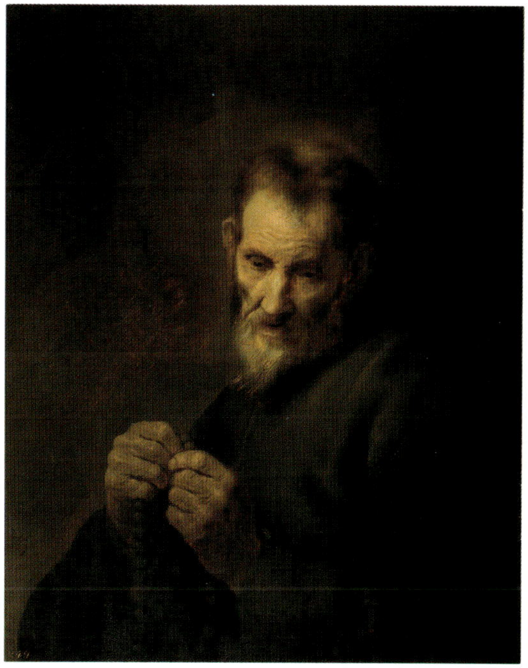

Hofstede de Groot saw this picture at Newbattle Abbey in 1893 and remarked that it was ' the most interesting piece in the collection' and classed it as 'one of the earliest known and one of the very few dated works of Jan Lievens, quite in his Leiden, Rembrandt style'. It is painted with a restricted palette of browns and greys, and Lievens used the technique of scratching through the paint to the red-brown ground to highlight hair, as seen in Rembrandt's *Self-portrait* of 1629 (Rijksmuseum, Amsterdam, no.A4691).

In 1629, the year *Portrait of a Capuchin Monk* was painted, Sir Robert Kerr was sent by Charles I to The Hague as a personal envoy, to convey his condolences to the king and queen of Bohemia on the death (by drowning) of their eldest son, who was Charles's nephew. Though it is tempting to suppose that Kerr may have acquired this painting directly from the artist, the available facts concerning his visit are somewhat confusing. Given the nature of his mission, it is quite likely that Sir Robert would have met the Prince of Orange's secretary, Constantin Huyghens (who, like Sir Robert, had a strong enthusiasm for the work of the metaphysical poet, John Donne). Huyghens certainly knew both Rembrandt and Lievens by this date and had just had his portrait painted by Lievens, which is now in Douai.[3] It is uncertain whether Sir Robert and Lievens (or indeed Rembrandt) met at this time, although Huyghens could certainly have provided the introduction.[4] It is known, however, that after his return to England, Sir Robert presented Charles I with three paintings then ascribed to Rembrandt (of which one was later recorded in 1649 as by Lievens). As discussed in the entry for one of these paintings (Catalogue no.46), Sir Robert may have bought these himself or may have been given them by the Prince of Orange to present to King Charles. Whoever did the actual buying, it would seem likely that Constantin Huyghens had something to do with the recommendation of the artists whom he had so strongly championed. The *Portrait of a Capuchin Monk* may have been given in gratitude to Kerr by Lievens if he, rather than Rembrandt, had earned the commission to paint pictures to be presented to Charles I. On the other hand it could have been a gift from Lievens in order to promote himself. (It has been suggested that it was through Sir Robert's agency that Lievens came to England, but there is no proof of this.) Alternatively, the painting could have been bought by Sir Robert or given to him by the Prince of Orange or by Huyghens as a gesture of diplomacy or friendship.

Whatever the details of its acquisition, the *Portrait of a Capuchin Monk* surely had a particular appeal for Sir Robert whose house, Newbattle Abbey, had once been home to a community of monks (even though Augustinian rather than Capuchin). The Lothian family also owned a *Portrait of an Old Man* attributed to Lievens.[5] One of the artist's relatively rare landscapes was owned by Sir James Erskine of Torrie.[6]

EXHIBITED: *Edinburgh 1883*, no.338 (as 'Unknown'); *RA* 1885, no.88 (as 'Unknown').

LITERATURE: *HdG 1893*, pp.216-17; H. Schneider, *Jan Lievens: Sein Leben und Seine Werke*, Haarlem, 1932, revised by R. E. O. Ekkart, Amsterdam, 1973, pp.107, 324; *Jan Lievens ein Maler im Schatten Rembrandts*, exhibition catalogue, Herzog Anton Ulrich-Museum, Braunschweig, 1979, p.15, repr. fig.1;. *Sumowski*, vol.3, no.1238, repr.p.1877‡; *Wenley*, no.249.

PRIVATE COLLECTION, ENGLAND

1 The painting was noted at Newbattle Abbey in about 1788 as 'a monk with his Beads', *Wenley*, no.249. It is possible, though unlikely, that the paintings by Lievens were purchased some time after Sir Robert's death to complement the portrait of him by then in the collection.

2 J. G. van Gelder, 'The Rembrandt Exhibition at Edinburgh', *The Burlington Magazine*, 92, 1950, p.328.

3 R. E. O. Ekkart, 'Rembrandt, Lievens and Constantin Huyghens', in *Rembrandt & Lievens in Leiden*, exhibition catalogue, Museum de Lakenhal, Leiden, 1991-2, pp.48-59.

4 However, it is strange that if they did meet *c.*1629, Sir Robert makes no reference to having made Lievens's acquaintance when he writes about him in 1654 (Catalogue no.30). Though Sir Robert was old, his correspondence does not lead one to presume that he had become particularly forgetful.

5 Newbattle Abbey, no.246. See *Wenley*, no.246, who states that the work is not listed until 1878 in the Great Hall at Newbattle Abbey and was perhaps sold in 1936, later possibly in a sale in Amsterdam, 11 December 1956. Hofstede de Groot could not decide if it was by Lievens or Salomon de Koninck.

6 *The Torrie Collection*, no.23. The National Gallery of Scotland's *Portrait of a Young Man* (no.1564) was only purchased in 1922 from London.

30 *Portrait of Robert Kerr 1st Earl of Ancram*

Oil on panel: 62 × 52 cm
Inscribed: *Earle of Ancram* at top left (twice) and *92* (Newbattle Abbey number) at bottom left (and again above this in smaller figures)
PROVENANCE: Commissioned in 1654 by Sir Robert Kerr, 1st Earl of Ancram (1578-1654), and given to his son, William, 3rd EARL OF LOTHIAN, at Newbattle Abbey near Edinburgh; thence by descent to the Marquess of Lothian; on loan to the Scottish National Portrait Gallery.

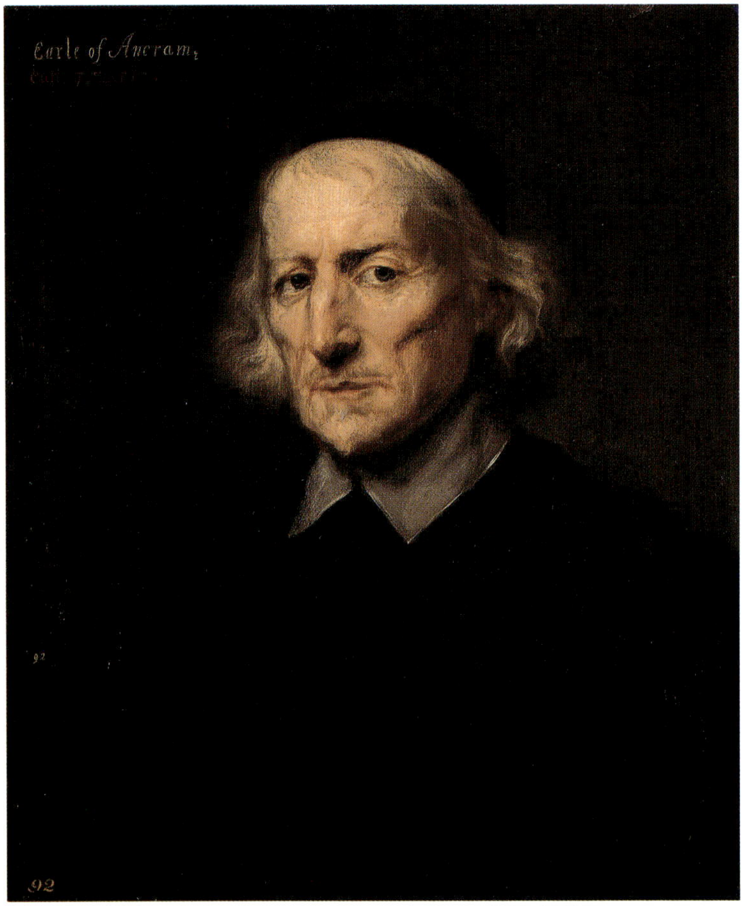

The portrait was painted while Sir Robert, a Royalist, was living alone in exile in Holland. The author of a 'Sonnet in praise of Solitude' in 1624, Sir Robert was preoccupied some 30 years later by 'the cold, cold days' when he was 'stryving by God's assistance to be readdy to die'.[1] His mind was evidently on this subject when he wrote from Amsterdam to his son William, 3rd Earl of Lothian, in Scotland on 30 May 1654: 'Though I be by God his mercy, alyve and in health, yet I grow very old, which showeth more in one year now than in thrie before, as you will see by the difference of my pictures, where of I have sent you one, and have another much older donne since, by a good maister, to bestow upon you iff I have my toung to my end, otherwayes you may call for it at this toun near the new markett, out of the hands of Mr Levinus, the Duke of Brandenburg's paynter. He duelt at the fleur-de-luce and you may be sure of a good one. He ist the better because he has so high a conceit of himself that he thinks here is none to be compaired with him in all of Germany and Holland, nor the rest of the 17 provinces'.[2] The earlier portrait to which Sir Robert referred was painted the year before in 1653 by Hercules Sanders (1616-63), and had been sent back to the family in Scotland (fig.52). The comparison with Lievens's portrayal all too poignantly shows the earl's ageing 'more in one year now than in thrie before' but it also captures his dignity in the face of death. Strangely, it was Oliver Cromwell, the Lord Protector, who paid Sir Robert's burial dues when he died in Amsterdam that year, perhaps as a mark of respect for Kerr's unswerving allegiance, albeit to his king.[3]

EXHIBITED: *Edinburgh 1883*, no.339; *The Age of Charles II, RA*, 1960, no.53; *The Orange and the Rose*, Victoria and Albert Museum, London, 1964, no.41; *Jan Lievens ein Maler im Schatten Rembrandts*, exhibition catalogue, Herzog Anton Ulrich-Museum, Braunschweig, 1979, no.38.

LITERATURE: *HdG 1893*, p.214; H. Schneider, *Jan Lievens: Sein Leben und Seine Werke*, Haarlem, 1932, revised by R. E. O. Ekkart, Amsterdam, 1973, pp.147, 334; *Sumowski*, vol.3, no.1294, repr. p.1933‡; *Wenley*, no.92.

THE MARQUESS OF LOTHIAN

1 A letter of 9 December 1653 (in Scottish Record Office, Edinburgh, SRO / GD40/2 / XIV -65-), quoted in *Border Story. The Name and House of Kerr at Monteviot, Jedburgh, Scotland*, Kelso, 1980, p.46 (unattributed).

2 *Correspondence of Sir Robert Kerr, First Earl of Ancram, and his son William, Third Earl of Lothian*, ed. D. Laing, Edinburgh, 1875, vol.2, p.383.

3 *Border Story, op.cit.*, p.46 (unattributed).

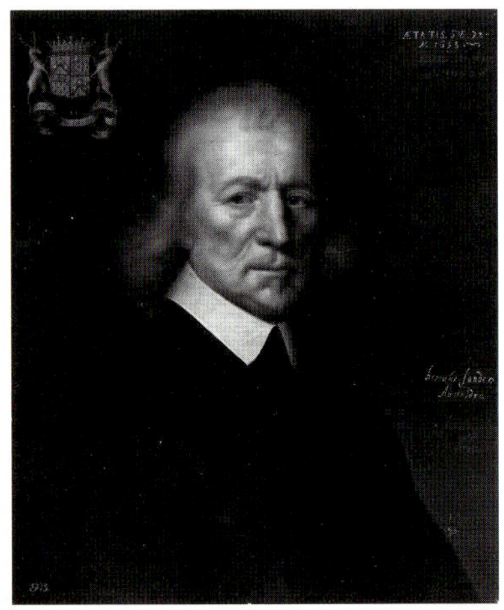

fig.52

1634–93. Born in Dordrecht, Maes trained with Rembrandt probably from the end of the 1640s. He had returned to Dordrecht by 1653 where he remained until 1674, then living in Amsterdam until his death. His early genre and biblical scenes and portraits are influenced by Rembrandt. Maes specialised in genre scenes in the late 1650s but then turned almost exclusively to portraiture.

31 *Dutch Family Group*

Oil on panel: 50.5 × 38 cm
PROVENANCE: In the collection of LORD CLERK OF ELDIN by 1819 (when exhibited), until sold at his sale by Winstanley, 16 March 1833 , lot 170 (engraved in catalogue by W. Geikie): Rt Hon. R. C. Nisbet Hamilton by 1856, when exhibited at the British Institution ; inherited by his daughter, MRS NISBET HAMILTON OGILVY by whom bequeathed to the National Gallery of Scotland, 1921 (no.1509).

A. Bredius, the famous Dutch art historian, saw this painting on 29 December 1883 when it was at the Royal Scottish Academy in Edinburgh and wrote that 'The Dutch Family is a fine specimen of Nic. Maes's early and best Time ... The picture belongs to about the year 1635 & may be reckoned among the best works of Maes'.[1] However, despite Bredius's dating of the work, it is perhaps from the 1650s as it is close in style to two other family groups of this period.[2] A spurious Rembrandt signature was removed from the picture when it was cleaned in 1952.

EXHIBITED: Royal Institution, Edinburgh, 1819, no.23, (as a Rembrandt from Lord Eldin's collection); British Institution, London, 1856, no.27 (attributed to Maes); *Edinburgh 1883*, no.266.

LITERATURE: *HdG*, no.937 (as Rembrandt); *Sumowski*, vol.3, 1983, p.2035, no.1438, repr. p.2164.

NATIONAL GALLERY OF SCOTLAND

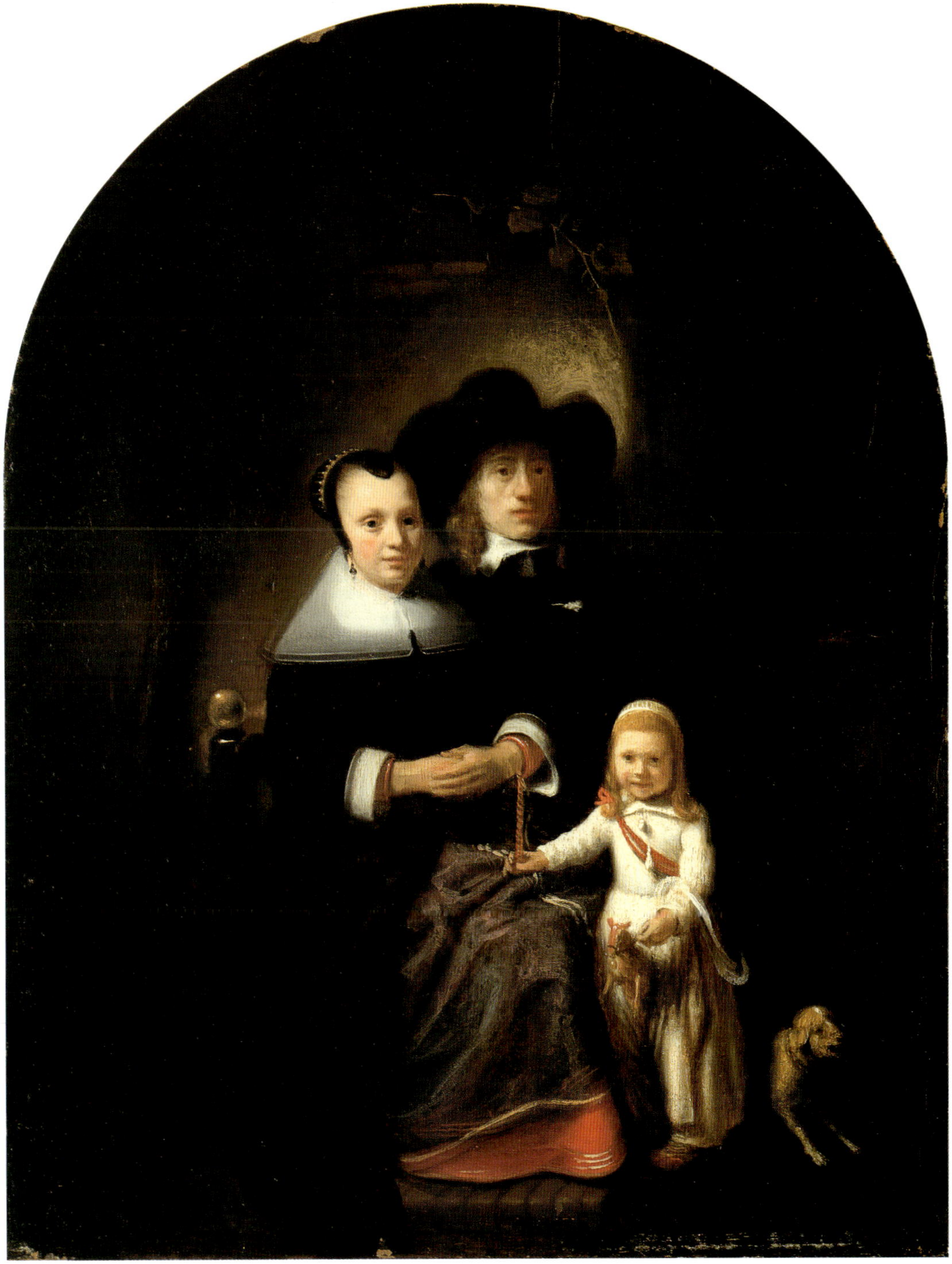

1 Quoted in a letter from Gilbert Ogilvy, 5 January 1921, in Gallery bequest files.
2 C. A. Staring, *Oud Holland*, LXXX, 1965, p.177, figs 1 and 2.

32 *A Young Girl Threading a Needle*

Oil on panel: 40.64 × 31.75 cm
Signed: *N. MAES* (*S* in reverse) and dated 1657
PROVENANCE: Brought to England in 1833 by Mr Chaplin from whom purchased by Lord Francis Leveson Gower, 1st Earl of Ellesmere;[1] Private Collection, Scotland.

The girl embodies the virtues of diligent domesticity, or what Simon Schama calls the 'Heroic housewife',[2] seen in many of Maes's works, including *A Young Girl Peeling Apples* which used to be in the collection of the 2nd Duke of Sutherland (now in the Metropolitan Museum of Art, New York, see fig.53). The girls' demure sweetness presumably succeeded in making the moral medicine go down more palatably.

As Haak points out, the type had its origins in sixteenth-century iconography, but Maes emphasises the Dutch character of the girl's goodness by including in the background a map of Holland (with the north shown on the right side). Maes used such motifs frequently, for example in *The Listening Maid* in the Wallace collection, London (no.P224), dated 1656, which shows another similar map,[3] while an earlier painting dated 1655 (*HdG,* no. 66) makes use of a comparable pose.[4]

EXHIBITED: *Manchester 1857*, no.1071 (*A Girl Sewing* lent by the Earl of Ellesmere); *RA 1952-3*, no.509.

LITERATURE: *Smith*, supplement, no.1; *Bridgewater House Catalogue 1851*, no.167; *Waagen*, vol.2; p.42; *HdG*, no.61; *Bridgewater House Catalogue 1926*, no.167; *Sumowski,* vol.3, no.1371, repr.p.2097; *Haak*, p.91, fig.141.

PRIVATE COLLECTION, SCOTLAND

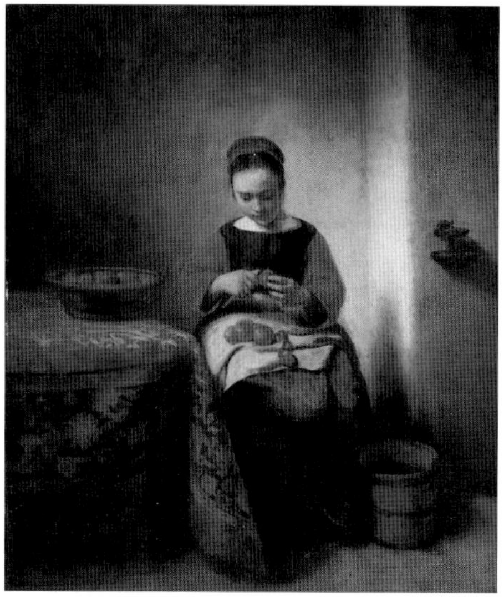

fig.53

1 *Bridgewater House Catalogue 1903*, no.66.
2 S. Schama, *The Embarassment of Riches*, London, 1978, p.398, quoting from Jacob Cats's poem of the same name.
3 *Ibid.*, p.460.
4 S. J. Gudlaugsson, *Oud Holland*, 83, 1968, p.13, pl.16.

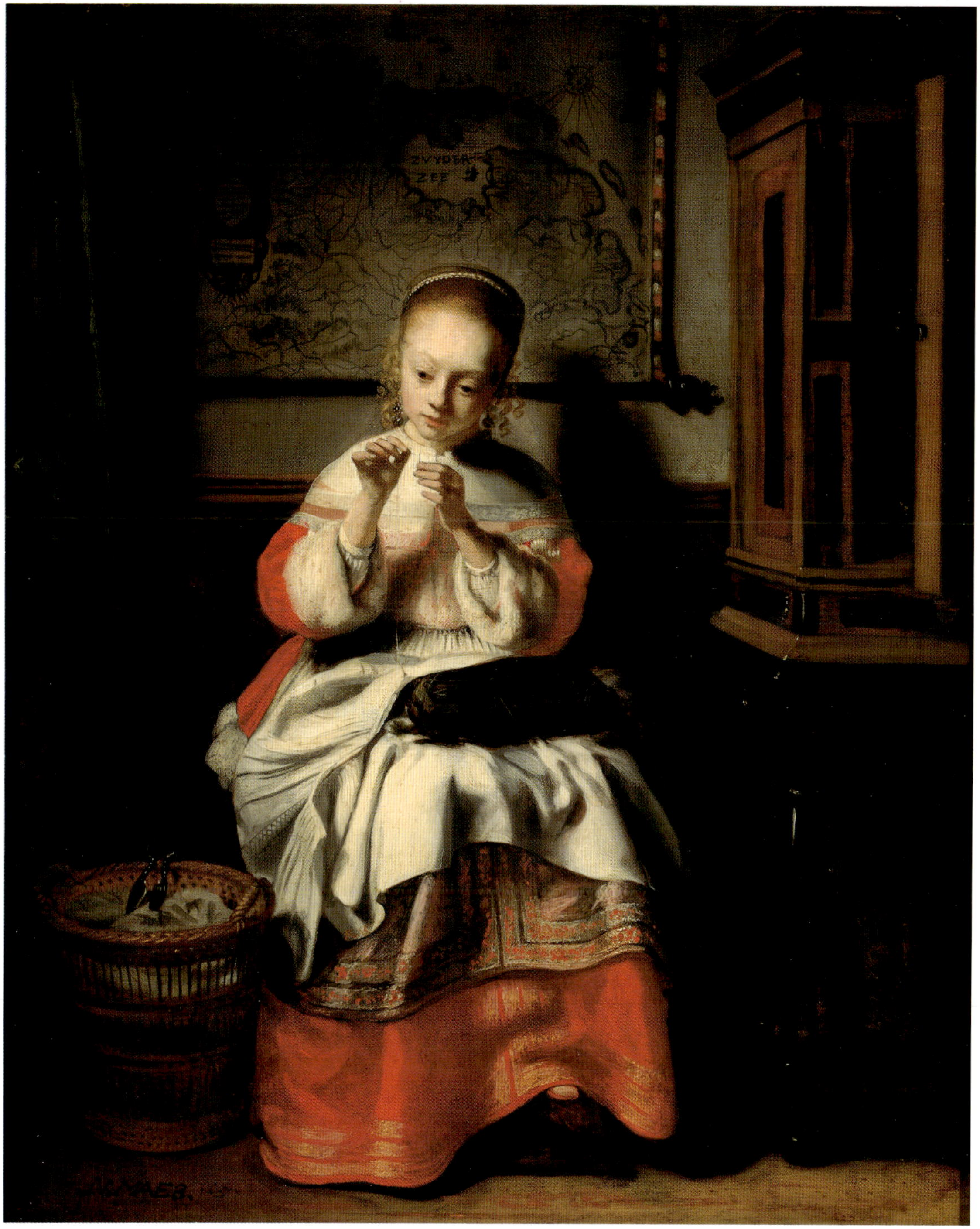
ZUYDER
ZEE

33 *The 1st Duke of Argyll*

Oil on canvas: 48.3 × 58.4 cm
Signed: *NMAES* at bottom right

34 *Colonel Charles Campbell*

Oil on canvas: 48.3 × 58.4 cm
Signed: *NMAES* at bottom left
PROVENANCE (for nos 33 and 34): The DUKES OF ARGYLL. Rev. G. Read in 1867.[1] The Duke of Argyll by 1950 at Inverary Castle.

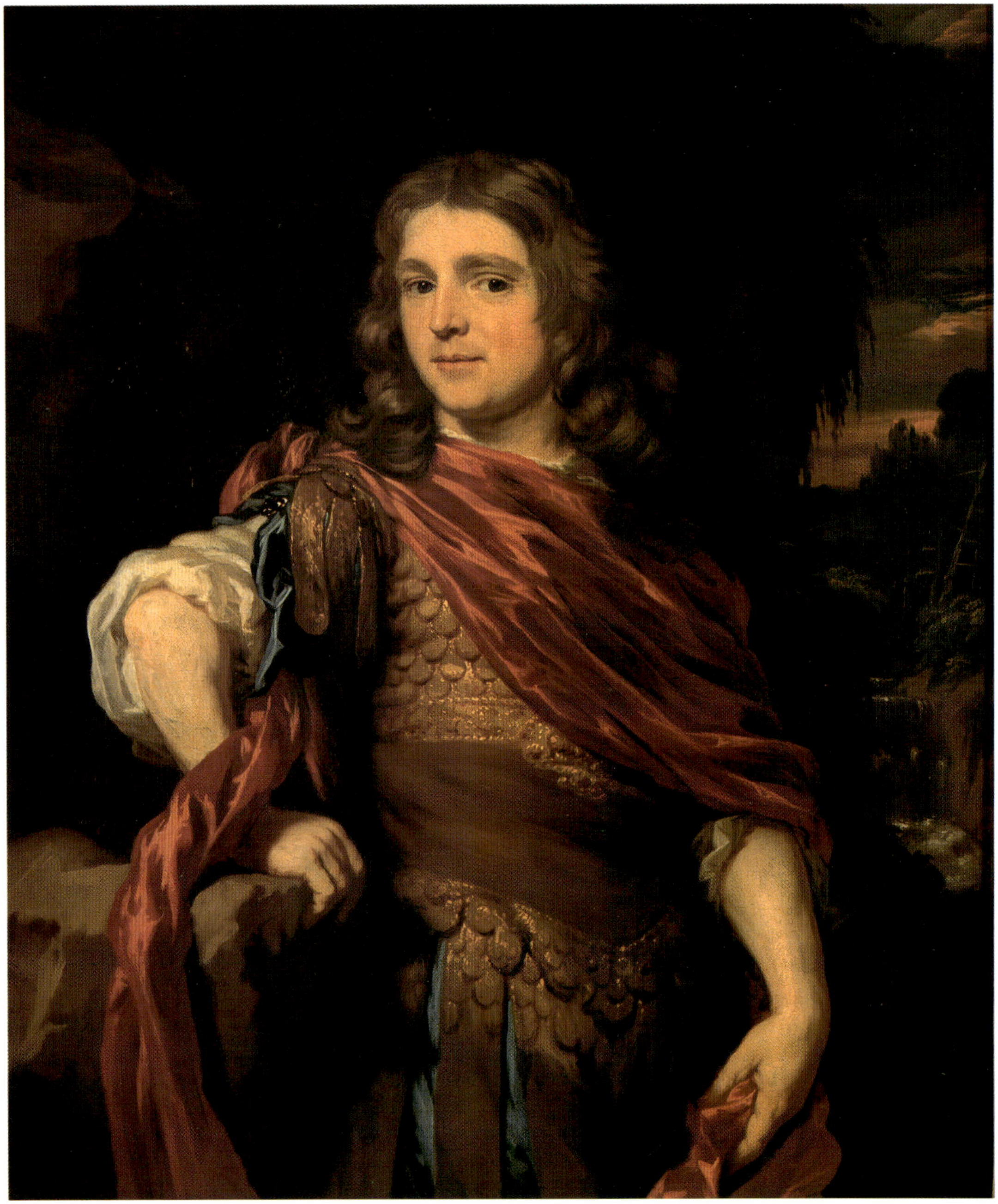

There is also a third portrait of the same size at Inverary Castle. The identification of the subjects of these three portraits is problematical. They were traditionally believed to represent the 1st, 2nd and 3rd Dukes of Argyll. The latter two were the 1st Duke's sons, John (*c.*1680-1743) and Archibald (1682-1761). However, they were too young to be identified as the two young men shown here.

A portrait of a member of the Argyll family by Maes (*HdG,* no.133) 'with a brown coat and a red cloak' (which cannot be any of the Inverary portraits because of the colours used) was reproduced in *The Connoisseur,* September 1916, and certainly shows the same sitter (but older) as that in Catalogue no.34. Though the portrait is there identified as the 9th Earl of Argyll, it seems likely that Catalogue nos 33 and 34 represent, as Waterhouse suggested, the 1st Duke of Argyll and his brother Charles Campbell.[2] Their father, the 9th Earl, escaped to exile in the Netherlands in 1681 by which time the sons would have been about 28 and 25. This is probably a little old for the two young men here, but both may have been to the Netherlands before this, perhaps with their father or a tutor (which might explain the identity of the third portrait). Stylistically the paintings could date from about 1675 when the 1st Duke (then the Marquess of Lorne) would have been about 22 and his brother 20. The portrait of the 1st Duke, still at Inverary, by John Medina, was probably painted in 1689 to commemorate his accession and shows a rather more portly character but wearing the same type of mock Roman armour.[3]

THE TRUSTEES OF
THE 10TH DUKE OF ARGYLL

1 *Waterhouse Notebooks*, vol.31, p.59, 21 June 1950: 'Three companion ¾ lengths, signed and said to be of the 1st Duke and his brother Col. Charles Campbell (two are said to represent the latter)...On the back of one of the Colonel Campbells is the label of a Dublin exhibition as lent by a Rev. George H. Read'. The label was inscribed '1867'.

2 *Ibid.*

3 *Holloway*, p.36 , fig.5.

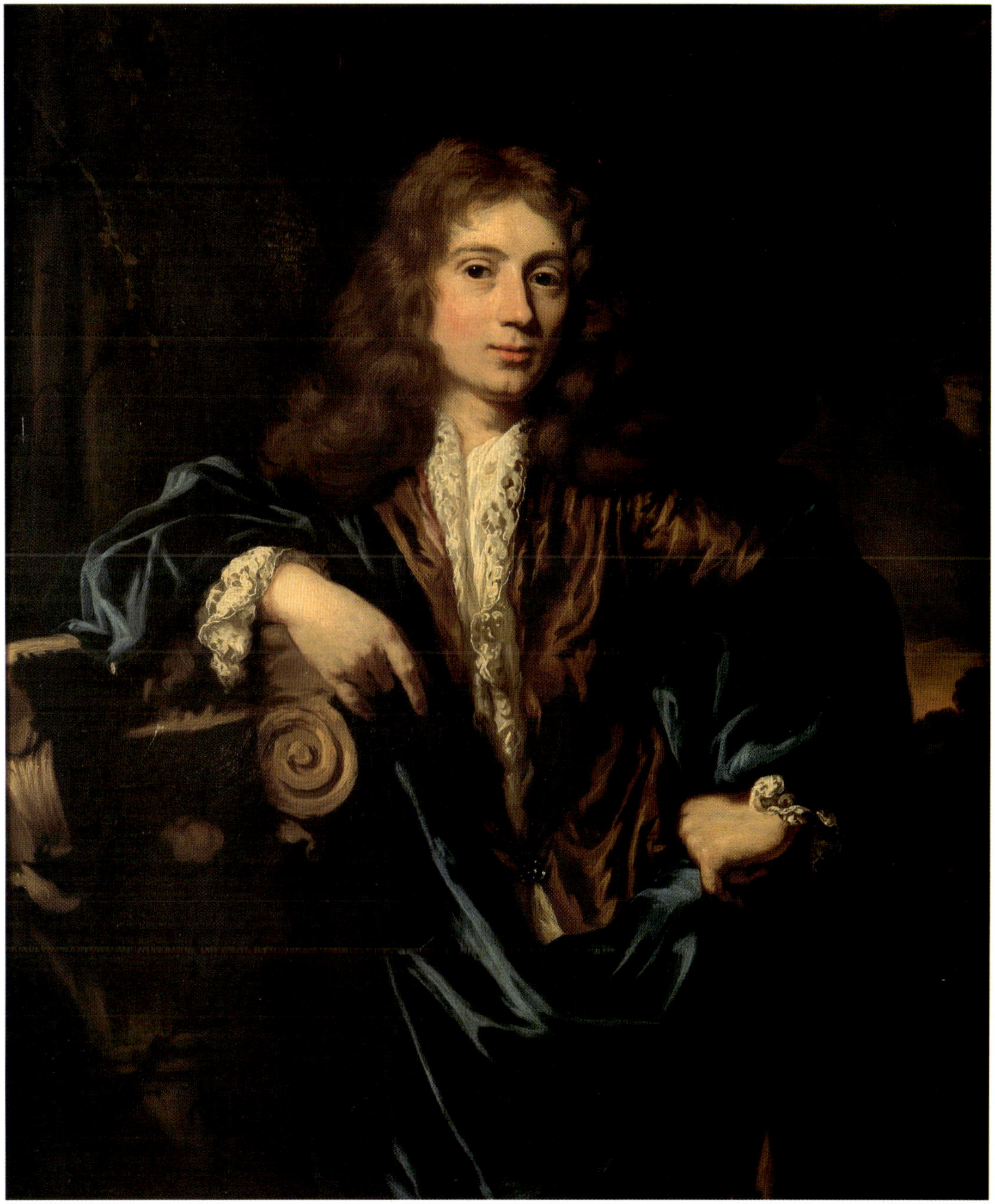

JACOB FRANSZ. VAN DE MERCK

c.1610-64. Born in Delft where he was living in 1631, Van de Merck is listed as a member of the painters' guild in The Hague in 1636. By 1640 he was in the guild at Dordrecht and then lived from 1658-63 in Leiden, where he died in September 1664. He is primarily known as a portrait painter.

35 *Still-life with Fruit and Parrot*

Oil on canvas: 170 × 136 cm
Signed and dated: *JvMerck 1654* across window-sill.
Traces of false signature: *J de Heem* at top right
PROVENANCE: Corehouse, Lanarkshire by 1850, when mentioned (as J. de Heem) in a manuscript inventory; by descent to Colonel CRANSTOUN of that Ilk.

The painting was acquired as a De Heem and is listed as such in 1850, hanging in the dining room at Corehouse[1] for which it was presumably purchased, admirably fulfilling its role as a large-scale decorative work. The house, designed by Blore, was finished about 1840 and this picture was probably acquired at about the same time.

Restoration revealed a false signature of Jan de Heem at the top right of the picture, which seems to have been covered with particularly dark (perhaps tinted) varnish.[2] Small pieces of Dutch newsprint were discovered as packing in the stretcher of the canvas and these date from after 1825, so it seems likely that at about this date the picture may have been given the deep brown tone ' of an old violin' (so praised by Sir George Beaumont and beloved of British collectors). It was also given the signature of Jan de Heem to make the work more marketable, concealing the name of Jacob van de Merck. Comparison with a signed *Fruit Still-life* in the Museum de Lakenhal, Leiden, is clearly by the same hand.[3] However, in scale and content, the Corehouse painting is considerably more ambitious than the artist's other four known signed still-life pictures.[4]

COLONEL CRANSTOUN OF THAT ILK

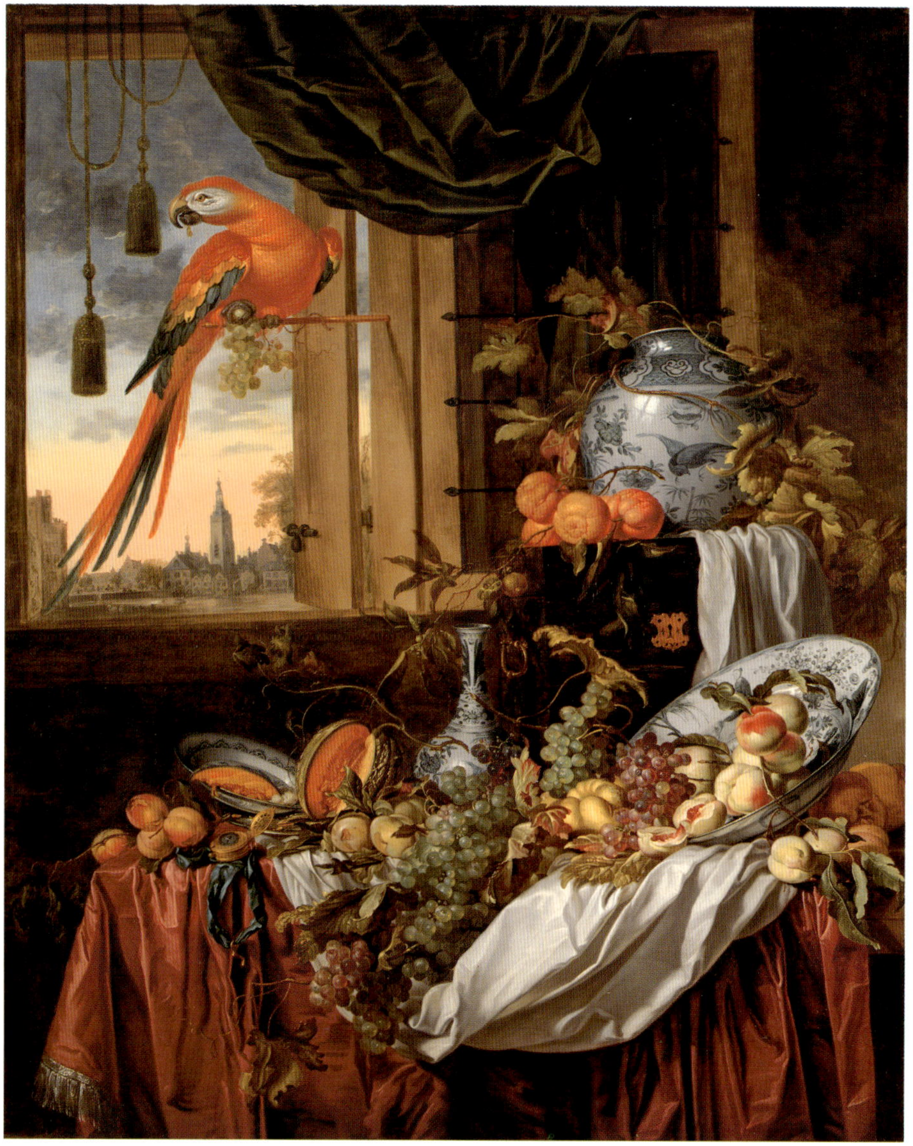

1 *Waagen*, vol.3, p. 312: 'Corehouse, seat of Lord Cranstoun in Lanarkshire', where he lists a Veronese but he did not actually visit the house.

2 Restoration carried out in 1992 by Nicola Christie, Assistant Conservator, National Galleries of Scotland.

3 See *Catalogus van de Schilderijen en Tekeningen*, Museum de Lakenhal, Leiden, 1983, no.592, p.214. The Lakenhal also has nine examples of Van de Merck's portraiture.

4 *Ibid.*, p.214; photographs in *RKD*.

GABRIEL METSU

1629-67. Born in Leiden where he worked almost exclusively until his move to Amsterdam by 1658. Believed by Houbraken to be a pupil of Gerard Dou, Metsu is best known for his genre scenes but also painted still-lifes and portraits. He died in Amsterdam where he is buried in the Nieuwe Kerk.

36 *A Cavalier on Horseback before an Inn*

Oil on canvas stuck on panel: 65 × 50 cm
Signed: G. *Metsu* above the door
PROVENANCE: Lubbeling sale; Lambert Witsen sale, Amsterdam, 25 May 1746, lot 5; Le Brun sale, 1778;[1] London sale, 1790, to Tassaert; perhaps London sale, 1794, from sale of Duc de Quesnoy, to Williamson; Morland sale, London, 1799, to Parke; 3rd Duke of Bridgewater;[2] Private Collection, Scotland.

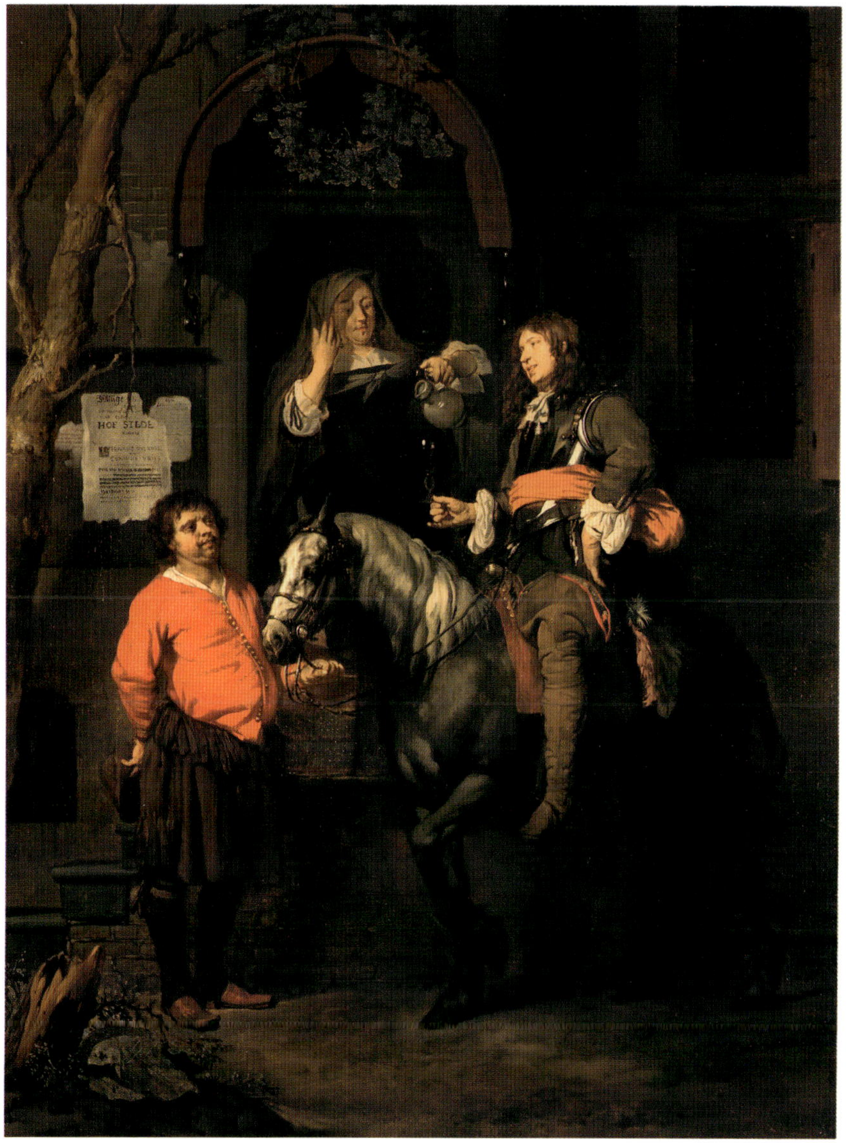

The wreath of foliage above the door appears to be made of vine leaves and is, therefore, a fitting adornment for the hostelry. It is also possible that the hostess's careful pouring of the wine may be a sign of moderation – as an advocation of temperance perhaps.[3]

A clear distinction can also be seen between the mounted cavalier and the lowly peasant who holds the horse, a contrast to which Metsu frequently draws attention in his paintings.[4] The notice which can be seen on the left of the door advertises a sale of the estate of a Cornelis Vries, whose name also appears in a document relating to Metsu.[5] Similar handbills can be found in other works by Metsu, such as in *The Sleeping Sportsman* in the Wallace Collection, London (no.P251), and *A Young Woman Selling Poultry* in the Gemäldegalerie, Dresden. The latter picture is signed and dated 1662 and *A Cavalier on Horseback before an Inn* is probably contemporaneous.

EXHIBITED: *Gabriel Metsu*, Museum de Lakenhal, Leiden, 1966, no.39.

LITERATURE: *Stafford Gallery Catalogue 1808*, no.192; *Stafford Gallery Catalogue 1818*, vol.3, pl.8 (which is marked 1816), no.74; *Smith*, no.38; *Bridgewater House Catalogue 1851*, no.194; *Waagen*, vol.2, p. 44; *HdG*, no. 198; *Bridgewater House Catalogue 1926*, no.194; F. W. Robinson, *Gabriel Metsu. A study of his place in Dutch genre painting of the Golden Age*, New York, 1974, p.83, p.149, fig. 81.

PRIVATE COLLECTION, SCOTLAND

1 Engraved by Tellier in the *Le Brun Gallery*.

2 *Bridgewater House Catalogue 1851* and *1926*, no.194, from which provenance details are taken. Three works by Metsu are listed in the *Catalogue of Pictures at Cleveland House* (unattributed), London, 1806, nos 109, 146 (a seller of herrings) and 169. It is not known whether 109 or 146 was A *Cavalier on Horseback* (Cleveland House was the former name of Bridgewater House).

3 *Haak*, p.91.

4 *Masters of Dutch Genre Painting*, no.70.

5 Robinson , *op. cit.*, p.83.

c.1590-before 1648. Mytens was born in Delft and trained in The Hague, probably with the painter Michiel van Miereveld, and was influenced also by the style of Jan Anthonisz. van Ravesteyn. He came to Britain c.1618 and worked for the British aristocracy, taking over after Paulus van Somer's death in 1621 as the leading portrait painter. He was appointed court painter to Charles I in 1625 but was subsequently superseded in popularity by Van Dyck. Mytens returned to The Hague c.1634.

37 *James, 3rd Marquis and 1st Duke of Hamilton*

Oil on canvas: 221 × 139.7 cm
Signed and dated: *D. Mijtens fe^t. anno 1629* on the base of the column
PROVENANCE: Commissioned by James, 1st Duke of Hamilton (1606-49), in 1629, and thence by descent until placed on loan at the Scottish National Portrait Gallery by whom purchased with the aid of the NHMF, the NACF and the Pilgrim Trust, 1987 (no.PG.2722).

This was not the first picture that Mytens painted for the Hamilton family. In 1622 he had painted a portrait of the sitter's wife, Lady Mary Fielding, aged nine (two years after her marriage!), and in 1624 he had portrayed the sitter's father.[1] Presumably as part of the same commission he also did a full-length portrait of James in 1624,[2] the year before his father died and he became the 3rd Marquis. James was in Scotland from early 1626, but returned to live in London on 20 October 1628. He was then made a privy councillor in both England and Scotland and this portrait by Mytens, painted the following year, celebrates all the elegance, arrogance and position of a favoured courtier. In the Civil War, James unsuccessfully tried to reconcile the Scottish Covenanters and King Charles I. Despite his own claim to the Scottish throne (next in line after the descendants of James VI), Hamilton remained loyal to Charles I, an allegiance which led to his own execution in 1649.

The first mention of the portrait in the Hamilton inventories occurs in a document written probably in 1649, which describes 'One picture of My Lord standing at length with his hett in his hand of Mittens'[3] and it appears also in a later inventory of 13 October 1704: 'A peice of James Duke of Hamilton a full length holding his hatt between his fingers leaning upon a stick by Mysens'[4] when it hung on 'the Great Stairs' at Kinneil Castle.

Other pictures by Mytens in the Hamilton inventories were noted in 12 August 1695 in 'A list of the right honourable the Earl of Arrans pictures at London' which included 'a head of James Duke of Hamilton by Mytens (no.2).[5] There was also an oval three-quarter length of the same sitter by 'Matings' in the 'Great Drawing Room' at Kinneil Castle as well as a small picture of the 'Earl of Newport at length' by 'Mitings' in the 'Great Bedchamber' there.[6] The work of Mytens and his studio was also popular amongst other Scots, as attested by a version of the portrait of the 1st Duke's father at Hopetoun House and another left to the Scottish National Portrait Gallery (PG 1056) by Mrs Nisbet Hamilton Ogilvy of Biel, near Edinburgh, and paintings in the collections of, for example, the Duke of Fife at Duff House in Banff, the Duke of Buccleuch at Drumlanrig Castle, the Earl of Mar and Kellie, Lt. Col. Stirling of Keir, Lord Kinnoull and Sir James Fergusson of Kilkerran .

EXHIBITED: *RA 1938*, no.75; *Edinburgh 1991*, no.10.

LITERATURE: O. Ter Kuile , 'Daniel Mijtens "His Majesties Picture-Drawer" ', *Nederlands Kunsthistorisches Jaarboek*, 1969, vol.20, pp.70-1, no.53, fig.32.

SCOTTISH NATIONAL PORTRAIT GALLERY

1 Ter Kuile *op. cit.*, no.44, fig.53, the picture in the collection of the Duke of Hamilton, Lennoxlove, East Lothian. There are many different versions (some by his studio) of the portrait of James, 2nd Marquis (1589-1625), which can be seen in the Royal Collection , the Duke of Hamilton's collection, Scottish National Portrait Gallery and in the collection of the Marquess of Linlithgow at Hopetoun House near Edinburgh (for versions see *ibid.*, nos 45, 46, 47, 48, 49, 50, 51, 51A).

2 Formerly in the collection of the Duke of Hamilton, now in the Tate Gallery, London (no.3474), *ibid.* no.52.

3 *Waterhouse Notebooks*, transcriptions of Hamilton inventories in the Getty Archive, Santa Monica, Document 10, no.85. There was also the painting of 'My Lady, to the middle, in a ruffe, with a feather in her head' , no.96, i.e.the portrait of Lady Mary Fielding mentioned above.

4 *Ibid.*, Document 8 , no.159.

5 *Ibid.*, Document 2, unnumbered paintings.

6 *Ibid.*, Document 8, nos 192 and 214. The Earl of Newport's portrait occurs again in a list of 1759 (Document 12, no.312) when it is valued at £1.

7 Ter Kuile, *op. cit.*, nos 47, 49, 3, 15 and 106, 21, 62, 63, 72.

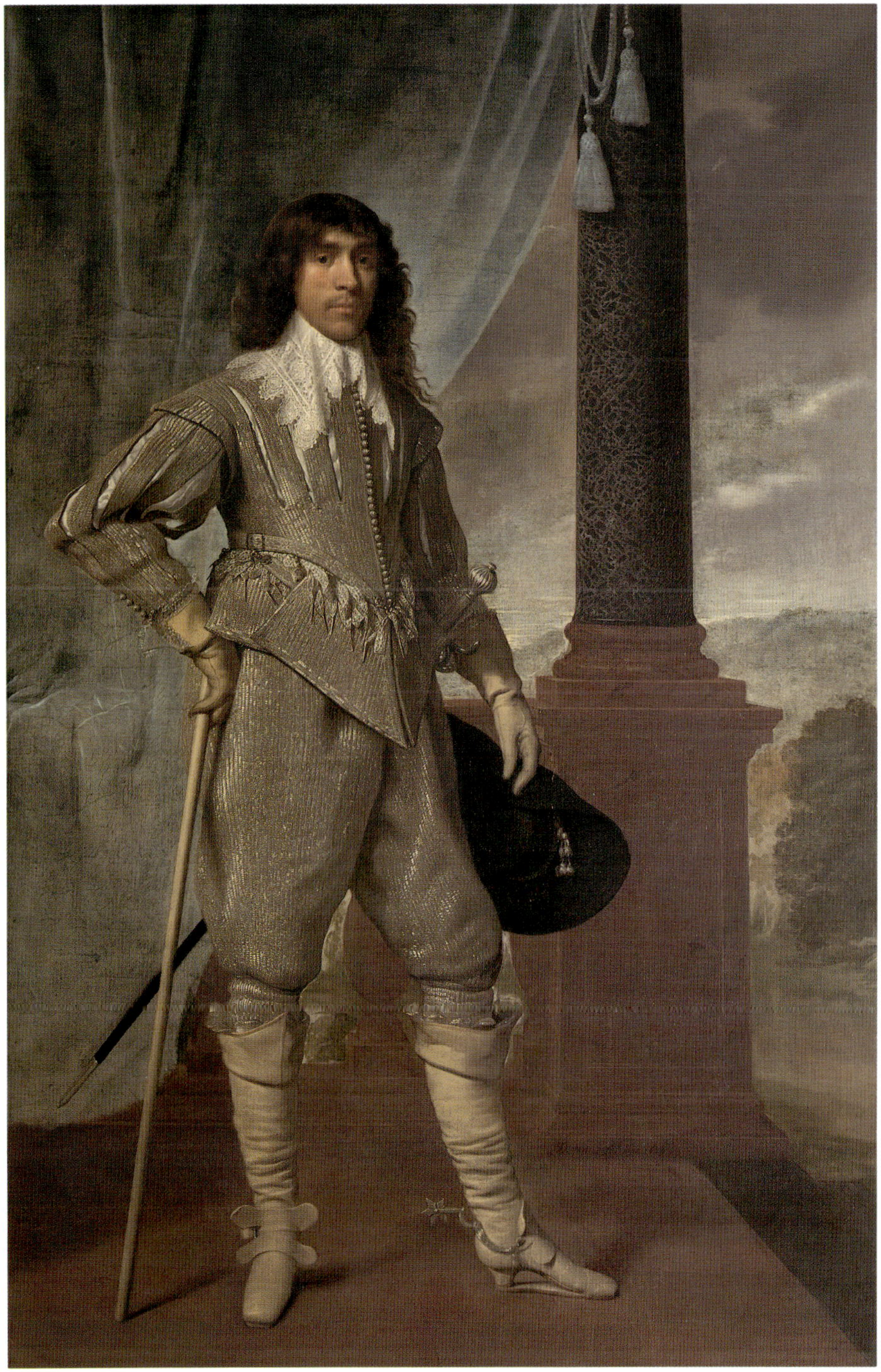

AERT VAN DER NEER

1603/4-77. Born in Amsterdam, Van der Neer is recorded as being about 38 years old on 22 July 1642 and his age has also been deduced from other documents. Probably brought up near Gorinchem, he may have trained under R. Camphuysen, who influenced his early landscapes, the first of which is dated 1633. His works did not fetch high prices and he was made bankrupt as an innkeeper, dying impoverished in Amsterdam. Van der Neer is now recognised as an accomplished master of moonlight, twilight and winter scenes.

38 *A Wooded River Landscape by Moonlight*

Oil on panel: 28.5 × 27.3 cm
PROVENANCE: Presumably purchased by George Brudenell, Duke of Montagu (1712-90), and inherited by his daughter and sole heiress, Elizabeth, wife of the 3rd DUKE OF BUCCLEUCH and thence by descent.

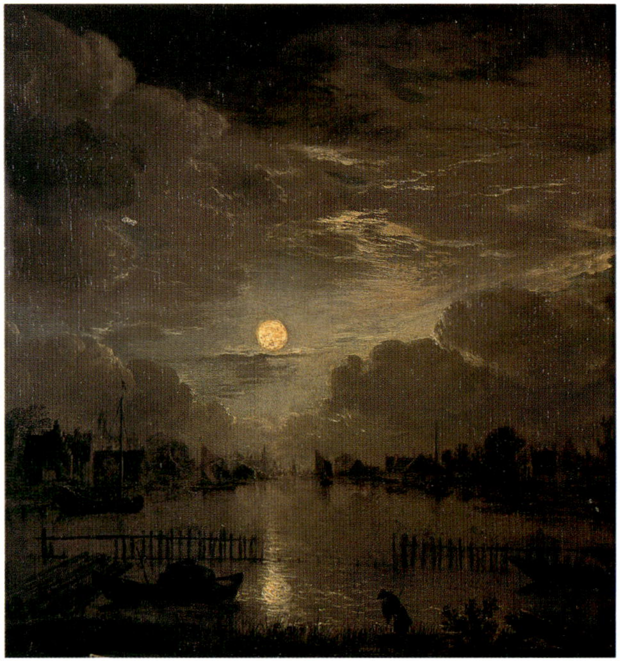

The picture now hangs in the boudoir at Drumlanrig Castle, in Dumfries and Galloway, where it is accompanied by another smaller work by the same artist, inherited from the Duke of Montagu. Adriaen van Ostade's *Peasants Playing Cards* (Catalogue no.41) hangs in the same room and such cabinet pieces of small scale and fine finish were much admired and acquired by British collectors. It is not known exactly when *A Wooded River Landscape by Moonlight* was brought to Scotland but it certainly hung at Montagu House in London until 1865 as it appears in an inventory of that date.[1] It was engraved by W. Mayor as a *Vue de Canal proche de Haarlem.* Another of Van der Neer's moonlit river scenes was in the collection at Amisfield by 1771 and exhibited in *Pictures from Gosford House,* no.32.

EXHIBITED: *Treasure Houses 1985*, no.306, p.373.

THE DUKE OF BUCCLEUCH AND QUEENSBERRY

1 *Treasure Houses, op. cit.* The painting is also in an inventory of Montagu House of *c.*1820.

39 *Moonlight Winter Scene on a Frozen Canal*

Oil on canvas: 67.3 × 103.2 cm
Signed with monogram
PROVENANCE: With John, 3rd EARL OF BUTE, before 1800 and thence by descent; Private Collection, Scotland.

The picture is mentioned in the 1800 catalogue of pictures at Luton Hoo (no.266) and also in the 1822 catalogue (no. 64), where it is recorded as hanging in the little breakfast room[1] and described as by 'Vanderneer, *A Frost Piece* – His landscape is varied and well chosen, touched with spirit and delicacy, has an expensive talent and in all parts of Europe his pictures are in great esteem'. Another *Frost Piece* (unnumbered) by the same artist is listed in the same catalogue as hanging in the best dressing room.

The painting was regarded by Bode as one of Van der Neer's best winter scenes. It shows 'kolf' players, skaters and a horse sled against a wide background with buildings in the distance at the right and left; an updated version of the type of broad panorama employed by Hendrick Avercamp in his winter scenes (e.g. Catalogue no.1). Though none of Van der Neer's paintings is dated by him after 1650, this is a mature work and probably dates from *c.* 1655-60, painted about the same time as the artist's *Skating Scene* in the Wallace Collection, London,[2] and his *View of a River in Winter* at the Rijksmuseum, Amsterdam,[3] with which this picture can most closely be compared.

The picture was exhibited with most of the pictures from the Bute collection at the Bethnal Green Museum from 1882-3 and was mentioned in a review in 1883: 'The best ice piece is Van der Neer's "Winter Scene in Holland" in a moonlit twilight, with figures skating on a smooth river: a town and a windmill are on the further shore. They harmonize exquisitely with the olive silver of the shining ice and the warm palours of the sky. The grading of the atmosphere and of the solid elements of this picture make it equal to the best Cuyps of the same subject.'[4]

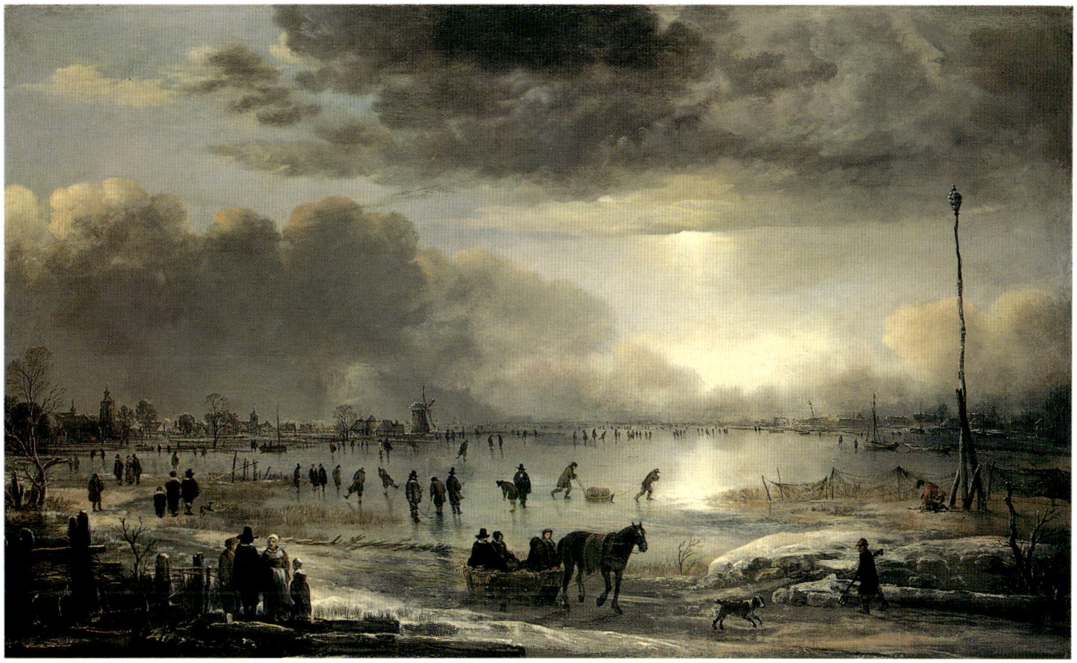

An almost identical composition was with Dr H. Steinmeyer in Berlin in 1938 (*RKD* photograph).

EXHIBITED: British Institution,1847, no.79; *RA,* 1870, no.18 (as by Arnold Van de Neer); *Bethnal Green 1882-3*, no.59; *Glasgow 1884*, no.118; *RA,* 1912, no.80; *Agnews*, no.16, repr. in colour as frontispiece.

LITERATURE: *Waagen,* vol.3, p.481; W. Bode, *Dutch and Flemish Painting,* London, 1909, p.185.

PRIVATE COLLECTION, SCOTLAND

1 The large landscapes by Cuyp (Catalogue no.16) and by Ruisdael (Catalogue no.57) in the current exhibition also seem to have hung in the same room.
2 No.P217; see J. Ingamells, *The Wallace Collection Catalogue of Pictures, Dutch and Flemish,* London, 1992, vol.4, pp.232-3.
3 No.C.191; see *Masters of Dutch Landscape*, no. 60.
4 'The Marquis of Bute's Pictures at Bethnal Green' (anonymous review), *The Athenaeum,* 6 January 1883, p.24.

HENDRIK TEN OEVER

1639-1716. Baptised in Zwolle, Ten Oeuver may have been a pupil of a Zwolle portraitist, Eva van Marle. He also studied with his cousin Cornelis de Bie on his move to Amsterdam shortly after 1657, returning to Zwolle after De Bie's death in 1664. He painted portraits and history pieces as well as landscapes both Dutch and Italianate, city views, still-lifes, game pieces and genre scenes.

40 *Canal Landscape with Figures*

Oil on canvas: 66.7 × 87 cm
Signed and dated: *Hten Oever / 1675* bottom left
PROVENANCE: Siegfried Bendixen from whom purchased in 1822[1] by SIR JAMES ERSKINE OF TORRIE, by whom bequeathed in 1825 to the University of Edinburgh which received the picture in 1836; placed on loan to the Board of Manufactures, Edinburgh, first at the Royal Institution, then at the National Gallery of Scotland for its opening in 1859 until 1983, when returned to the University of Edinburgh.

The picture was painted in the year of Ten Oever's wedding to Geertruidt van der Horst whom he married on 16 November 1675.[2] It shows a distant view of the artist's home town of Zwolle. The naked figures bathing in the light of the setting sun make the scene something of a curiosity. Such nudity, except in historical or mythological contexts, is rare in Dutch art[3] and its closest precedent is in Paulus Potter's *Cow Reflected in the Water* of 1648 in The Mauritshuis, The Hague (no.137), which also shows nudes in a contemporary Dutch setting.

This is one of the few works from the Torrie collection whose provenance is traceable. Sir James Erskine bought 14 Dutch and Flemish paintings from Siegfried Bendixen, an engraver in Hamburg, for a total of £215 in 1822, and one of the works was *Canal Landscape with Figures.* Erskine presumably believed it to be by Aelbert Cuyp (who influenced Ten Oever), and the picture was exhibited as by Cuyp in 1830. It is probably the painting mentioned by Waagen in his notes upon the Torrie collection as ' Albert Cuyp. – A landscape. Too heavy in tone and too decorative in treatment to be by him'.

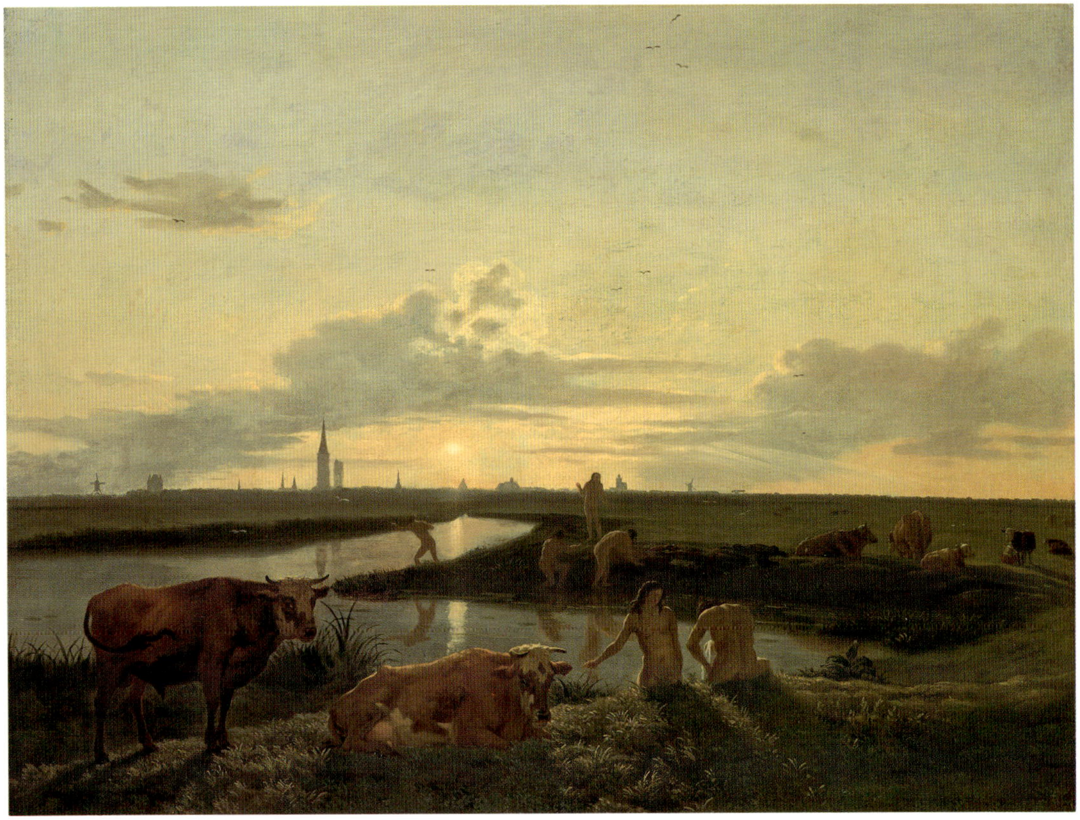

EXHIBITED: Royal Institution, Edinburgh, 1830, no.98 (as Cuyp); Royal Institution, Edinburgh, 1850, no.22 (as Cuyp); *Hendrik ten Oever*, Zwolle, 1957, no.43, repr.; *The Torrie Collection*, no.27, pl.4; *Masters of Dutch Landscape*, no.62.

LITERATURE: *Waagen*, vol.3, p.273, no.15; *HdG 1893*, p.132.

THE TORRIE COLLECTION
THE UNIVERSITY OF EDINBURGH

1 *Pictures for Scotland*, p.16 and note 2.

2 Ten Oever painted another version of this picture the following year which omits the bathers, replacing them with less unorthodox, clothed figures. See *Masters of Dutch Landscape*, p.389, fig.1.

3 *Ibid.*, p.389.

ADRIAEN VAN OSTADE

1610-85. Son of Jan van Ostade, Adriaen was baptised in Haarlem where, according to Houbraken, Frans Hals was the master of both Ostade and Adriaen Brouwer in about 1627. Ostade is first recorded as an artist in 1632. He spent most of his life in his home town as an important member of the Haarlem guild and had many pupils, including his brother Isack, Jan Steen, Cornelis Bega and Cornelis Dusart. An etcher and painter, he specialised in genre peasant scenes which show the influence of Brouwer, though not of Hals.

41 *Peasants Playing Cards*

Oil on panel: 31.1 × 22.9 cm
Signed and dated: *A Ostade / 1667* at centre right
PROVENANCE: Presumably purchased by George Brudenell, Duke of Montagu (1712-90), and inherited by his daughter and sole heiress, Elizabeth, wife of the 3rd DUKE OF BUCCLEUCH, thence by descent.

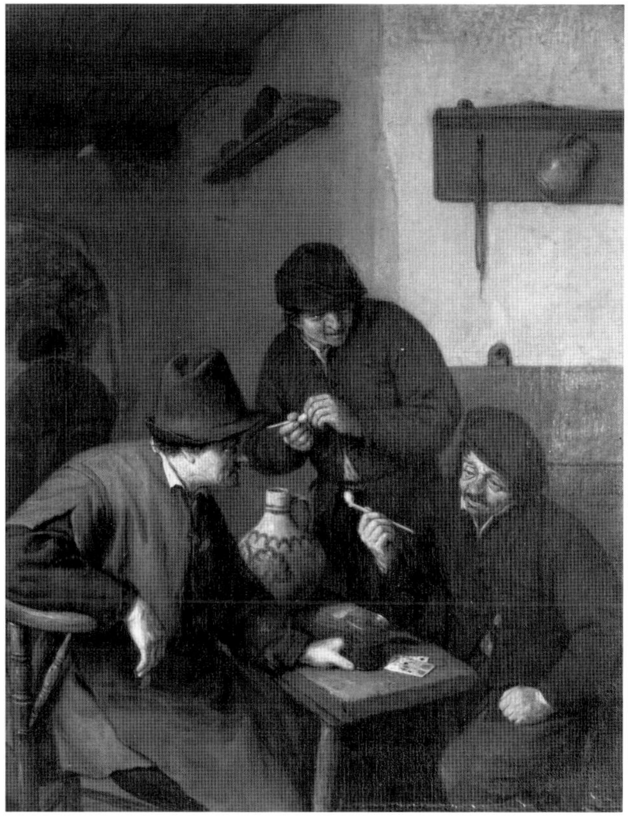

This painting hung at Montagu House,[1] where it was called *Three Boors Smoking*, and now hangs in the boudoir at Drumlanrig Castle where it is accompanied by another interior by Ostade (which also came from Montagu House).[2] There is another version of *Peasants Playing Cards* which was listed as in the James collection in 1971.[3]

One of the first records of paintings by Ostade in Scotland is in a list of the collections of the Duke of Hamilton dated 2 April 1698: 'A piece of perspective by Ostade' and a 'A Dutch Home by Ostade'. [4] Further works are listed in an inventory of pictures in the duke's appartments at the Palace of Holyrood House on 5 October 1704: 'A Horse and Forge done by Oasteard' (no.31) and 'A Dutch piece done by Oastad' (no.34), as well as an unattributed painting of 'A Dutch piece smoaking a pipe of tobacco' (no.46) hanging close by in 'My Lady Dutchess' Closet'. Such small genre pieces gained in popularity in Britain in the eighteenth century and they continued to be sought after in the nineteenth century. Ostade was particularly admired by Sir David Wilkie who had been encouraged to study the Dutch artist's work by Sir George Beaumont.[5] When he visited the Louvre in 1814, Wilkie was impressed by the Ostades, which he pronounced 'very fine specimens' and later noted that they improved greatly on further viewing.[6] While Ostade was not the only painter he praised, it is difficult to imagine many of Wilkie's genre scenes of interiors without the example of such pictures as *Peasants Playing Cards* and *Peasants before a Fire* (Catalogue no.42).

THE DUKE OF BUCCLEUCH AND QUEENSBERRY

1 Montagu House, no.31.
2 Montagu House, no.225.
3 Photograph and letter in Gallery files sent by C. Duits. The version is *HdG*, no.347.
4 *Waterhouse Notebooks*, transcriptions of Hamilton inventories in the Getty Archive, Santa Monica.
5 A. Cunningham, *The Life of Sir David Wilkie*, London, 1843, vol.1, p.148.
6 *Ibid.*, pp.398 and 422.

42 *Peasants before a Fire*

Oil on panel: 35.9 × 32.7 cm
Signed and dated: *AV Ostade 1668* (*AV* in ligature) on a plank left of centre foreground
PROVENANCE: G. Braamcamp sale, Amsterdam, 31 July 1771, lot 156, bought by Fouquet with pendant; Prince de Conti sale , Paris, 8 April 1777, lot 308, bought by Dubois; Poullain sale, Paris, 15 March 1780, lot 46; Prol(e)y in 1786; Harris, London, sold 1805; de Blyny; J. F. Tuffen sale, Christie's, London, 11 April 1818, lot 104 (as from Orléans collection), bought by Pinney; Sir Simon Clarke by 1829 and sold at his sale, Christie's, London, 8 May 1840, lot 34, to Colliard;[1] Schneider sale, Paris, 6 April 1876, lot 26, bought by Lord Dudley; Earl of Dudley sale, Christie's, London, 25 June 1892, lot 16, bought by Agnews, London, from whom acquired by WILLIAM MCEWAN in 1893; inherited by his daughter the Hon. Mrs Greville by whom bequeathed to The National Trust at Polesden Lacey in 1942.

There is an unidentified seal on the reverse of the panel with a bird holding a branch in its beak, a windmill (?) and a monogram (*JMB* or *JSCB*). A painting which was listed as a pendant at the Braamcamp sale has not been traced.

This was the only Ostade owned by William McEwan but he did possess other interior scenes such as *La Partie de Tric-trac* and *The Card Players* by David Teniers the Younger, as well as *The Game of Cards* by Cornelis de Man and an interior by Pieter de Hooch of *The Golf Players* which was formerly in the collection of Sir Hugh Hume Campbell.

EXHIBITED: British Institution, London, 1815, no.90; *RA 1952-3*, no.501.

LITERATURE: J. F. de Bastide, *Catalogue Raisonné du Cabinet de M. Braamcamp*, Amsterdam, 1766, pp.67-8; *Smith*, no.29 and supplement no.133; *HdG*, no.747; F. St J. Gore, *Catalogue of the Paintings at Polesden Lacey*, National Trust guidebook, 1976, no.49; *Polesden Lacey*, National Trust guidebook, 1985, no.49.

THE NATIONAL TRUST
POLESDEN LACEY

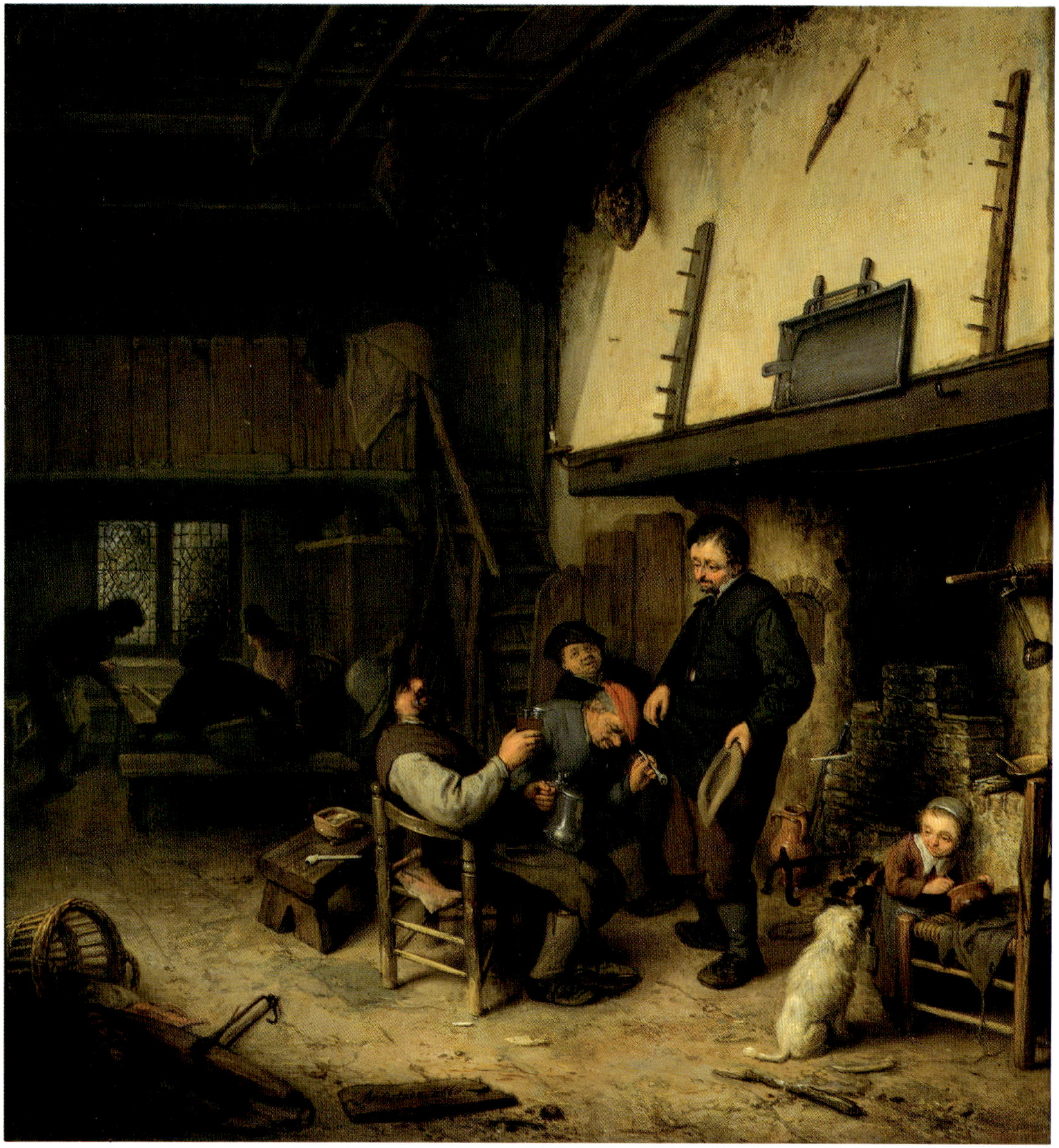

1 F. St J. Gore, *op. cit.*, p.25, notes that Colliard is listed as the purchaser in Christie's annotated catalogue but that Smith says that it was bought by J. Burchard. Hofstede de Groot wrote in his copy of the catalogue that it was sold 'to Colliard via Nieuwenhuys for Sir J. Barchard according to Smith'.

CORNELIS VAN POELENBURGH

c.1593-1667. Born in Utrecht, Poelenburgh was the son of the canon of the Catholic cathedral in that city. He trained with Abraham Bloemart and was in Rome by 1617, where he was probably a member of the Schildersbent, a group of Netherlandish painters. He also visited Florence but returned to Holland before 1627, travelling to London in 1637 where he lived for most of the time until 1641. Much influenced by his stay in Rome, Poelenburgh specialised in Italianate landscapes but also painted portraits and religious and mythological scenes.

43 *Bathsheba*

Oil on panel: 39 × 31 cm
PROVENANCE: The EARL OF WEMYSS AND MARCH by 1771 (Amisfield catalogue) and thence by descent.

This painting shows the passage described in 2 *Samuel* 11, v.2-4: 'It happened late one afternoon when David arose from his couch and was walking upon the roof of the king's house, that he saw from the roof a woman bathing; and the woman was very beautiful'. He sent messengers to Bathsheba and summoned her to sleep with him but in pictorial tradition this is normally shown by a letter, which in this picture lies upon the parapet. [1] The sculpture of Leda and the Swan and other elements, such as the peacock, are probably included as symbols of David's lust for Bathsheba.

Poelenburgh's cabinet paintings were collected from an early date in Britain and there were (and still are) many of his works in Scottish collections. The Duke of Hamilton's inventories[2] list several paintings by Poelenburgh. One was in the collection by 14 August 1695, a 'small landskipe with a sleeping Venus and Cupid by Poelenberg' (no. 18) and at Kinneil Castle on 13 August 1704[3] there was a 'Landskipp of 6 boys and a woman, a boy playing upon a pipe ... by Cornelis Poulengborch' (no.261) and 'a little square piece with several naked figures by Poolenbergh' (no.276). The Marquess of Bute also owned *The Flight into Egypt* of 1625, now in the Centraal Museum, Utrecht (no.8391), while Brodie Castle has the artist's *Tobias and the Angel* (Brodie Castle inventory, no.97). A large *Finding of Moses* was sold at Lord Clerk of Eldin's sale in Edinburgh on 16 March 1833, lot 151.

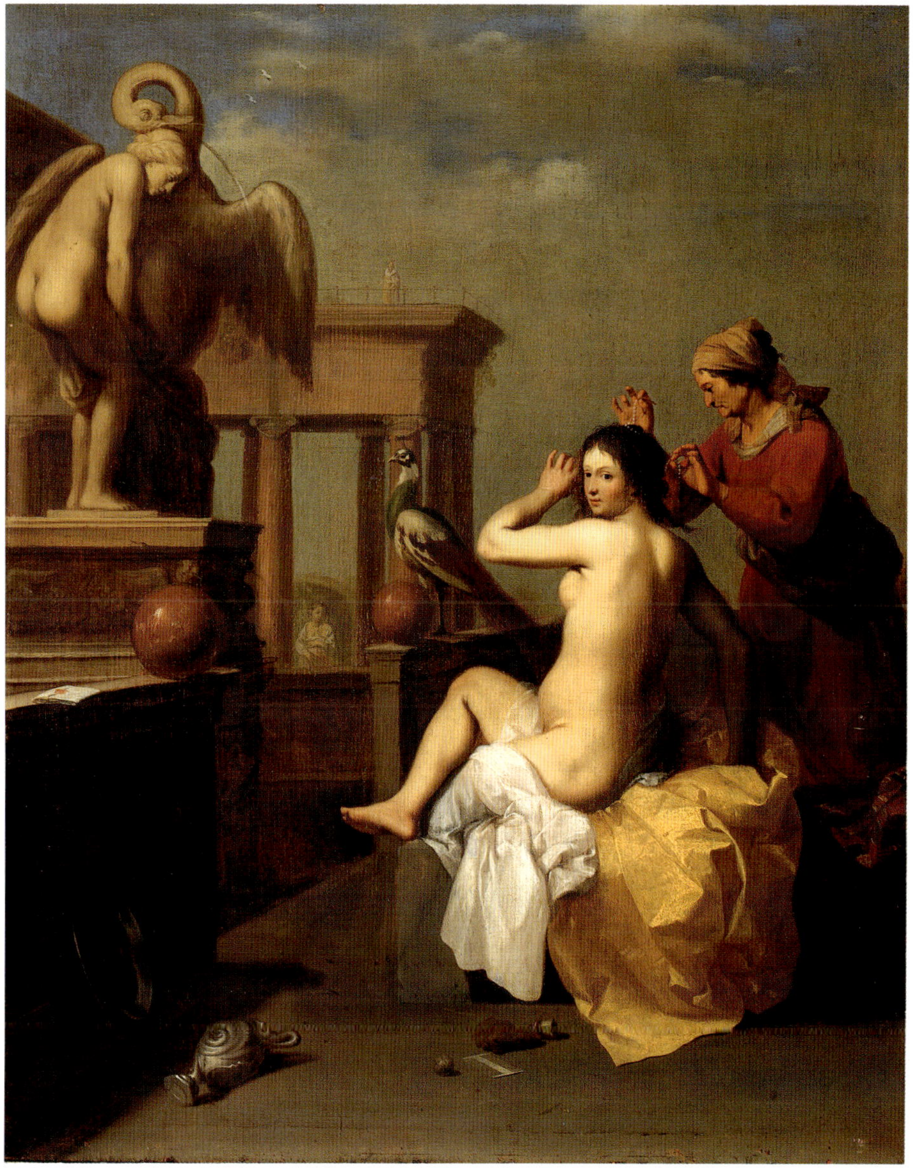

LITERATURE: *Catalogue of Pictures at Amisfield*, 1771; *Inventory of Pictures at Gosford House*, 1948,[4] no.404 (as French School).[5]

THE EARL OF WEMYSS AND MARCH

1 *Rembrandt 1991*, no.39.
2 *Waterhouse Notebooks*, transcriptions of the Hamilton inventories in the Getty Archive, Santa Monica.
3 *Ibid.*
4 The Gosford inventory also notes another Poelenburgh, *Venus and Adonis*, no.219.
5 The *RKD* ascribed the *Bathsheba* to a follower of Poelenburgh, François Verwilt (*c.* 1620-91), on the basis of a black and white photograph before cleaning.

ADAM PYNACKER

c. 1620-73. Born in Schiedam, his date of birth is deduced from a later document of 22 January 1652 which noted his age as 31. Pynacker is reputed to have visited Italy and his first dated work of 1650 is an Italianate scene. He is recorded as being in Delft from 1649-51 and in 1657 and in Schiedam in 1651, 1652 and 1658 (though he may not have settled in either place). He worked in Lenzen from 1654-5 and moved to Amsterdam c.1661 where he spent most of his time until his death. He was much influenced by the work of Jan Both and Jan Asselyn but developed his own distinctive style of Italianate landscape.

44 *A Forest Glade*

Oil on canvas: 90 × 81.2 cm. Signed: *A Pynacker* (*AP* in monogram) indistinctly on boulder, bottom right
PROVENANCE: Probably Pierre de Grandpré sale, Paris, 16 February 1809, bought by A. de la Hante;[1] SIR JAMES ERSKINE OF TORRIE by whom bequeathed in 1825 to the University of Edinburgh which received the picture in 1836; placed on loan to the Board of Manufactures, Edinburgh, first at the Royal Institution, then at the National Gallery of Scotland for its opening in 1859 until 1983, when returned to the University of Edinburgh.

Waagen described this picture as ' A wooded landscape, with hilly distance; in front a shepherd-boy with his dog and a cow. In this solidly painted picture, which represents a fresh morning light, the master appears in his most favourable aspect', but this was refuted by Hofstede de Groot who dismissed it as 'genuine ... and as usual boring'. Harwood dates it to about 1657, noting that the picture includes one of the first instances of Pynacker's recurring motif of a gnarled decaying birch tree stump, and also the foliage of wild cabbage in the foreground.[2] *A Forest Glade* may have had a companion work but this has been lost.[3]

EXHIBITED: *Birmingham 1989*, no. 88; L. B. Harwood, *Reflections on Italy; Adam Pynacker*, R. L. Feigen & Co., London, 1991, no.8.

LITERATURE: *Waagen*, vol.3, p.273; *HdG 1893*, p.133; *Harwood*, no.58.

THE TORRIE COLLECTION
THE UNIVERSITY OF EDINBURGH

1 *Harwood*, p.78.
2 Harwood, 1991, *op. cit.*, p.26.
3 *Ibid.*, note 10. *Landscape with Woods and Undergrowth* was also sold at the Grandpré sale to A. de la Hante and was regarded by Hofstede de Groot (*HdG*, no.178) as a companion to the Edinburgh painting.

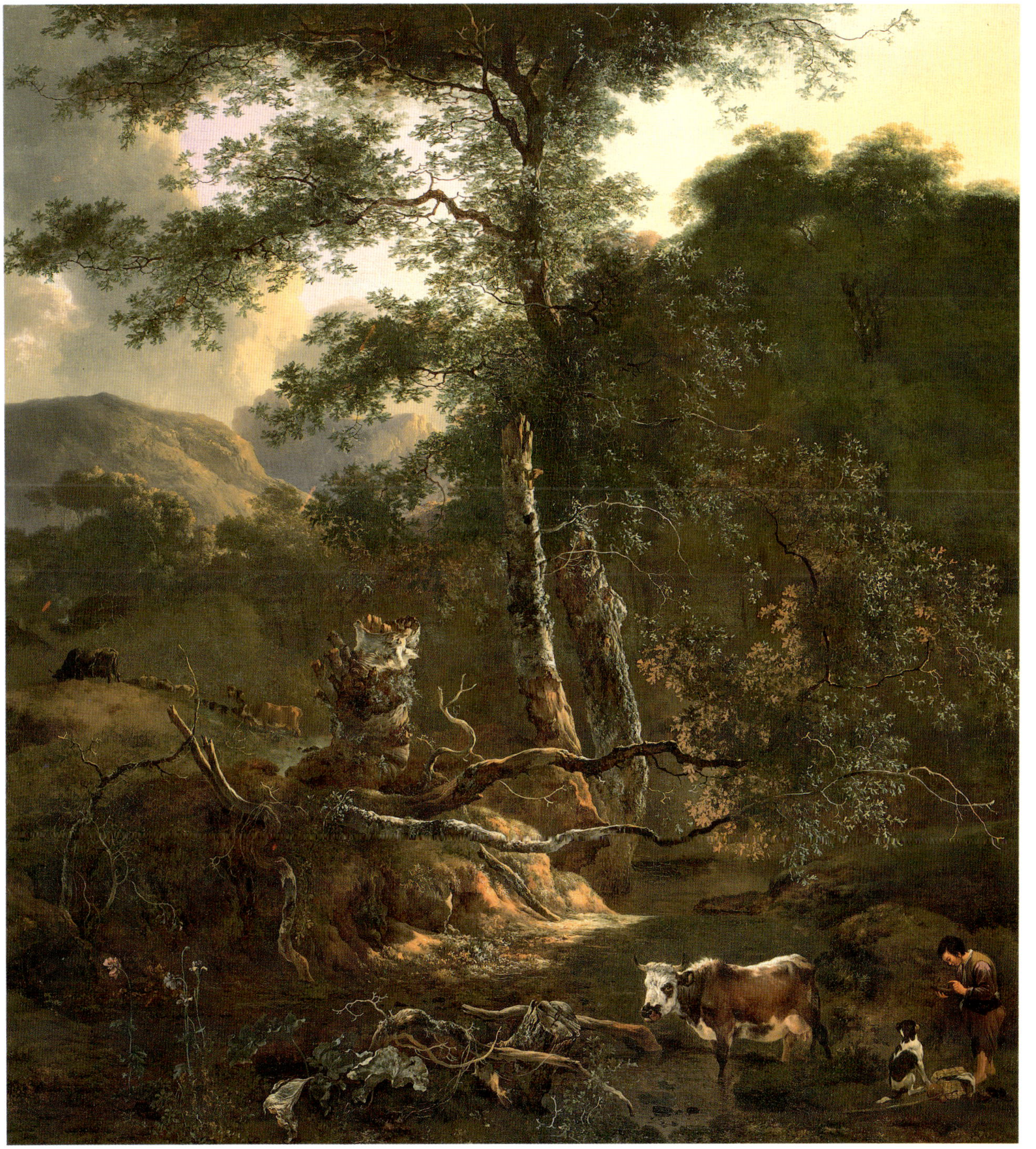

45 *Landscape with Stone Bridge*

Oil on canvas: 77 × 63.2 cm
Signed: *APynacker* (*AP* in monogram) bottom right
PROVENANCE: J. Kleinenbergh, Leiden sale, 19 July 1841, lot 192, to C. S. Roos; purchased by A Brondgeest Gallery on behalf of Baron Verstolk van Soelen, The Hague (d. 1845), from whose estate purchased in 1846 by Thomas Baring, Humphrey Mildmay and Samuel Jones Loyd (later Lord Overstone); Lord Overstone, London; his daughter, Lady Wantage, London, by 1883; Private Collection, Scotland and placed on loan at the National Gallery of Scotland, 1988.

Described by Waagen as a 'View on the Tiber ... Of great effect and very careful execution, but somewhat cold in the shadows'. The site was later identified as the bridge over the River Tyeron at Francheville near Lyons, where Pynacker may have travelled on his way to Italy in the 1640s. However, a precise location has not been generally agreed. Pynacker may have elaborated upon reality in this composition and uses the bustling foreground figures to balance the calmness of the smooth river framed by the bridge.

EXHIBITED: *Manchester 1857*, no.725; *RA 1938*, no.265; *RA 1952-3*, no.472; *Manchester 1957*, no.111; *Italianiserende Landschapschilders*, Centraal Museum, Utrecht, 1965, no.111; *Art in Seventeenth-Century Holland*, National Gallery, London, 1976, no.84; *Agnews*, no.24.

LITERATURE: *Waagen 1857*, p.136; *HdG*, no.76; *Wantage Catalogue*, no.182; *Masters of Dutch Landscape*, p.396, fig.1; *Harwood*, no.43.

PRIVATE COLLECTION, SCOTLAND

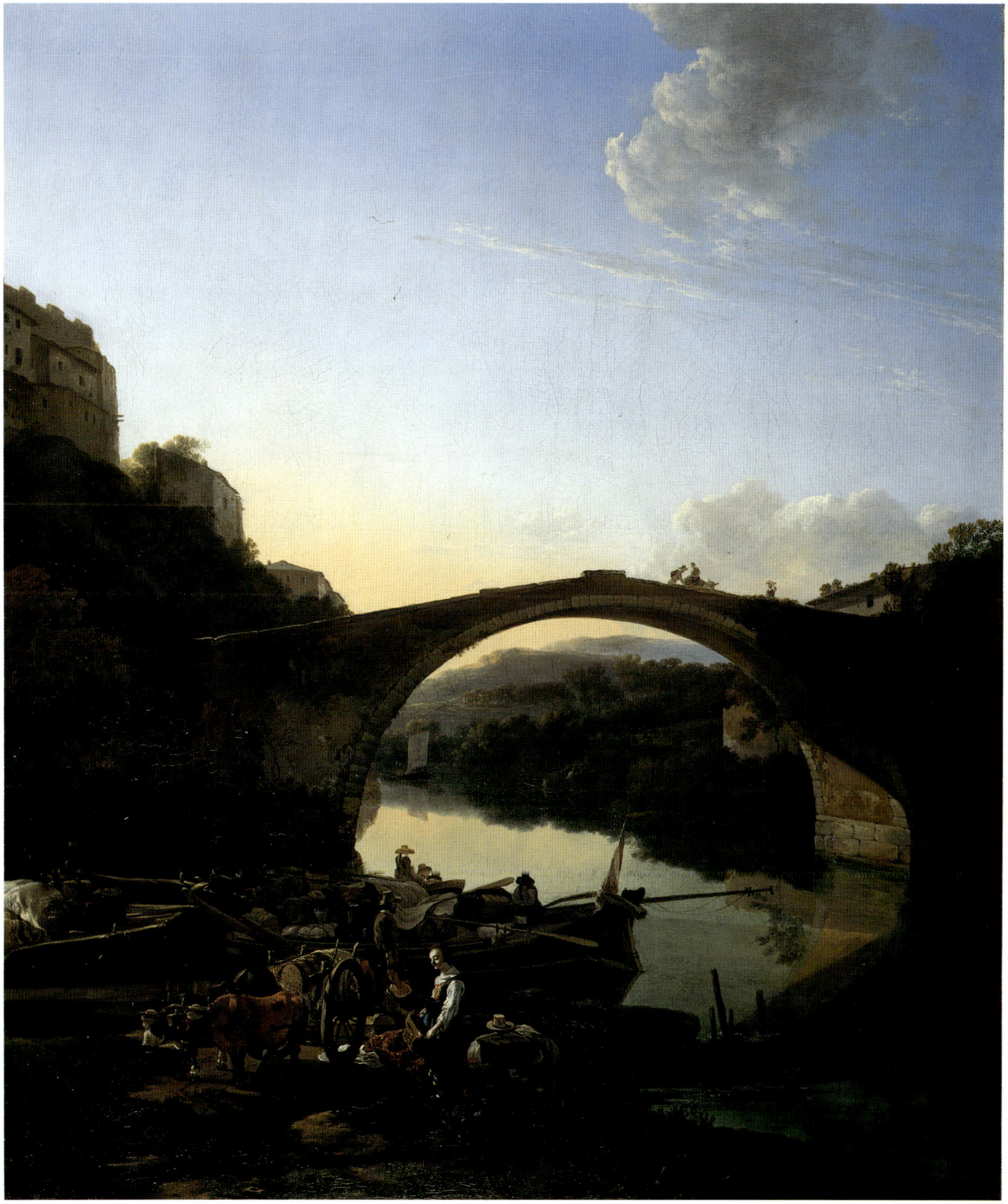

1606-69. Rembrandt Harmensz. van Rijn was born in Leiden, the son of a miller. He was inscribed at the University of Leiden in May 1620 but, from c.*1621, trained for about three years with Jacob Isaacz. van Swaneburgh in Leiden and then for a few months with Pieter Lastman in Amsterdam. He then established his own studio in Leiden, and during this period worked closely with Jan Lievens and trained Gerrit Dou. Probably in the winter of 1631-2 Rembrandt settled in Amsterdam where his portraits were in great demand. In June 1634 he married Saskia van Uylenburgh who bore him a son, Titus, in 1641 before her death the following year. His daughter, Cornelia (baptised in 1654), was the child of his second, common-law, wife Hendrijke Stoffels. Rembrandt's commissions declined from the late 1630s though he continued to maintain a large and busy studio. He declared insolvency in 1656. His last dated work is of 1669, the year of his death, and he was buried in the Westerkerk in Amsterdam on 8 October.*

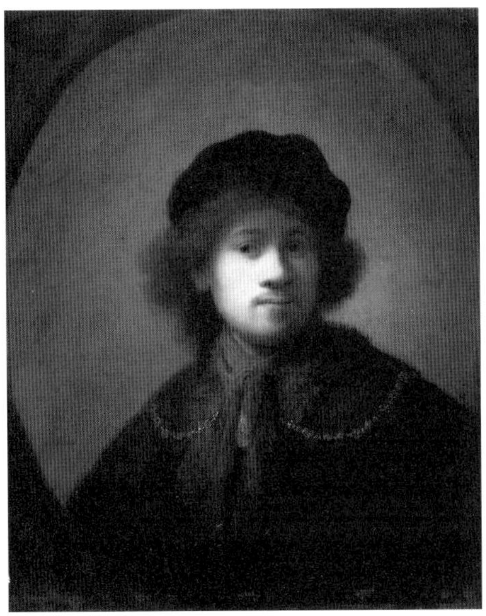

fig.54

46 *An Old Woman: 'The Artist's Mother'*

Oil on panel: 61.3 × 47.3 cm

PROVENANCE: Presented by SIR ROBERT KERR, 1st Earl of Ancram, to Charles I certainly before 1639;[1] sold to Bass, 19 December 1651, during the Commonwealth;[2] returned to the Royal Collection at the Restoration and thence by descent.

Technical examination shows that the panel was first used for a study of an old man, perhaps an evangelist (placed the other way up on the panel).

The sitter has traditionally been called 'Rembrandt's Mother' but, although the same model figures in other works by Rembrandt and his studio (see, for example, fig.58, *An Old Woman Reading*), there is no proof for such an identification.

The back of the panel bears the 'CR' brand of Charles I and also a label which reads ' Given to the King by Sir Robert Kerr'. It has been presumed that as the donor is simply named 'Sir Robert Kerr', the gift must have been made before he was created 1st Earl of Ancram in June 1633. The picture is identical to that recorded in Abraham van der Doort's catalogue of the Royal Collection of *c.*1639 as 'Done by Rembrandt and given to the kinge by my Lo: Ankrom' and was in the Long Gallery at Whitehall where it hung 'Betweene the ..ffowerteene and last wind dowes an old woeman with a great scarfe uppon her heade with a peaked falling band In a Black frame'.[3] Sir Robert gave two other pictures to Charles I which were also then ascribed to Rembrandt, and the three works are the first recorded 'Rembrandts' to have come to Britain. One was almost certainly the *Self-portrait* now at the Walker Art Gallery, Liverpool (fig.54) and the other a painting which is now lost. Van der Doort had described the latter as '... a young Scholler Sitting upon a Stoole In a purple cap and black gown reading in a book by a Seacole fire ...' but by 1649 it was listed as 'A student sittinge by ye fyer: done by Lievens'.[4] This is likely to have been the picture listed in 1641 as a work by Jan Lievens which the Prince of Orange bought and presented to the British Ambassador who gave it in turn to the King of England.[5] As discussed in connection with Lievens's *Portrait of a Capuchin Monk* (Catalogue no.29), Sir Robert had travelled to The Hague in 1629 as a personal envoy of King Charles I. It may be that the three paintings listed by Van der Doort were indeed given by the Prince of Orange, or by his secretary Constantin Huyghens, to Sir Robert to convey to Charles I. However, *An Old Woman* has been ascribed a date of not earlier than 1630 in the *Rembrandt Corpus.* If true, this would mean that the panel would have had to come to Britain after Kerr's visit to the Netherlands (but still before June 1633), although perhaps there is no reason why the paintings might not have been promised to Kerr on his visit in 1629 and sent on separately to London after completion. The similarity between the work of Rembrandt and that of Lievens, particularly in the period *c.*1629-30, has led to much discussion of the authorship of this painting, which was thought to be by Rembrandt in the first volume of the *Rembrandt Corpus* but ascribed to Lievens by the time the second was published.[6]

EXHIBITED: *The Queen's Pictures. Royal Collectors through the Centuries,* National Gallery, London, 1990, no.12.

LITERATURE: C. White, *The Dutch Pictures in the Collection of Her Majesty the Queen,* London, 1982, no.158, pp.101-3; *Rembrandt Corpus,* vol.1, no.A32, pp.315-21 and vol.2, no.A32, pp.839-40.‡

HER MAJESTY THE QUEEN

1 The picture is listed in Abraham van der Doort's catalogue of Charles I's collection, *c.*1639. Transcribed in *The Walpole Society,* ed. O. Millar, vol.37, no.101, p.60.

2 'The Inventories and Valuations of the King's Goods', ed. O. Millar, *The Walpole Society,* vol.43, p.265.

3 See note 1 for reference.

4 O. Millar (ed.), *op. cit.*, no.97, p.304.

5 I. I. Orlers, *Beschrivinge der Stadt Leyden* , Leiden, 1641; *Rembrandt Corpus,* vol.2, p.839.

6 The poor condition of the Walker Art Gallery picture makes similar re-evaluation difficult.

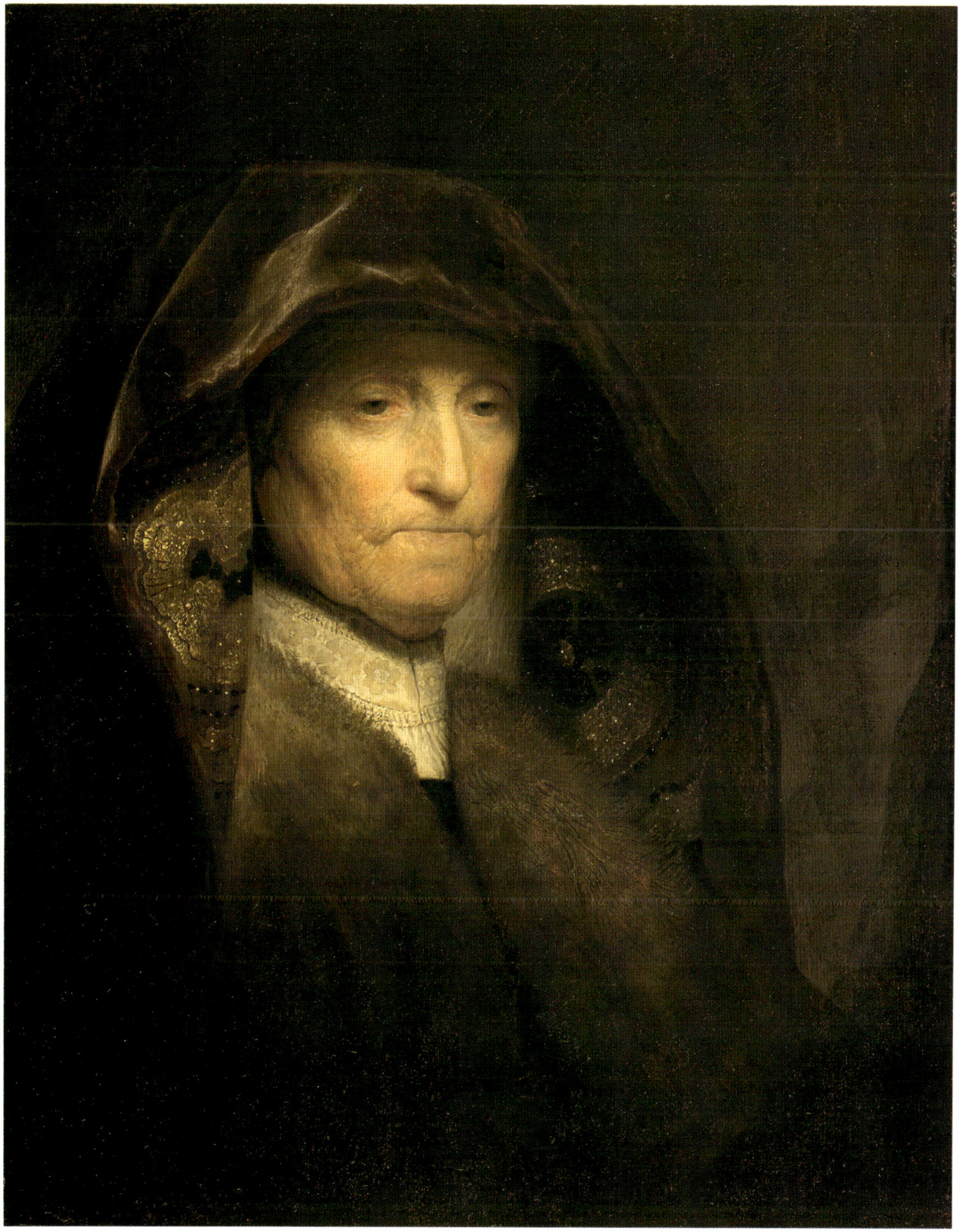

47 *A Portrait of the Artist as a Burgher*

Oil on panel: 64.4 × 47.6 cm
Signed and dated: *RHL van Ryn / 1632* at centre right
PROVENANCE: In the collection of Philippe, Duke of Orléans (d.1723), Paris (as a pendant of the *Bust of a Young Woman*, now in the Allentown Art Museum, Pennsylvania, no.61.35.G); Louis-Philippe ('Philippe Egalité'), Duke of Orléans, until 1792 when purchased by Thomas Moore Slade on behalf of the 7th LORD KINNAIRD, together with Thomas Hammersley and William Morland and exhibited for sale by private contract at 125 Pall Mall, London, April-June 1793, no.68, valued at 200 guineas. Bought (with its 'pendant' from Charles Birch by Lord Egremont, Petworth, 27 January 1800, for 50 guineas; thence by descent to Lord Leconfield, Petworth, by whom sold privately, 1927. Viscount Rothermere by whom sold at Christie's, London, 6 December 1946, no.65, purchased by SIR WILLIAM BURRELL, who presented it to Glasgow Art Gallery and Museum in 1946.

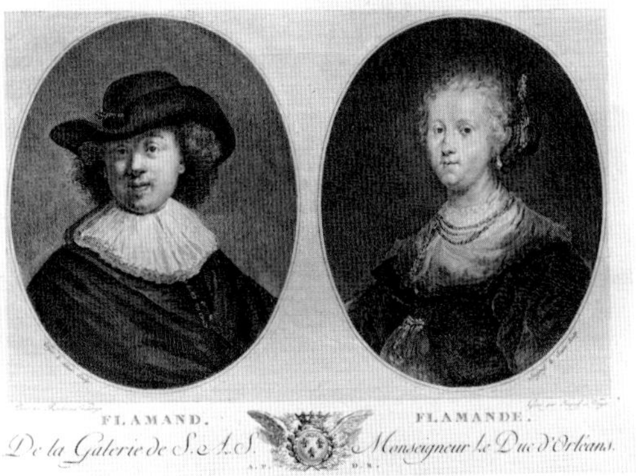

fig.55

1 *Rembrandt Corpus*, vol.2, no.C59, pp.686-90.
2 *The Artist as a Burgher* was etched by Voyez le Jeune in the *La Galerie du Palais-Royal...*, Paris, 1786-1808, vol.3, pl. 9.
3 *Rembrandt Corpus*, vol.2, p.234, fig.5.
4 R. Marks, *Burrell: Portrait of a Collector* (2nd edn), Glasgow, 1988, p.178. (The Hals is not mentioned in *Slive*.)

As with Catalogue no.46, technical investigation has revealed that there is another composition underneath this work, probably also a self-portrait. Since there is no bevelling on the panel, it may originally have been rectangular and cut into an oval at a later stage (although the edges do not appear to have been sawn after painting so this is uncertain). The portrait is unusual in showing the artist in rather formal dress with an elaborate collar, cloak and hat. At the start of his career in Amsterdam in the early 1630s, it is likely that Rembrandt was purposefully portraying himself in the garb of a gentleman, rather than in his more accustomed and more humble painter's beret. By the eighteenth century this picture was presumably considered so unlike a Rembrandt self-portrait that it was given a spurious female companion (which is no longer believed to be by Rembrandt),[1] with which it was engraved when in the collection of the Duke of Orléans (see fig.55).[2] *A Portrait of the Artist as a Burgher* relates to a very similar proof print now in the Bibliothèque Nationale, Paris, for an etching dated 1631.[3]

Sir William Burrell used Partridges of Bond Street to bid for him at the auction and he paid them £13,125, including their commission. This was the highest price Burrell had paid to date for a single purchase in a period of over 60 years of collecting (although he was to spend £14,500 for his *Portrait of a Man* by Frans Hals two years later in 1948).[4] Bought as a pendant for his new Rembrandt, Burrell's *Portrait of Saskia* was also purchased in 1946 from Partridges for £11,000. Now kept in the reserve at the Burrell collection, this is of dubious authenticity.

EXHIBITED: 125 Pall Mall, London, 1793, no.68; *RA* Winter Exhibition 1899, no.41; *RA 1938*, no.123; *The Burrell Collection*, McLellan Galleries, Glasgow, 1949, no.570; *Edinburgh 1950*, no.4; *A Selection from the Burrell Collection*, McLellan Galleries, Glasgow, 1951, no.382; *Primitives to Picasso, RA* 1962, no.124; *Glasgow's European Treasures*, Glasgow Museum and Art Gallery, 1972-3, no.105; *Treasures from the Burrell Collection*, Hayward Gallery, London, 1975, no.12.

LITERATURE: *HdG*, no.573; *Rembrandt Corpus*, vol.2, no.A58, pp.230-7.‡

THE BURRELL COLLECTION
GLASGOW ART GALLERY AND MUSEUM

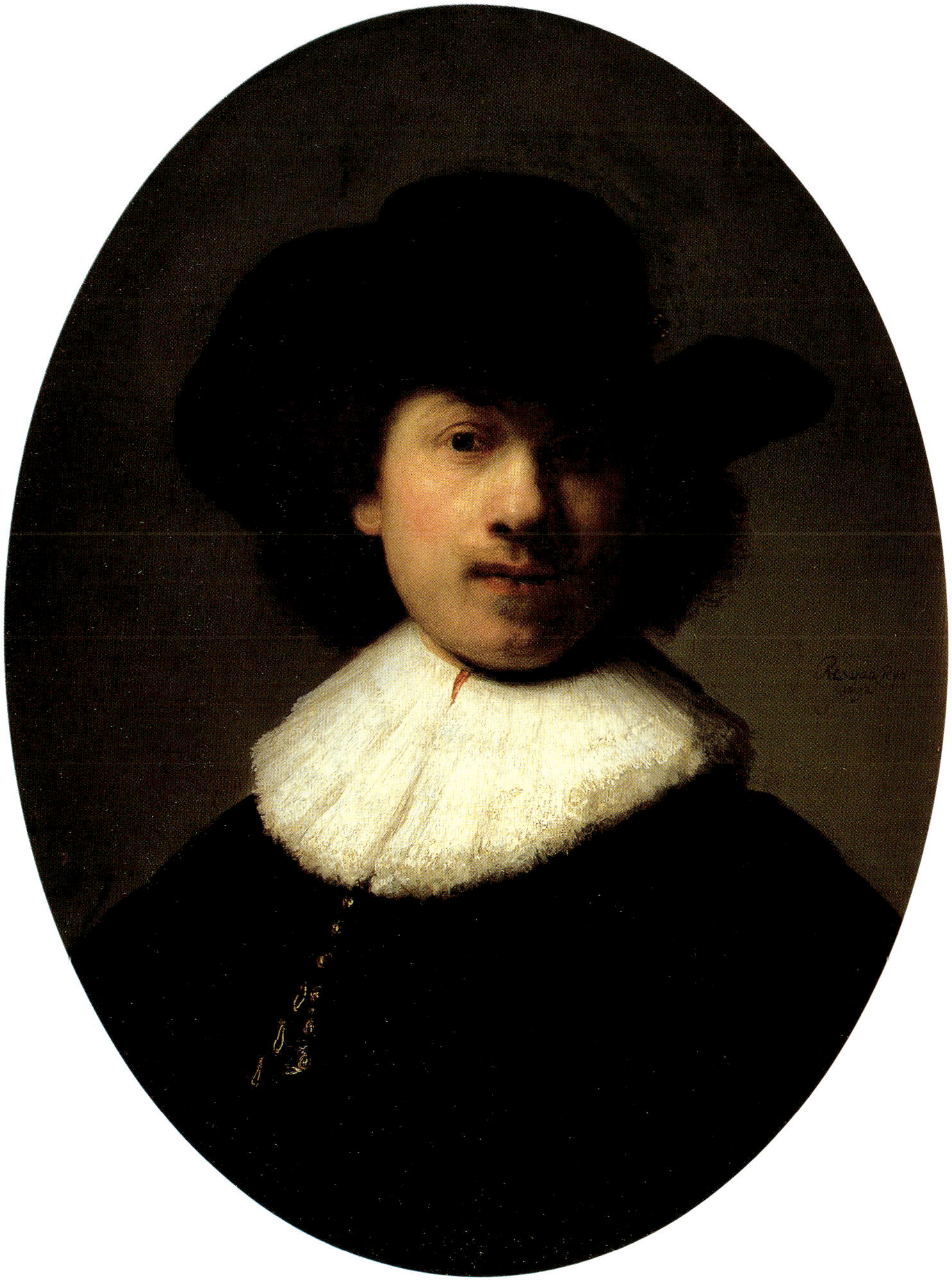

48 *The Entombment of Christ*

Oil on panel: 32.2 × 40.5 cm
PROVENANCE: Probably identical with a sketch described in an inventory of Rembrandt's possessions, 25-6 July 1656.[1] Perhaps mentioned in the collection of Robert Strange, London, by 1769;[2] his sale Christie's, London, 7-9 February (sold on 8 February) 1771, lot 61, catalogued as *The Entombing of Lazarus*, purchased for 12 guineas by William Hunter, by whom bequeathed to The University of Glasgow in 1783.

The exact purpose and date of this panel have been much debated, though not its authenticity. It relates to a completed painting on canvas, *The Entombment* (92.6 × 68.9 cm) which was half-finished by 1636 and delivered to Prince Frederik Hendrik in 1639. It is now in the Alte Pinakothek in Munich.[3] Though the two compositions differ, the same shroud-slung body of Christ dominates both designs. The Hunterian panel may have acted as a loose preliminary study for the Munich canvas, which would indicate a date of 1635 or before, although the authority of the panel's brushwork and the assured handling of light and shade has led to the disputed suggestion that the panel postdates the Munich picture and is a reworking of it, perhaps painted as late as 1639.[4] The panel is, however, in grisaille. It is possible that it may have served as a study for an etching which for some reason was not executed. Of Rembrandt's works in grisaille, only one, the *Ecce Homo* (National Gallery, London) was certainly used thus, but his few other grisailles, which may perhaps also have served this purpose, are *The Entombment* panel, *Joseph Relating his Dreams* (Rijksmuseum, Amsterdam), *John the Baptist Preaching* (Gemäldegalerie Berlin-Dahlem) and *The Lamentation* (National Gallery, London).[5]

L. Simond, author of the *Journal of a Tour and Residence in Great Britain during the years 1810 and 1811...*, visited Hunter's collection on 25 August 1810 but mistakenly located the panel, writing that 'A merchant of this town, Mr Gordon, has a small collection of very good pictures ... a Rembrandt, (Lazarus in his Tomb), the colouring merely black and white, mellowed with yellow, and his usual glorious outline, of the greatest effect.'[6] There was also a painting described as Rembrandt's *The Entombment of The Saviour Unfinished* in Edinburgh in 1827 when it was in the collection of Francis Grant who etched it for his catalogue (see fig.56).[7] It is tempting to suggest, since it was on panel and was described as unfinished, that this was a study for the Munich painting but it was almost certainly a copy, although the quality of the other paintings in the sale was high.

EXHIBITED: *Edinburgh 1950*, no.13; *Glasgow University's Pictures*, no.12, pl.XII.

LITERATURE: *Waagen*, vol.3, p.283; *HdG 1893*, pp.146-7; *HdG*, no.139; J. G. van Gelder, 'The Rembrandt exhibition at Edinburgh', *The Burlington Magazine*, 92, 1950, pp.327-9; *Rembrandt Corpus*, vol.3, no.A105, pp.65-9.‡

THE HUNTERIAN ART GALLERY
GLASGOW

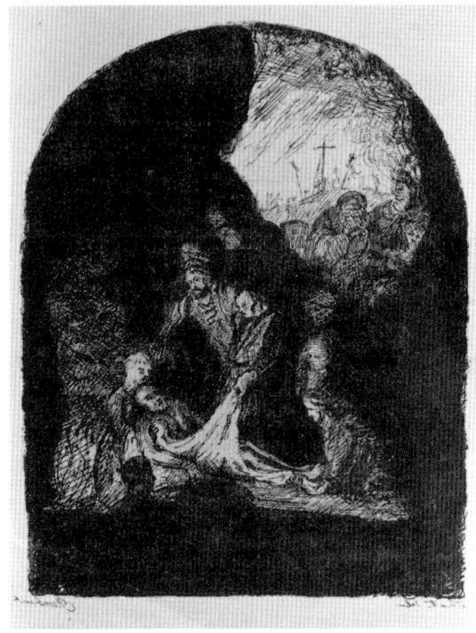

fig.56

1 *Rembrandt Corpus*, vol.3, p.69.
2 *Ibid.* Listed as *The Entombing of Lazarus* and measuring 'One foot three inches and a half wide, by one foot half an inch high' (32.3 × 40 cm) in R. Strange, *A Descriptive Catalogue of a Collection of Pictures ... collected during a Journey of Several Years in Italy*, London, 1769, no.59. The dimensions match the Hunterian panel almost exactly.
3 *Rembrandt Corpus*, vol.3, no.A 126, pp.271-9.
4 *Ibid.*, pp.67-8.
5 *Ibid.*, pp.67-8. See nos A.89, A66, A106 and A107.
6 (L.Simond), *Journal of a Tour and Residence in Great Britain during the years 1810 and 1811, by a French Traveller...*, London 1815, vol.1, pp.286-7.
7 *Catalogue of Pictures principally of the Italian schools, The Property of a Gentleman, now exhibiting for sale in the Calton Convening-Room*, Edinburgh, 1827, no.13, p.8, repr. p.9.

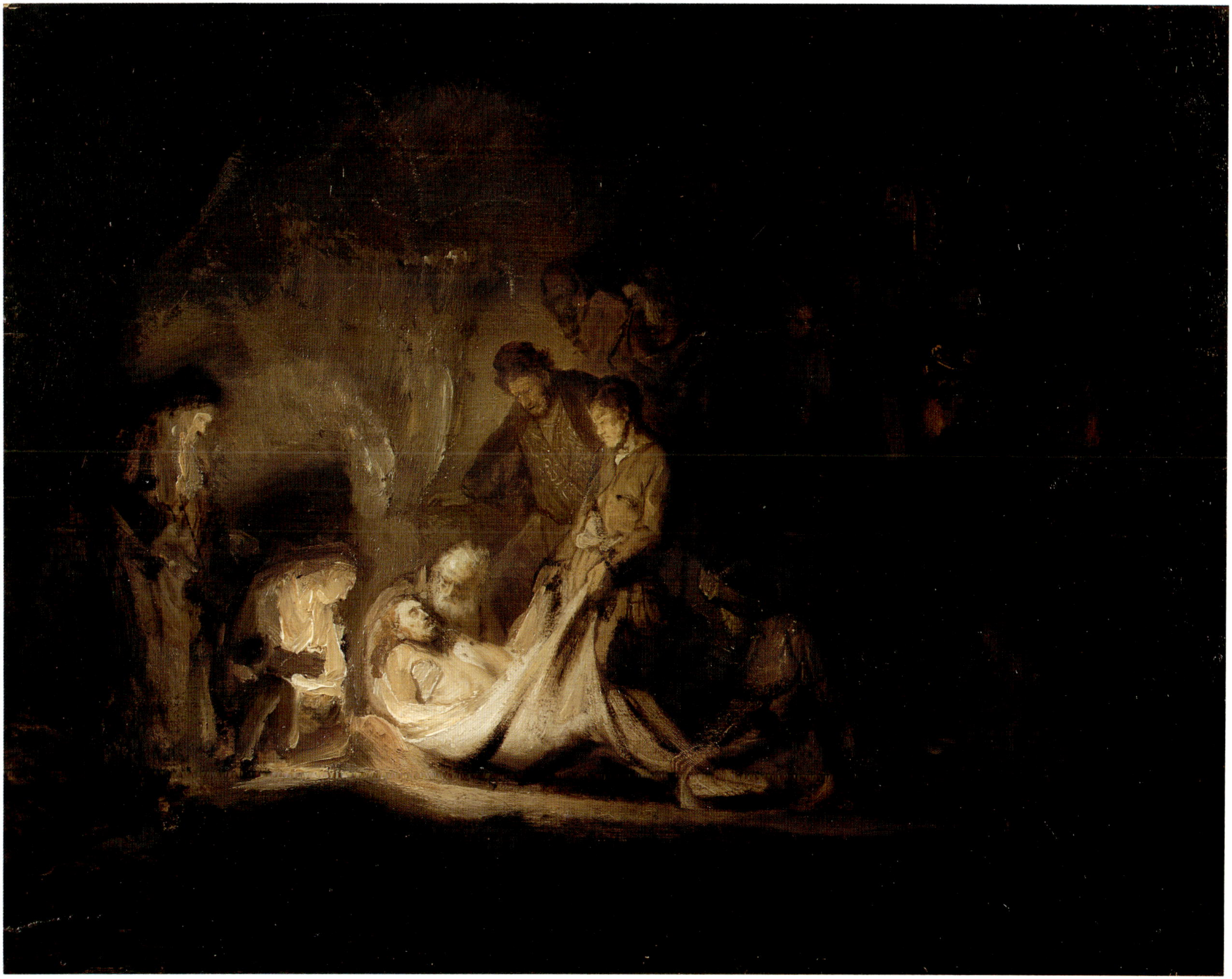

49 *Flora*

Oil on canvas: 123.7 × 97.5 cm
Signed and dated : *Rem [b.] a [...] 1635* at bottom left at right of staff (inscription by another hand but perhaps copied from original signature if the painting was cut down)
PROVENANCE: Duc de Tallard sale, Paris, 22 March-13 May 1756, lot 156; sold to Remy for 602 francs, 'pour l'Angleterre'. Collection of George Brudenell, Duke of Montagu (1712-90) by *c.*1780,[1] and inherited by his daughter and sole heiress, Elizabeth, wife of the 3rd DUKE OF BUCCLEUCH and thence by descent, purchased from the 8th Duke of Buccleuch by the National Gallery, London, in 1938 (no.4930).

There is still some debate as to whether this is an allegorical portrait of Rembrandt's first wife, Saskia van Uylenburgh. The subject of the picture is a personification of the goddess Flora (associated with the Spring) or an arcadian shepherdess,[2] and her features may have been based on those of Saskia. The Buccleuch picture probably dates from 1635 as stated by the inscription, although not written by Rembrandt himself. (He had painted a *Flora*, now in the Hermitage, St Petersburg, in the previous year 1634).[3] Technical investigation of the Buccleuch picture has revealed that the subject was originally of a *Judith* about to drop the head of Holofernes into a sack, watched by an old maidservant. Rembrandt later altered his design, retaining most of the upper part of Judith but painting over other parts of the picture and perhaps reducing the size slightly.[4]

The painting was brought from Montagu House in London to Scotland sometime before 1857, when Waagen lists it as hanging in the gallery at Dalkeith Palace near Edinburgh, and described it as 'of marvellous power and transparency and careful finish'. It was still at Dalkeith Palace in 1893 when it was seen by Hofstede de Groot.

EXHIBITED: *Manchester 1857*, no.666 (as *Female Portrait*); *RSA*, 1883, no.421:[5] *RA 1899*, no.77; *RA 1929*, no.154; *Amsterdam 1932*, no.6; *RA 1938*, no.129; NACF exhibition, National Gallery, London, 1945-6, no.4; *Rembrandt, Art in the Making*, National Gallery, London, 1988-9, no.5; *Rembrandt 1991*, no.23.

LITERATURE: *Waagen*, vol.3, p.314, and *Waagen 1857*, p.436; A. Francis Steuart, *Catalogue of the Pictures at Dalkeith House*, Dalkeith, 1890, p.45 (hanging on the west wall of the gallery) ; *HdG 1893*, p.213; C. Brown, 'Rembrandt's "Saskia as Flora' X-rayed", in *Essays in Northern European Art presented to Egbert Haverkamp-Begemann on his Sixtieth Birthday*, Doornspijk, 1983, pp.48-51; *Rembrant Corpus*, A112, pp.148-60‡; *MacLaren and Brown*, no.4930.

THE NATIONAL GALLERY, LONDON

1 *MacLaren and Brown*, p.358, note 34 cites a manuscript list of paintings in the collection of the Duke of Montagu *c.*1780, no.114.
2 *Ibid.*, pp.355-6 for identification of subject.
3 *Rembrandt Corpus*, vol.2, no.A93, pp.495-503, also with discussion of subject.
4 For a full discussion of Rembrandt's alterations see *Rembrandt, Art in the Making*, National Gallery, London, 1988-9, no.5.
5 J. M. Gray, *Notes of the Edinburgh Loan Exhibition of 1883*, Edinburgh, 1883, pp.16-17 : 'From the Duke of Buccleuch ... comes another of the finest works in the exhibition, No.421, a perfect example of Rembrandt ... erroneously described in the catalogue as 'The Artist's Second Wife, in the Character of a Jewish Bride', but is manifestly a fancy portrait of Saskia van Ulenburg, his first wife ... the wonder of the picture consists in the treatment of the splendid drapery, in the most masterly and delicately perfect richness of its detail, which never for a moment interferes with the breadth and harmonious lighting of its subject'.

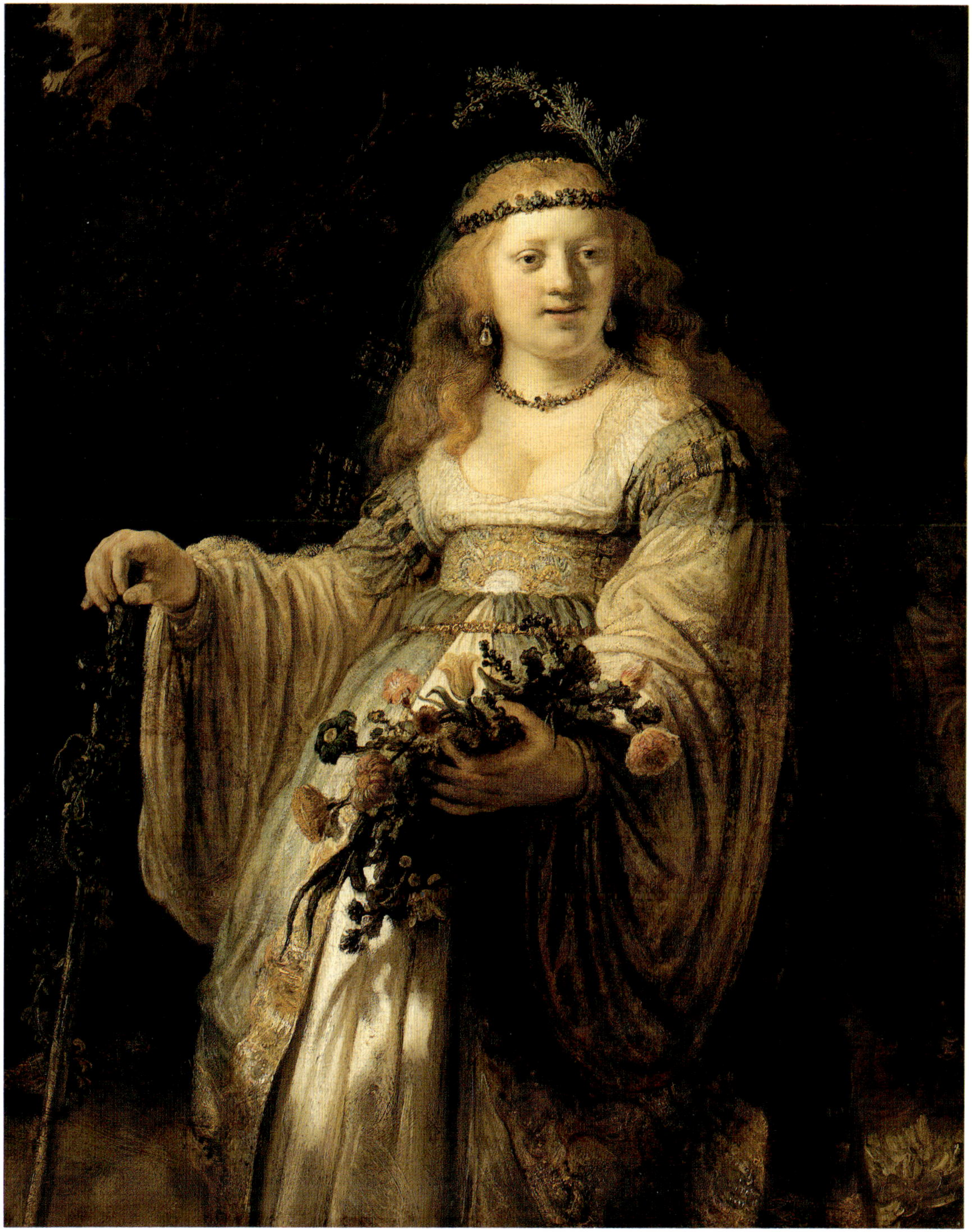

50 *A Woman in Bed*

Oil on canvas: 81.1 × 67.8 cm (arched top).
Signed and dated: *Rembra... / f. 164.* at bottom left
PROVENANCE: [1] Collection of François Tronchin, Geneva, by 1757,[2] given (in exchange) to Count Vitturi, Venice, by 1765;[3] Thomas Moore Slade by *c.* 1776 by whom sold to Viscount Maynard *c.*1790; Sir Henry St John Mildmay before 1836 and purchased from his collection by Samson Wertheimer of Bond Street, in his sale, Christie's, London, 19 March 1892, lot 706, bought in at £5250; C. J. Wertheimer from whom purchased by the Rt Hon. WILLIAM MCEWAN in 1892 for £5775[4] and presented by him to the National Gallery of Scotland in the same year (no.827).

(The canvas was laid on boards at one time, perhaps by the artist himself.) Though the last digit of the date is now illegible, the painting probably dates from *c.*1645.[5] The woman was once thought to have been Hendrijke Stoffels, Rembrandt's common-law wife, but there is no mention of her in Rembrandt's household before 1649. This means that the model is more likely to have been Geertje Dircx. who lived with Rembrandt *c.* 1643-9. The picture is likely to be connected with a story from the *Apocrypha*, probably that of Sarah watching as her bridegroom Tobias vanquishes the devil that has killed her previous seven husbands on their wedding nights (*Tobit*, VIII, v.1-4). Rembrandt's composition is perhaps based on Pieter Lastman's painting of the same subject (Boston Museum of Fine Arts, no.62.985, fig.57) and the pose is reminiscent of Rembrandt's *Danäe* in the Hermitage, St Petersburg (which, though dated 1636, had been reworked in *c.*1645-50).

After William McEwan's gift of the portraits of *A Dutch Gentleman* and *A Dutch Lady* to the National Gallery of Scotland in 1885 (Catalogue nos 20 and 21), he presumably felt that Scotland's national collection was still lacking an example by Holland's most renowned painter. He deposited a sum of £5000 with the Trustees of the National Gallery of Scotland with a view to purchase a Rembrandt when one of suitable quality should become available. Sir George Reid, President of the Royal Scottish Academy, was appointed to decide which work to buy. *A Woman in Bed* had been praised by both John Forbes White and Frederick Lord Leighton,[6] and when it came up for auction in Samson Wertheimer's sale, the Gallery attempted to secure it with McEwan's £5000. The picture was bought in at £5250 but Charles Wertheimer decided to sell the painting a few days later once the Gallery had raised more funds by contacting McEwan, who immediately provided the extra £775 required. [7]An anonymous review in *The Art Journal* of 1897 (p.246) described the opening of newly refurbished rooms in the National Gallery of Scotland on 10 May 1897. After 'a re-classification of works' the paintings were rehung 'under the able direction of Sir George Reid PRSA and Mr R. Gibb RSA'. Pride of place was the first gallery which was made over to Dutch and Flemish seventeenth-century painting including 'the great Vandyks and Rembrandt's "Hendrijke Stoffels" recently presented by Mr. William McEwan M.P.', together with the portraits by Frans Hals.

EXHIBITED: British Institution, London, 1865, no.109; *RA*, 1883, no.235; *RA 1929*, no.115; *Amsterdam 1932*, no.24; *Amsterdam 1969*, no.7; *Rembrandt 1991*, no.36.‡

LITERATURE: *Smith*, no.151; *HdG 1893*, p.133; *HdG*, no.305; *Gerson*, no.227; *Tümpel*, no.23.

NATIONAL GALLERY OF SCOTLAND

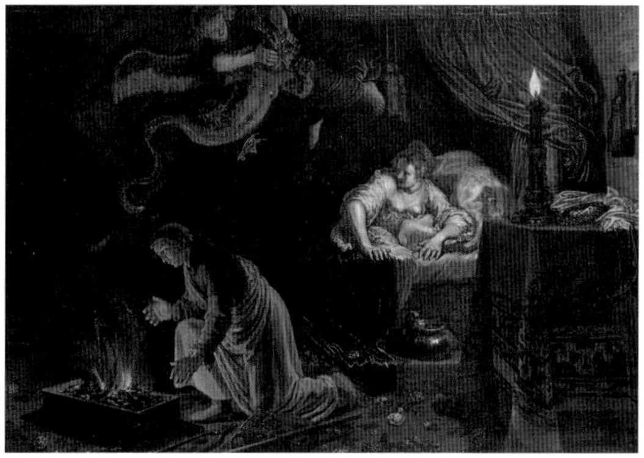

fig.57

1 Contrary to the provenance given by *HdG* and *Rembrandt 1991*, H. Macandrew notes (in Gallery file) that he could find no record of this painting in the British Museum Library version of the sale catalogue of the collection of the Prince de Carignan, Paris, 30 July 1742.

2 *A Woman in Bed* is shown in the background of a pastel portrait by J.-E. Liotard of Tronchin, dated 1757, which is now in Cleveland Museum of Art (no.78.54).

3 *Rembrandt 1991*, p.230. Listed in a manuscript catalogue of Tronchin's collection in 1761, no.25, the picture was no longer there by 1765, for it does not appear in Tronchin's printed catalogue of that date.

4 R. Gibb, *Catalogue of the National Gallery of Scotland*, 35th edn, Glasgow, 1899, p.65.

5 *Rembrandt 1991*, p.230.

6 *Pictures for Scotland.* p.84. John Forbes White mentions the picture in his article on Rembrandt for the *Encyclopaedia Britannica.*

7 *Ibid.*

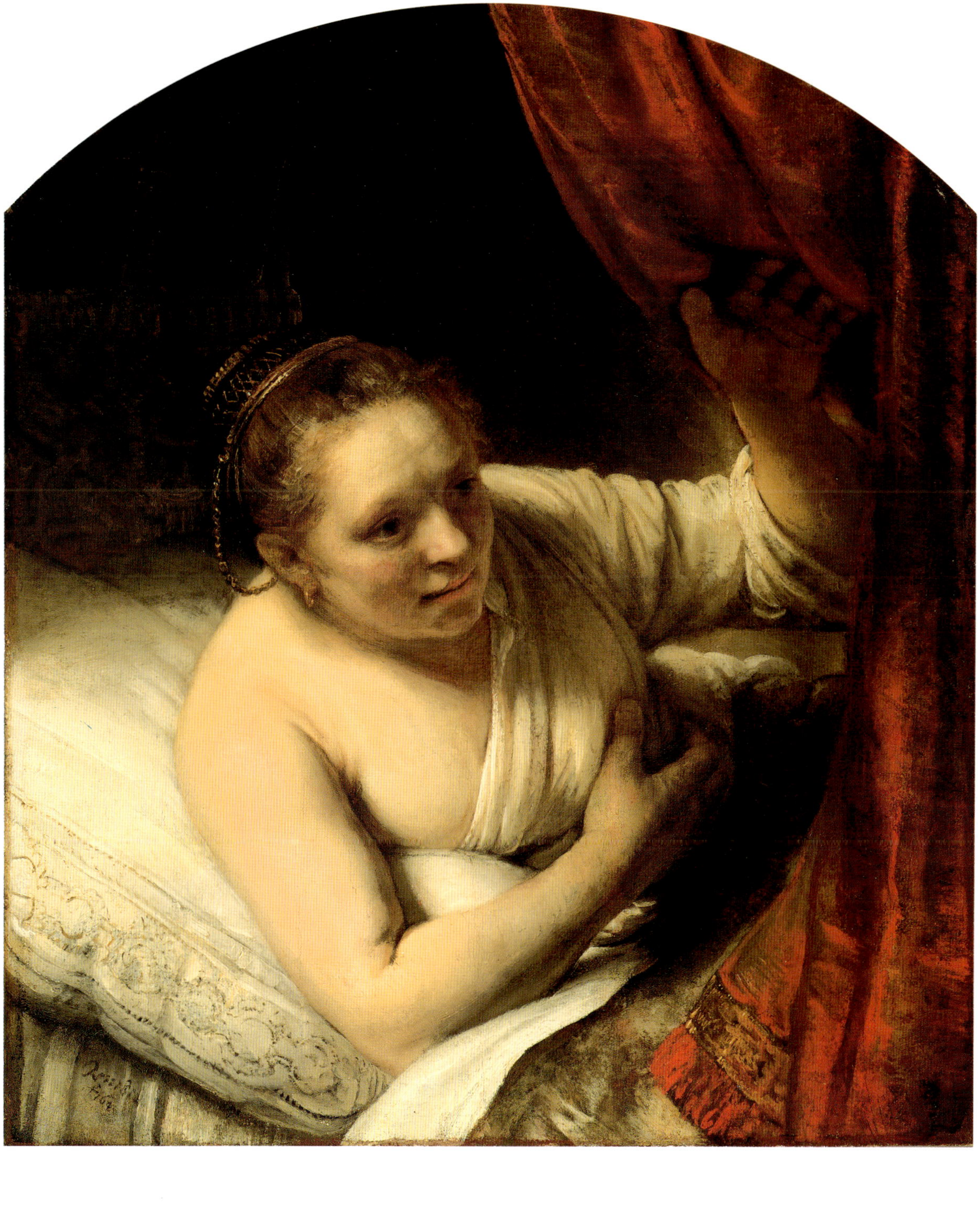

51 *Titus at his Desk*

Oil on canvas: 77 × 63 cm
Signed and dated (probably by another hand): *Rembrandt f. 1655* at bottom left
PROVENANCE: Thomas Barnard (1728-1806), Bishop of Limerick; inherited by his son, Andrew Barnard (d.1807), and his wife Lady Anne (1750-1825, née Lady Anne Lindsay, eldest daughter of James Lindsay, 5th Earl of Balcarres); inherited by the Lindsay family in 1825[1] and thence by descent to the EARLS OF CRAWFORD AND BALCARRES and purchased from the family by the Vereigning Rembrandt and 120 Friends of the Museum and given to the Stifting Museum Boymans, 1940 (no.St.2).

The picture shows Rembrandt's son, Titus, as he pauses from study, holding a portable pen and ink case in his left hand. It has been suggested that the painting may represent more than just a straightforward portrait of Titus as a daydreaming scholar. A personification of *Melancholia* may also be intended, the state of mind that was believed to be characteristic of the creative genius and vital for the imagination.[2] Rembrandt painted other likenesses of his son, notably that of 1657 in the Wallace Collection, London (no.P29),[3] which shows Titus wearing a similar crimson beret, and that of 1660 in the Rijksmuseum, Amsterdam (no.A3138), in which the young man wears the costume of a monk.

Rembrandt and his first wife, Saskia van Uylenburgh, had four children but only Titus (1641-68) survived, the other three dying in early infancy. Saskia died only a few months after the birth of Titus, in 1642 and Titus was looked after first by Geertje Dircx. until 1649, and then by Hendrijke Stoffels, who became Rembrandt's common-law wife. After Rembrandt declared himself insolvent in 1656, Hendrijke and Titus were legally responsible for the administration of Rembrandt's business from the end of 1660, employing Rembrandt to work for them and thereby protecting him from his creditors. Rembrandt's financial problems were already becoming apparent before this. Schwartz suggested that this painting might almost be entitled 'Titus Writing his Will' for in 1655 (the year inscribed on this work), Rembrandt transferred ownership of his house on the Breestraat to his son, who was then required to make a will leaving all his property to Rembrandt in the event of Titus's early death.[4] Titus trained with his father though very little is known of his work today except three of his paintings listed in the inventory of Rembrandt's sale in 1658 (of puppies, of a book and of a head of the Virgin).[5] He seems to have continued to assist with his father's business affairs after Hendrijke's death in 1663. Titus died only a few months after his marriage in 1668 to Magdalena van Loo (a relative of his mother's family), and before the birth of their daughter Titia.[6]

This picture was in the collection of Thomas Barnard, Bishop of Limerick, whose only son, Andrew, married Lady Anne Lindsay in 1793. She left Scotland to join her husband who became a colonial secretary for Lord Macartney at the Cape of Good Hope, but returned after her husband's death there in 1807. She inherited her husband's property including the *Titus* which hung at their house in 21 Berkeley Square, where Alexander William (1812-80), 25th Earl of Crawford and 8th Earl of Balcarres, recalled seeing it in 1827.[7] His father, James (1783-1869), 24th Earl of Crawford and Lord Lindsay, exhibited *Titus* at the British Institution in 1866 where it was listed as '"A Boy Writing" property of Lord Lindsay'. He became Baron of Wigan in 1826 and was presumably responsible for later taking the picture from London to the family house there, Haigh Hall in Lancashire. Hofstede de Groot noted that the *Titus* was at Haigh Hall in his entry for the painting and it was recorded as being sent from there to exhibition at the Royal Academy in London in 1929. The Crawford family also owned the portrait of *Margaretha de Geer* (now in the National Gallery, London, no.5282), ascribed to Rembrandt, which was given to the Earl of Crawford by Lady Wantage in 1920, and was sold by him in 1941. Lord Crawford exhibited this work at the Royal Academy (no.111) in 1929 together with *Titus at his Desk* (but the *Margaretha de Geer* did not hang at Haigh Hall at that time). Both pictures were cleaned by Martin de Wild some time prior to 1928.[8]

EXHIBITED: British Institution, London, 1866, no.75; *Amsterdam 1898*, no.90; *RA 1899*, no.23; *Loan exhibition of Old Masters*, Agnews, London, 1922, no.13; *RA 1929*, no.108 (when noted as from Haigh Hall at Wigan); *Amsterdam 1932*, no.86; *De Hollandse Schilderkunst ...*, Palais des Beaux-Arts, Brussels, 1946, no.86; *Dutch Painting: The Golden Age...*, Metropolitan Museum of Art, New York, Toledo Musum of Art, Ohio, Art Gallery of Toronto, 1954-5, no.65; *Rembrandt*, Nationalmuseum, Stockholm, 1956, no.33; *Rembrandt ...*, Rijksmuseum, Amsterdam, and Museum Boymans-van Beuningen, Rotterdam, 1956, no.70; *Meesterwerken ... uit de verzameling van het Museum Boymans-van Beuningen*, The Hermitage, Leningrad, 1986, no.26; *Een gloeiend palet*, Museum Boymans-van Beuningen, Rotterdam, 1988, no.22; *Rembrandt 1991*, no.42.‡

LITERATURE: *HdG*, no.702; *Gerson*, 325; *Barker*, pp.27, 40-2, *Tümpel*, no.184.

BOYMANS-VAN BEUNINGEN MUSEUM
ROTTERDAM

1 *Barker*, p.27.
2 *Rembrandt 1991*, p.257.
3 J. Ingamells, *Rembrandt 1892* exhibition catalogue, Wallace Collection, London, 1992, no.3.
4 G. Schwartz, *Rembrandt, zijn leven, zijn schilderijen*, Maarssen, 1984, p.296.
5 *Rembrandt 1991*, p.256 and notes 3, 4, 5.
6 *Ibid.*
7 *Barker*, p.40. A letter written in 1827, while Alexander William was still at Eton notes: 'In regard to the pictures at Berkeley Square, they have nearly all got their names and painters written at the bottom of the frame in Lady Anne's writing, so that it is easy to tell the lower row, but those above being beyond my reach render it impossible. There are some by very eminent masters ... Breughel ... Vander Heem, de Steen, Metzi, 2 Rembrandts, Schalken ... Van de Velde etc.'. He made a list of pictures owned by the Crawford family, begun in March 1827, in which he described one of Lady Anne's contributions to the collection as 'Rembrandt a boy reading beaut. below name' (*Barker*, p. 42).
8 A letter of 14 February 1928 from Lord Crawford (in Gallery files) states that Martin de Wild cleaned ' Both my Rembrandts, the Pieter de Hooghe, Hobbema, Van de Velde and other pictures of first rate importance'.

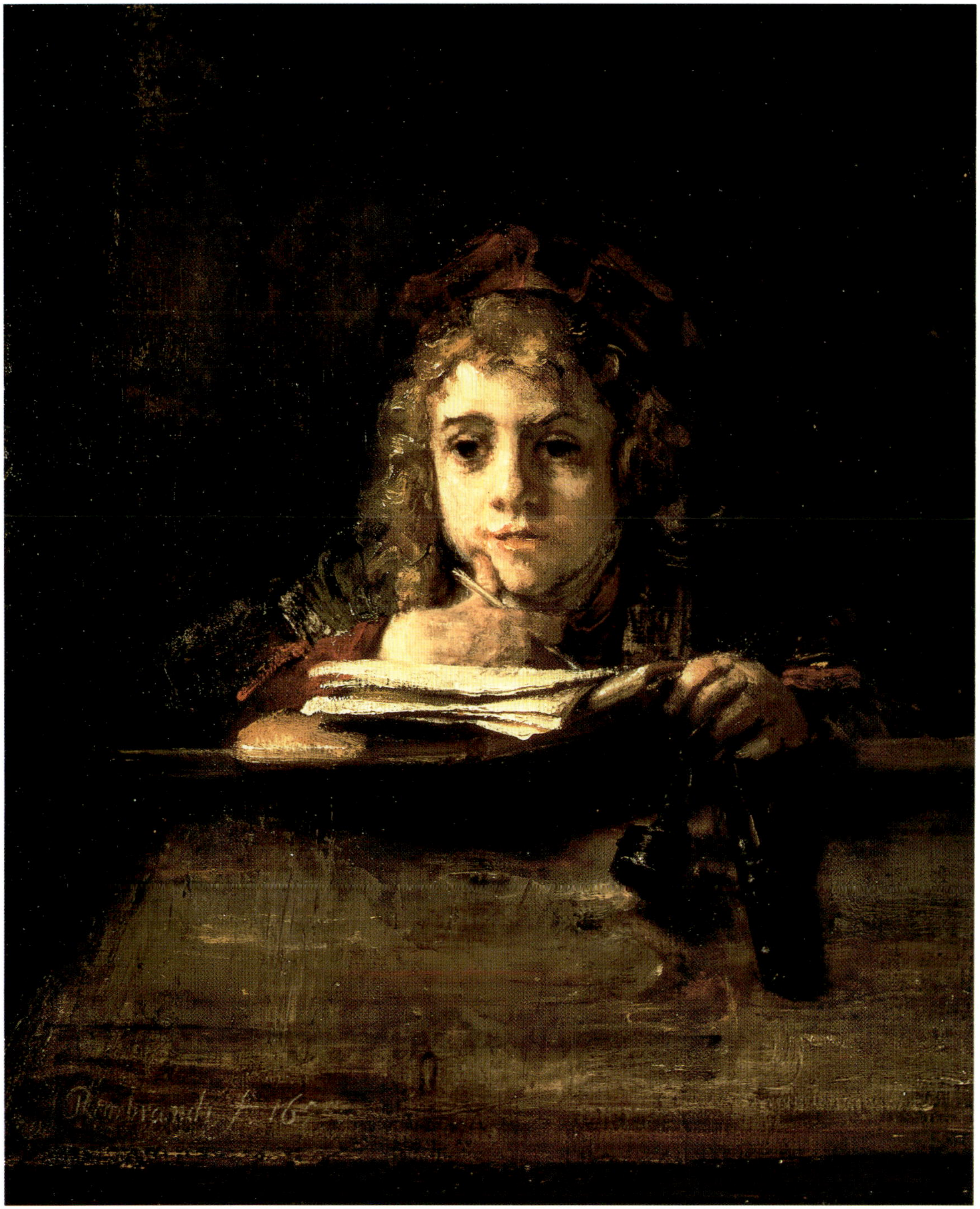

52 *Self-portrait aged 51*

Oil on canvas: 52.2 × 43 cm
Signed and dated: *Rembrandt / f. 1657* at bottom right
PROVENANCE: Countess of Holderness sale, Christie's, London, 6 March 1802, lot 56, where probably purchased by the 3rd Duke of Bridgewater (d. 1803);[1] Earl Gower, 1st DUKE OF SUTHERLAND, inherited by Lord Francis Leveson Gower, 1st Earl of Ellesmere, and thence by descent to John, 5th Earl of Ellesmere and later 6th Duke of Sutherland, who placed it on loan to the National Gallery of Scotland in 1946.

The painting is dated the year after Rembrandt was forced to seek a *cessio bonorum*, a declaration of legal insolvency which meant that all his property was required to be sold to raise money for his creditors. Rembrandt's possessions, including his large art collection, were sold in 1658 (mostly at a fraction of their real worth).

A photograph of this painting made some time before 1909[2] suggests that it was originally larger on all four sides. The photograph shows what appear to be strips of canvas added to the present format of the painting (the edges of which do not appear to have been cut down to any great extent). The largest strip was added to the bottom of the canvas, smaller strips to the left and right and a very narrow strip along the top. The *Stafford Gallery Catalogue* of 1818 provides measurements which, converted from the imperial, are approximately 66 × 53 cm, meaning that the picture was then about 15 cm taller and about 10 cm wider. There is some confusion as to when the strips were removed.[3] Whenever this occurred, it is likely that the reason for removal was that the strips were not considered to be authentic, although a picture such as *A Man in Armour* (*Alexander the Great*), in Glasgow Art Gallery would suggest that Rembrandt did occasionally resort to the use of such strips to enlarge his canvas.[4] The picture was relined and restored by Martin de Wild in 1933,[5] and close inspection shows that it is likely that he 'strength-ened' certain lines, for instance around the outline of the nose, in a characteristic gingery-brown overpaint which was also found on his restoration of Cuyp's *The Fleet Landing at Nijmegen* (Catalogue no.14). De Wild also favoured a varnish which was particularly rich in linseed oil and has a tendency to discolour.[6]

EXHIBITED: *Edinburgh 1945*, no.186; *Edinburgh 1950*, no.30; *RA 1952-3* , no.180.

LITERATURE: *Stafford Gallery Catalogue 1808*, no.134; *Stafford Gallery Catalogue 1818*, vol. 3, no.66, p. 98 (size as 1ft 8¾in × 2ft. 2in.); *Smith*, no.204; *Bridgewater House Catalogue 1851*, no.186; *HdG*, no. 553; *Bridgewater House Catalogue 1926*, no.186; *Gerson*, no.329; *Tümpel*, no.170.

THE DUKE OF SUTHERLAND

1 De Groot notes that the painting was bought by Earl Gower at the Holderness sale for £81 81s, but the fact that the picture was in the collection of his second son, Lord Francis Leveson Gower (who took the name of Egerton, later Earl of Ellesmere), rather than the collection of his first son, George Granville Leveson Gower (later 3rd Marquis of Stafford and 2nd Duke of Sutherland), probably implies that the picture was in the collection of the 3rd Duke of Bridgewater which was inherited by Lord Francis after his father Earl Gower's death in 1833. (The pictures acquired by Earl Gower himself seem to have been inherited by his first son.

2 W. R. Valentiner, *Klassiker der Kunst in Gesamtaugaben; Rembrandt's Gemälde*, Stuttgart and Leipzig, 1909, p.401.

3 *Edinburgh 1950*, no.30, states that the additions were removed when the picture was cleaned ın 1933 (and that the additions were at the right and at the bottom). However, the measurements given in 1909 (next to the photograph showing the additions) are 51 × 43.5 cm, which are almost identical to the measurements today. It is difficult to know whether the strips had already been removed by 1909 (contrary to what is stated in the *Edinburgh 1950* catalogue) meaning that an old photograph must have been used in the 1909 publication, or whether only the centre of the painting was measured and the strips ignored.

4 *Rembrandt 1991*, no. 43; C. Brown and A. Roy, 'Rembrandt's "Alexander the Great" '. *The Burlington Magazine*, May 1992, pp.286-97.

5 *Edinburgh 1950*, no.30.

6 These points have contributed some doubts as to the authenticity of the portrait.

53 *Self-portrait*

Oil on canvas: 84 × 66cm
Signed and dated: *Rembrandt f. 1659* at centre left
PROVENANCE: George Brudenell, Duke of Montagu (1712-90) by 1767[1] and inherited by his daughter and sole heiress, Elizabeth, wife of the 3rd DUKE OF BUCCLEUCH and thence by descent, sold by the 7th Duke of Buccleuch in 1928 to Colnaghi's, London; Knoedler's, New York, in 1920 by whom sold to Andrew W. Mellon, by whom given by deed of gift to the National Gallery of Art, Washington DC, in 1934 and received in 1937 (no.1937.1.72).

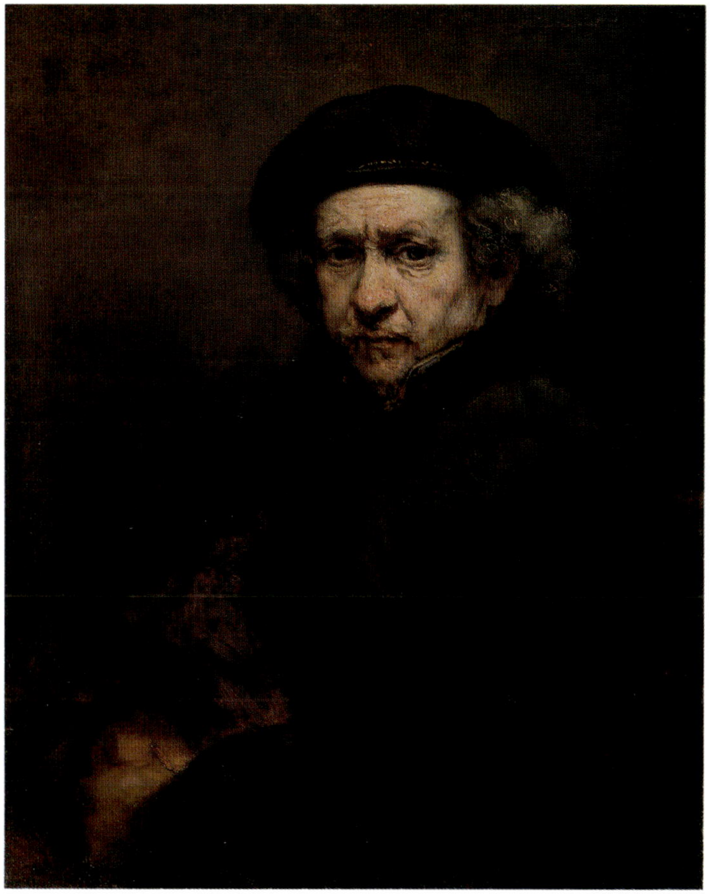

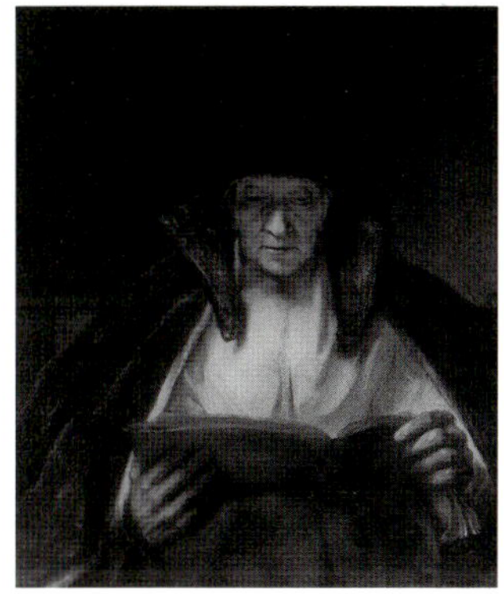

fig.58

Hofstede de Groot noted that the picture was later enlarged, particularly at the bottom and also at the sides, and that the beret was a later addition.[2] The painting was restored in 1992.

This work long enjoyed critical acclaim while in the collection of the Duke of Buccleuch, and a letter written on 28 November 1928 to Colnaghi's from Charles Holmes, then Director of the National Gallery, London, declares that he had 'always regarded this as one of the three supreme self-portraits of Rembrandt; the other two being of course the Frick picture and the Iveagh picture'. He asked if the painting could go on show at the National Gallery before it was shipped to America as it would be 'tragic that a portrait like this should leave the country until people here have had an opportunity of seeing it'.[3] Holmes also said that the only reason London did not buy the Buccleuch picture was that it was of the same date and too similar to the *Elderly Man as St Paul* already in the gallery (no.243). However, there have now been doubts raised as to the authorship of the Buccleuch picture.[4]

The Dukes of Buccleuch also owned two other Rembrandts: *Flora,* which once hung at Dalkeith Palace near Edinburgh (Catalogue no.49), and *An Old Woman Reading,* which still hangs at Drumlanrig Castle (see fig.58).[5] They do not all appear to have been kept together though, and the *Self-portrait* seems to have hung at the Buccleuch's London residence, Montagu House. Since *An Old Woman Reading* was thought to represent the artist's mother and the *Flora* was seen as Saskia, the Buccleuch collection theoretically had portraits of mother, son and wife (all of which were exhibited at the Royal Academy in 1899, nos 8, 77 and 6).

EXHIBITED: *RA,* Winter Exhibition 1872, no.181; *Amsterdam 1898,* no.102; *RA 1899,* no.6; Detroit Institute of Art, 1930, no.62; *Rembrandt* ..., Rijksmuseum, Amsterdam, 1935, no.26; *The World's Fair,* New York, 1939, no.307; *Rembrandt in the National Gallery of Art,* National Gallery of Art, Washington DC, 1969, no.19; *Masterpieces of Western European Painting...,* The Hermitage, Leningrad, 1989, no.13.

LITERATURE: *Smith,* no.215; *HdG,* no.554; *Portrait of the Artist by Rembrandt* (unattributed), M. Knoedler and Co., London, 1929; *Gerson,* no.376; K. Roberts, review of *Gerson, The Burlington Magazine,* May 1972, p.353; *Tümpel,* no.A72.

NATIONAL GALLERY OF ART
WASHINGTON DC

1 When engraved in mezzotint as from the Duke of Montagu's collection by R. Earlom in 1767. It was also engraved by H. Dawe in 1834.
2 *HdG,* no.554.
3 Letter in picture file in National Gallery of Art, Washington DC.
4 For example, in *Tümpel.*
5 *Treasure Houses 1985,* no.292, F. Russel states that *An Old Woman Reading* and the Buccleuch *Self-portrait* were purchased together for £140, as recorded in a Montagu House inventory.

54 *Self-portrait as the Apostle Paul*

Oil on canvas: 91 × 77 cm
Signed and dated: *Rembrandt f. 1661.* centre left by the shoulder. (Also inscribed on a fragment of the former stretcher, built into the new one: *From the Corsini Palace of Rome / brought to England by William Buchanan Esq in Summer 1807*)
PROVENANCE: Fournier collection, Paris;[1] Palazzo Corsini, Rome,[2] from where purchased by William Buchanan in 1807; in the collection of Lord Kinnaird of Rossie Priory near Dundee by 1809 (see below) and thence by descent until purchased in 1936 by J. G. Bruijn; placed in the Rijksmuseum, Amsterdam, in 1956 by Mrs Bruijn-van-der Leeuw of Muri near Bern, Switzerland, and donated by her and her husband to the museum in 1961 (no.A4050).

De Groot states that the picture was in Kinnaird's collection by 1811 and that Smith recorded that it was sold in the Kinnaird collection in 1813 for £ 215.[3] In his memoirs, William Buchanan claimed to have sold the painting for 500 guineas.[4] Whatever price Lord Kinnaird paid, he must have secured the picture by 1809, the date when it was engraved in mezzotint by C. Turner in a rare book of twelve plates of examples from the *Kinnaird Collection or Cabinet Picture Gallery.*[5]

The subject has been identified with the Apostle Paul on account of the handle of a sword projecting from Rembrandt's coat and the manuscript he holds which is written in Hebrew script, both of which have been considered as the Apostle's attributes.[6] Waagen described it as a 'man with a white cloth round his head' rather than as a portrait of Rembrandt or, indeed, as a portrait of an Apostle, but he praised it as 'most spiritedly treated with the broad touch of his later time'. It was the only Dutch painting in the Kinnaird collection mentioned by Waagen, while Hofstede de Groot, who went to Rossie Priory, the family seat near Dundee, in 1893, also noted Lord Kinnaird's other Rembrandt, a portrait of 'a lady of 40 to 50 years old'. This was the portrait of *Haesje van Cleyburg*, now also in the Rijksmuseum, Amsterdam (no.4833), which was purchased from Lord Kinnaird in 1985.[7]

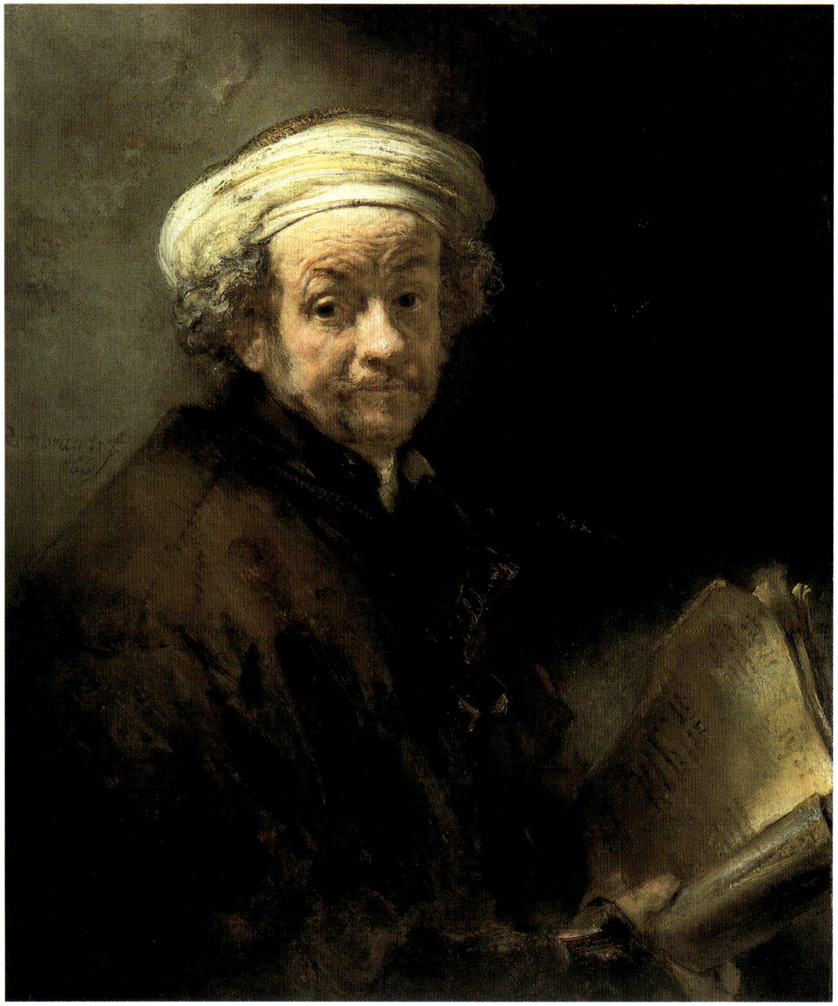

EXHIBITED: *RA* Winter exhibition, 1878, no.171; *RA 1899*, no.71; *RA 1929*, no.113; *Amsterdam 1932*, no.33; *Drie eeuwen portret in Nederland*, Rijksmuseum, Amsterdam, 1952, no.149; *Amsterdam and Rotterdam*, no.149.

LITERATURE: *Kinnaird Collection or Cabinet Picture Gallery* (unattributed and unpaged), published by subscription by E. Orme, London, 1809, pl.2 (by C. Turner); *Smith*, no.209 ; *Waagen 1857*, p.447; *HdG 1893*, p.228; *HdG*, no.575; E. J. Meijer, 'De Schenking De Bruijn-Van der Leeuw aan het Rijksmuseum', *Bulletin van het Rijksmuseum*, 1961, no.9, pp.47-8; J. Rosenberg, *Rembrandt. Life and Work*, London, 1964, pp.52-3 and p.347, note 3; *Gerson*, no.403; P. J. J. van Thiel, 'Zelfportret als de apostel Paulus. Rembrandt van Rijn', *Openbaar Kunstbezit*, no.13, February 1969, pp.1a-1b; *Tümpel*, no.175; H. Perry Chapman, *Rembrandt's Self-portraits*, Princeton,1990 pp.120-7.

THE RIJKSMUSEUM, AMSTERDAM

1 *HdG*, no.575.
2 When copied by Sir Joshua Reynolds : *Reynolds* exhibition catalogue, *RA*, 1986, p.21 and note 47.
3 *HdG*, no.575.
4 W. Buchanan, *Memoirs of Painting, with a chronological history of the Importation of Pictures by the Great Masters into England since the French Revolution*, London, 1824, vol.2, p.179.
5 Turner's plate is inscribed 'Rembrandt A Portrait of himself. Brought from the collection of the Corsini family at Rome by Mr Buchannan. 3' by 2'6⅛. Pubd.Jan. 2. 1809'. The mezzotint is listed in A. Whitman, *Masters of Mezzotint*, London, 1898, p.83, no.421.
6 J. Rosenberg, *op. cit.* and H. Perry Chapman, *op. cit.*
7 *Rembrandt Corpus*, vol.2, no.A103, and *Waterhouse Notebooks*, vol.22, p.80.

55 *Carcass of an Ox*

Oil on panel: 73.5 × 51.4 cm
Signed and incompletely dated: *Rembrandt. f. 16* in centre of black band of paint running along bottom of painting
PROVENANCE: Perhaps Jan Maurits Quinkhard sale, Amsterdam, 15 March 1773, lot 11. Jan van Dijk sale, Amsterdam, 14 March 1791, lot 49. Perhaps Jan Wubbels sale, Amsterdam, 16 July 1792, lot 276 (sold to Ten Kate for 160 guilders). Perhaps sold in Amsterdam, 14-15 August 1793, lot 106, sold to Schot. Collection of the dealer, Woodburn, London, by 1836;[1] S. Woodburn sale, London, 16 May 1854, lot 173. JOHN GRAHAM GILBERT; his wife by whom bequeathed to Glasgow Art Gallery and Museum in 1877 (no.600).

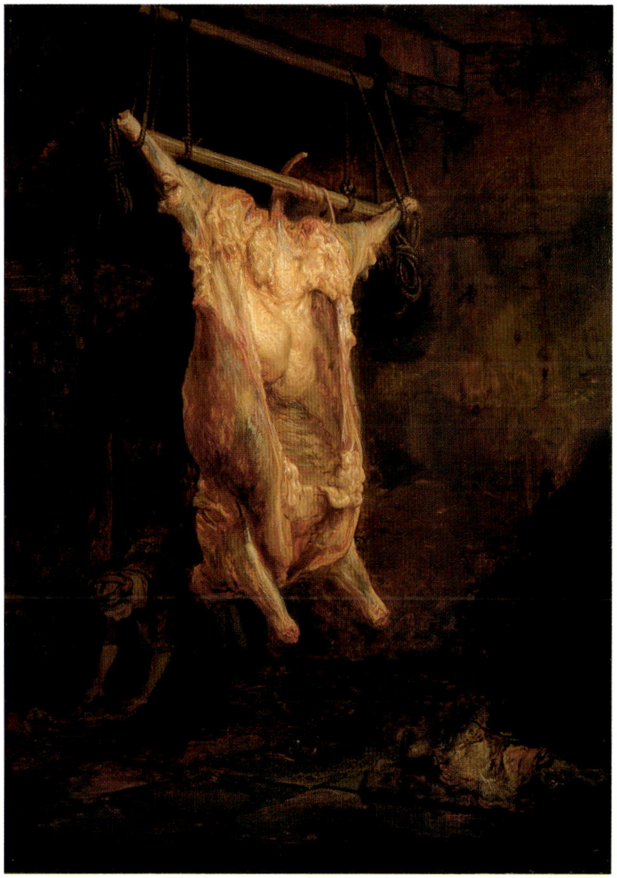

Hofstede de Groot remarked that this work was more carefully finished than Rembrandt's famous painting of the same subject in the Louvre which is dated 1655, and as a result dated the Glasgow picture earlier, to about 1640. Although not by Rembrandt, the painting is loosely inspired by the master's work of this period. Carel Fabritius (1622-54) has been suggested as a possible artist.[2] He was working in Rembrandt's studio in the early 1640s (after Fabritius's marriage in September 1641, when he moved to Amsterdam). An inventory of the estate of his wife made in 1643 does include a painting of 'a slaughtered pig'.[3]

While the Glasgow painting and Rembrandt's famous composition of 1655 are similar, there is no reason to suppose that there was a single prototype. The subject of a slaughtered pig or ox was first found in the work of artists such as Pieter Aertsen, Joachim Bueckelaer and Martin van Cleve and was not uncommon in Dutch seventeenth-century art. The scene may have been intended as a 'vanitas'. Sometimes children are shown in the background of such compositions with a balloon made of the animal's bladder, perhaps as a visual reminder that 'homo bulla est' – man is as ephemeral as a bubble.[4]

John Graham Gilbert owned other works ascribed to Rembrandt now in Glasgow Art Gallery and Museum. The most famous of these is *The Man in Armour* (no.601) now identified with Rembrandt's *Alexander the Great*.[5] The *Head of a Bearded Man* (no.599), however, is probably a studio replica of a picture now in Groningen. Graham Gilbert's admiration for Rembrandt was such that he seems to have painted his own copies, also now in Glasgow: a *Margaretha de Geer* (no.557) after the 1661 portrait in the National Gallery, London, a *Rabbi* (no.602) after a portrait in Dresden Musem and a *Self-portrait* (no.598) after the picture in the Royal Collection.[6]

EXHIBITED: *Amsterdam 1898*, no.76; *RA 1899*, no.44; *Amsterdam 1932*, no.12.

LITERATURE: *Smith*, no.619; *HdG 1893*, p.143; *HdG*, no.971; *Glasgow Catalogue*, vol.1, no.600, p.109, vol.2, p.71; *Rembrandt Corpus*, vol.3, no.C122.‡

GLASGOW ART GALLERY AND MUSEUM

1 *Smith*, no.619.
2 *Rembrandt Corpus*, vol.3, p.768.
3 *Ibid.* 'Een do. van een geslegen varcken' in the inventory drawn up on 24 April 1643, after his first wife's death.
4 *Ibid.*, p.769, where the possible symbolism of the subject is discussed at length.
5 *Rembrandt 1991*, no.43 and C. Brown and A. Roy, 'Rembrandt's "Alexander the Great"', *The Burlington Magazine*, May 1992, pp.286-97.
6 *Glasgow Catalogue*, p.115.

JACOB VAN RUISDAEL

c.1628/29-82. Born in Haarlem, but the exact date of his birth is uncertain. A date is suggested by a document that gives his age as 32 on 9 June 1661. Jacob was the son of Isaack Jacobsz. van Ruisdael (a frame maker and landscape painter) and the nephew of the artist Salomon van Ruysdael, and probably trained with both of them. He became a member of the guild in Haarlem in 1648. However, his earliest works date from 1646, and few are dated after 1653. He travelled to Bentheim c.1650, probably with Nicolaes Berchem, and was living in Amsterdam by June 1657, probably remaining there until his death. He was skilled as an etcher and draftsman and painted most categories of landscape. He influenced many artists and Hobbema was one of his pupils. He may have practised as a doctor from 1676 but the documentary evidence for this is inconclusive.

56 *The Banks of a River*

Oil on canvas: 134 × 193 cm
Signed and dated (indistinctly): *JvRuisdael 1649* [1] (*JvR* in monogram) at bottom left

PROVENANCE: SIR JAMES ERSKINE OF TORRIE by whom bequeathed in 1825 to the University of Edinburgh which received the picture in 1836; placed on loan in 1845 to the Board of Manufactures, Edinburgh, first at the Royal Institution, then at the National Gallery of Scotland for its opening in 1859 (no.75) where it has remained.

The basic composition of *The Banks of a River* is adapted from a painting of two years earlier, *River Landscape with a High Sandy Bank* (Hage Collection, Nivaagaard, Denmark).[2] However, the dramatic high sky and extensive panorama give this picture a grandeur unmatched by the earlier work in either scale or effect. Ruisdael used drawings of Rhenen on the Neder Rijn as the inspiration for the town in the distance, and the tower of the church of St Cunera and twin towers of Rhenen's watergate are clearly visible.[3] He also adapted various motifs from the work of Cornelis Vroom. The figures in *The Banks of a River* are probably painted by another artist, possibly Ruisdael's friend, Nicolaes Berchem, or, more probably, Philips Wouverman.[4] Sir James Erskine also owned another painting by Jacob van Ruisdael. A manuscript catalogue of some of his works left to his sister records: '... a Woodland Scene by Jacob Ruysdael, the figures by A. van de Velde, ... 27" × 32"... a belt of trees with the skyline showing through.. The whole picture has fine colour and is in good condition. From Sir James Erskine's Collection. Valued at £60 by W. S. Woodburn in 1825. There are two examples of this master in the N. G. of Scotland, given by Sir James Erskine'. [5]

EXHIBITED: *Ruisdael 1981*, no.9, pp.44-5, repr.‡; *The Torrie Collection*, no.34; *Dutch Landscape; The Early Years, Haarlem and Amsterdam 1590-1650*, National Gallery, London, 1986, no.105.

LITERATURE: *Smith*, supplement, no.32; *Waagen*, vol.3, pp.273-4; *HdG 1893*, p.133; *HdG*, no.703; *Rosenberg*, p.22; *Walford*, pp.71-2, fig.59.

THE TORRIE COLLECTION
THE UNIVERSITY OF EDINBURGH

1 Revealed by cleaning in 1962.
2 *HdG*, no.694; *Ruisdael 1981*, p.45, repr.
3 *Walford*, p.71.
4 *Ruisdael 1981*, p.45.
5 Rev. Canon Harper, *Catalogue Raisonné of the Erskine of Torrie Institute, Dunimarle 1912*, unpublished manuscript, photocopy at the Royal Commission on Ancient and Historical Monuments of Scotland, Edinburgh, p.220.

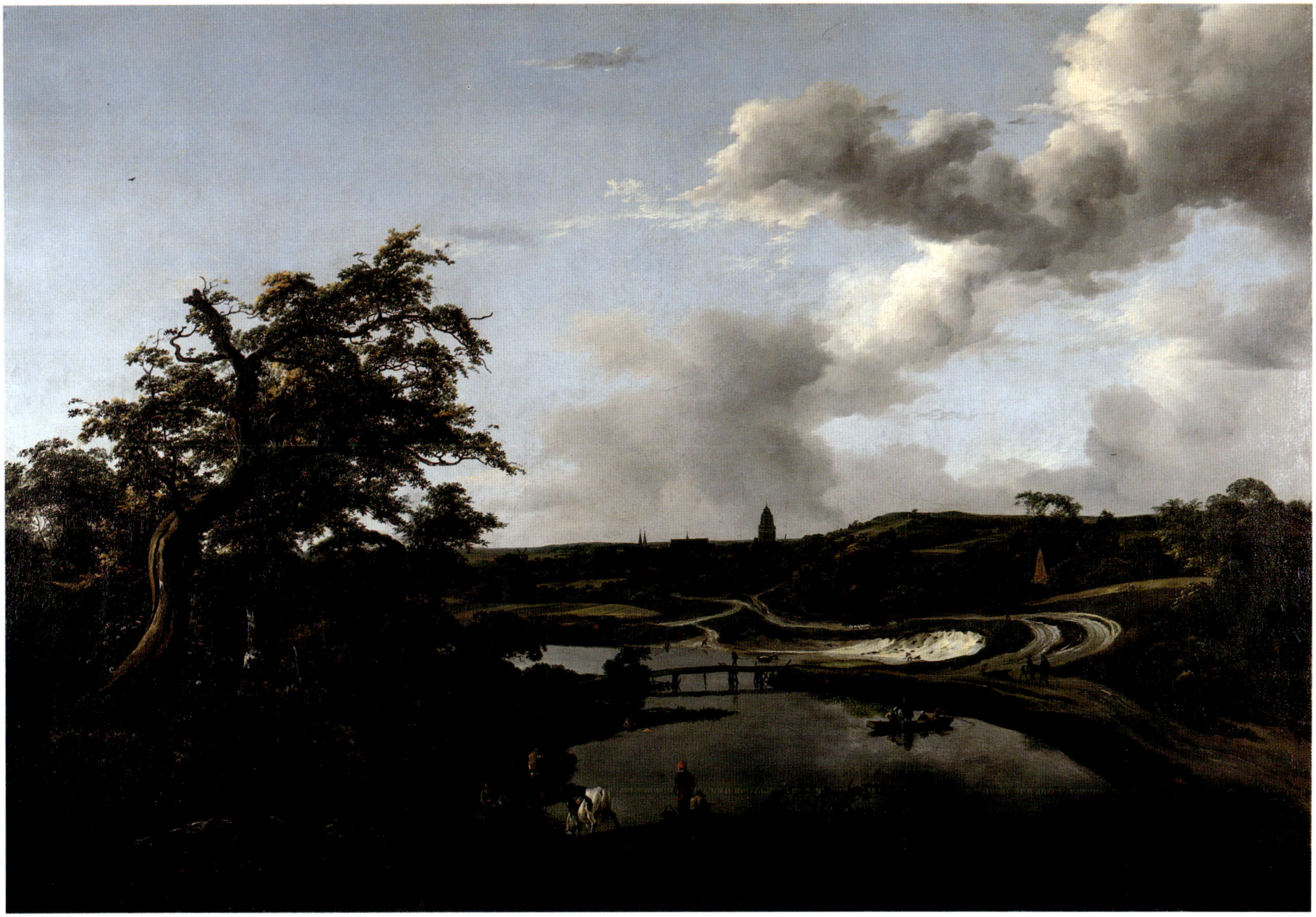

57 *Egmond aan Zee*

Oil on panel: 49.8 × 68.3 cm
Signed: *JR* (in monogram) with traces of what may have been a date at bottom right
PROVENANCE: In the collection of ARCHIBALD MCLELLAN by 1842[1] and by whom bequeathed in 1854 to Glasgow Art Gallery and Museum (no.34).

Hofstede de Groot called this 'One of the strong pieces of the collection; a very fine view'.[2] Egmond is on the coast to the east of Alkmaar and provided the young Ruisdael with much of his early subject matter, along with Haarlem and the coast near Naarden. Perhaps influenced by C. J. Visscher's print of *Egmondt op Zee* of 1615, Ruisdael painted several views of Egmond, travelling there with his father in about 1646. Only two of his views are dated, that in the A. F. Philips collection at Eindhoven of 1646 (which shows almost the same view as the Glasgow picture),[3] and that in the Currier Art Gallery, Manchester, New Hampshire, which is dated 1648.[4] Although the Glasgow picture was once thought to be dated 1655, the date is unreadable and the composition is most likely to be earlier than this, perhaps *c.*1648. Walford suggests that it is rather more assured in handling than the 1648 version and proposes a possible date in the late 1640s or even the early 1650s. The church that forms the focus of these pictures was already damaged when Ruisdael painted it, and collapsed in 1743.

LITERATURE: *Smith*, supplement, no.117; *Waagen*, vol.3, p.287; *HdG 1893*, p.144; *HdG*, no.47; *Glasgow Catalogue*, vol.1, p.123, vol.2, repr. p.75; *Ruisdael 1981*, p.31‡; *Walford*, pp.51-2 and note 10.

GLASGOW ART GALLERY AND MUSEUM

1 *Smith*, supplement, no.117, as a view of Katwijck.
2 *HdG 1893*, p.144, no.419, also as a view of Katwijck though he alters this to a view of Egmond in *HdG*, no.47.
3 *Rosenberg*, no.29. See, also, *Walford*, p.51.
4 *HdG*, no.49, and *Ruisdael 1981*, p.41 and repr. p.40.

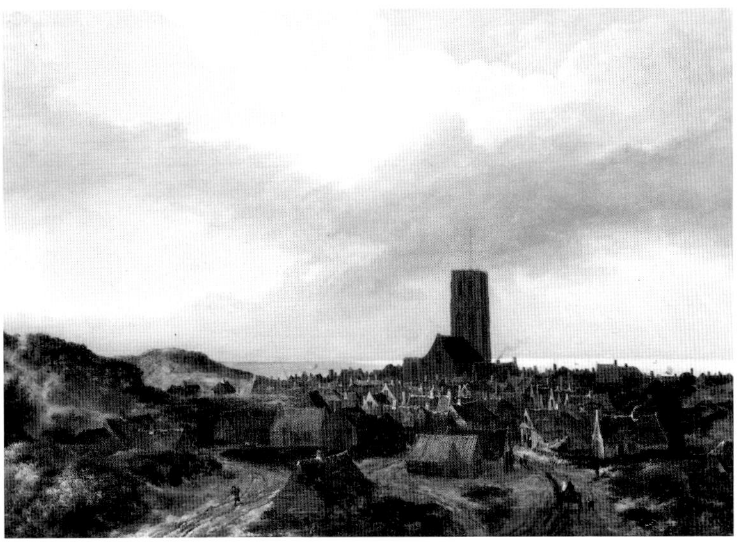

58 *Ruins by a River*

Oil on canvas: 53.7 × 63.8 cm
Signed: *JvR*.....? (*JvR* in monogram) at bottom left
PROVENANCE: In the collection of the 7th EARL OF WEMYSS AND MARCH at Amisfield by 1771[1] and thence by descent; placed on loan to the National Gallery of Scotland in 1957.

Hofstede de Groot observed the 'effect of this piece is mainly in the contrast between the red stone colour of the ruins and the green of the trees'.[2] He saw the picture twice, once at Gosford House, and by mistake described it twice in his survey of Ruisdael's work. The painting is probably datable on stylistic grounds to the 1650s or early 1660s and the figures may be by Ruisdael, as Hofstede de Groot believed.

EXHIBITED: *Manchester 1857*, no.851; University of Edinburgh exhibition, 1953, no.22; *Pictures from Gosford House*, no.36.

LITERATURE: *Waagen 1857*, p.440; *HdG*, nos 685 and 754 both refer to this picture; *HdG 1893*, p.218.

THE EARL OF WEMYSS AND MARCH

1 From a manuscript list of paintings at Amisfield House dated 1771, no.24.
2 *HdG 1893*, p.218..

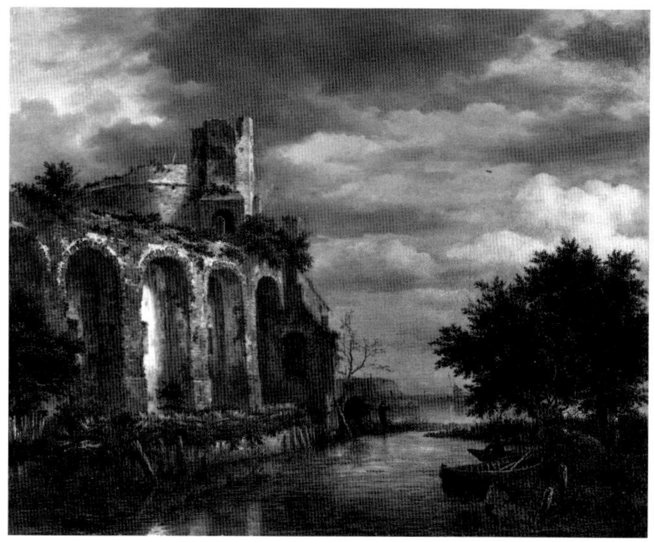

59 *Mountain Landscape with Waterfall*

Oil on canvas: 118 × 178 cm
Signed: *J v Ruisdael* (*JvR* in monogram) at bottom right
PROVENANCE: In the collection of the MARQUESS OF BUTE by 1835[1] and thence by descent; Private Collection, Scotland.

In works such as this, Ruisdael was considerably influenced by the painter Allart van Everdingen (1621-75) who had visited Scandinavia in 1640-4[2] and whose characteristic subjects were such waterfalls and pine trees. Ruisdael started to paint in this style from the mid to late 1650s (though his first dated picture in this style was painted in 1659) [3] and this picture was probably painted *c.* 1656-8. The composition is very closely based on a drawing by Ruisdael now in the Pierpont Morgan Library, New York (see fig.59).[4]

This is probably the picture listed in an 1822 inventory[5] as hanging in the little breakfast room at Luton Hoo, a 'Ruysdael Landscape – His landscapes are from nature representing torrents, and waterfalls. Trees delicately handled. Skies clear, water transparent, and every part has the look of true nature – no Painter ever possessed a greater degree of admiration and the very high prices given for his works at this day are proof of their merit'. When Waterhouse saw the painting in July 1949 he called it a 'Norwegian Landscape, *HdG,* no.760, quite accurately described: ... waterfall bottom centre with some huge tree trunks dashing downstream. The castle is perhaps not ruined: the character is Norwegian from the pines. A little brackish but really a very noble example'.[5]

EXHIBITED: *Bethnal Green 1882-3,* no.219; *Glasgow 1884,* no.145; *Edinburgh 1949,* no.29 (along with no.28, the artist's *Distant View of Haarlem*).

LITERATURE: *Smith,* no.198; *Waagen,* vol.3, pp.480-1; 'The Marquis of Bute's Pictures at Bethnal Green – first notice' (anonymous review), *The Athenaeum,* 30 December 1882, p.905; *Richter,* no.145; *HdG,* no 760; *Walford,* p.104, fig.97.

PRIVATE COLLECTION, SCOTLAND

1 When recorded by Smith as being in the Bute collection.
2 See *Masters of Dutch Landscape,* pp. 306-11.
3 A picture by Van Everdingen from the Bute collection was also exhibited in *Edinburgh 1949,* no.14. For literature on the artist's relationship with Ruisdael see A. I. Davies, *Allart van Everdingen,* Harvard dissertation, 1973, New York, 1978, pp.217-29.
4 *Walford,* p.104.
5 *Masters of Dutch Landscape,* no.85.
6 *Waterhouse Notebooks,* vol. 30, July 1949, p.58.

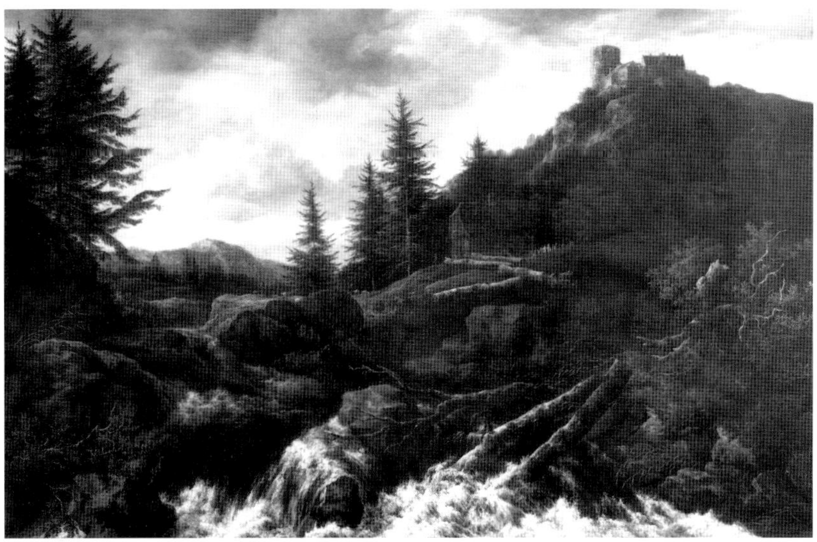

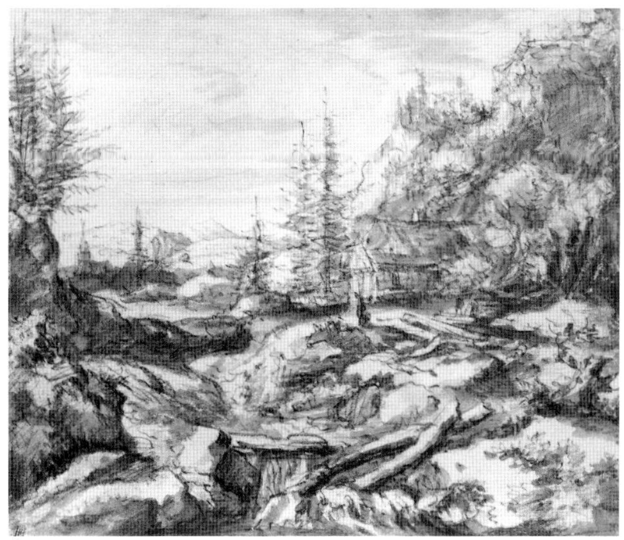

fig.59

60 *Rocky Landscape with Waterfall*

Oil on canvas: 106.7 × 150.5 cm
Signed: *JvRuisdael* (*JvR* in monogram) on rock in centre
PROVENANCE: Purchased *c.*1810 from a collection at Alkmaar by Walker; J. Campbell, London, 1831; bought by John Smith and sold to Héris of Brussels; Baron J. G. Verstolk van Soelen, The Hague, 1835, no.45; from whose estate purchased in 1846 by Thomas Baring, Humphrey Mildmay and Samuel Jones Loyd (later Lord Overstone); Lord Overstone, London; his daughter, Lady Wantage, London; Private Collection, Scotland.

Gerson believed this to be painted in the late 1660s[1] and Slive also ascribes it to this period (or to the early 1670s), when Ruisdael abandoned the Scandinavian scenery and roaring torrents of his earlier paintings (such as that in Catalogue no.59). Though the waterfall is still 'strewn with the most improbable boulders' as Walford points out,[2] the rushing water is more decorative than destructive and the hills less steep and craggy. Waagen was most impressed by the painting, pronouncing it 'in every respect one of the finest known to me of the master. The water is of most admirable animation, with the utmost breadth and softness of execution. The individuality of every portion is more marked, and the number of details more numerous, than in any other picture on so large a scale by Ruysdael that has come before me'.

In 1721, Houbraken had remarked that Ruisdael was particularly known for his painting of 'water splashing and foaming as it dashed upon the rocks so naturally, delicately and transparently that it appears to be real'.[3] Both he and the writer Jan Luyken seem to have made puns upon the meaning of Ruisdael's name, using the Dutch 'ruis' (noise) and 'dael' (valley), for valleys noisy with water were considered Ruisdael's hallmark.[4] Luyken employed the emblem of a waterfall with the motto 'Tot verdooving' (Until deafening) as a symbol of the deafening noise of man's world against the calm silence of God, and in 2 *Samuel* 22, v.2-33 God is described as the 'rock', 'stronghold and refuge' which alone is able to withstand the 'waves of death' and 'the torrents of perdition' that assail mankind. It is likely that Ruisdael's contemporaries would have been aware of such visual allusions in his work.[5]

EXHIBITED: British Institution, London, 1847 no.23 and 1848 no.25; *Manchester 1857*, no.702; *RA*, Winter exhibitions 1871, 1888, no.67, 1907, no.107; *RA 1952-3*, no.302; *Ruisdael 1981*, pp.106-7, repr.‡

LITERATURE: *Smith*, no.129; *Waagen 1857*, p.141; *Wantage Catalogue*, 1902, no.200; *HdG*, no.252; *Rosenberg*, no.194.

PRIVATE COLLECTION, SCOTLAND

1 Note on photograph in Gallery files.
2 *Walford*, p.144.
3 Quoted in *Masters of Dutch Landscape*, p.451 and note 8.
4 *Ibid.*, note 9.
5 Discussed in *Walford*, p.143.

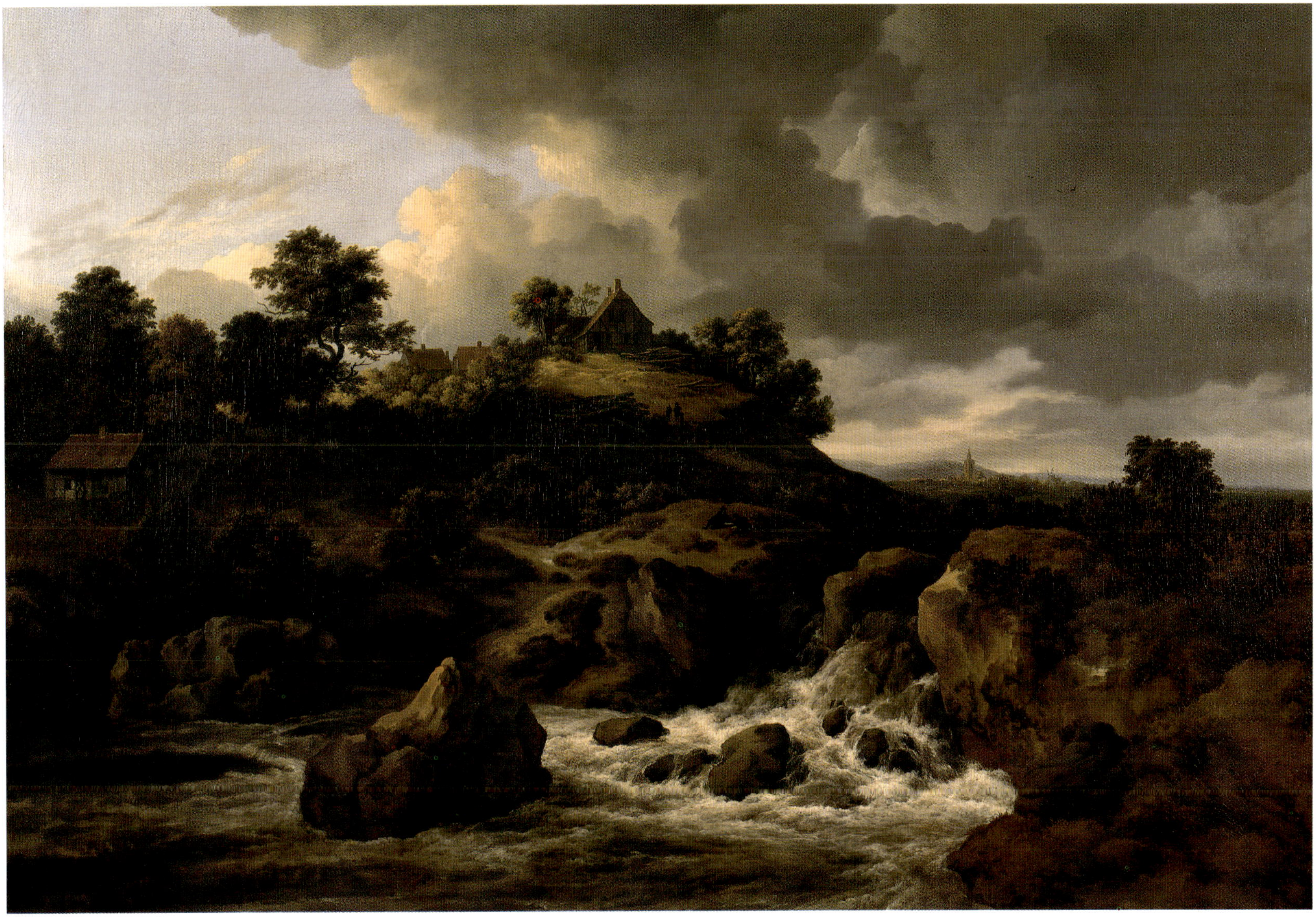

61 *A View of Haarlem from the Bleaching Grounds*

Oil on canvas: 41.9 × 41.9 cm
Signed: *J v Ruisdael* (*JvR* in monogram)
PROVENANCE: In the collection of the 7th EARL OF WEMYSS AND MARCH at Amisfield by 1771[1] and thence by descent.

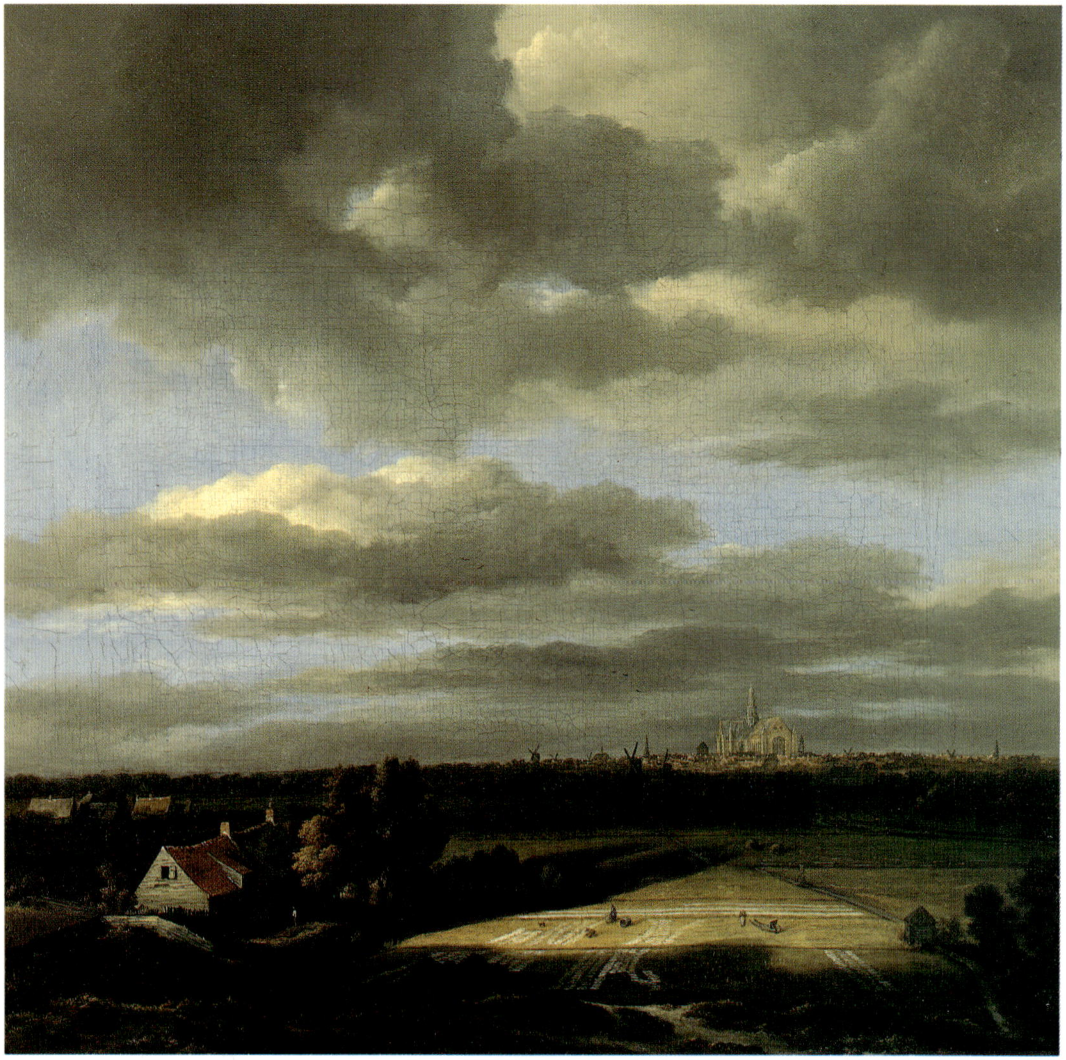

This painting was almost certainly intended as a pair to *A Distant View of Alkmaar* (Catalogue no.62). Rosenberg dates both pictures to 1676-81, believing that Ruisdael was also responsible for the staffage and suggests that, although the artist's late work can be uneven, these pictures show that he was still capable of high quality towards the end of his life.

The painting shows the town of Haarlem in the distance with the dominant church of St Bavo's, where Ruisdael was to be buried and which Pieter Saenredam also painted (Catalogue nos 65 and 66). In the foreground are long strips of linen stretched out in the sun to bleach. A thriving textile town, Haarlem was also the centre of the linen bleaching industry in an age of elaborate ruffs and collars. Ruisdael painted such bleaching grounds frequently.

Catalogue nos 58 and 59 were listed as being by 'Vanderwarf' in the 1771 list but it seems that the 7th Earl was, in any case, an admirer of Ruisdael's work, for in addition to these pictures he owned the landscape *Ruins by a River* (Catalogue no.58), as well as a *Winter Landscape*.[2]

EXHIBITED: *Pictures from Gosford House*, no.25.

LITERATURE: *Waagen 1857*, p.437; *HdG*, no.64; *HdG 1893*, p.218;.*Rosenberg*, no.47; *Walford*, pp.177-80, repr. fig.182 in colour.

THE EARL OF WEMYSS AND MARCH

1 From a manuscript list of paintings at Amisfield House dated 1771, no.25 (Collectors Index).

2 The *Winter Landscape* was exhibited in *Manchester 1857*, no.970, and in *Pictures from Gosford House*, no.24.

62 *A Distant View of Alkmaar (?)*

Oil on canvas: 41.9 × 41.9 cm
Signed: *J v Ruisdael* (*JvR* in monogram)
PROVENANCE: In the collection of the 7th EARL OF WEMYSS AND MARCH at Amisfield by 1771[1] and thence by descent.

This picture was probably intended as a pendant to *A View of Haarlem* (Catalogue no.61). It was previously titled *A View of Haarlem from the Dunes at Overveen,* but Walford believes it shows the town of Alkmaar as the church is too squat to be St Bavo's. It closely resembles a painting at the Boston Museum of Fine Arts (no.39.794) which has been identified with Alkmaar, north of Haarlem.[2] However, the church in the foreground remains unidentified and if this is Alkmaar, the artist may have taken a certain topographic licence with the scene.

EXHIBITED: *Pictures from Gosford House*, no.27.

LITERATURE: *Waagen 1857*, p.437; *HdG*, no.63: *HdG 1893*, p.218; *Walford*, pp.177-80.

THE EARL OF WEMYSS AND MARCH

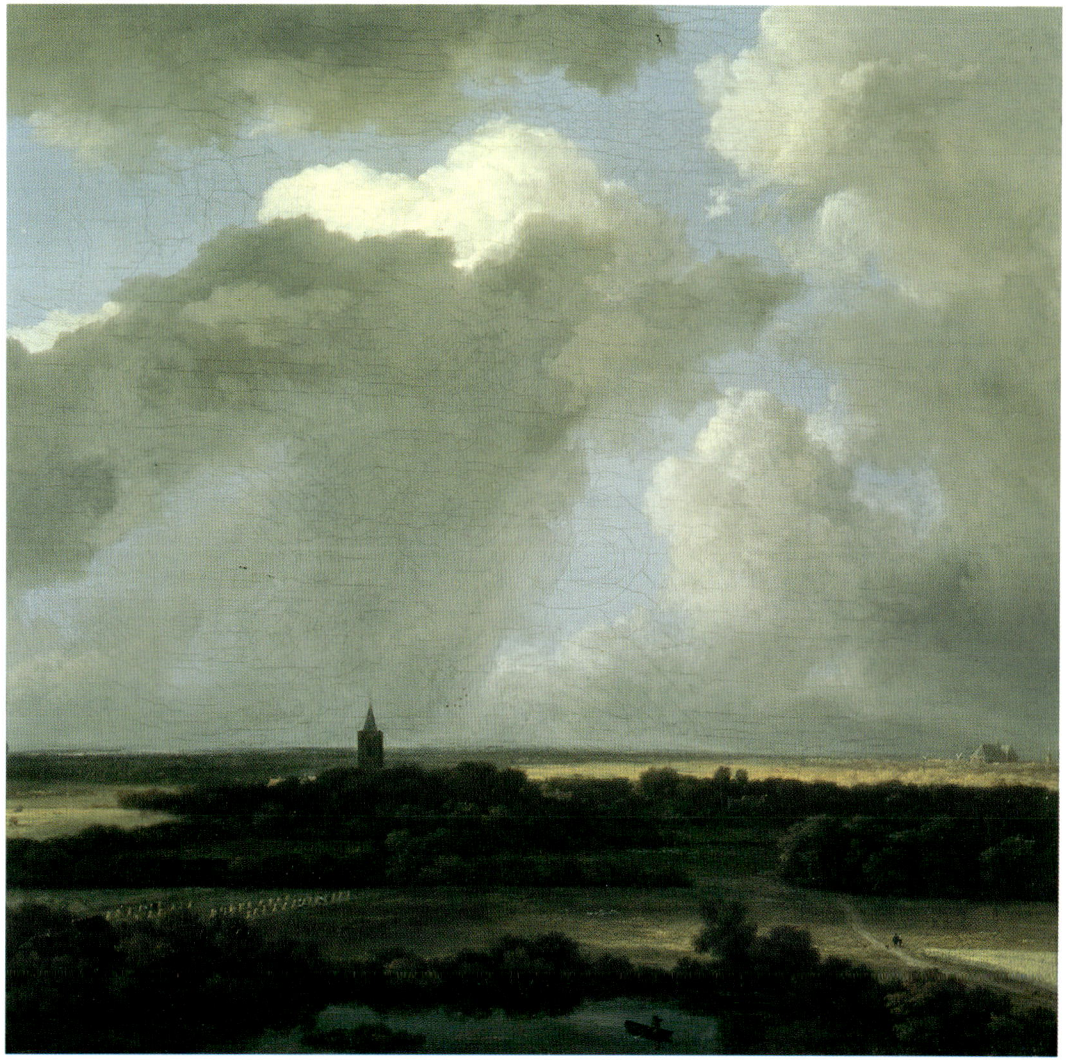

1 From a manuscript list of paintings at Amisfield House dated 1771, no.26, as by 'Vanderwarf' (see Collectors Index).

2 *Walford*, p.180. See, also, *Masters of Dutch Landscape*, no.89.

SALOMON VAN RUYSDAEL

1600/03?-70. Born in Naarden, Salomon abandoned the family name of De Go(o)yer for Ruysdael (never spelling it 'Ruisdael', the surname his brother Isaack and nephew Jacob used). Salomon lived in Haarlem throughout his life and became a member of the painters' guild there in 1623, his first dated work being painted two years later. His teacher is not known but his early work is close to that of Esaias van de Velde, who was in Haarlem from 1612-18. With Jan van Goyen and Pieter Molijn, Ruysdael became one of the foremost landscape artists, painting in carefully restricted tones.

63 *The Ferry Boat*

Oil on panel: 71.2 × 115.57 cm
PROVENANCE: In the collection of the 7th EARL OF WEMYSS AND MARCH at Amisfield by 1771[1] and thence by descent.

Stechow dates this painting to 1632.[2] Ruysdael's work and that of Jan van Goyen were extremely similar at this stage and Hofstede de Groot thought that this picture was by Van Goyen, although he pronounced it 'very much a Salomon Ruisdael style'.[3] The ferry boat is a motif he used often. A painting showing the same scene from a slightly altered viewpoint is in the Alte Pinakothek in Munich (*Stechow*, no.329) while the ferry recurs in later paintings such as *River Scene with a Ferry* of 1649 (*Stechow*, no.356.), which contains a similar pattern of cottage, bystanders, tree and ferry though painted in more lively colours.[4]

Such 'tonal' landscapes do not seem to have been in great demand until the nineteenth century and therefore the presence of a Salomon van Ruysdael in a collection in Scotland at such an early date as 1771 is unusual (furthermore the 7th Earl also owned two early tonal landscapes by Van Goyen).[5] Works by Salomon van Ruysdael are recorded in the collections of the Duke of Hamilton (*Stechow*, nos 224C by 1882 and no.396 by 1887), the 2nd Marquess of Breadalbane (*Stechow*, no.479), William McEwan (*Stechow*, no.460C) and the Earl of Stair at Lochinch (*Stechow*, no.485A).

EXHIBITED: *Pictures from Gosford House*, no.31; *Thomson*, no.38; *Agnews*, no.38.‡

LITERATURE: *HdG*, no.547 (as Van Goyen); *HdG 1893*, p.219; *Stechow*, no.409.

THE EARL OF WEMYSS AND MARCH

1 Amisfield list 1771, no.34.
2 Stechow, *op. cit.*
3 *HdG 1893*, p.219.
4 Exhibited in *Dutch Landscape the Early Years*, National Gallery, London, 1986, no.58.
5 See *Pictures from Gosford House*, p.6.

64 *Waterside with Trees*

Oil on panel: 32.8 × 51.1 cm
Signed and dated: *SvR* (in monogram) *1633* on riverbank at right
PROVENANCE: The Earl of Mar and Kellie, Alloa House, sold Sotheby's, London, 22 June 1960, lot 5; bought by C. Duits (£3800). P. de Boer, Amsterdam; purchased by the Stichting Johan Maurits van Nassau and lent to The Mauritshuis, The Hague, 1960 (no.941).

Like the Weymss picture (Catalogue no.63), this composition is characteristic of the work of Salomon van Ruysdael in the 1630s.[1] The colouring is cool and almost monochromatic, the eVect achieved by slight variations in tone.

It is not known when *Waterside with Trees* entered the collection of the Earl of Mar and Kellie. It may have been part of the property which came into his ownership through the Earls of Kellie, such as the canvas by Jacob de Wet (Catalogue no.73). Alternatively, it could have been a Mar family picture at Alloa House.

EXHIBITED: Dordrecht, 1964, no.66, repr.44.

LITERATURE: *Stechow*, no.498A.‡; *Hollandse Schilderkunst, Landscappen 17de Eeuw*, The Mauritshuis, The Hague, 1980 , pp.95-6, repr. p.217.

THE MAURITSHUIS, THE HAGUE

1 For examples of related compositions see *Hollandse Schilderkunst, op. cit.*, p.95, referring to *Stechow*, nos 549, 322, 439, 440 and 325.

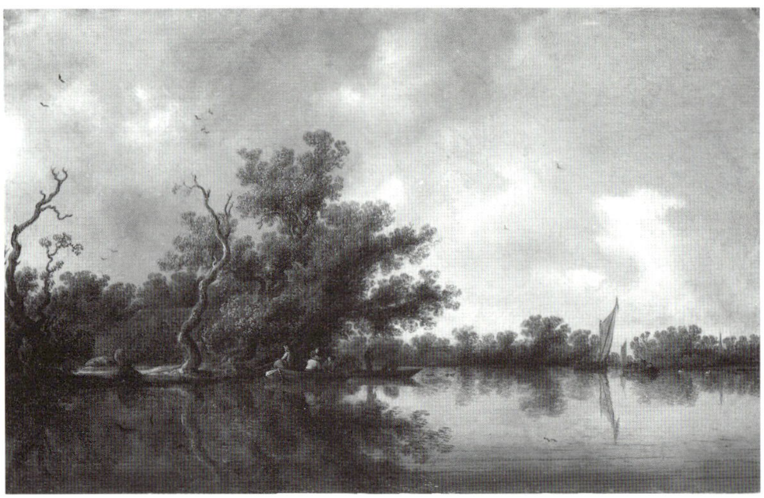

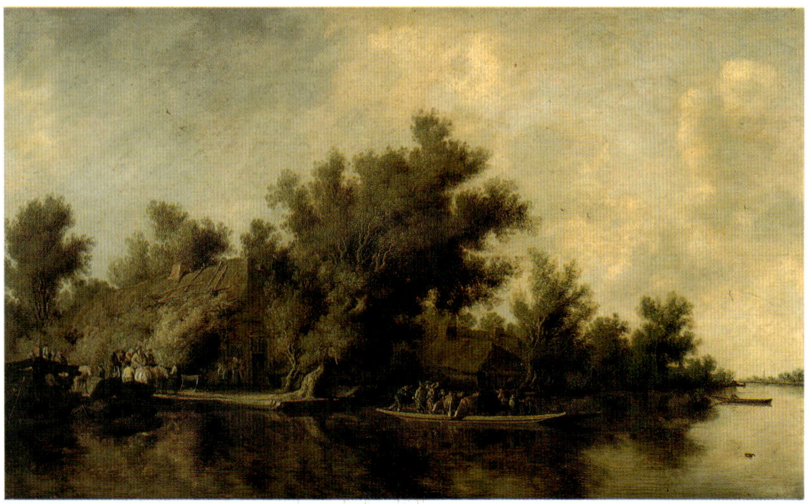

1597-1665. Pieter Saenredam was born in Assendelft, the son of Jan Saenredam, the engraver. He entered the studio of Frans Pietersz. de Grebber in Haarlem in May 1612, working there until 1622. The following year he became a member of the painters' guild in Haarlem where he spent most of his life. He knew the architects and painters Salomon de Bray and Jacob van Campen; the latter drew Saenredam's portrait in 1628. Saenredam's earliest dated picture (of 1626) was The Expulsion from the Temple *but he later came to specialise in architectural painting and drawing.*

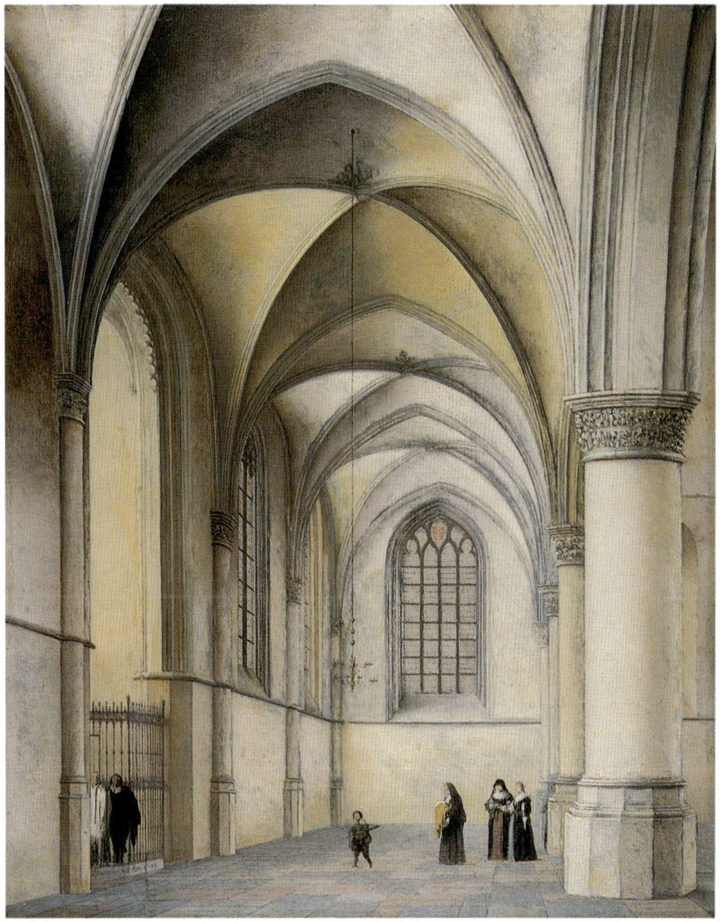

65 *South Aisle of St Bavo's Church, Haarlem*

Oil on panel: 42.8 × 33.6 cm
Signed and dated: *P. Saenredam fecit Anno 1633* on left on the step into the chapel
PROVENANCE: Hendrick Houtkamp sale, Alkmaar, 19 March 1776, lot 154; Nicolaas Nieuhoff sale, Amsterdam, 14 April 1777, lot 177; bought by Jan Gildemeester, his sale, Amsterdam, 11 June 1800, lot 193, bought by Yver; J. B. P. Le Brun, Paris, 1792; W. EUING , by whom bequeathed to Glasgow Art Gallery and Museum in 1874 (no.383).

This early work is a view of the church where Saenredam himself was later buried on 31 May 1665. The scene depicts a baptism, near the chapel for that purpose renovated by Lieven de Key in 1593. Of the two men on the right, the one in white wears the vestments of a Catholic priest. It may be that the picture was commissioned for a Catholic patron but it would have been impossible for a Catholic ceremony to have then taken place in St Bavo's, a Protestant church since 1578. Saenredam owned a large collection of mainly seventeenth-century drawings and mementos of St Bavo's and it is possible that he may have based the baptism group on one of these[1] or simply used his imagination. Saenredam's compositional drawing (dated 11 October 1631) for the painting was lost in Berlin in 1945, but there is a drawn copy after the painting in the Graphische Sammlung Albertina in Vienna and painted copies in Dulwich College and in the Six collection in Amsterdam.[2]

Saenredam's views of churches seem to have been popular in Scotland by the latter half of the nineteenth century. At least four works were owned by W. A. Coats (Catalogue no.67) and two by Arthur Kay, both of which are now in the National Gallery, London. Kay was particularly fond of one of his Saenredams, *View of the Buurkerk, Utrecht* (National Gallery, London, no. 1896), writing that the 'condition of the picture was extraordinary: it was absolutely untouched, even the most delicate tracery of the windows was still there ... The white walls had the surfaces broken up with infinite knowledge and care. So lovely was the atmosphere of this little masterpiece that one felt inclined to walk upon tiptoe towards the distant window'.[3] This picture, which was in Kay's collection by 1899,[4] was perhaps the first Saenredam recorded in Scotland as it was brought by Charles Galli to Edinburgh by 1826 and exhibited for sale at the Royal Institution (no.35).

EXHIBITED: *Pieter Jansz. Saenredam 1597-1665*, Museum Boymans-van Beuningen, Rotterdam, 1937-8, no.9; *Pieter Jansz. Saenredam,* Utrecht, 1961, no.63; *Edinburgh 1984*, no.23; *Rotterdam*, no.13, pp.100-3.‡

LITERATURE: *HdG 1893*, p.144; *Glasgow Catalogue*, p.126; G. Schwartz and M. J. Bok, *Pieter Saenredam. The Painter and his Time*, London, 1990, no.62, p.262.

GLASGOW ART GALLERY AND MUSEUM

1 Schwartz and Bok, *op.cit.*, pp.74-5.
2 *Rotterdam*, p.102.
3 A. Kay, *Treasure Trove in Art*, Edinburgh and London 1939, pp.64-5.
4 *MacLaren and Brown*, p.408, note 16.
5 *Ibid.*, p.407.

66 *The Interior of St Bavo's Church, called the 'Grote Kerk', at Haarlem*

Oil on panel: 174.8 × 143.6 cm
Signed, dated and inscribed: *Dit is de Cathedrale grote kerck / van haerlem, in hollandt. / Pieter Saenredam, dese met schilderen / voleijnt, den 27 februarij. 1648* bottom left corner

PROVENANCE: Possibly the work referred to in a letter from Saenredam to Constantin Huygens of 21 May 1648 as being on offer to the Stadholder Prince William II[1] and probably the picture which was purchased from the burgomaster of Amsterdam, Andries de Graeff, by the States of Holland and West Friesland to present as part of the 'Dutch Gift' to Charles II on the restoration of the monarchy. Described in an inventory of Charles II's collection of *c.*1666-7;[2] last recorded in the Royal Collection in an inventory of 28 October 1714. Perhaps in the sale of William van Huis, London, on 6 August 1722, lot 137.[3] Major Sir Thomas Neave, 5th Baronet (1874-1914); Asscher and Welker, London, in 1934 from whom purchased by the 4th MARQUESS OF BUTE and by descent to the 6th Marquess at Mount Stuart, Rothesay, by whom sold to Agnews, London; purchased by the National Gallery of Scotland with the aid of the NHMF, the NACF and the Pilgrim Trust in 1982 (no.2413).

The inscription states: 'This is the Cathedral Great Church of Haarlem in Holland. Pieter Saenredam finished painting this, the 27 February 1648', while the graffiti drawing of the man with a bird may represent St Bavo whose emblem was the falcon. Made up of six vertical planks of oak (each approximately 24 cm wide), this is the largest painting on panel by Saenredam to have survived.

The composition differs from that in Catalogue no.65 in showing the view from the choir looking down the nave of the church towards the west. Saenredam made a free drawing of the general composition on 25 August 1635 which he followed with a more careful preparatory drawing on 15 December 1635, of which two fragments, which make up the lower part of the overall design, survive. [4] On one of these, now in the Ian Woodner family collection, New York (fig.60), a small circle can be seen just at the right of the far group of three men. This was what Saenredam called the 'oog' or eye, the vanishing point on the 'horizon' chosen by the artist, where the perspective (orthogonal) lines converge. Saenredam then used such precise drawings to form the basis of the composition of his pictures. In the Bute painting, however, he subtly manipulated the dimensions of the church, thickening the columns and raising the arches in the foreground while making the distant arch lower and shortening the height of the figures. The intended effect succeeds in making the church seem vast, dwarfing the men within it. [5] The fifteenth-century organ is recorded in a detailed drawing in the Lugt collection, Institut Néerlandais, Paris. (The organ itself was demolished in the eighteenth century and another built at the west end of the nave of the church.) The picture of the church exterior which can be seen above the door on the left is now at the Frans Hals Museum in Haarlem and is attributed to Pieter Gerritsz.

EXHIBITED: *The Orange and the Rose*, Victoria and Albert Museum, London, 1964, no.65, pl.VII; *Edinburgh 1984*, no.17, p.21 and pp.22-38‡; *Edinburgh 1991*, no.12.

LITERATURE: R. Ruurs, 'Review of Dutch Church Painters. Saenredam's Great Church at Haarlem in Context' in *Oud Holland* 99/2, 1985, pp.161-4; G. Schwartz and M. J. Bok, *Pieter Saenredam. The Painter and his Time*, London, 1990, no.58, pp.261, 128, 152, 178, 206.

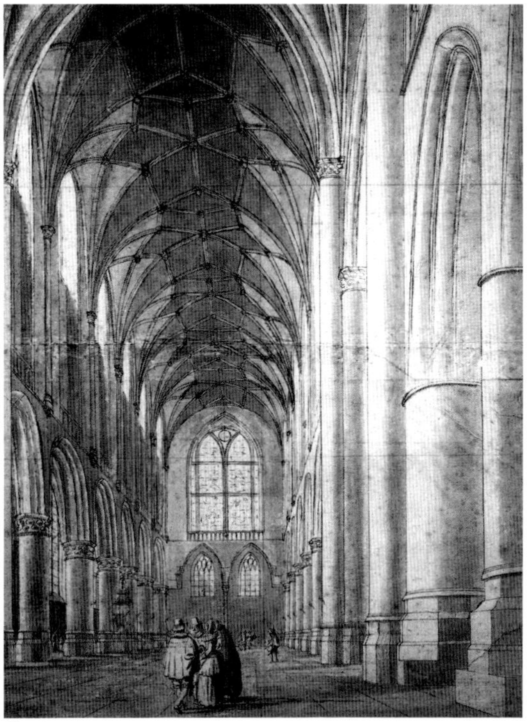

fig.60

1 Saenredam's letter is now lost but was transcribed in 1866 and is quoted in P. T. A. Swillens, *Pieter Jansz. Saenredam, schilder van Haarlem 1597-1665*, Amsterdam, 1935, p.143, in which Saenredam writes of 'mijn laest gemaeckte groote kerck'.

2 As no.137 and described as 'Peter Sauredam. Harlaem Church. A prospective. Dutch p'sent' which first hung in the King's Privy Gallery at Whitehall.

3 As 'Sanredam. The Church at Haerlem'. Suggested by Dr Lorne Campbell in a letter of 11 November 1983 in Gallery files. He noted that the Breughel (lot 60) in this sale could have been the painting now in the Frick Collection, New York, which was once in the Royal Collection.

4 See *Edinburgh 1984*, nos 18 (Gemeentearchief, Haarlem), 19 (Gemeentearchief, Haarlem) and 20 (Ian Woodner family collection).

5 For a detailed discussion of how Saenredam altered the perspective studies in this composition see *Edinburgh 1984*, pp.24-5 and 28-33. The review of this by R. Ruurs, *op.cit.*, suggests that the alterations are due to Saenredam's *onhandigheid* or 'clumsy' drawing.

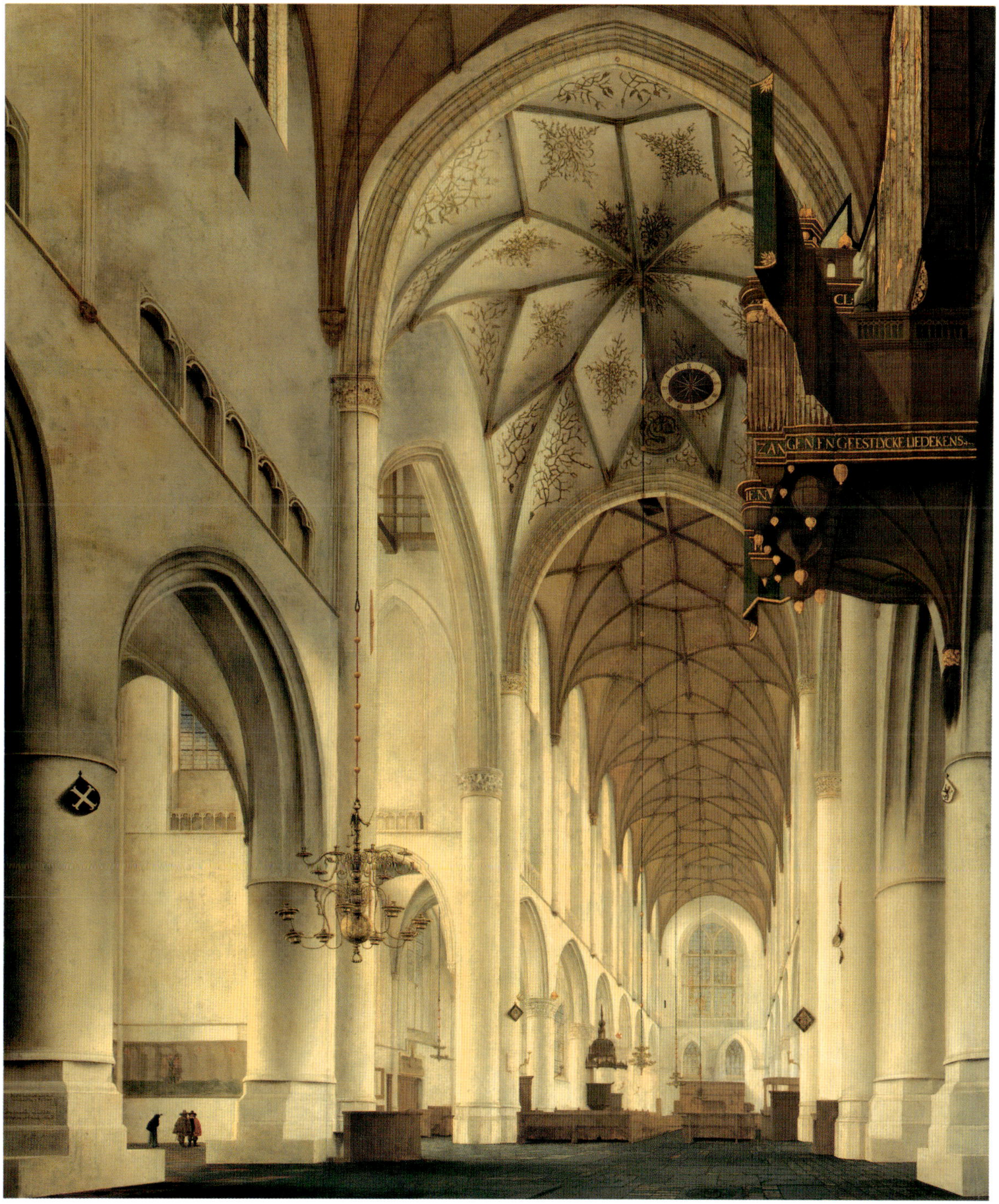
ZANGEN EN GEESTLYCKE LIEDEKENS

67 *Nave of the Buurkerk, Utrecht, viewed from North to South.*

Oil on panel: 40.7 × 33.5 cm
Signed and dated: *Pr Saenredam f / Ao 1654 4/21* at lower left on column
PROVENANCE: W. A. COATS by 1904, sold after W. Paterson's exhibition of the late W. A. Coats's collection at the Royal Society of British Artists, London, January 1927, no.179, for £250 ; Asscher and Welcker Gallery, London; Dr F. H. Fentener van Vlissingen, Esch, acquired in 1936; Private Collection, the Netherlands.

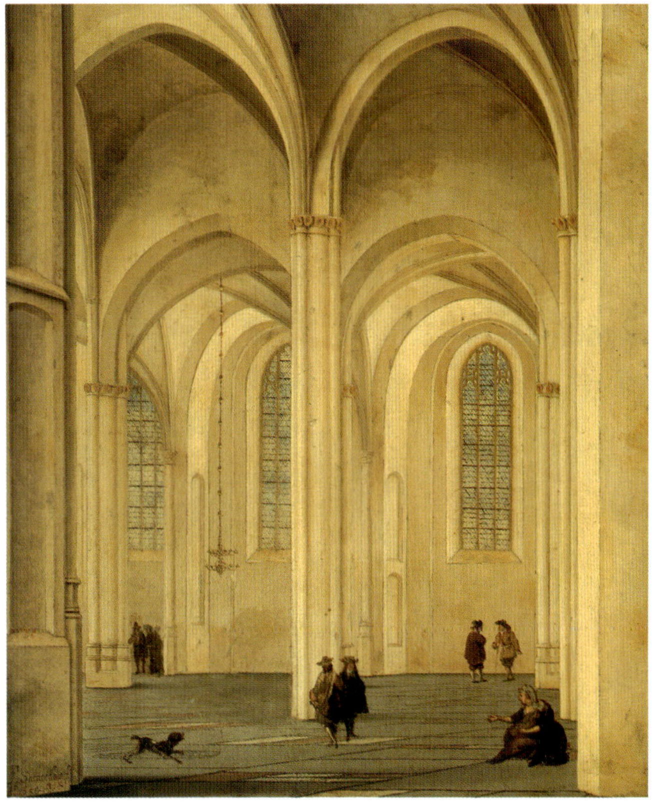

In 1636, Saenredam made site drawings at the Buurkerk (of which two survive).[1] He then painted five pictures, of which four are known today. (One of these, painted in 1644, now in the National Gallery, London, was formerly in the collection of Arthur Kay.)

William Coats obviously admired the work of Saenredam for he owned four paintings by him. These were dispersed after his death and this is the only painting which today can certainly be traced to his collection for it is illustrated in Coats's catalogue, published for him in 1904 by William Paterson (where it was the only Saenredam to be included). However, a manuscript inventory in the family's possession shows that this painting *Interior of Haarlem Cathedral*, which hung in the hall at Dalskairth, was also accompanied by two *Church Interiors* which hung in the dining room, and another *Church Interior* in the billiard room. All four were exhibited at the Royal Society of British Artists in London in January 1927 (nos 152, 175, 179, 181), by William Paterson. An annotated list describes no.152 as valued by Paterson for probate at £80; it was later sold at Christie's, London, 10 June 1927, lot 133, described as a *Church Interior with Gravediggers* (45.7 × 34.9 cm) and was bought by Asscher and Welker for £17. Paterson did probate valuations for the other paintings: no.175 for £30, no.179 (i.e. Catalogue no.67) for £100 and no.181 for £80. In the event, only two seem to have sold at the sale at the end of the exhibition at the Royal Society for British Artists in January 1927 (the precise date of sale is not known); no.179 (Catalogue no. 67) sold for £250 and no.181 for £80. It is not known when no.175 was sold but it seems likely that this is the *North Aisle of the Mariakerk* now in Los Angeles Museum of Art in the Carter collection.[2] The provenances of the two missing Coats's Saenredams have occasionally been confused with other pictures. The Mauritshuis's view of the outside of the Mariakerk (no.974) could not have been in Coats's collection since his paintings were clearly listed as church interiors.[3]

EXHIBITED: *Tentoonstelling van oude kunst uit particulier bezit en stad en provincie*, Centraal Museum, Utrecht, 1938, no.93; *Pieter Jansz. Saenredam*, Centraal Museum, Utrecht, 1961, no.123; *Rotterdam*, no.22.‡

LITERATURE: *Catalogue of the Collection of Pictures of the French, Dutch, British and Other Schools, Belonging to W. A. Coats*, published by W. B. Paterson, Glasgow, 1904 (described as 'Interior of Haarlem Cathedral. signed *1654 4/21*'), pl. XXXIV; *Catalogue of pictures and drawings being the Entire Collection of the late W. A. Coats Esquire, exhibited at the Royal Society of British Artists, Suffolk Street, London SW1*, published by W. B. Paterson, January, 1927, no.179; G. Schwartz and M. J. Bok, *Pieter Saenredam. The Painter and his Time*, London, 1990, no.123, pp.154, 210, 276.

PRIVATE COLLECTION
THE NETHERLANDS

1 Schwartz and Bok, *op.cit.*, p.155, figs 174 and 175.
2 *Rotterdam*, no.17.
3 *Rotterdam*, no.20. The Mauritshuis picture was probably the first of two Saenredams sold together as lot 66: *A Church Scene with Figures amongst Trees* at Christie's, London, 4 February 1927, and sold to Skilleter. The other picture in this lot is now at the Rijksmuseum Twenthe, Enschede. This largely anonymous sale has been assumed to have included Coats's pictures but there seems no proof of this.

JAN STEEN

1625/6-79. Jan Havicksz. Steen was born in Leiden and was inscribed 'aged twenty' at the university there in November 1646. He may have trained with Nicolaus Knüpfer and Adriaen van Ostade, and with Jan van Goyen whose daughter Steen married in 1649. He lived and worked in The Hague, Delft, Warmond and Haarlem but seems to have returned to Leiden in 1670, and may later have kept an inn in the city before his death there. Particularly well known for his genre scenes, Steen also painted biblical, mythological and historical works, as well as portraits and some landscapes.

68 *A School for Boys and Girls*

Oil on canvas: 81.7 × 108.6 cm

PROVENANCE: G. Braamcamp by 1752; his sale, Amsterdam, 31 July 1771, lot 211, bought by J. Greenwood.[1] Marquis of Camden sale, Christie's, London, 12 June 1841, lot 70, bought by Seguier for Lord Francis Egerton, later 1st Earl of Ellesmere; thence by descent to the 5th Earl of Ellesmere, later 6th DUKE OF SUTHERLAND, by whom placed on loan at the National Gallery of Scotland in 1946; purchased by Private Treaty from the Ellesmere Trustees with the aid of the NHMF 1984 (no.2421).

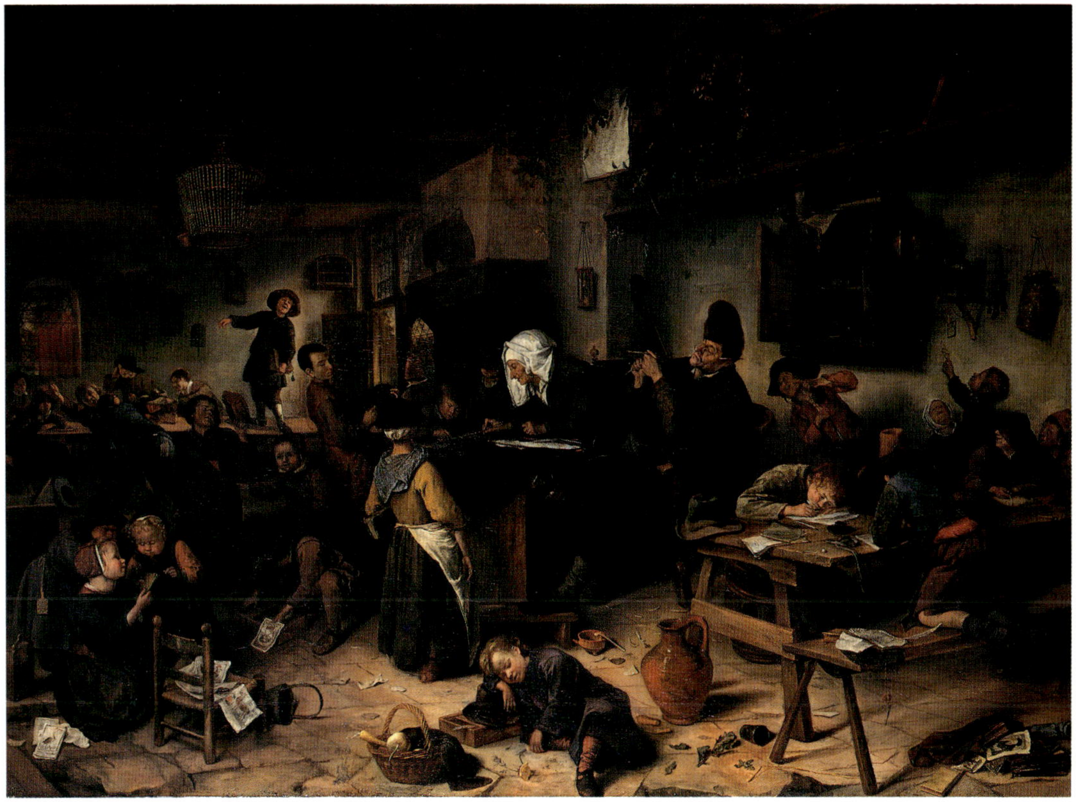

This is the largest and most elaborate of several schoolroom scenes by Steen and was painted *c.*1670. Adriaen Brouwer and his circle seem to have been the first to depict the theme of the unruly school.[2] Here classroom chaos is studiously ignored by the schoolmaster and his wife who make no attempt to regain order. Educational illustrations are strewn about the room while a print of a scholar, perhaps after Holbein's portrait of Erasmus of Rotterdam, is clearly discarded under the bench at the right. A small boy offers a pair of spectacles to an owl perched near a lamp, acting out a Dutch proverb: 'What use are glasses or light if the owl does not want to see?'.[3] (The owl was also recognised as a symbol of wisdom, the attribute of the goddess Athene.) It has been suggested that Steen loosely based the composition of this painting on a print of Raphael's *School of Athens*, a witty comparison whose irony Steen would have relished.[4] Such allusions in the work combine to warn of the evils of inattentiveness and of the rejection of study, so that Steen manages to teach a humourous but moral lesson by showing pupils learning nothing.

A School for Boys and Girls was seen in the Gallery at Bridgewater House in London in 1931 by Ellis Waterhouse who noted that the painting had recently been cleaned by Martin de Wild.[5]

EXHIBITED: *Manchester 1857*, no.935, lent by the Earl of Ellesmere; *Edinburgh 1945*, no.153; *RA 1952-3*, no.562; *Jan Steen*, The Mauritshuis, The Hague, 1958-9, no.52, pl.53.

LITERATURE: *Waagen*, vol.2, p.45; *Smith*, no.20 and supplement, no.10; *Bridgewater House Catalogue 1851*, no.153; *HdG*, no.287 (confused with the *Village School* in Dublin);[6] *Bridgewater House Catalogue 1926*, no.153; *Masters of Dutch Genre Painting*, pp.318-20, fig.3‡; *Haak*, p.430, fig.943; S. Schama, *The Embarrassment of Riches*, London, 1988, p.558, fig.288.

NATIONAL GALLERY OF SCOTLAND

1 C. Bille, *De tempel der kunst. Het kabinet van der Heer Braamcamp*, Amsterdam, 1961, vol.2, pp. 51, 118.

2 M. F. Durantini, 'The Child in Seventeenth Century Dutch Painting', *Studies in the Fine Arts. Iconography.* No. 7, Ann Arbor, 1983, pp.130-6.

3 'Wat baet er kaers en bril als den uyl niet sien will', approximately the equivalent of 'You can lead a horse to water but you cannot make him drink'.

4 G. Smith, 'Jan Steen and Raphael', *The Burlington Magazine*, March 1981, pp.159-60.

5 *Waterhouse Notebooks*, vol.6, p.112, 21 December 1931.

6 H. Potterton, *Dutch Seventeenth and Eighteenth Century Paintings in the National Gallery of Ireland*, Dublin, 1986, pp.145-8.

69 *The Fishmonger*

Oil on panel: 54 × 42.2 cm
Signed: *J Steen* (*JS* in monogram) on front edge of wheelbarrow to right
PROVENANCE: Perhaps purchased by the 3rd Duke of Bridgewater (1736-1803); recorded in the collection.of Earl Gower, probably by 1808 and certainly by 1813;[1] Private Collection, Scotland.

Steen painted many such 'Marketing Scenes' as Hofstede de Groot termed them. These included hawkers, pedlars and vendors and were particularly popular in the 1660s. Steen's ability to paint everyday scenes with gentle humour and keen observation is well demonstrated in this fine panel. The adults at the centre of the compositon, engrossed in the selling of fish, are cleverly offset by the children who are equally caught up in wonderment at the catch. It is possible that the subject conjured up the biblical story of 'The Feeding of the Five Thousand' in the minds of the devout. As well as serving as a symbol of the early Christian church, fish was also eaten as a form of religious observance.

The subject matter of this panel is similar to *A Woman at her Stall with Fish and Fruit*, by the artist Gabriel Metsu, which also appeared in the *Stafford Gallery Catalogue 1818*, vol.4, pl.38, no.73.

LITERATURE: Possibly *Stafford Gallery Catalogue 1808*, no.187 (as 'A Woman selling Fish'); *Stafford Gallery Catalogue 1818* , vol.3, pl. 17, no.133; *Smith*, no.177; *Bridgewater House Catalogue 1851*, no.191; *HdG*, no. 253; *Bridgewater House Catalogue 1926*, no.191.

PRIVATE COLLECTION, SCOTLAND

1 *Bridgewater House Catalogue 1851* and *1926*, where the entries are *not* marked with an asterisk meaning that the picture came into the collection during the lifetime of the 3rd Duke of Bridgewater. *The Itinerant Fishmonger*, as it had been called, may have been the picture listed as *A Woman Selling Fish* by Jan Steen in the *Stafford Gallery Catalogue 1808* and was certainly in the collection by 1813 as it was engraved with two other works on a plate noting publication in that year, published later in the *Stafford Gallery Catalogue 1818*. Hofstede de Groot's statement (*op. cit.*, p.76) that the picture was in the sale of W. A. Verbrugge at The Hague, 27 September 1831, is therefore incorrect.

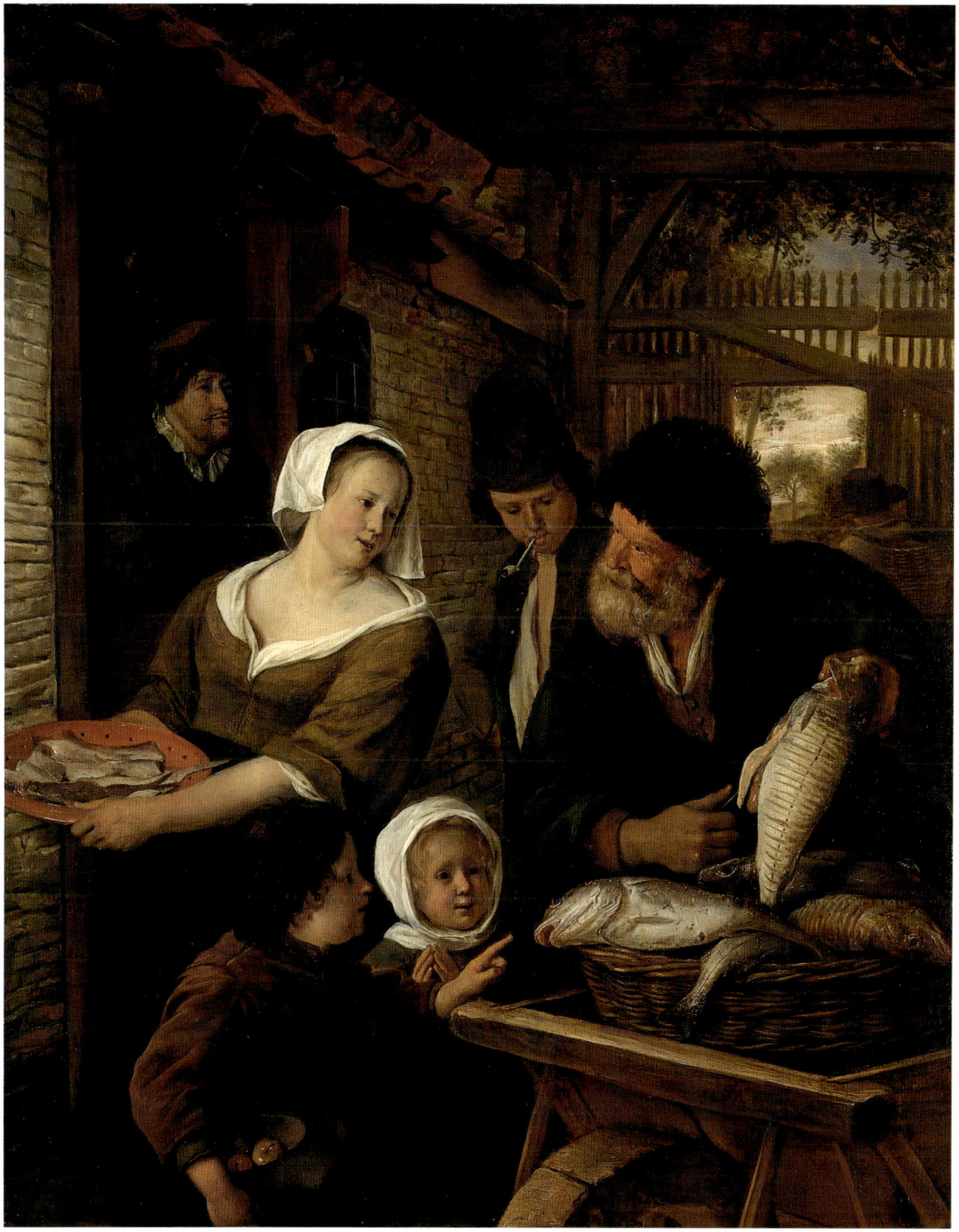

WILLEM VAN DE VELDE THE YOUNGER

1633-1707. Baptised in Leiden, Willem moved with his family to Amsterdam where his younger brother, Adriaen, was born. Both boys became artists, probably first trained by their father, though Willem is recorded as a pupil of the marine artist Simon de Vlieger. He lived and worked in Amsterdam from about 1652 until 1671 but, after the French invasion of 1672, decided to accompany his father to England. There both were employed by Charles II in 1674, Willem mainly executing paintings from his father's designs. Though they visited the Netherlands occasionally, they lived in England until their deaths, employed by the court where their paintings were much admired, copied and imitated.

70 *Fishing Boats in a Calm*

Oil on canvas: 41.9 × 56.2 cm
Signed and dated: *W. V. Velde 1658* on the spar at bottom left
PROVENANCE: SIR JAMES ERSKINE OF TORRIE by whom bequeathed in 1825 to the University of Edinburgh which received the picture in 1836; placed on loan to the Board of Manufactures, Edinburgh, first at the Royal Institution, then at the National Gallery of Scotland for its opening in 1859 until 1983, when returned to the University of Edinburgh.

Willem van de Velde painted such tranquil scenes mainly in his early career and his first such works date from *c.*1653. The stern of what appears to be a prince's yacht can be seen at the left with its elaborate carving and coat-of-arms.[1]

Such marines have long been collected by the Scots, whose own boats were often built by the Dutch.[2] There were certainly paintings by Van de Velde in the collection of the Duke of Hamilton by 10 July 1699 (nos 10 and 50) while on 5 October 1704 a 'small sea piece' was in the duchess's closet and a 'picture of a shipp in a tempest' (no.113) was hanging in the duke's closet at Holyrood House in Edinburgh.[3]

Sir James Erskine also included two more marine paintings as part of the Torrie bequest: Ludolf Backhuizen's *A Squall* which was exhibited at the Royal Institution in Edinburgh in 1819 (no.3) and an unidentified *Sea Piece.*[4] The manuscript inventory of the collection at Dunimarle includes another marine by 'Backhysen' which had 'belonged to Sir James's Collection'.[5]

EXHIBITED: *The Torrie Collection*, no.44, pl.10.

LITERATURE: *HdG*, no.190.

THE TORRIE COLLECTION
THE UNIVERSITY OF EDINBURGH

1 G. Keyes, *The Mirror of Nature. Dutch Marine Art of the Seventeenth Century*, Minneapolis Institute of Art, 1990 exhibition catalogue, no.35, p.163. The yacht was built for the Stateholder Frederick Henry but completed for his son and successor, William II, whose arms it showed.

2 T. C. Smout, 'Scottish-Dutch Contact', p.22.

3 *Waterhouse Notebooks*, transcriptions of Hamilton inventories in the Getty Archive, Santa Monica.

4 *The Torrie Collection*, nos 1 and 11.

5 Rev. Canon Harper, *Catalogue Raisonné of the Erskine of Torrie Institute, Dunimarle 1912*, unpublished manuscript, photocopy at the Royal Commission on Ancient and Historical Monuments of Scotland, Edinburgh, p.60.

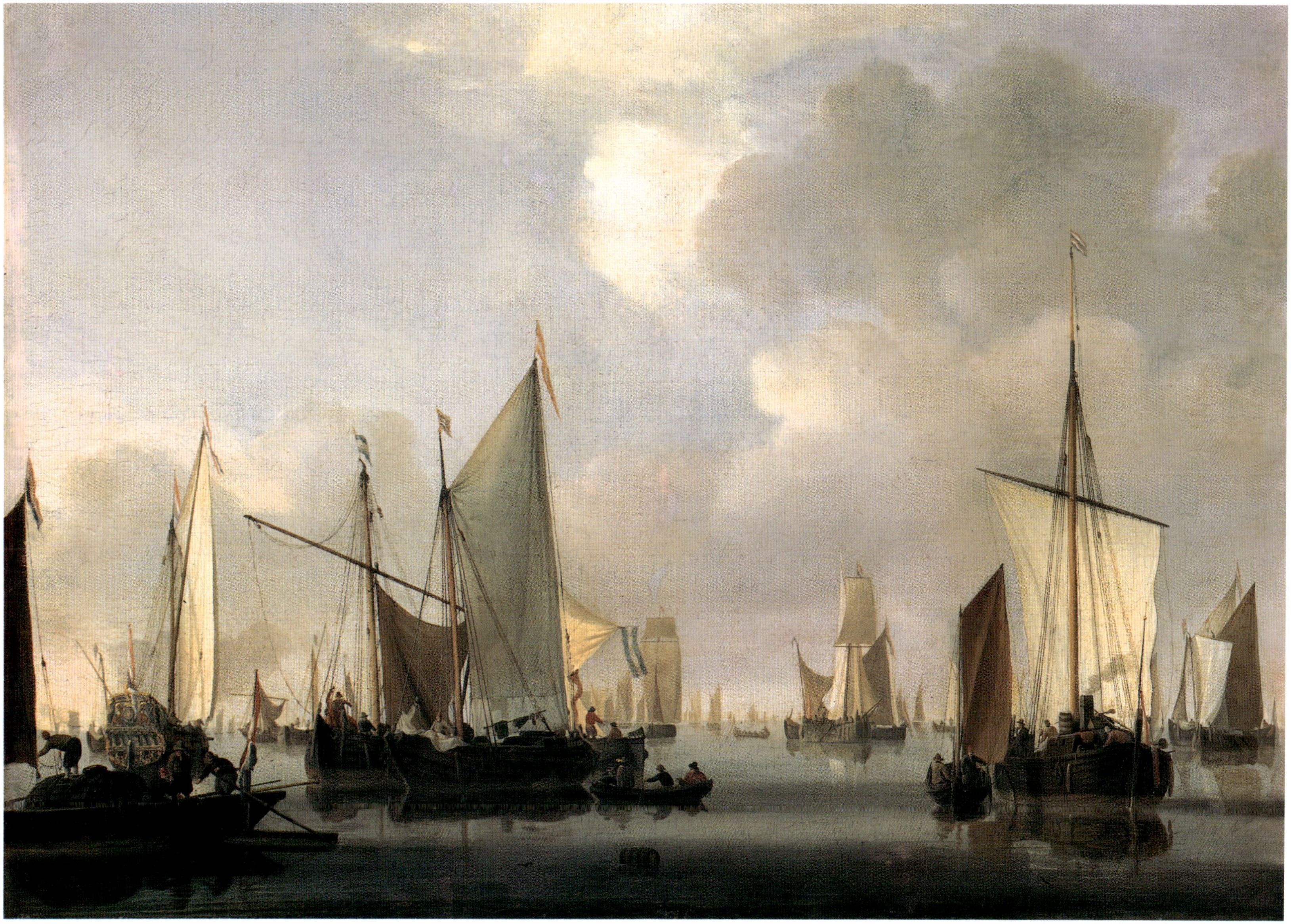

JAN VERMEER

1632-75. The son of Reynier Vos, or Vermeer, a silk weaver who may have dealt in paintings, Johannes (or Jan) Vermeer was baptised in Delft. (His family also seems to have been involved in counterfeiting.) Vermeer married in 1653, the year in which he entered the Delft guild of painters and acted as a document witness with Gerard ter Borch. He was an adviser on the authentication of paintings at The Hague in 1672 but, although he was an important guild member, he had financial problems, and his widow sought a declaration of bankruptcy the year after his death. It is not known who taught him, but Leonaert Bramer, who vouched for Vermeer's character at his betrothal, may have been an early master.

71 *Christ in the House of Martha and Mary*

Oil on canvas: 160 × 142 cm
Signed: *IV Meer* (*IVM* in monogram) on stool at bottom left

PROVENANCE: In the collection of a Bristol family by the 1880s; sold by a Bristol dealer with two Raeburns for £140 to Arthur Leslie Colley from whom bought by the dealers Forbes and PATERSON, London, in 1901; bought the same year by W. A. COATS; presented by his two sons in memory of their father to the National Gallery of Scotland in 1927 (no.1670).

The scene illustrates *Luke* 10, v.38-42 and the composition may be based on an engraving by G. van Velden after Otto van Veen of about 1597-8[1] while the arrangement of the figures may be influenced by a now lost *Magdalene Washing the Feet of Christ* by Leonaert Bramer.[2]

Cleaning of the painting in 1901 revealed a signature which was identified as that of Vermeer by N. Forbes Robertson[3] while, more recently, examination of the pigments used has shown that this is the only painting by Vermeer in which indigo is present but ultramarine is absent.[4] The picture is the largest and perhaps the first surviving work by Vermeer and certainly belongs to a small group of early works dating from *c.*1654-6, the *Diana Reposing* at The Mauritshuis, The Hague, and *The Procuress* (signed and dated 1656), at the Dresden Gemäldegalerie.[5]

Scarcely more than 30 paintings by Vermeer are now known and this is the only work to have come to Scotland (although ARTHUR KAY did claim to have persuaded the dealers Lawrie and Co. to offer *A Young Woman Standing at a Virginal* to the National Gallery, London).[6] A letter from W. A. Coats at Skelmorlie Castle dated 2 October 1903[7] notes that 'My large Vermeer of Delft was sold to an old lady by a dealer in 1884 for £10 and resold for £13 – Colley bought it from a dealer who bought it from its owner, a Bristol man called Abbot.[8] It was offered to his brother and himself one after the other by his mother's trustees but they all refused it, he himself saying "Take the beastly thing away!" Colley saw it in the dealer's shop and at once bought it, seeing it packed up and taking it away. There was a big sale that day in the same street and several London dealers were in this dealer's place the same day but too late'. Coats's decision to buy the picture is remarkable for, though Vermeer had become popular after his 're-discovery' by Thoré-Bürger in the 1860s, this was hardly a 'typical' work for a private collector to purchase. Coats's *Vertumnus and Pomona* by Cesar van Everdingen (now in the J. Paul Getty Museum, Malibu) is another large figure painting of a type rarely seen in Scotland. Such purchases by Coats indicate his refreshingly unorthodox taste in Dutch art.

LITERATURE: *HdG*, no.1; *The Catalogue of the Collection of Pictures of French Dutch British and Other Schools belonging to W. A. Coats*, 1904, pl. XXXVII; A. B. de Vries, *Jan Vermeer van Delft*, 2nd edn, London, 1948, p.80, pl.2; P.T.A. Swillens, *Johannes Vermeer: Painter of Delft 1632-1675*, 1950, pp.161-4, pl.34 (as Johan van der Meer); A. Blankert, *Vermeer of Delft*, Oxford, 1978, pp.13 and 155, no.1, pl.1; A. Blankert, J. M. Montias and G. Aillaud, *Vermeer*, Paris, 1986, no. 1, p.171, repr. pl.2.

NATIONAL GALLERY OF SCOTLAND

1 Blankert et al., *op. cit.*, p.79.
2 Repr. in *Bulletin des Musées Royaux*, Brussels, 1957, 3-4, p.163.
3 *The Morning Post*, 14 January 1927, p.9.
4 H. Kühn, 'A Study of the Pigments and the Grounds Used by Jan Vermeer', *National Gallery of Art Report and Studies in the History of Art*, vol.2, Washington DC, 1968, pp.168-9. It may be that this was for reasons of economy. The painting is very large and indigo was considerably cheaper than ultramarine.
5 A. Wheelock, in *Artibus et historiae*, no.14, VII, 1986, pp.71-89, adds to this group by attributing a painting of *St Praxedis* dated 1655 to Vermeer. (This is rejected by Blankert et al., *op. cit.*, p.163, note 5.)
6 A. Kay, *Treasure Trove in Art*, Edinburgh and London, 1939, p.53.
7 Letter amongst Coats family papers. I am most grateful to Frances Fowle for kindly providing me with this information.
8 It has not yet proved possible to trace this family.

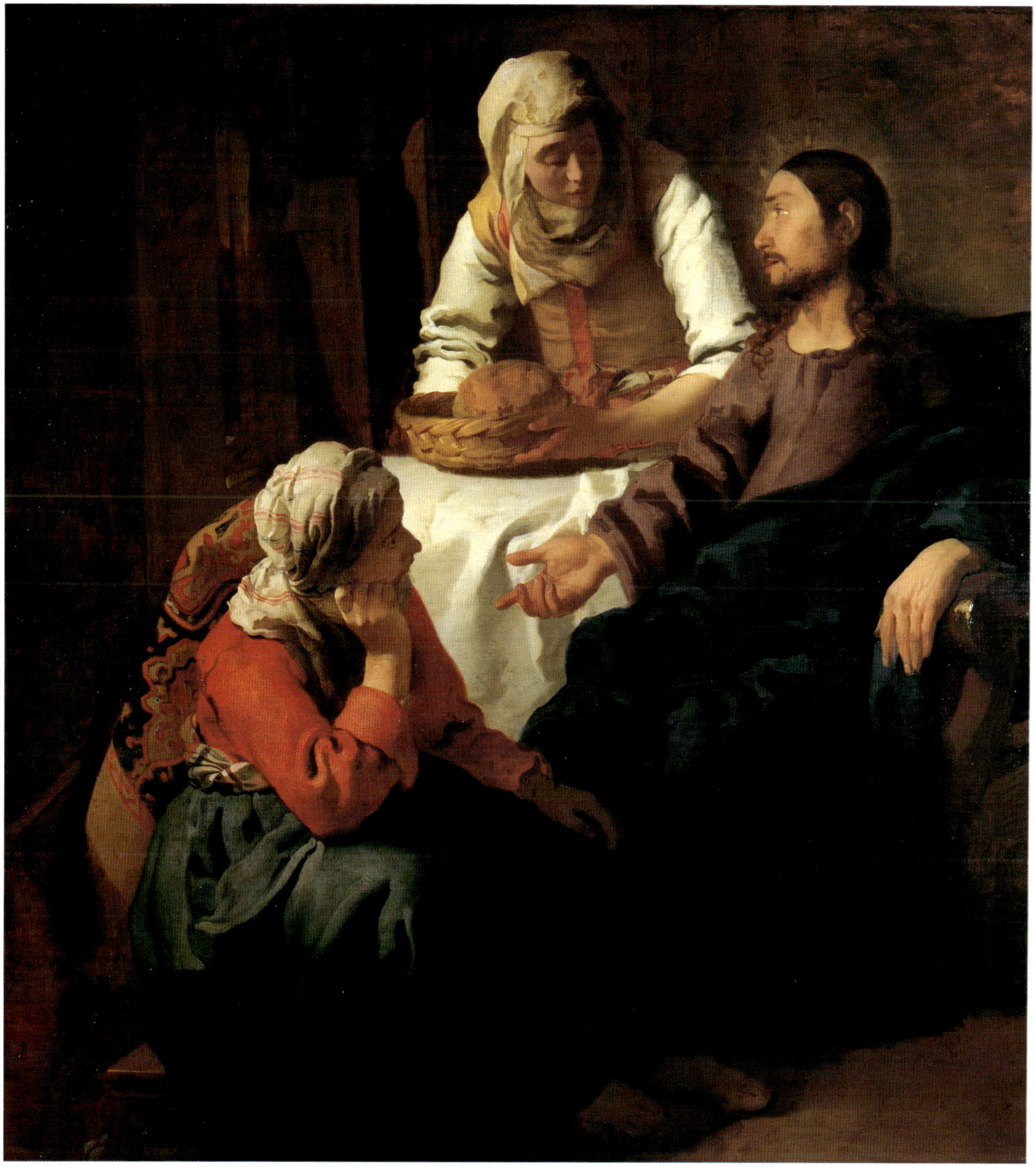

WILLEM VAN DER VLIET

c. 1584-1642. Born in Delft and a pupil of Miereveld, Van der Vliet was best known for his portraiture. Houbraken noted that he also painted history and genre scenes but these are now relatively scarce.

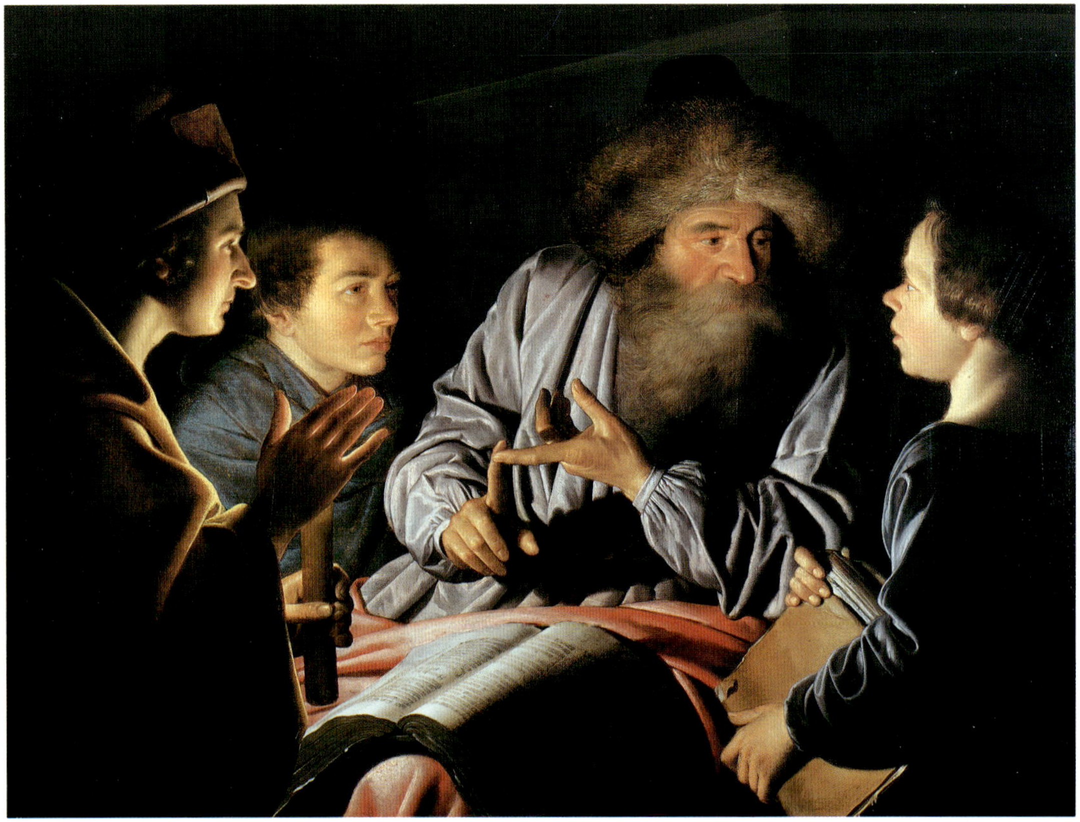

72 *Philosopher and Pupils*

Oil on panel: 85.09 × 113.03 cm
Signed and dated: *W. Van der Vliet fecit, 1626* at top right
PROVENANCE: William, 22nd Brodie of Brodie, *c.*1824, and by descent to Ninian, 25th Brodie of Brodie; made over to The National Trust for Scotland, 1980.

In an inventory made at Brodie Castle in May 1852 the painting appears as 'No. 15 Schoolmaster and Pupils, Ghivando della Notte' (assumed to be by Gerrit Honthorst) and hung in the drawing room. It was later tentatively attributed to Hendricksz. Volmarijn[1] but recent cleaning revealed the signature of Van der Vliet.[2]

Despite the rarity of works by Van der Vliet, there was another painting by him in Scotland. *The Steadfast Philosopher*, signed and dated 1627, was reputedly brought back by Adam Drummond, 9th Baron of Lennoch, on his return from studying at Leiden University.[3] The model for the philosopher in the Brodie picture is perhaps the same as that used for Van der Vliet's *Man Holding a Bag of Bones*, *The Steadfast Philosopher* and *A Teacher Instructing his Pupils*.[4]

EXHIBITED: *Manchester 1957*, no.137 (as Volmarijn); *Agnews*, no.34 (as Volmarijn); *Pride of Place - Treasures from the National Trust for Scotland*, The Burrell Collection, Glasgow, 1991, repr. p.4.

LITERATURE: L.J. Slatkes, review of B. Nicolson's *The International Caravaggesque Movement*, Oxford, 1979, in *Simiolus*, no.12, 1981-2, p.178; C. Wansink, 'Some History and Genre Paintings by Willem van der Vliet', *Mercury*, no.6, 1987, repr. p.4.

THE NATIONAL TRUST FOR SCOTLAND

BRODIE CASTLE

1 B. Nicolson, *The International Caravaggesque Movement*, Oxford, 1979, p.108.
2 Slatkes, *op. cit.*, had attributed the work to Van der Vliet prior to restoration.
3 Now Private Collection, New York. See Sotheby's sale, London, 9 March 1983, lot 69, repr. in colour. A letter in the *RKD* files suggests that it may have come into the collection somewhat later and notes a label in French on the back of the picture.
4 Wansink, *op. cit.*, figs 5, 7, 10.

JACOB JACOBSZ. DE WET

c.1640-97. Jacob Jacobsz. de Wet was the son of the Haarlem artist Jacob Willemsz. de Wet (c.1610-c.1671) who had been a student of Rembrandt in Amsterdam. Training under his more able father, Jacob emulated the style of his father's lighter mythological paintings and the work of the two has often been confused. He became Court Painter to Charles II and was brought to Scotland in 1673 by the architect Sir William Bruce, and was probably accompanied by the sculptor Jan van Santvoort. De Wet seems to have made various trips back and forth to Scotland, for, although he was recorded as a painter in Cologne in September 1677, he was certainly back in Edinburgh in February 1684. He returned to Haarlem in 1691, dying in Amsterdam on 11 November 1697.

73 *Mount Olympus*

Oil on canvas: 163.2 cm in diameter (circle slightly uneven)

PROVENANCE: Presumably commissioned for Kellie Castle in Fife by the 3rd EARL OF KELLIE, *c.*1675; thence by descent to Lady Janet Erskine, wife of Captain Wilmot of Portarlington, Ireland; their daughter Mrs Wilmot Chelwoode; John H. Lorimer; Dr Hew Lorimer; acquired with Kellie Castle by The National Trust for Scotland, 1970.[1]

This painting is a version of De Wet's *Apotheosis of Hercules* in Charles II's bedchamber in the Palace of Holyrood House. The subject is the same, though reduced in size and with fewer figures, showing Hercules with his club and lion skin being helped up by Mercury onto Jove's crowded cloud.[2] De Wet was commissioned to paint various allegories and mythological scenes at Holyrood and was then employed to paint 110 portraits of the Kings of Scotland in the Long Gallery there. He signed the contract for this on 26 February 1673, when he is described as 'In dwellar in the cannongate' as 'His majesties pictur drawer in Scotland'.[3] He was paid an annual salary of £120 for the pictures which had to be completed in two years. With little leniency but some justification, Hofstede de Groot pronounced them 'unbelievably bad fantasy portraits'.[4]

When the 3rd Earl of Kellie returned from his exile in the Netherlands to Fife in 1661, he was rewarded for his Royalist loyalty by being appointed Constable of Edinburgh Castle. He would therefore certainly have been involved with the organisation of the refurbishment of Holyrood for Charles II, and must have seen De Wet's work there, and perhaps also at William Bruce's own house at Balcaskie (about a mile from Kellie) which was decorated by De Wet in 1674. As well as working for Bruce, De Wet had also signed a contract with Sir Patrick Lyon, 1st Earl of Strathmore, in January 1688 to paint 34 *Scenes from the Life of Christ and the Twelve Apostles* for the chapel at Glamis Castle (which are still *in situ*), as well as ceiling decorations there. He was employed in 1685 by the Duke of Hamilton who is recorded as owning some of his work,[5] and further Scottish collectors of his painting included the Earl of Seafield, the Makgills of Cousland and the Clerks of Penicuik.[6] The varying quality of the paintings ascribed to the artist in Scotland suggests that De Wet had some sort of workshop here which may well have continued to produce works after his return to the Netherlands.

When the title of Earl of Mar and Kellie was granted (see Collectors Index), the family abandoned Kellie Castle and most valuable items were removed, probably to Alloa House. *Mount Olympus* was taken to Ireland on the marriage of Lady Janet Erskine to Captain Wilmot of Woodbrook House, Portarlington, then in Queen's County. Professor James Allan Lorimer, who restored Kellie in the 1870s, knew of its existence and, through the agency of the painter John H. Lorimer (who lived at Kellie from 1916 until his death in 1936), it was brought back from Ireland although it is not known if it was given or purchased .The painting was reinstated into the ceiling of the Vine Room, once the bedroom of the countess, where it is framed by its original seventeenth-century plasterwork.

THE NATIONAL TRUST FOR SCOTLAND
KELLIE CASTLE

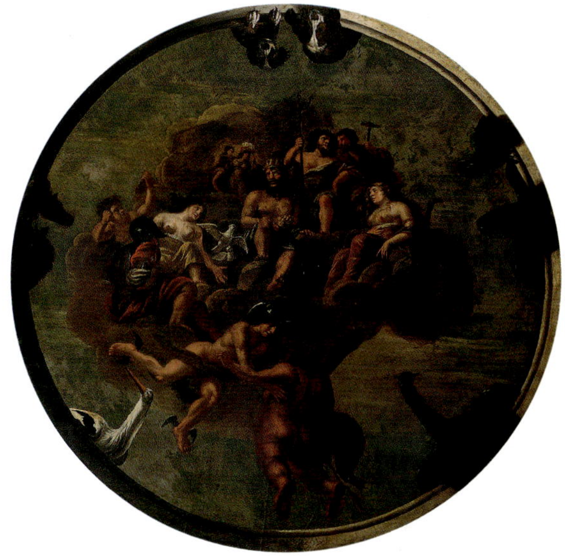

1 I am most grateful to Dr Stefanie Blackden at Kellie Castle for providing me with much of the above information.

2 On 13 February 1949 Waterhouse remarked of the Holyrood pictures: ' The De Wet's one needn't at the moment bother about - tho' the overmantles, esp. Finding of Moses, and Hercules, are rather good' (*Waterhouse Notebooks*, vol.29, p.56).

3 *Holloway*, p.149. With bibliography including P. Haverkorn van Rijkswijk, 'De Schilder Jacob de Wet in Schotland', *Oud Holland*, 1899 (Nendeln reprint, 1976), p.191 and J.G. Dunbar, 'Lowlanders in the Highlands; Dutch craftsmen in Restoration Scotland', *Country Life*, 8 August 1974, pp.372-6.

4 *HdG 1893* , p. 135, 'ongeloofelijk slechte fantasieportretten'.

5 *Waterhouse Notebooks*, transcriptions of the Hamilton inventories in the Getty Archive, Santa Monica. De Wet was commissioned to work at Chelsea Palace on 12 August 1695. *The Battle of Bothwell Bridge* by 'De Wett' (no.10) and a round work valued at £5 by De Witt (no.255) appear in an inventory of 7 June 1759.

6 *Holloway*, pp.24-7. The Earl of Seafield's *Still-Life with Skull*, signed 'De Witt pinxit' (repr. p.26, no.16) is De Wet's only known still-life, while the Penicuik picture of *The Highland Wedding* (repr. p.27, no.17) provides an extraordinary link between the Dutch and Scottish artistic tradition and looks forward to the compositions of Alexander Carse and David Allan.

JAN WIJNANTS

c. 1631/2-84. Born in Haarlem, Jan was the son of an art dealer of the same name (though the spelling Wynants occurs on some works). Jan remained in Haarlem until 1659, but moved to Amsterdam by the spring of 1660. Often in debt, Wijnants is described as 'a painter and a publican' in April 1672 and his wife is recorded as cleaning pictures in 1680. He specialised in painting landscapes (usually dune scenes near Haarlem), but the figures are often by other artists such as Adriaen van de Velde, who was perhaps his pupil, or Johannes Lingelbach. Wijnants's later work shows the influence of Jacob van Ruisdael and Philips Wouvermans.

74 *A Wooded Landscape with a River*

Oil on canvas: 94 × 116 cm
Signed: *J wÿnants F* bottom left
PROVENANCE: J. Wi(l?)tsen sale, Amsterdam, 16 August 1790, lot 85, bought by Yver; Marquis de Montcalm sale, London, 4 May 1849, lot 113, bought by Farrer; SIR HUGH HUME CAMPBELL BY 1856;[1] C. J. Nieuwenhuys sale, Christie's, London, 17 June 1886, lot 118 (bought in), C. J. Nieuwenhuys sale, Christie's, London, 25 June 1887, lot 99, to Sir Henry Page Turner Barron by whom bequeathed in 1901 to the National Gallery of Ireland (no.508).

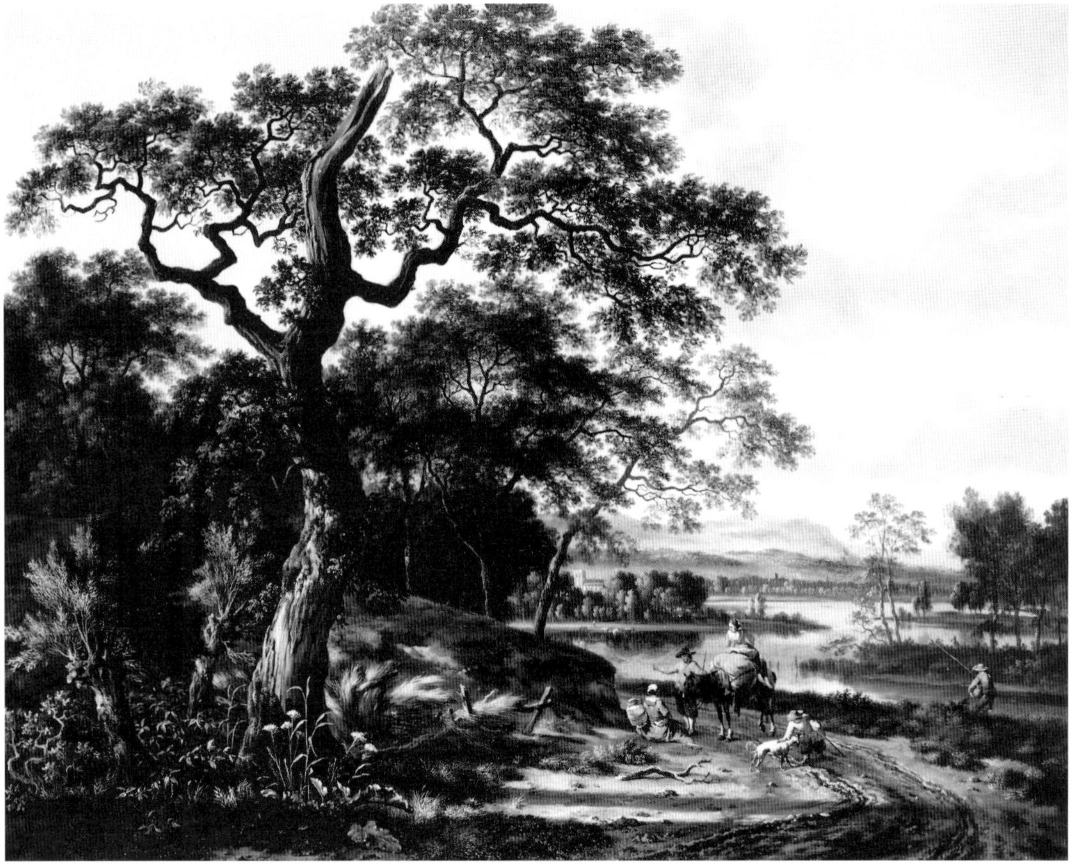

Hofstede de Groot believed the figures to be painted by Lingelbach, likening them to those found in a landscape in the Royal Collection of 1669.[2] Paintings of 1659, 1667 and 1668 anticipated this composition.[3] The form of signature on the Dublin painting relates to that used on a document signed by Wijnants in 1679, indicating that this is a late work. Waagen called it 'a fine specimen of the master in his free manner' when he saw the painting at Marchmont House in Berwickshire, where Sir Hugh Hume Campbell also owned Wijnants's, *Landscape with Woman Driving Sheep through a Ruined Gateway.* This was sold at Christie's, London, on 16 June 1894, lot 52, and is now in the National Gallery, London (no.2532).

EXHIBITED: British Institution, London, 1856, no.12 (as in collection of Sir Hugh Hume Campbell); *Masters of Dutch Landscape*, no.118.‡

LITERATURE: *Waagen*, vol.4, p.442; *HdG*, no.458; H. Potterton, *Dutch Seventeenth and Eighteenth Century Paintings in the National Gallery of Ireland*, Dublin, 1986, no. 508.

NATIONAL GALLERY OF IRELAND
DUBLIN

1 Potterton, *op. cit.*, note 1, states that *Redford* (vol.2, p.349) wrote that the painting was in a sale of Campbell's pictures in 1872, but no such sale is listed, nor is a sale of the previous year on 8 June 1871, an alternative suggested by Hofstede de Groot (*HdG*, no.458.). It does not appear in the sale of 16 June 1894.

2 *White*, no.264.

3 *Masters of Dutch Landscape*, p.526; the paintings are in Dresden Gemäldegalerie, no.1941A; Budapest, no.507; and the Louvre, Paris, no.1967.

DOMENICUS VAN WIJNEN (CALLED ASCANIUS)

1661-c.1700. Born in Amsterdam in 1661, Van Wijnen studied in The Hague with a history painter Willem Doudyns. Van Wijnen was then in Rome from 1680-90, becoming a member of the Schildersbent, a group of Netherlandish artists, by whom he was nicknamed Ascanius (the son of Aeneas in Virgil's Aeneid*). Three of his pictures were engraved in a book about the Schildersbent written by C. de Bruyn, who visited Rome in 1675, but little else is known about Van Wijnen's work or life and his paintings are scarce.*

75 *The Temptation of St Anthony*

Oil on canvas: 72 × 72 cm
Signed: *DVW AEscanius* (*DVW* in monogram) on stone steps at left
PROVENANCE: J. M. Birckenstock sale, Artaria, Vienna, March 1811, lot 121 (a now lost pendant, lot 120, was sold separately); bought by S. Sharp by whom exhibited in 1868; ARTHUR KAY, by whom presented to the National Gallery of Ireland, 1901 (no.527).

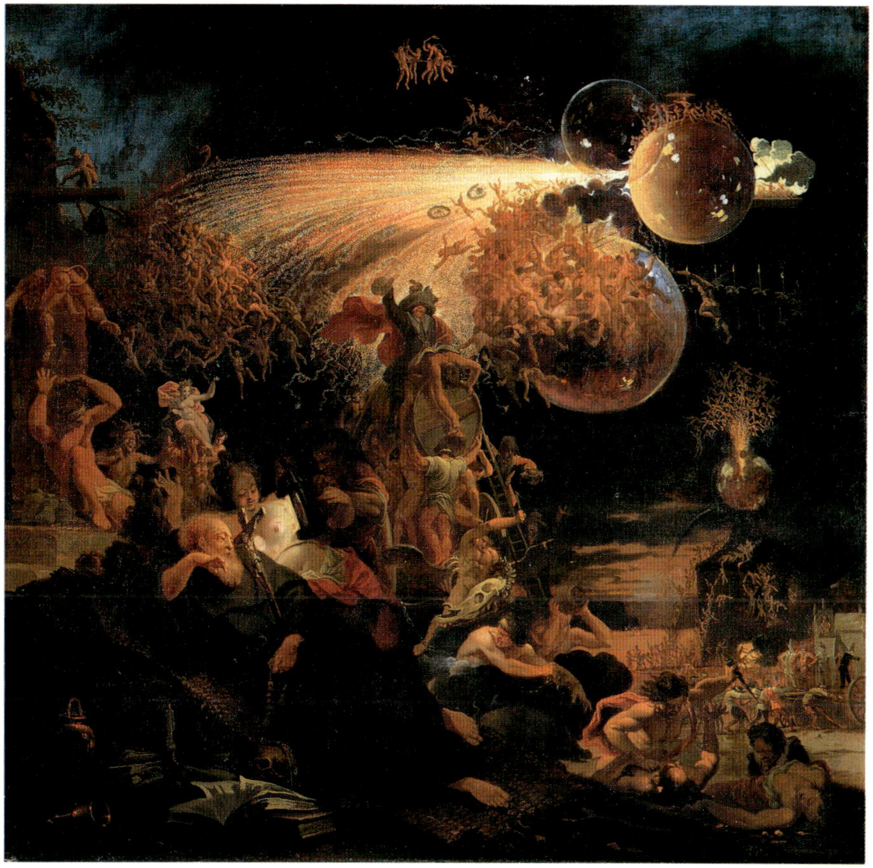

In a letter of 1 May 1901 to Sir Walter Armstrong, then Director of the National Gallery of Ireland, Kay wrote: ' In reply to yours of the 12th I have found no definite idea as to what is going on among the "subordinate adventurers and adventuresses" probably the cardinal sins, murder, rape etc. It is really a most amusing and interesting picture; and I believe unique as the priesthood destroyed all the works of Ascanius they could lay hands on. He was a sort of 17th century Wiertz, only better'.[1]

Kay was not quite correct in believing the picture to be unique for there is another painting of the *Temptation of St Anthony* by Van Wijnen (owned by Alexander Kemény, Bojnice, Czechoslovakia), although there are some variations in composition.

He was, however, right in his identification of 'sins' in the painting. St Anthony was a hermit who withdrew into the desert to escape the seven deadly sins who here surround him. Lust is represented by a young woman with a lantern, Avarice as an old man with his moneybags, Envy the old woman with snake-like locks and Pride the naked woman held up by men. Gluttony is shown by the drinkers in the middle of the picture, Anger by those fighting on the right while Sloth is the pig by them. The subject of St Anthony was popular with the artists who specialised in fantastical scenes, such as Hieronymous Bosch and his followers, who seem to have influenced Van Wijnen in both theme and style.

EXHIBITED: *National Exhibition of Works of Art*, Leeds, 1868, no.835; *Bosch, Goya et la Fantastique*, Galerie des Beaux-Arts, Bordeaux, 1957, no.168; *Gods Saints and Heroes. Dutch Paintings in the Age of Rembrandt*, National Gallery of Art, Washington DC, Detroit Institute of Arts, Rijksmuseum, Amsterdam, no.88; *Dutch Painting of the Golden Age from the National Gallery of Ireland*, Smithsonian Institution travelling exhibition, 1987, no.37.

LITERATURE: J. W. Salomonson, 'Domenicus van Wijnen', *Niederdeutsche Beiträge zur Kunstgeschichte*, Berlin, 1985, no.24, repr. p.135; H. Potterton, *Dutch Seventeenth and Eighteenth Century Paintings in the National Gallery of Ireland*, Dublin, 1986, no. 527, pp.185-7, fig. 187.‡

NATIONAL GALLERY OF IRELAND
DUBLIN

1 In picture file at National Gallery of Ireland.

1566-1638. Born in Utrecht, Wtewael trained until the age of 18 with his father who was a glass painter. He studied for two years with Utrecht masters, then travelled in France and Italy, where he was influenced by Mannerist painting. He was living in Utrecht again by 1592, helping to establish an artists' guild there in 1611, but seems to have stopped painting after about 1630 to become a wealthy flax merchant in his native city.

76 *The Adoration of the Shepherds*

Oil on canvas: 75 × 97 cm
Signed: *IOACHIM WTE WAEL FE* at right , on the base of the column
PROVENANCE: LORD KINNAIRD; Kinnaird sale, Christie's, London, 21 June 1946, lot 7, bought by Kauffman; Grete Ring, London, 1947; purchased in 1948 with the France fund for the Ashmolean Museum, Oxford (no.A770).

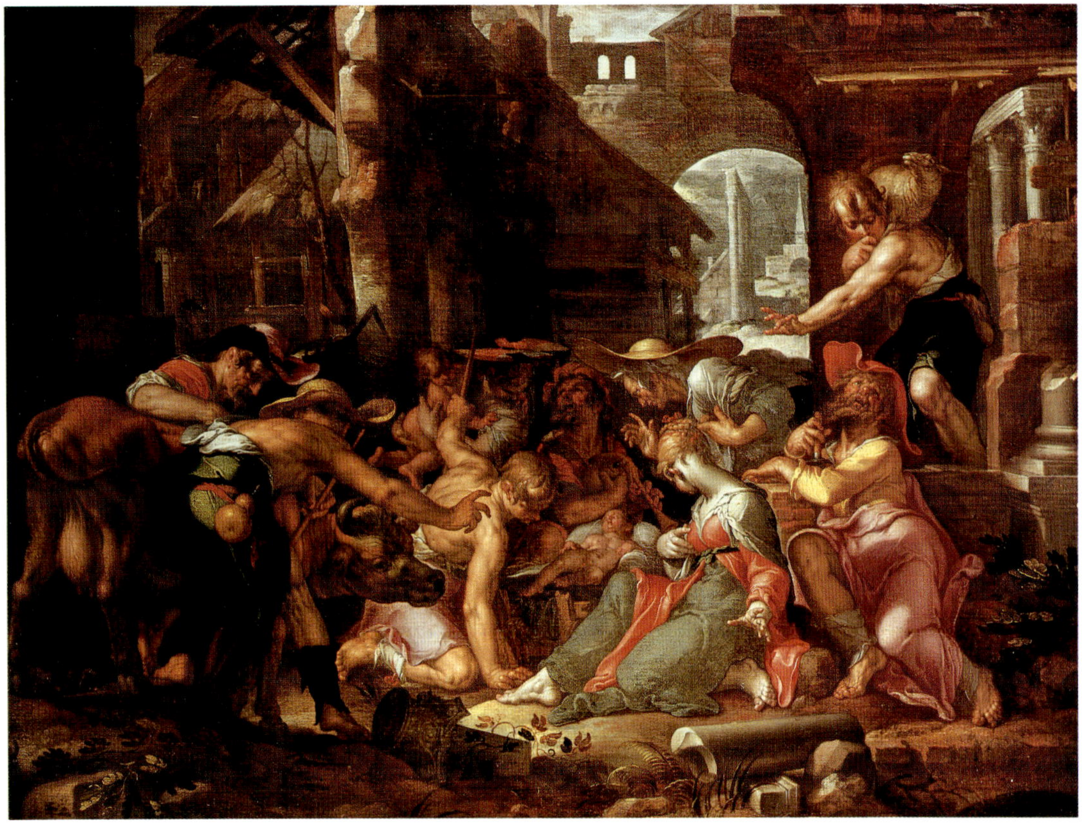

Wtewael depicted this subject many times over a period of years and nine paintings of varying size are known, ranging from a small picture on copper, a larger work on panel to a canvas of more than two metres square.[1] These are reworkings rather than straightforward copies of the composition and give an insight into Wtewael's stylistic development. The earliest *Adoration of the Shepherds* is probably that dated 1598 in the Centraal Museum, Utrecht, while the Oxford picture has been dated to *c.*1606 on the basis of stylistic similarity to a dated *Annunciation to the Shepherds* in New York.[2] Though the poses are complicated, they do not have the frenetic exaggeration of Wtewael's early work at its most Mannerist.

A related design to the Oxford picture in pen, ink and wash (see fig.61) was bequeathed to the National Gallery of Scotland by David Laing.[3] The Pushkin Museum, Moscow, has a painted copy of the composition (no.1870).

At the Kinnaird sale, *The Adoration of the Shepherds* was considered to be the work of Abraham Bloemart, who painted *St John Preaching* (Catalogue no.3), one of Lord Kinnaird's syndicate purchases from the Orléans collection.

EXHIBITED: *RA 1952-3*, no.33; *Dutch Pictures in Oxford*, Ashmolean Museum, Oxford, 1975, no.10; *Netherlandish Mannerism in British Collections*, Entwhistle Gallery, London, 1990, no.10.

LITERATURE: A. W. Lowenthal, *Joachim Wtewael and Dutch Mannerism*, Doornspijk, 1986, no.A-42.

THE VISITORS OF THE ASHMOLEAN MUSEUM, OXFORD

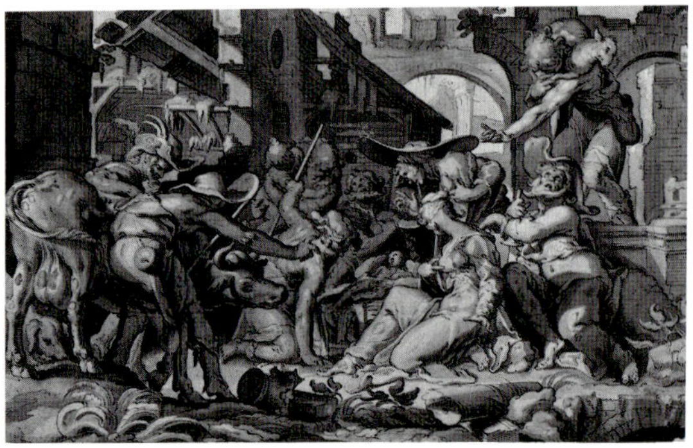

fig.61

1 *Netherlandish Mannerism in British Collections, op. cit.*, p.72.
2 Lowenthal, *op. cit.*, p.116, comparison with A41, p.115.
3 *Andrews*, vol. 1, p.105, vol 2, no.RSA453, fig.722.

Index of Collectors

SMALL CAPITALS are used in the text to indicate cross references within this index.

ROBERT ALEXANDER

Robert Alexander (d.1775) was a banker in Edinburgh and friend of Alexander Runciman. He owned a considerable number of paintings, most notably Rembrandt's *Judas Repentant, Returning the Pieces of Silver* (*Rembrandt Corpus*, vol.1, no.A15), now in an English private collection. Alexander's taste encompassed the Italian, French and English schools, marble busts and statues, as well as Dutch and Flemish paintings. The sale of most of the collection 'brought from his late residence in Edinburgh', at Christie's, London, 31 March and 1 April 1775, included landscapes by Keirincx, Cuyp, Salomon Ruysdael and a Ruisdael *Waterfall*, as well as paintings by Van der Neer, Wouvermans, Weenix, Schalcken, Ostade, Bakhuizen, Hondecoeter and Beerstraten. As well as Rembrandt's *Judas* (1 April, lot 66) and *Rembrandt's Mother* (31 March, lot 46), there was *The Raising of Lazarus* by Cornelis van Haarlem (1 April, lot 62), an artist whose works are rarely found in Scotland. The total of 144 lots (sold over two days) realised £1592 15s. Further sales took place at Christie's, London, on 6-7 March 1776 and 25-26 February 1788.

EARL OF ANCRAM

See EARLS AND MARQUESSES OF LOTHIAN

THE DUKES OF ARGYLL

The Netherlands were a refuge for the Argylls. The 9th Earl (1629-88) was hounded by Charles II and escaped across the North Sea in about 1681. He spent most of his exile in Friesland but went to Rotterdam on learning of the death of Charles II. His eldest son, Archibald Campbell (b.*c*.1653), became 10th Earl in 1689, after the execution of his father the previous year and was later 1st Duke of Argyll. He was certainly in Holland in 1688, while his younger brother, Colonel Charles Campbell (b.*c*.1655) was in Amsterdam on 17 April 1685, attending a meeting of Scottish refugees there. It may be that he had accompanied his father, the 9th Earl, for the years of his exile in Holland. (See Catalogue nos 33 and 34.)

The 1st Duke's eldest son, John Campbell (1680-1743), became 2nd Duke of Argyll and 1st Duke of Greenwich but was succeeded by his brother Archibald (1682-1761), who at the age of about 17 was sent to study law at the University of Utrecht. The 2nd and 3rd Dukes were brought up at Ham House (now owned by the National Trust), the Richmond seat of their grandmother, the Duchess of Lauderdale, which boasted one of the first and finest cabinets of Dutch seventeenth-century paintings in Britain.

The Argyll collection was clearly considered of sufficient importance to be included amongst those few whose pictures were to be engraved by Gambarini in 1631 (*The Walpole Society*, vol.XXIV [Vertue IV], p.19). It is known that the 2nd Duke kept paintings at Adderbury, the house he rebuilt in Oxfordshire (inherited by his daughter, the Countess of Dalkeith, mother of the 3rd Duke of Buccleuch). He may have owned Jacob van Ruisdael's *A Wooded Landscape with a Waterfall*, now in the collection of the DUKE OF BUCCLEUCH at Bowhill. This may be the 'good Ruysdael' listed at Adderbury in 1768 by Walpole. It is worth noting that the 2nd Duke's nephew was John, 3rd EARL OF BUTE, one of the most important eighteenth-century collectors of Dutch art in Britain.

Many of the Dutch pictures were dispersed after the death of John Campbell, 4th Duke of Argyll (1693-1770). One sale at Langford's, Covent Garden, London, 19-23 March 1771, listed 11 works by Rubens as well as three pictures ascribed to Rembrandt : 'An old man's head' (lot 57), 'a portrait' (lot 58), and 'A lady's head highly finished' (lot 59). The largest Argyll sale of 140 paintings was held at Phillips, London, 25-6 May 1798. Lot 104 was Rembrandt's *Bearded Man in a Cap* (National Gallery, London, no.190), which was in the Argyll collection before 1781, while lot 136 was perhaps Lievens's *Landscape with Tobias and the Angel* (National Gallery, London, no.72). The sale also included works by Dou, Hals, Ostade, Poelenburgh, Van Goyen and Van der Neer. When Farington visited Inverary Castle on 13 October 1801, he did not mention any Dutch pictures.

Scots Peerage, vol.1, pp.318-93; *The Walpole Society*, vol.XVI, p.66; *Waterhouse Notebooks*, vol.31, pp.59-69; N. Grant, *The Campbells of Argyll*, London, 1975; G. Harvey Johnston, *The Heraldry of the Campbells*, Argyll, 1977; *Holloway*, pp.51-67; J. Cornforth and G. Hughes-Hartman, *Inverary Castle*, guidebook, Derby, 1986; *Holmes*, p.314.

MRS ROBERT BAILLIE-HAMILTON

Née Mary Gavin Pringle, the Hon. Mrs Robert Baillie-Hamilton married Major Robert Baillie-Hamilton in 1861. He was the son of the 10th Earl of Haddington, George Baillie (1802-70), who had assumed the name Baillie-Hamilton on succeeding to the title of 10th Earl of Haddington at Mellerstain, Berwickshire. (For Mellerstain, see *Holmes*, p.318.) Mrs Baillie-Hamilton was the niece of JOHN, 5TH MARQUESS OF BREADALBANE, of Taymouth Castle, whose pictures she inherited in 1878 on the death of her mother, Lady Elizabeth Maitland Pringle, sister of the Marquess. Mrs Baillie-Hamilton lived at Langton, Duns in the Borders (also part of her mother's estate) and died on 12 April 1912. An inventory of her pictures is in the Getty Archive, Santa Monica (Waterhouse collection), and included many Dutch paintings. A Wouverman now in Minneapolis Museum of Art was owned by her husband Robert, who exhibited it at the *RA* in 1881 (no.73), along with five other paintings, including a Teniers (no.99). Twelve paintings from their collection were also exhibited at the *RSA* in 1883, including two Cuyps (nos 403 and 412), two Jacob van Ruisdaels (nos 329 and 418), a Van der Neer (no.355), a Bakhuizen (no.205), a Van Huysum (no.308) and the Minneapolis Wouvermans (no.334). A large sale of the Baillie-Hamiltons' pictures (cited as 'from the Marquis of Breadalbane's collection') was held at Christie's, London, on 5 June 1886. The couple had no children and the estate passed to Mrs Baillie-Hamilton's sister, Magdalen Breadalbane, Lady Harvey. Her heir, Lieut. Col. the Hon. Thomas George Breadalbane Morgan-Grenville-Gavin sold some of the pictures at Christie's, London, 27 March 1925. The title page of the sale catalogue notes that 'The majority of these Pictures were the property of the 2nd Marquess of Breadalbane at Taymouth Castle; a number of them had been brought there in 1860 from the Marquess of Breadalbane's appartments at Holyrood Palace'.

WILLIAM BEATTIE

A Glasgow collector, Beattie lent a Rembrandt *Self-portrait* to the Glasgow International Exhibition of 1901 as well as four Italian paintings, and furniture, glass and bronzes to decorate the East and West exhibition rooms (exhibition catalogue, pp.106-7). He also owned Nicolaes Maes's *Portrait of a Lady*, now at the Columbia Museum, which was sold by the executors of William Beattie's estate at Christie's, London, 18 July 1924, lot 80, as well as a *Portrait of a Lady* by Van der Helst, lot 79.

JOHN BELL

A reference (kindly provided by F. Fowle) to John Bell (d.1881) of North Park, Glasgow, is in *The Bailie* of January 1881. He was on the General Committee of the fund-raising Fine Art Loan Exhibition at the Corporation Galleries in Glasgow in 1878, along with Thomas Coats, JOHN GRAHAM-GILBERT, ROBERT NAPIER and WILLIAM MCEWAN. Bell owned about 800 paintings which included works from the Italian and Spanish schools as well as Dutch and Flemish paintings. Some of his collection was sold after his death by Morrison, Dick, McCulloch of 98 Sauchiehall Street, Glasgow, 1-5 February 1881. His collection included a Van Goyen now in the Metropolitan Museum of Art (no.65.181.11), and the Philips Koninck in the Ashmolean Museum, Oxford (no.A719). The Koninck had formerly been in the collection of ROBERT NAPIER. A much larger sale of the remainder of his collection was held at Christie's, London, 24-5 June 1881, and the proceeds were bequeathed, as the catalogue stated, 'for the express purpose of Dedication to the corporation of Glasgow for a Public Museum'. Lot 357 was *Anna and the Blind Tobit* (then thought to be by Rembrandt but since given to Dou) now at the National Gallery, London (no.4189). 127 of the 190 paintings sold were attributed to the Dutch and Flemish schools. The total sum raised at the sale was £9735 14s 6d, though only 16 lots in Bell's sale were deemed worthy of listing in *The Athenaeum,* 2 July 1881, p.22.

(John Bell is not to be confused with John Charles Bell of Broughty Ferry, Dundee, who collected contemporary Scottish pictures which were sold at Dowells, Edinburgh, 17 March 1877.)

JOHN, 5TH MARQUESS OF BREADALBANE

The title of Earl of Brea d'Albane and Holland (Scottish Peerage) was created in 1677 for John Campbell of Glenorchy (*c*.1635-1716).

Born in Dundee and educated at Eton, John, 5th Marquess (1796-1862), lived in Edinburgh and Taymouth Castle, Tayside. He was the MP for Okehampton from 1820-6 and for Perthshire from 1832-4. He was also President of the Society of Antiquaries of Scotland and was made Lord Rector of the University of Glasgow in 1841. His marriage to Eliza, sister of the 10th Earl of Haddington, was childless and, on his death in Switzerland in 1862, his collection was left to his sister Elizabeth Maitland Pringle who died in 1878. (See, too, the entry for MRS ROBERT BAILLIE-HAMILTON.)

Scots Peerage, vol.2, p.211.

WILLIAM BRODIE OF BRODIE

William, 22nd Laird of Brodie (1799-1873), purchased many of the Dutch paintings which hang in Brodie Castle in Forres, Morayshire. These may have been intended to complement the extravagant refurbishment of the castle which was undertaken in the 1820s by William Burn. Brodie Castle has been in the care of the National Trust for Scotland since 1980. Unfortunately, despite extensive family archives, information on the pictures is scarce. The numerous Dutch works, including a *Portrait of Dr Talpen* by Ferdinand Bol, dated 1669, portraits by J. G. Cuyp and landscapes by Poelenburgh are listed by C. Wright, *Birmingham 1989*, p.287.

C. Hartley, *Brodie Castle,* National Trust for Scotland guidebook, Edinburgh, 1986 (with a detailed bibliography, p.24).

THE DUKES OF BUCCLEUCH AND QUEENSBERRY

The Countess of Dalkeith, mother of the 3rd Duke of Buccleuch, was the daughter of the 2nd DUKE OF ARGYLL and inherited his house at Adderbury in Oxfordshire, as well as the paintings kept there. These probably included Jacob van Ruisdael's *A Wooded Landscape with a Waterfall* (fig.5), which now hangs in the hall at Bowhill. However, the majority of Dutch pictures in the Buccleuch collection were inherited from George Brudenell (1712-90). He was the 4th Duke of Cardigan, and was married to Mary Montagu, only daughter of the 2nd Duke of Montagu. Brudenell was later created 3rd Duke of Montagu (also called 1st Duke of the second creation of the title). He owned Montagu House in London and Boughton House in Northamptonshire. The Duke's son, John Montagu, Lord Brudenell, had died in 1770 and so at the Duke's death in 1790 his collection and property passed to his remaining child, Elizabeth, who in 1767 had married Henry, 3rd Duke of Buccleuch (1746-1812). He had also succeeded to the title of 5th Duke of Queensberry in 1810 (when, at the death of the 4th Duke of Queensberry, the title reverted under limitation to the male heirs of Lady Jane Douglas). The large Montagu estates (with Boughton House) therefore formally passed to the Buccleuch family after the Duchess Elizabeth's death in 1827 (though some sources give her date of death as 1824). The Buccleuch houses in Scotland benefited from the Montagu paintings which were hung in Drumlanrig Castle near Dumfries, Bowhill near Selkirk and Dalkeith Palace near Edinburgh. Pictures were also kept at Montagu House in London. The most important Dutch school paintings inherited from the Montagu collection were Rembrandt's *Flora,* his *Self-portrait* (Catalogue nos 49 and 53) and his *An Old Woman Reading* (fig.58), which now hangs at the foot of the main stairs at Drumlanrig Castle. The many other works included smaller cabinet paintings such as Van der Neer's *Wooded River Landscape by Moonlight* (Catalogue no.38), Ostade's *Peasants Playing Cards* (Catalogue no.41), Pieter de Hooch's *Woman Knitting* (*Sutton,* no.103, sold 1965), and Pynacker's *Landscape with Mules* (*Reflections of Italy : Adam Pynacker,* exhibition, R. L. Feigen and Co., London, 1991, no.3).

Rembrandt's *Flora* and Ruisdael's *A Wooded Landscape with a Waterfall* were seen by Waagen in the Gallery at Dalkeith Palace by 1857, together with Wouverman's *Stag Hunt,* and a Wijnants' *Landscape* (these four being the only works of the Dutch school that Waagen mentioned there). Hofstede de Groot listed rather more works including a Dou, a Van Mieris, and an Adriaen van de Velde (it is quite possible that these pictures were already at Dalkeith during Waagen's visit but he did not see fit to remark upon them). A catalogue of pictures at Dalkeith written in 1890, however, noted portraits by Mierevelt and Wissing (p.28), a '*Landscape with Seated Figure in the Foreground* by Ruysdael', and a Vroom (p.36), as well as Rembrandt's *Flora* (p.45), another 'Ruysdael' and the Wijnants (p.48), Wouverman's *Stag Hunt* (p.49), a Van de Velde (p.56), a Molijn (p.57) and a Poelenburgh (p.72). The Duke's dressing room was filled with Dutch pictures by Hondecoeter, Van Mieris, Jan Weenix and Frans Hals (pp.82-3) and elsewhere throughout the house were many more paintings which, though unnamed, have titles which suggest the work of Dutch or Flemish artists.

Waagen 1857, pp.435-7; W. Fraser, *The Scotts of Buccleuch*, 2 vols, Edinburgh, 1878; A. F. Steuart, *Catalogue of the Pictures at Dalkeith House*, Dalkeith, 1890; *HdG 1893*, pp.213-14; Duke of Buccleuch, *Catalogue of Pictures in Montagu House* (private publication, giving Montagu House inventory numbers), 1898; *Scots Peerage*, vol.2, pp.225-49; *Waterhouse Notebooks,* vol.13, p.85, vol.27, p.47, and vol.30, pp.70 ff.; *Holmes,* Boughton p.46, Bowhill p.302, Dalkeith p.307, Drumlanrig pp.307-8; *Boughton House*, guidebook (unattributed), St Ives, 1981; *Bowhill*, guidebook (unattributed), Derby, 1981; *Drumlanrig Castle*, guidebook (unattributed), Selkirk, 1989; B. Fredericksen, 'Leonardo and Mantegna in the Buccleuch collection', *The Burlington Magazine*, February 1991, pp.116-18.

SIR WILLIAM BURRELL

Sir William Burrell (1861-1958) was an astute Glasgow shipping magnate whose canny business practice was reflected in his approach to collecting. In 1902 Sir Robert Lorimer described the Burrell method as 'the nimblest I've ever struck. He sells his fleet when there is the periodical boom and then puts his money into 3% stock and lies back until things are absolutely in the gutter – soup kitchen times – everyone starving for a job. He then goes like a roaring lion. Orders a dozen large steamers in a week, gets them built at rock bottom prices, less than half what they'd have cost him last year. Then by the time they're delivered to him things have begun to improve a little bit and there he is with a tip top fleet of brand new steamers and, owing to the cheap rate he's had them built at, ready to carry cheaper than anybody' (Mallalieu, *op. cit.*, p.75). Burrell's collection was bought and sold along the same lines; his final tally (recorded by him in 28 notebooks with columns for date, price, provenance and comments) was 8000 objects, but a much larger number passed through the collection. He was praised by Lord Clark as 'not simply an amasser' but 'an aesthete'. As with other collectors of the period, such as W. A. COATS or ARTHUR KAY, Burrell's purchases were wide ranging. He exhibited not only paintings but also furniture, bronzes, glass and silver at the Glasgow International Exhibition of 1901, to which he was the greatest contributor, lending over 200 items. Sir Robert Lorimer acted as his adviser and travelling companion for a time (although their relationship was to prove stormy). The search for new additions to the collection was thorough for, as Lorimer remarked, 'You never saw such a chap as that Burrell. He's been all over the place on business since we were in Holland', describing how they went to a sale of the contents of a Dutch castle in July 1899 and soon afterwards visited the Low Countries again, adding to their purchases at Dordrecht, Gouda, Meppel, Utrecht, Delft and Brussels (Marks, *op. cit.*, p.92). It is likely that Burrell's affairs in shipping also put him into contact with a number of businessmen in the Netherlands who may well have owned Dutch paintings themselves.

Burrell's interest in seventeenth-century Dutch pictures was only a small part of his passion for acquisition, but it was an interest that started early. Two portraits of Dutch children dated 1622 and 1635 (Burrell Collection, Glasgow), acquired in Holland in the 1890s, are amongst the first recorded paintings that Burrell bought. His most important purchase was undoubtably Rembrandt's *A Portrait of the Artist as a Burgher* (Catalogue no.47), while other acquisitions were of varying quality. He bought a *Portrait of a Man* by Frans Hals on 5 April 1948 for £14,500, the most he paid for anything in all his years of collecting. Burrell's files also record some of his sources. An *Interior of the Oudekerk in Delft* (no.654), ascribed to Hendrick van Vliet, was bought in March 1902 for £90 from the famous Glasgow dealer, Alexander Reid (whose portrait by Van Gogh is owned by Glasgow Museums and Art Galleries), and in the same year another Van Vliet (no.305) of the same subject was acquired. (W. Liedtke, *Architectural Painting in Delft*, Groningen, 1982, appendix II, nos 225 and 49.) Burrell showed a liking for Dutch still-lifes, owning pictures by Jan de Heem (no.36), Willem Kalf (no.64), and Abraham van Beyeren (no.37). He also acquired Jacob Duck's *Cavalier Drinking* in 1916 (for £262 10s) and a Joos van Craesbeek at a dealers' fair nearly 30 years later in 1945. The remainder of his Dutch collection of paintings consisted mainly of portraits, including *Jacob Trip* by Maes (no.25, formerly with David Croal Thomson, from whom he bought a number of paintings), a Van Ravesteyn and an Eeckhout (nos 657 and 656). Despite the uneven quality of his Dutch pictures, it is important to remember that they were not made in isolation. Burrell bought Dutch seventeenth-century stained glass, clocks and furniture, textiles, as well as other pieces of decorative art. He also collected a fine and wide range of Hague school pictures to follow the earlier paintings and to complement his large number of pictures from the Barbizon school and contemporary Scottish masters.

R. Marks, *Burrell. Portrait of a Collector*, 2nd edn, Glasgow, 1988 (with bibliography); *Birmingham 1989*, p.279; H. Mallalieu, 'The Junior Burrell', *Country Life*, 11 January 1990, pp.74-6; picture files in the Burrell Collection, Glasgow.

THE EARLS & MARQUESSES OF BUTE

John, 3rd Earl of Bute (1713-91), was born in Edinburgh and brought up on the Isle of Bute, though he spent most of his life at the Court of George III in London, where he became Prime Minister, a post from which he resigned in 1763. He was a Trustee of the British Museum in 1765 and President of the Society of Antiquaries of Scotland in 1780. His son, John, Lord Mountstuart (1744-1814) succeeded him, becoming 4th Earl and 1st Marquess of Bute. He followed his father's example in collecting, both men being advised in their purchases by Captain William Baillie (1723-1810). Cuyp's *Landscape with Rider and Peasants* (Catalogue no.16), was already in the collection by 1764, and the first manuscript catalogue of the collection was written in about 1799. Although not the first, it was arguably the greatest collection of seventeenth-century Dutch paintings in Britain and influenced the taste of other great collectors of the late eighteenth and early nineteenth century, such as the Prince Regent, the 1st Earl of Ellesmere and the 3rd and 4th Marquesses of Hertford. The Dutch and Flemish paintings were much praised by Waagen, who stated that 'Of all the collections formed in England before the first French Revolution, it is the most important in works of this class; so that for productions of many of the first masters it may vie even with the finest collections formed since that Revolution – such as those of Sir Robert Peel, Lord Ashburton, and the Marquis of Westminster; nay, it contains fine works of several good masters of whom there are no specimens at all in those collections'. The collection had previously been reorganised in 1822 when it was catalogued, the same year in which a large number of pictures were sold at Christie's, London, on 7-8 June. The Christie's catalogue, comprising 173 lots (a total of 201 paintings), notes that 'although the principal Chef d'Oeuvres which give such celebrity to the Bute collection are not included in this assemblage, the Connoisseurs will nevertheless be gratified by finding in it a great Variety of Gallery and Cabinet Specimens by the most distinguished Masters ... and in the purest State of Preservation'.

The Bute pictures were hung at Luton Hoo in Bedfordshire, the house designed and built for Lord Bute by Robert Adam on an estate purchased in 1763. However, the house was badly damaged by a large fire in 1843 and sold the following year. Most of the collection was later exhibited in turn at Bethnal Green Museum in London in 1882-3, in the Corporation Galleries (now the McLellan Galleries) in Glasgow in 1884 and at Manchester in 1885. The catalogues of these exhibitions show the great range and number of paintings in the Bute collection, for despite putting 201 pictures up for sale in 1822, there were still 294 paintings from the collection available for exhibition at Bethnal Green in 1882-3.

Although the Bute collection was originally bought for Luton Hoo, Scotland considered offering to house the paintings as early as 1845, two years after Luton Hoo was burnt. A letter from Patrick Shaw of February 1845, in the archives of the Royal Scottish Academy, suggested that the President 'waited on him [the Marquess] personally on the occasion of his reaching Edinburgh in May ... This might prevent any interim disposition of the pictures and probably save his Lordship some expense in preparing a gallery at Bute which I understand was some time ago his intention'. Minutes of the Academy for 30 May 1845 record how 'some conversation took place on the propriety of a deputation of the Academy waiting upon the Marquess of Bute in reference to requesting the loan of the Looten Collection of Pictures, in case of their proceeding to build their new galleries. The Depute President gave it as his opinion that in the present state of indecision as to the building it was premature to wait for this purpose upon his Grace'. Only a couple of years later the Royal Institution and the Board of Manufactures (later to become the National Gallery of Scotland) made a similar proposal. In 1847, they applied to exhibit pictures from the Bute estate in the Royal Institution Galleries during the minority of the new Marquess (G. Harvey, *Notes on the Early History of the Royal Scottish Academy*, 2nd edn, Edinburgh, 1873, p.115). However, the offer was refused and the Bute collection was eventually moved to the family homes in Scotland. A number of the Dutch and Flemish pictures were later exhibited at the National Gallery of Scotland in 1949 and Saenredam's *The Interior of St Bavo's Church, called the 'Grote Kerk', at Haarlem* (Catalogue no.66), bought by the 4th Marquess of Bute in 1934, was acquired by the National Gallery of Scotland in 1982.

Waagen, vol.3, pp.474-85; Christie's, London, 7-8 June 1822 (sale of Italian, French, Flemish and Dutch paintings from Luton Hoo); 1822 catalogue of Luton Hoo collection (copy made in 1949 by E. K. Waterhouse in archive of National Gallery of Scotland); 'The Marquis of Bute's Pictures at Bethnal Green', anonymous review, *The Athenaeum*, 30 December 1882, pp.904-5; 'The Marquis of Bute's Pictures at Bethnal Green', anonymous review, *The Athenaeum*, 6 January 1883, pp.23-4; *Bethnal Green 1883*; *Richter*; *Glasgow 1884*; *Scots Peerage*, vol.2, pp.285-312; *Waterhouse Notebooks*, vol.14, pp.45-8, vol.30, pp.57-66; *Edinburgh 1949*; *DNB* entry for John Stuart, 3rd Earl of Bute; *Holmes*, Luton Hoo p.170, Mount Stuart p.320; M. Hall, 'Luton Hoo, Bedfordshire', *Country Life*, 23 January 1992, pp.50-3.

SIR HUGH HUME CAMPBELL

Sir Hugh Purves Hume Campbell (1812-94), 7th Baronet, of Marchmont House, Berwickshire, and (in 1877) 18 Hill Street, Berkeley Square, London, was MP for Berwickshire. His portrait was painted by Sir John Watson Gordon and was engraved by Edward Burton in 1861. Waagen mentions Campbell's 'choice selection of Dutch masters' (acquired from 1850 onwards), which included Cuyp's *Baptism of the*

Eunuch, now at Anglesey Abbey (National Trust), Ruisdael's *Forest Scene* at the National Gallery of Art, Washington DC, and Wijnants's *Wooded Landscape* in the National Gallery of Ireland. Campbell exhibited works from his collection at the British Institution in 1855, 1857, 1866 and at the *RA* in 1877. After his death, his paintings were sold at Christie's, London, 16 June 1894. Many were purchased by George Salting who bequeathed them to the National Gallery, London, in 1910, including a Maes (no.2581), a Wijnants (no.2532) and a Steen (no.2559). De Hooch's *Kolf Players,* bought by WILLIAM MCEWAN and now at Polesden Lacey, was also in Sir Hugh's collection.

(The household accounts of Sir Hugh's ancestor, Hugh Campbell, covering the years 1737 to 1746, are in the Victoria and Albert Museum.)

Waagen 1857, pp.441-3; M. Warrender, *Marchmont and the Humes of Polwarth,* Edinburgh, 1894 (dedicated to Sir Hugh).

SIR ARCHIBALD CAMPBELL

Sir Archibald Campbell (1769-1846/8), of Succoth at Garscube, was listed as present (but unharmed) when the floor collapsed at LORD CLERK OF ELDIN's sale of pictures in Edinburgh in 1833. A keen collector of paintings, Sir Archibald owned a number of Dutch pictures including *The Liberation of St Peter,* now given to Abraham Bloemart and his studio in the Cincinnati Art Museum, which was on loan to Glasgow Art Gallery *c.*1950-73 (this picture apparently had a stretcher label with the words 'Gomm coll/ No.16 MARQUESS OF LOTHIAN, Newbattle, Dalkeith', *Dutch, Flemish and German Paintings in the Cincinnati Art Museum,*1987, no.3, p.18, note 6.). The picture was with Sir George Ilay Campbell by 1868 and went by descent to Sir Ilay M. Campbell (creators of the gardens at Crarae in Argyll) by 1947. Flinck's *Sleeping Cupid* of 1655 (*Sumowski,* vol.2, no.651) was also in this collection before its sale at Christie's, London, on 2 December 1977, lot 24. Cuyp's *Horsemen Crossing a Ford* (*HdG,* no.597) was in the collection, as well as a Pynacker, *Shepherd and Lady Driving Cattle* (*HdG,* no.146, *Harwood,* no.D 53).

Waagen, vol.3, p.294; *Waterhouse Notebooks,* vol.22, pp.97-108, 16 July 1937; sales of *Old Master drawings from the property of Sir Ilay Campbell,* 26-7 March 1974, and *Old Master Paintings,* 3 May 1974, were held at Christie's, London.

THE CLERKS OF PENICUIK

John Clerk (1611-74), whose family were originally from Kilhuntly in Badenoch, was the first laird of Penicuik (near Edinburgh). He acted as a factor in Paris, shipping goods from Europe to Scotland, particularly for the then EARL OF LOTHIAN. It is known that he had contacts all over the Netherlands and it seems that his collection at Penicuik was largely a product of his entrepreneurial dealings from the 1640s. The extraordinary wealth of family archives (now at the Scottish National Record Office) enables a fairly detailed picture of these transactions. There are transcripts of inventories of pictures at 'Newbiging This First day off Januar 1665' (GD18/1788) which included the 'pictur off 2 Mort heads with a scroll of paper and some dutch wreating on it with some Books done on cloth and batert on wood in a rudish cullort wooden Frame. Wery well done -40 lib Scots originall-Be Rembrant van vyn'. John Clerk of Penicuik can therefore lay claim to having imported the first Rembrandt to Scotland, if his attribution is trustworthy. There was also a 'werie Curious Large perspective on wood in a Blak ebone Frame-with some little Figures on it wery weel done Be poelenburgh ... weell worth 30 lib sterlin' and a 'young philosopher leaning on a glob poynting & counting with his Fingers' valued at '36 lib. Scots', a sea piece by Vroom, and a painting of two mice by 'Elie Vooncq'. A transcript (GD 18/4653) shows what Clerk was importing from the Continent to sell in Scotland three years later. It contains a list 'of the most famous painters' who 'hath lived in Europe these many years bygon', and is an 'extractst off the Original catalogue sent to Scotland in december 1668' of 'Most Curious rare pictures', including a 'poelembourgh', a 'jacob pynai', and a 'Jean van Goyen', as well as works by Abraham Bloemart, Cornelis van Haarlem and Lucas van Leyden. Pictures were by no means Clerk's sole merchandise and the lists also describe a delightful miscellany including combs and mousetraps. John Clerk's son (1649-1722) was created Sir John, a baronet of Nova Scotia, in 1679. He studied in Paris, visiting much of France and the Netherlands. His son, Sir John, 3rd Baronet (1676-1755), travelled still more extensively. He was a student at the age of 19 at Leiden University and studied with Herman Boerhave (Smout, 'Scottish-Dutch Contact', p.27). In 1695 he sat for a portrait drawing to Willem van Mieris (fig.4), still in the family collection. Family portraits were commissioned from the Dutch artist Jacob de Wet and the Clerks also owned De Wet's *Highland Wedding* (Catalogue no.73, note 6). These are first listed in the collection in 1724 but were presumably painted before 1691 when De Wet returned to the Netherlands. Other papers at the Scottish Record Office list the collection in 1676 (ExGD18/2567), 1727 (GF/2107), 1739 (GD18/4666), 1752 (GD18/2337) and 1873 (GD18/176011). The family lent pictures to the *Edinburgh 1883* exhibition, amongst which were Reinier Zeeman's *View of Amsterdam,* no.256, and Hondecoeter's *Cocks Fighting,* no.374. Waterhouse noted in 1949 that two Rembrandts (*HdG,* nos 169a and 397) had been sold to L. Douglas in about 1909 (vol.29, p.59).

J. M. Gray, *Notes on the Art Treasures at Penicuik House, Midlothian* (private publication), Edinburgh, 1889; *Waterhouse Notebooks,* vol.29, pp.58-63, vol.31, pp.33-5; I. S. Hodkinson, 'Varied Taste in a Scottish Collection', *Country Life,* 29 August 1968, pp.492-4; I. G. Brown, *The Clerks of Penicuik : Portraits of Taste and Talent,* Edinburgh, 1987 (with useful short bibliography); *Holmes,* p.321.

JOHN, LORD CLERK OF ELDIN

Lord Clerk of Eldin (1757-1832) was a descendant of the CLERKS OF PENICUIK and was one of the most famous advocates in Scotland, as well as owning one of the most important collections of Dutch and Flemish paintings in the country. As a founding director of the Royal Institution in Edinburgh, he exhibited numerous Dutch paintings there in 1819 at the first exhibition of 'Ancient Masters' (nos 12, 13, 16, 23, 31, 48 and 56), as well as lending five Dutch paintings the following year (nos 24, 27, 29, 38 and 84). Lord Eldin encouraged young artists to avail themselves of his collection and in *A Memoir of the late Andrew Geddes Esq. A. R. A.* by Mrs Geddes, London, 1844, pp.7-9, it is described how Lord Clerk lent the young painter Geddes drawings and paintings by the 'Old Masters' to copy and learn by.

A drawing by Cornelis Beelt from the collection of DAVID LAING and now in the National Gallery of Scotland (D 1705) was purchased from the late Lord Eldin at his sale at Picardy Place, Edinburgh, 14-29 March 1833. The catalogue of this sale was illustrated with engravings and gives a good idea of the extent of his collection. This sale, incidentally, drew such crowds that when a fine Teniers was put up on the easel ('View of an interior with Boors regaling ... painted in his best style; both the figures and details highly finished- soft yet spirited') half of the floor caved in, taking many with it and causing the publication of an anonymous pamphlet, *A concise and accurate account of the Accident that occurred at the sale of the late Lord Eldin's Pictures on Saturday 16th March ... by a sufferer,* Edinburgh, 1833. Amongst those listed as escaping 'with slight injury or altogether unhurt' were SIR ARCHIBALD CAMPBELL, DAVID LAING, FRANCIS GRANT and a Mr Ewing, 'from Glasgow, nephew of Mr Ewing of Melville Street' (perhaps WILLIAM EUING). It is thought that a number of the pictures were destroyed by the debris.

W. A. COATS

William Allan Coats (1853-1926) was the third generation of the Coats family to make money from the manufacture of Coats' sewing thread. William himself was an acknowledged expert in the use of dye. The company, J. and P. Coats of Paisley, later became Coats Patons PLC, now registered in Glasgow. A letter from a manager there in 1984 (in Gallery files) quotes company records about William Allan Coats: 'In his leisure he either cultivated his artistic tastes, being noted as a connoisseur of paintings, or put to sea in one of his yachts'. Until William, there had been no real tradition of collecting pictures in the family but his father, Thomas, who ran the Ferguslie Thread Works in Paisley with his brother Peter, was a knowledgeable and enthusiastic collector of Scottish coins. William, however, developed a taste largely for 'Old Master' Dutch paintings, as well as Barbizon and Hague school pictures and contemporary Scottish art, particularly works by Joseph Crawhall. Many French nineteenth-century works were purchased from Alexander Reid in Glasgow (Glasgow Museums and Galleries). Coats was reputedly his best client and also a friend of SIR WILLIAM BURRELL. Old Master paintings were bought from fellow Scots, Forbes and Paterson at 5 Old Bond Street, London, or from Paterson's shop in 33 Renfield Street in Glasgow. (It was WILLIAM PATERSON who later catalogued, valued and sold much of Coats's collection.) This combination of interests reflects the pattern of purchasing in Glasgow and, to a certain extent, Scotland as a whole, at the end of the nineteenth century. Coats seems to have formed most of his collection in the 1890s and he stopped working in 1901. The catalogue of his pictures which was published in 1904 contains the highlights of his collection (although it is not comprehensive), but he probably did not buy much after this date.

Coats owned at least four pictures by Saenredam (Catalogue no.67), a *Young Man in a Plumed Hat* by Frans Hals (now discredited, in the Edsel Ford Collection, Detroit, *Slive,* vol.3, p.140, no.D31) as well as Cesar van Everdingen's *Vertumnus and Pomona,* now in the Getty Museum, Malibu. (This latter painting cannot, therefore, have been in Paris in 1911 or 1914 as listed in its provenance, as it was already in the Coats collection by 1904 where it remained until 1927.) He also owned Vermeer's *Christ in the House of Martha and Mary* (Catalogue no.71) and Salomon Koninck's *Old Woman Weighing Gold* (*Sumowski*, vol.3, no.1110) which hung at his home, Skelmorlie Castle, Dalskairth, in Dumfries and Galloway. His sons sold many of the pictures after his death, Thomas living at Leverholme, Nitshill, Renfrewshire.

Catalogue of the Collection of Pictures of the French, Dutch, British and Other Schools, Belonging to W. A. Coats, published by W. B. Paterson, Glasgow, 1904; *Catalogue of Pictures and drawings being the entire collection of the late W. A. Coats, Esqre. Exhibited at the Galleries of the Royal Society of British Artists, Suffolk Street, London,* published by W. B. Paterson, London, January 1927; *Waterhouse Notebooks,* 17 January 1927, p.61; sale of some pictures from the Coats' collection at Christie's, London, 4 February 1927; catalogue of sale of Coats's pictures, Christie's, London, 10 June 1927; Thomas H. and Major J. A. Coats sale at Christie's, London, 12 April 1935; *Pictures for Scotland,* p.85; *Holmes,* p.323; R. Marks, *Burrell : Portrait of a Collector,* 2nd edn, Glasgow, 1988, pp.65-6.

THE CRANSTOUNS OF COREHOUSE

Corehouse near the Falls of Clyde was built by Edward Blore from 1824-7 and was restored by Scotland's Historic Buildings in 1984. Waagen did not visit the house although he notes that a Veronese hung there. The Royal Institute of British Architects, London, possesses Blore's original drawings for layout of the house, which show that certain items of furniture (such as a large Dutch cabinet) were included from the start as part of the brief. It seems that this attention to the detail of how the house would look when complete and furnished was of great importance to the architect, and the large still-life then believed to be painted by Jan de Heem (Catalogue no.35) was almost certainly acquired with the intention of enlivening the dining room (where it is listed in a manuscript inventory of the collection of 1 November 1850 as '1 large Fruit piece with name of the painter de Heem the elder'). The collection came from various sources, some paintings inherited from Edmunstone ancestors and others from George Cranstoun, Senator of the College of Justice and scholar of Greek, at whose Edinburgh house in Charlotte Square friends such as Sir Walter Scott would gather for literary salon evenings. A portrait by Mytens of John, 2nd Lord Cranstoun, and a *Child and a Goat* (believed to show the 4th Lord Cranstoun as a boy) by Abraham Hondius were acquired by Colonel Charles Cranstoun from the ennobled branch of the family which became extinct on the death of the 11th Lord Cranstoun in 1869, and from whose daughter the pictures were purchased.

Waagen, vol.3, p.312; *Irving,* p.78; *Scots Peerage,* vol.2, pp.585-602.

THE EARLS OF CRAWFORD AND BALCARRES

George, 22nd Earl of Crawford died without issue in 1808 and the title reverted to the descendants of the 1st Earl, being inherited by Alexander Lindsay, Earl of Balcarres, who was the direct heir of John Lindsay of Balcarres, second son of David, 9th Earl of Crawford. Alexander Lindsay (1752-1825) became the 23rd Earl of Crawford and Lord Lindsay (though he was still called Earl of Balcarres). He was a Representative Peer for Scotland and the Civil Governor of Jersey and then Jamaica. After returning to Britain in 1801, he sold the barony of Balcarres to his brother Robert and, in order to supervise his wife's collieries in Lancashire, settled at Haigh Hall in Wigan (which was sold in the 1940s and is now owned by the local council). His son James (1783-1869) was born in Scotland but was created Baron Wigan of Haigh Hall in 1826, winning an appeal to be called Earl of Crawford and Lord Lindsay in 1848. He spent most of his time in Lancashire but bought an estate at Dunecht in Aberdeenshire where he built a large house. His son Alexander William, Lord Lindsay (1812-80), became 25th Earl of Crawford in 1869. He married his cousin Margaret, the daughter of James Lindsay of Balcarres, and it was their only son, the 26th Earl, who later bought back the landed barony of Balcarres from his mother's brother, Sir Coutts Lindsay, and also became a Knight of the Thistle. The 25th Earl, however, was most renowned as a collector of books and of Italian paintings, and wrote *Sketches of the History of Christian Art*, London, 1847, an important early study of Italian art. Unsurprisingly, his collecting interests tended towards Italy, but his interest in the family's collection prompted him to discover the provenance of some of the pictures when still a schoolboy (*Barker*, p.41). In March 1827 he noted the 'Orig. Balcarres collection collected in Holl^{d}, by Alex. & Colin E[arl]s of B[alcarres] in the finest time of ye school', and stated that other sources of the 394 pictures in the collection were from Haigh, from the sales of Astley of Dukinfield and Sir Richard Clayton at Adlington, the Muncaster collection, and Lady Anne Barnard, *née* Lindsay, who inherited Rembrandt's *Titus at his Desk* (Catalogue no.51).

A number of Dutch and Flemish pictures came into the collection at a later date, inherited by David Alexander Edward Lindsay, 27th Earl, who was born at Dunecht. Some of these were originally from the estate of Baron Johan Gijsbert Verstolk van Soelen of The Hague, who had died in 1845, and whose estate was put up for sale the following year and purchased by a 'triumvirate' of Humphrey Mildmay, Thomas Baring and Samuel Jones Loyd. Samuel Jones Loyd was created 1st Baron Overstone in 1850, and at his death in 1883 many paintings were inherited by his daughter, Harriet Sarah, Lady Wantage, who had married Robert James Loyd-Lindsay, 1st Baron Wantage in 1858. Lord Wantage inherited his father-in-law's property, owning it until his death in 1901 when it went to his wife. At her death in 1920, the pictures were left to her nephew (the great-nephew of Lord Overstone), David, 27th Earl of Crawford. Some of the Dutch pictures were sold a few years afterwards. Jan Steen's *Soo de Ouden Songen* (now in the Allentown Art Museum, Pennsylvania) was sold in 1926 and the *Portrait of Margaretha de Geer* attributed to Rembrandt (National Gallery, London, no.5282) was sold in 1941. Hobbema's *The Water Mill* (*HdG,* no.86) was sold to H. E. ten Cate in 1936 and is now in the Toledo Museum of Art (no.67.157). The De Hooch (Catalogue no.25) and Rembrandt's *Titus at his Desk* (Catalogue no.51) were cleaned, as well as other paintings in the collection, by Martin de Wild sometime before 1928.

Scots Peerage, vol.3, pp.1-51; *Waterhouse Notebooks,* vol.22, pp.43-4 and vol.27, p.27; sale of paintings belonging to the Earl of Crawford and Balcarres, 11 October 1946, Christie's, London; *Pictures for Scotland,* p.144; *Barker*; H. Brigstocke, *The Bulletin of the John Rylands University Library of Manchester,* vol.64, Spring 1982; H. Brigstocke, *William Buchanan and the Nineteenth-century Art Trade,* private publication for the Paul Mellon Centre for Studies in British Art, 1982.

THE EARLS OF DALHOUSIE

Dalhousie Castle, Midlothian, contained a few Dutch pictures amongst its collection of predominantly Italian, Flemish and Scottish art. A manuscript list of paintings made in 1824, now at the Scottish Record Office (GD45/19/189/1) shows that the 9th Earl (1770-1838) owned 'A Betrayal of Christ,-Style of Honthorst' (no.19) and paintings of the Dutch school (nos 32, 33 and 46), as well as a number of unattributed pictures whose titles suggest Dutch or Flemish authorship. Though Dalhousie did not perhaps have exceptional Dutch paintings, it certainly contained one of the most important collections of Dutch seventeenth-century drawings in Scotland, probably formed by George Ramsay, 8th Earl (1739-87). Acquired almost entirely as by Rembrandt, the drawings were mainly the work of his pupils such as Nicolaes Maes and Ferdinand Bol. With their collector's mark of a 'D' with crown above, they were bound in an eighteenth-century album, a pair to another containing Italian sixteenth- and seventeenth-century drawings. George Gilbert Ramsay, later 15th Earl of Dalhousie in 1928 (at the death of his father who had been painted by Sargent, *Treasure Houses 1985*, no.569), sold the drawings in 1922 to P. & D. Colnaghi, London. They were then purchased by the dealer Cassirer in Berlin who subsequently split up the drawings to sell them separately. They still appear on the market, for example a drawing by Bol of a *Sleeping Figure* (a study for a larger early drawing of the *Liberation of St Peter*) sold at Sotheby's, New York, 8 January 1991, lot 28. Most of the collection was sold at Sotheby's, London, on 23 February 1955.

(On the death of William, Earl of Panmure, in 1782, the estates came to his nephew George, 8th Earl of Dalhousie. There are inventories of the contents of Panmure House in the Scottish Record Office, of 1686 (GD45/857), 1695 (GD45/18/864), 1705 (GD45/18/882) and 1762 (GD45/18/2411).)

Irving, p.89; *Scots Peerage*, vol.3, pp.87-110.

GEORGE DUNCAN

George (1791-1878) was the younger son of William Duncan (1741-99) and Amelia Guthrie (1754-1817) and was married in Edinburgh on 18 November 1823 to Hester Wheeler. He died, without issue, on 6 January 1878 at his house in Dundee, The Vine, which was built in 1836 and still stands with its Graeco-Egyptian façades to south and east.

Duncan was a Liberal MP for Dundee from 1841-57. He was much praised for his support of free trade and educational reforms and founded an Industrial School in Ward Road, Dundee, in 1856, which later became the College of Technology. He was closely involved with the Dundee, Perth and London Shipping Company by whom he was presented with articles of silver plate in 1834 in recognition of 'His Valuable Services in the Introduction of Steam Navigation between Dundee and London'. Dundee Museum also has a silver salver given to Duncan by the 'Seaman Fraternity of Dundee' in the same year. His public career is described at length in the *Dundee Advertiser* of 7 January 1878.

Duncan had a keen interest in art and became the principal benefactor of Dundee Art Gallery to which he bequeathed at least 33 pictures, ten of which were mentioned by Hofstede de Groot. The gallery received the paintings in 1878, five years after its foundation, and the works formed the nucleus of its collection of seventeenth-century Dutch and Flemish pictures. Unfortunately there is very little known about how Duncan's collection was formed and the pictures' provenances, although a fragment of an 'Adrian Brouwer', which had been given to Duncan by a Dr Keith of Aberdeen in 1850, was recorded in the possession of a relative in 1973.

HdG 1893, pp.147-8; transcript of Duncan's will, dated 14 February 1878, Dundee Sheriff's Office. (I am most grateful to Elisabeth Cumming who provided much of the biographical information on Duncan.)

SIR LAWRENCE DUNDAS

A member of the cadet branch of the Scots family of Dundas, Sir Lawrence (*c.*1710-81) made between £600,000 and £800,000 in Flanders as the Commissary-General of the army during the Seven Years War. He was made a baronet in 1762 and was MP for Linlithgow (1747-8) and for Edinburgh (1768-81). He commissioned William Chambers to design his city 'palace', Dundas House, in St Andrew's Square in Edinburgh (now the head office of the Royal Bank of Scotland), and his country house of Kerse was designed by Robert Adam. Though there is no proof that Dutch paintings hung in his properties in Scotland, Dundas was renowned for his fine collection of seventeenth-century Dutch pictures, some of which, including *The Calm* by Jan van de Cappelle, were shown in Johann Zoffany's painting of the interior of the Pillar Room at 19 Arlington Street, Dundas's London home. (The Zoffany and the Van de Cappelle were placed on temporary loan at the National Gallery of Scotland in 1992.)

T. Harris, 'Pictures from Aske Hall loaned by the Marquess of Zetland', *The Connoisseur*, no.CLII, 1963, p.36; D. Sutton, 'The Nabob of the North', editorial, *Apollo*, September 1967, p.169; John Harris 'The Dundas Empire', *Apollo*, September 1967, pp.177-9; *Treasure Houses 1985*, nos 281 and 282, pp.356-7.

THE EARLS OF ELGIN

One of the earliest records of Dutch paintings in the Elgin collection is in the 1819 Royal Institution catalogue of 'Ancient Pictures' which lists Dusart's *Dutch Boor*, Poelenburgh's *Repose in Egypt* and A. Ostade's *Dutch Boor* (nos 34, 73 and 81). These were exhibited by Thomas, 7th Earl of Elgin (1766-1841), who was responsible for bringing to Britain the Elgin marbles from the Parthenon in Athens. It may be that an interest in Dutch pictures had been instigated by Lord Elgin's wife Mary who collected Dutch seventeenth-century painting, though the marriage was later dissolved (see MRS NISBET HAMILTON OGILVY OF BIEL).

Waagen states that he did not see Lord Elgin's pictures at Broomhall in Fife, and none of the works he saw on loan at the McLellan Gallery in Glasgow was Dutch. The collection did, however, include Rembrandt's *Portrait of a Young Woman* (formerly thought to show Saskia van Uylenburgh), which is now in the Rijksmuseum, Amsterdam. It was listed by Hofstede de Groot who praised it, but did not believe it to represent Saskia. A letter from Lord Elgin to Duveen of 1933 (copied in Rijksmuseum files) states that 'there is probably no doubt' that his 'great grandfather Thomas [the 7th Earl] purchased the picture, because most of the collection at Broomhall dates from his time, and, as you know, he was rather a famous collector of works of art'. Waterhouse recorded that most works acquired at this time for the Elgin collection were bought from Quentin Crawford via Lebrun in Paris.

Waagen 1857, pp.443-5; *Irving*, pp.126-7; *HdG 1893*, pp.222-4; *Scots Peerage*, vol.3, pp.466-97; *Waterhouse Notebooks*, vol.30, pp.193-204; J. Mordaunt Crook, 'Broomhall, Fife', *Country Life*, 29 January 1970, pp.242-6; *Holmes*, p.303.

SIR JAMES ERSKINE OF TORRIE

The family was descended from Colonel Erskine who represented Culross in Parliament from 1689-97. Sir James (1772-1825) succeeded his brother William, 2nd baronet, who died in 1813 from pleurisy. Their father, Sir William (1728-95) who was created 1st baronet in 1791, commanded the 15th Light Dragoons and was Lieutenant Colonel of the 26th Regiment of Foot. He was an army man for 50 years, serving in America, Flanders, Germany and the Netherlands. Sir James was also in the army, serving with the Duke of Wellington, and was in Paris at the fall of Napoleon. The Dunimarle catalogue (see below) describes him as 'an eminent art critic and patron – he collected Dutch and other masterpieces' (p.47). He certainly bought paintings and furniture in Paris and there were custom house receipts listing his acquisitions there, as well as purchases made elsewhere in Europe, including one for 'Vendu à son Excellence Monsieur le Lieutenant Géneral James Erskine-Deux tableaux l'un de Teniers et l'autre de

) Jan Both pour D(M)1300- C de Brun pour J. B. Pascal, Berlin le 7 Janvier 1820' (p.230). He also bought 11 pictures from John Wood, a dealer in Hamburg in 1822. It seems that Sir James employed a picture expert to advise him, a Mr Pizzette of 16 Foley Road, London (pp.60, 229) and Andrew Wilson was also recorded as fulfilling this role. Though it is not known when Sir James first started to acquire Dutch paintings, many were in the collection by 1819 when exhibited at the Royal Institution, Edinburgh, in 1819 (amongst which were nos 3, 6, 20, 43, 45). His collection hung at Torry (Torrie) House, near Culross, Fife, which was designed in the gothic style.

Sir James had no children and though there was a sale of some of his pictures at Christie's, London, on 22 March 1823, and some paintings were left to his sister, Mrs Sharpe Erskine of Dunimarle, he bequeathed the majority of the collection to the University of Edinburgh in his will dated 10 April 1839. Mrs Sharpe Erskine owned various Dutch works purchased by her brother, including a Bakhuizen (dated 1651), landscapes by Hobbema, Ruisdael and Aert van der Neer, as well as two Jan Boths and four Wouvermans. She founded the Erskine of Torrie Institute at Dunimarle Castle in Fife in 1872 as a memorial to her distinguished family, of whom by that time she was the last. The best of Sir James's Dutch pictures, however, went to his brother, John Drummond Erskine (also childless), who had a life interest in what has now come to be known as the Torrie Collection, which eventually came into the ownership of the University of Edinburgh on his death in 1836. However, there was little space to display the collection and it was placed on loan, first at the Royal Institution and later in 1859 at the newly built National Gallery of Scotland. The pictures were later returned to the University in 1983, with the exception of Jacob van Ruisdael's *The Banks of a River* (Catalogue no.56) which has remained.

Waagen saw the pictures on his visit in 1850 (vol.3, p.268), and described them as 'genuine and good', 'especially of the Netherlandish school of the 17th century', noting that the University 'greatly to their credit, have placed them in the Royal Institution, and thrown them open for the enjoyment of the public and the instruction of the artists'.

Catalogue of the Collection of Pictures and Marbles and Bronzes bequeathed to the University of Edinburgh by Sir James Erskine of Torry, Bart. (unattributed), Edinburgh, 1837; *Waagen*, vol.3, pp.272-6; *HdG 1893*, pp.130-5 (when in the National Gallery of Scotland); 'Catalogue Raisonné of the Erskine of Torrie Institute drawn up by the Revd. Canon Harper, Dunimarle 1912', photocopy of manuscript, Royal Commission on Ancient and Historical Monuments of Scotland, Edinburgh; *The Torrie Collection*; *Pictures for Scotland*, pp.15-16.

WILLIAM EUING

A Mr Ewing, 'from Glasgow, nephew of Mr Ewing of Melville Street', was recorded as being present at the sale of LORD CLERK OF ELDIN's pictures in Edinburgh in 1833 and escaped unhurt when the floor collapsed. This was presumably William Euing (d.1874), the insurance broker from Glasgow, who presented a number of works, including four Dutch paintings, to Glasgow Art Gallery and Museum at Kelvingrove in 1856 (the year after the Gallery's first published catalogue) and bequeathed others on his death in 1874. From his substantial collection of lesser Dutch seventeenth-century masters, Euing's first gift included works by Palamedesz., no.344, Hackert, no.345, and Lingelbach, no.342, while his bequest included a large number of works by Flemish and Dutch artists including a panel by Pieter Saenredam (Catalogue no.65). He also owned some eighteenth- and nineteenth-century Dutch painting, including examples by Jacob van Strij, Aert Schouman, Jan Verheyen and Hermanus Koekkok the elder. A photograph of him as an elderly man appears in the *Memoirs and Portraits of One Hundred Glasgow Men* (inscribed Maclure and Macdonald).

J. Maclehose, *Memoirs and Portraits of One Hundred Glasgow Men*, Glasgow, 1886, vol.1, pp.123-6; *Trust disposition ... by William Euing, Esq., insurance broker, Glasgow, dated 15 June 1869, and subsequent dates*, 1874, p.7; *Glasgow Catalogue*, pp.9 and 164 (for list of his Dutch pictures).

CHARLES GALLI

Perhaps primarily a dealer, Galli bought a number of important Dutch paintings in about 1824, said to have been the entire collection of a Van der Pot (or Pott), now believed to be a Heer Rom Pot, in Rotterdam. The pictures included Hobbema's *Avenue at Middelharnis*, and Saenredam's *Interior of the Buurkerk at Utrecht* (now both at the National Gallery, London), and they were brought to Edinburgh where they were exhibited for sale in the rooms of the Royal Institution in 1826. The auction was held on 17 and 19-21 January 1826 by Francis Wright and the catalogue was published by Oliver and Boyd in Edinburgh. The introduction noted that the 'various Collections from which this Gallery was formed were most of them of the highest celebrity, particularly that of the Royal Society of Physicians of Amsterdam, – a Collection well known to every admirer of the Fine Arts, and which was publicly sold within the last six months. There are a few of the finest specimens from the Collections of the Baron Luckhurst and Mynheer Vander Pott of Rotterdam, two celebrated Collections which Mr Galli purchased about two years ago'. Of 227 lots, 144 were of the Dutch or Flemish school, the remainder being mainly Italian paintings. (An annotated copy of the Royal Institution exhibition catalogue of 1824 shows that Galli also bought contemporary Scottish pictures, purchasing Walter Geikie's *Selling Fruit*, no.9, for £16 16s and Robert Gibb's *View of Aberlady Bay*, no.44, for £5.)

JOHN GRAHAM-GILBERT

John Graham (1794-1866), better known as John Graham-Gilbert, was a portrait painter and a member of the Royal Scottish Academy. He was born in Glasgow, the son of a West India merchant. Though working for a time in his father's business, he resisted making this his career, and studied instead to become an artist. He went to London in 1818 where he became a student at the Royal Academy and where he won the silver medal for the best drawing from the antique, and in 1821, the gold medal for the best history painting. He later went to study for two years in Italy and was in Rome in 1826. He returned to Scotland in 1827 when he set up as a successful portrait painter in Edinburgh, where he remained for about seven years. In 1834 he married the niece of Mr Gilbert of Yorkhill, the heiress to a large fortune. He adopted his wife's surname at marriage and moved to Glasgow, where he spent the rest of his life. Although much influenced by his stay in Italy, Graham-Gilbert was an avid collector of Dutch and Flemish painting and, after his death, his widow arranged to leave many of these to the Corporation of Glasgow. Though not all of Graham-Gilbert's collection was in her bequest (an Abraham Storck, for example, is still with family descendants), 47 Dutch and Flemish pictures came to the city at her death in 1877. The most important of these were undoubtably Rembrandt's *Man in Armour* (*Alexander the Great*) and Rubens's *Nature adorned by the Graces*, both of which he bought from Samuel Woodburn. (See, also, Catalogue no.55.)

Thirty-Ninth Annual Report of the Royal Scottish Academy, Edinburgh, 1866, pp.14-16; *Catalogue of the oil paintings forming the Graham-Gilbert Bequest to the Corporation of Glasgow*, Glasgow, 1877; *Irving*, p.179; J. Maclehose, *Memoirs and Portraits of One Hundred Glasgow Men*, Glasgow, 1886, vol.1, pp.145-8; *Glasgow Catalogue*, pp.9 and 165 (with full list of his Dutch paintings); *DNB*, pp.365-6.

FRANCIS GRANT

Born in Edinburgh, Francis Grant (1803-78) was the fourth son of Francis Grant, Laird of Kilgraston, and brother of General Sir James Hope Grant. Though he trained at the bar, Francis later became a portrait painter and was a member of the Royal Scottish Academy 'very early in its history' (*RSA Annual Report*, 1878). He moved to London in 1834 where he became President of the Royal Academy and was knighted. He was photographed (in calotype) on 12 September 1845. (S. Stevenson, *David Octavius Hill and Robert Adamson*, exhibition catalogue, Scottish National Portrait Gallery 1981, p.65.) In a diary entry for 26 March 1831, his friend Sir Walter Scott noted that as well as being 'passionately fond of fox-hunting', Grant 'had also a strong passion for painting, and made a little collection'. He first exhibited at the Royal Academy in London in 1832, and became a full academician in 1851. Since it is known that Grant had a small collection of pictures when he was quite young, it is believed that he probably owned the paintings put up for sale at the Calton Convening-Room, Edinburgh, in 1827 (before he went to live in London). Scott (quoted in *DNB, op. cit.*) stated that the young Grant had decided that as the fourth son, he would do as well to spend his settlement of £10,000 and then earn his own living and it appears that part of the money was used to buy pictures. Some of the illustrations in the catalogue are done by 'F. Grant', sometimes in reverse. The pictures were predominantly Italian works such as Guido Reni's *Head of St John*, which had been purchased in Rome by Gavin Hamilton. However, the collection did include some Dutch and Flemish pictures. There were three works ascribed to Rembrandt, an *Entombment* (Catalogue no.48, fig.56), a *Philosopher in his Study* (an 'early picture, highly finished' of *c*.30 x 45 cm), and a '*Prison picture*'. Given the high quality of Grant's Italian paintings, it is possible that the attributions given to some of the Dutch pictures were correct.

(A Francis Grant of 5 Manor Place is listed as being present at LORD CLERK OF ELDIN's sale in 1833 and a Francis Grant was also responsible for writing in the same year *The Catalogue of Pictures Ancient and Modern in Kinfauns Castle*, Perth, 1833.)

Catalogue of Pictures principally of the Italian schools, The Property of a Gentleman, now exhibiting for sale in the Calton Convening-Room, Edinburgh, 1827 (annotated copy in Gallery library notes ownership of a Francis Grant); *Fifty-First Annual Report of the Royal Scottish Academy, Edinburgh*, 1878, pp.12-13; *DNB*, pp.386-7.

THE DUKES OF HAMILTON

The Hamilton collection was chiefly built up by James, 3rd Marquis, later 1st Duke of Hamilton (1606-1648/9), although his father also owned pictures. Some 600 paintings hung at his residence in London, Chelsea Palace, which was built in 1638, and he certainly had pictures before this, including various Dutch and Flemish paintings mentioned in an inventory of 14 March 1624. The 1st Duke was painted by Daniel Mytens in 1629 (Catalogue no.37) and intriguingly, in an undated inventory made before 1649, there is mention of 'an old piece of the Offring of the three kings given by Statholder', no.14 (*Waterhouse Notebooks,* transcriptions of the Hamilton inventories at the Getty Archive, Santa Monica, Document 9). The family's Dutch connections were increased when the Duke's brother William (1616-51), who became 2nd Duke of Hamilton on James's execution at the hands of the Parlimentarians, was sent abroad after his education at Glasgow University, returning in 1637. He was in Campvere by June 1649, where he lived for a time, and was also at The Hague with Charles II in 1650, where he wrote his will. It is possible that he acquired Dutch paintings there, returning to Scotland where he died after a battle in 1651. His niece Anne then inherited the Hamilton estates on her uncle James's death and her husband William (1634-94) was made 3rd Duke of Hamilton in 1660. He was one of the first Scots to welcome the arrival of the Prince of Orange, and was President of the Convention of Estate which acknowledged William and Mary as British sovereigns. He won back the Hamilton estates, employing the painter Jacob de Wet in 1685 and began the main building of Hamilton Palace in Lanarkshire in 1693. Some pictures were kept by his son William (1658-1712) in London, and an inventory of 14 August 1695 lists the Mytens *Portrait of the 1st Duke* (no.2), now in the Scottish National Portrait Gallery, the *Battle of Bothwell Bridge* by De Wet (no.10, which is perhaps the *Portrait of the Duke of Atholl* in front of the battle, illustrated in *Holloway*, p.28, fig.3). There was 'a little head' by Rembrandt (no.19), as well a 'small landskipe with a sleeping Venus and Cupid by Poelenberg' (no.18). Pictures then seem to have been sent to Scotland and there is a list of paintings shipped to Kinneil on 8 January 1697 which included 'An ould man's head by Goltius' (no.7) and a 'Merevelt' (no.14). A list of pictures (already in Scotland?) of 10 July 1699 included works by Van de Velde (nos 10 and 50), 'Three Dutch Boors' (no.52), and a Goltzius 'head' (no.48). As Hereditary Keeper of the Palace of Holyrood House, the Duke of Hamilton took over the apartments originally refitted for Charles II and these were furnished for the Duke and Duchess, the family later employing William Adam to renovate the rooms on the first floor in the 1740s. Pictures were installed in Holyrood and were listed on 5 October 1704, including works by Bloemart (nos 7, 26, 107), a Rembrandt of 'an oval of a boy with a Turband' (no.27), a Frans Hals (no.28), and two Ostades (nos 31 and 34) while the pictures at Kinneil Castle were listed on 13 October 1704. The bulk of the Hamilton collection was later housed at Hamilton Palace, where it was listed extensively by Waagen, who regarded the works of art there as the 'chief object' of his visit to Scotland made shortly before the death of the 10th Duke, Alexander (1767-1852), who had married Susan, William Beckford's second daughter and co-heir. At that time the palace was the most sumptuous in Scotland but it was sold on 12 November 1919 and later demolished, though the dining room, with its rich Dutch-influenced oak panelling carved by William Morgan before 1700, can now be seen at the Boston Museum of Fine Art. The duke's hunting lodge, Chatelherault, named after the duchy awarded in 1548, still stands on the former estate outside Glasgow and has recently been renovated. A small part of the Hamilton collection is now in Brodick Castle on the Isle of Arran, owned by the National Trust for Scotland. It is likely that the small Van Poelenburghs there date back to seventeenth-century collecting (as the early inventories show works by this artist), and possibly some of the other Dutch pictures, such as Gerard Dou's *Portrait of an Old Woman*, which may have been 'A Dutch Woman's head' (no.314) in the Holyrood list of 5 October 1704.

Inventory of pictures at Hamilton Palace, Beckford MSS, Box 25-77, pp.50-67, Bodleian Library, Oxford; inventories of pictures owned by the Dukes of Hamilton, transcriptions in *Waterhouse Notebooks* in the Getty Archive, Santa Monica; *Waagen*, vol.3, pp.295-309 (for collection at Hamilton Palace); Christie's, London, sale, 17 June-20 July 1882 (for prices and buyers see *Illustrated London News*, 15 July 1882, vol.81, p.66); *Scots Peerage*, vol.4, pp.339-97; *Sale of Paintings by the Trustees of the late Duke of Hamilton*, Christie's, London, 6-7 November 1919; *Waterhouse Notebooks*, February 1949, vol.29, pp.46-9 (on Hamilton pictures at Holyrood); R. K. Marshall, *The Days of Duchess Anne*, Edinburgh, 1973; A. A. Tait, 'The Duke of Hamilton's Palace', *The Burlington Magazine*, July 1983, pp.394-402; *Holmes*, Brodick Castle p.303, Chatelherault p.305, Hamilton Palace p.313; *Brodick Castle, Arran*, National Trust for Scotland guidebook, Edinburgh, 1987; *Gow*, pp.44-8 (with illustrations of the Hamilton apartments at Holyrood) and pp.104-7 (with photographs) on the dissolution of Hamilton Palace.

THE EARLS OF HOPETOUN AND MARQUESSES OF LINLITHGOW

Descended from the Hopes of Craighall in Fife, the Hope family had notable branches both in Scotland and in the Netherlands. Henry Hope settled in Amsterdam at the beginning of the seventeenth century and his family became perhaps the most important bankers in Holland in the eighteenth century. (There is still the bank Mees & Hope in Amsterdam today.) Henry's nephew, Sir James Hope (1614-61), was a lawyer and politician. He started mining lead and its ore commercially at Leadhills, which proved most profitable, with most of the production being sent for sale in the Netherlands. Both nephew and uncle remained in close contact in pursuing their business interests in both countries. Sir James died at Granton of the 'Flanders sickness' on his return from the Netherlands on business. These links continued for generations as successive members of the family went to the University of Leiden to study law. As Basil Skinner points out (*op. cit.*, p.370), the portraits of John Hope (1650-82) and his wife, Lady Margaret Hamilton, by Karel de Moor were certainly painted in the Netherlands. The branch of the family which remained in Scotland was enobled, becoming the Earls of Hopetoun in 1703 and created the Marquesses of Linlithgow in 1902. Hopetoun House (likened to the Dutch palace of Het Loo, p.45), was built for the family by Sir William Bruce and was decorated with allegorical, mythological and historical works by the Dutch painter Philips Tideman, pupil of Gerard Lairesse. These were described by Hofstede de Groot in 1893. Although the whereabouts of the paintings he noted as hanging on the staircase at Hopetoun are no longer known, some 18 overdoors and overmantels still survive *in situ*, the remnants of a commission of 37 canvases ordered from Amsterdam in 1703. The cupola of the main staircase at Hopetoun was also decorated in the Dutch style (as revealed by recent restoration) although it is probable that this was done somewhat later, perhaps by a Scottish artist. The house was furnished with a number of Dutch paintings and pieces of furniture including a fine Dutch clock. The family had also inherited a number of pictures, predominantly landscapes, which had been bought by the 2nd Marquess of Annandale in the Low Countries in 1727. There is an inventory of paintings at Hopetoun made in 1817. Shortly after this, many paintings were purchased for the recently refurbished house, perhaps also *The Riding Lesson* by Cuyp (Catalogue no.15), which later hung in the Red Drawing Room. The Earl of Hopetoun showed several paintings in the first Royal Institution exhibition in Edinburgh in 1819: S. de Koninck's *Portrait of an Old Lady with a Book* (no.38), S. van Hoogstraten's *Portrait of a Lady* (no.40), Van de Velde's *Sea Piece* (no.72), as well as two works by Teniers, and a Guido Reni.

(See T. C. Smout, 'Scottish-Dutch Contact', p.25, for information on the Amsterdam Hopes. Also see D. Watkin, *Thomas Hope and the Neo-Classical Idea*, London, 1968.) For the Scottish Hopes: *Waagen*, vol.3, pp.309-12; *HdG, 1893*, pp.221-2; *Scots Peerage*, vol.4, pp.487-505; *Waterhouse Notebooks*, vol.22, pp.65-72 and vol.31, pp.28-9; B. Skinner, 'Philip Tideman and the allegorical decorations at Hopetoun House', *The Burlington Magazine*, August 1964, pp.368-73; *Holmes*, p.314.

DR WILLIAM HUNTER

Born in Long Calderwood, Lanarkshire, William Hunter (1718-83) studied Arts and Divinity at the University of Glasgow before commencing his studies in medicine in which he was renowned for his pioneering work in obstetrics and for advanced teaching methods in anatomy. He moved from Scotland to London in 1741 and became the first Professor of Anatomy appointed by Sir Joshua Reynolds for the Royal Academy at its founding in 1768. His interests ranged far outside medicine and his friends were important figures in the fields of literature, art, politics and science. His eclecticism is well represented in the collections which later made up the Hunterian Museum and which included zoological specimens, ethnography, pathology, geology and anatomy as well as outstanding coins, books, manuscripts, and his pictures (now in the Hunterian Art Gallery). Hunter had intended to make these collections part of his foundation of a medical school in London, subject to the granting of a site on Crown Land, which was refused in 1765. Hurt by this, and supposedly on the advice of Dr Samuel Johnson, Hunter bequeathed his collections to the University of Glasgow, with a life interest to his nephew, Matthew Baillie, who sent them to Scotland in 1807. The bequest was accompanied by £8000 to provide a building to house the collection and a further £500 per annum for its maintenance. The Hunterian Museum, built by William Stark, was opened in 1808, the first public museum in Scotland, and the third in Britain after the Ashmolean Museum in Oxford (opened 1683) and the British Museum (opened 1759). The most important Dutch pictures that Hunter acquired are undoubtedly Rembrandt's *The Entombment of Christ* (Catalogue no.48) and Philips Koninck's *Panoramic Landscape* (fig.8).

Waagen, vol.3, p.283; *Irving*, p.225; *HdG 1893*, pp.146-7; A. McLaren Young, *The Art Collections, The University of Glasgow*, Glasgow, 1951; *Glasgow University's Pictures*.

ARTHUR KAY

Kay (1860-1939) was born in Yorkshire but lived much of his life in Scotland. He bought his first painting at the age of 15 for his father's collection and later stated that the 'beautiful examples of the Netherlands, Italian and British schools' at the McLellan Gallery in Glasgow had provided his first ideas on art. He went to Glasgow University and later married Katharine Cameron, the painter and sister of Sir David Young Cameron (the artist and Trustee of the National Gallery of Scotland from 1920 until 1944). He travelled abroad, mainly in Europe, studying music with Franz Liszt and developing his eye for art (although he also set his sights on big game in Africa and travelled to Australia). Kay's collecting activities are recorded in his book *Treasure Trove in Art* with the enthusiasm of a true hunter as he displays his trophies, recounting the tales of their capture and, indeed, recalling those that got away. His collection was large and he bought and sold a great deal, spending the best part of his time stalking through dealers (pretending he was interested in anything but his chosen picture to put them off the scent) as well as giving (sometimes unsought) advice on the purchases of others, including Glasgow Art Gallery. Arthur Kay owned five paintings now in the National Gallery, London: two Saenredams, a Van Os, a Pynas and a Heda (see Public Collections). He also gave a Van Wijnen to the National Gallery of Ireland (Catalogue no.75) and a Van Beyeren to Glasgow Art Gallery and Museums while, interestingly, his gift to the National Gallery of Scotland was not Dutch but by Gouw Ferguson, the Scot whom Hofstede de Groot thought painted like a Dutchman. Kay also owned an authentic replica of Pieter Codde's *Preparations for a Carnival* at the Gemäldegalerie Berlin-Dahlem, which was on the Amsterdam art market in 1928 (Berlin files). (A. Chastel's *Fables, Formes, Figures*, Paris, 1978, vol.2, fig.312, also shows a Molenaer *Vanitas*, formerly in the collection of 'A. Kay, Edinburgh'.) Ten paintings from his collection are now in South Africa. Not all these have been traced but they include a Van Aelst and two works by Van Beyeren which were presumably sold by Kay (probably via Sir Hugh Lane) to Max Michaelis, who presented them to the Union of South Africa in 1913. The Michaelis collection is at the Old Town House in Greenmarket Square in Cape Town and the three pictures listed were among a series of still-lifes which formerly hung in Kay's dining room and which are mentioned by Hofstede de Groot after he visited Kay's collection in Glasgow in 1897. Kay's interests were not only in painting, however, and he owned ivories, bronzes, glass, embroideries, books and prints, common interests with his contemporary SIR WILLIAM BURRELL.

Kay's address in the catalogue of the Glasgow 1901 exhibition (to which he lent many items) is given as 21 Winton Drive, Glasgow, and as 72 Queen Street, Glasgow, in 1901, but he was certainly living in Edinburgh after the First World War. He was a member of the Society of Antiquaries and was elected an honorary member of the Royal Scottish Academy and Chairman of the Scottish Modern Arts Association.

HdG 1893, pp.224-5; *The Bailie*, Glasgow, no.1483, vol.LVII, 20 March 1901, p.3; A. Kay, *Treasure Trove in Art*, published by Oliver and Boyd, Edinburgh and London, 1939; Arthur Kay's sale of Old Masters and Old Drawings, Christie's, London, 11 and 12 May 1911; Arthur Kay sale, Christie's, Derby House, London, 8 and 9 April 1943; R. Marks, *Burrell: Portrait of a Collector*, 2nd edn, Glasgow, 1988, pp.62-5.

THE EARLS OF KELLIE

See also THE EARLS OF MAR

Thomas Erskine and James VI were childhood playmates and it was said that King James later owed his life to Thomas, who killed Sir Alexander Ruthven in 1600 at the Gowrie conspiracy in Perth. His reward was the Lordship and lands at Dirleton in 1603, and he was created Viscount Fentoun in 1606, a Knight of the Garter in 1613 and 1st Earl of Kellie in 1619. (He purchased Kellie Castle from Patrick, 6th Lord Oliphant, in 1613.) Thomas, 1st Earl, died in London in 1639 but was buried in Pittenweem in Fife. His son already having died, his first grandson Thomas inherited the earldom, followed by the second grandson, Alexander, who became the 3rd Earl. Alexander was a supporter of Charles II and was captured at the battle of Worcester. He was in the Dutch service and was married abroad in 1661 to Anna Kirkpatrick (later, after her death, marrying Mary Dalzell of Glenae in 1665). On his return to Edinburgh he was created Constable of the city in recompense for his services to the Crown. The family continued to live at Kellie, though a later Earl, Thomas (who died in Brussels in 1781), sold most of the estate surrounding the castle in 1769, and the building fell into disrepair after the death of the 10th Earl in 1829. The family descent was dogged by a lack of direct heirs and, on 23 March 1830, John Miller Francis Erskine, 9th Earl of Mar, claimed the Earldom of Kellie as the only surviving collateral male heir and became 11th Earl of Kellie in 1834. The castle was taken on long lease by Professor James Allen Lorimer (father of the architect Sir Robert) in the 1870s, and was later purchased by the Lorimer family in 1948 who owned it until 1970 when it was made over to the National Trust for Scotland.

Scots Peerage, vol.5, pp.81-97; Dr H. Lorimer, *Kellie Castle and Garden*, National Trust for Scotland guidebook, Edinburgh, 1985. (See also Catalogue nos 64 and 73.)

SIR ROBERT KERR

See THE EARLS AND MARQUESSES OF LOTHIAN

LORD KINNAIRD

In 1791 or probably 1792, George, 7th Baron Kinnaird (d. 1805), together with Thomas Hammersley and William Morland, employed Thomas Moore Slade of Chatham, Kent, to purchase the Flemish and Dutch paintings from the collection of Louis-Philippe ('Philippe Egalité'), Duke of Orléans. The pictures were brought to England in 1792 and were exhibited for sale by private contract in London, from April-June 1793 at 125 Pall Mall. Those works which remained unsold were exhibited for sale again in London in May 1795. The Kinnairds were related by marriage to the Ransom family, now of Barclay's bank, and the Kinnaird records, now held at Barclays, chart some of the financial dealings of the family, including providing an idea of the large outlay required for the purchase of the Orléans pictures. (These have been researched by B. Fredericksen at the Getty Provenance Index.) None of the paintings appears to have been kept by Lord Kinnaird for himself but some did come to Scotland, for example, Bloemart's *St John Preaching* (Catalogue no.3), and Rembrandt's *Portrait of the Artist as a Burgher* (Catalogue no.47). Waagen saw the Kinnaird collection but only mentions a Rembrandt 'Portrait of a man', actually the *Self-portrait as the Apostle Paul* (Catalogue no.54). Hofstede de Groot, however, also described Rembrandt's *Portrait of Haesje van Cleyburg* which is now in the Rijksmuseum, Amsterdam.

Charles, the 8th Baron (1780-1826), a parliamentary representative for Scotland, also purchased paintings (at exorbitant prices) and was forced to sell much of the collection at Grosvenor Street in 1813. (W. T. Whitley, *Art in England 1800-1820*, Cambridge, 1928, pp.212 ff.) He bought Jan Steen's *The Doctor's Visit* (now in the Johnson collection in Philadelphia), a month before his marriage to Olivia Fitzgerald in May 1806 (perhaps as a wedding present). The majority of the collection has been dispersed from Rossie Priory, for example the large number of paintings sold at the Kinnaird sale at Christie's, London, 21 June 1946.

Kinnaird Collection or Cabinet Picture Gallery, unattributed and unpaginated, London, 1809; *Waagen 1857*, pp.445-8; *HdG 1893*, pp.227-8; *Waterhouse Notebooks*, vol.22, pp. 73-87; H. Brigstocke, *William Buchanan and the Nineteenth-century Art Trade*, private publication for the Paul Mellon Centre for Studies in British Art, 1982, p. 469.

THE EARLS AND MARQUESSES OF LOTHIAN

Sir Robert Kerr, 1st Earl of Ancram (1578-1654), seems to have travelled first to the Netherlands under less than favourable circumstances as it is traditionally recorded that in his youth he killed a certain Charles Maxwell, and was forced to go into exile in Holland for six months. He was said to have bought pictures there which he presented to Prince Charles. He was made Lord of the Bedchamber to the Prince of Wales in 1618 and had his portrait painted by John Eycke to commemorate the appointment. After the prince became King Charles I, Sir Robert was sent to Holland on a diplomatic mission in 1629 to give the King's condolences to Charles's sister Elizabeth of Bohemia (the Winter Queen) and her husband on the death of their son by drowning. Following this visit, paintings then ascribed to Rembrandt were presented to Charles I (Catalogue no.46) by Sir Robert, who was created 1st Earl of Ancram in 1633. The defeat of the Royalists later forced Lord Ancram into exile in the Netherlands. Here his portrait was painted by Jan Lievens (Catalogue no.30) in 1654, the year of his death. Sir Robert's son, William Kerr, 3rd Earl of Lothian (*c.*1605-75) seems to have been purchasing paintings in the 1650s and 1660s via agents in Paris and the Low Countries (such as Mouat, who bought for him in Holland, and John CLERK OF PENICUIK who shipped works from France). It was the 3rd Earl who sent his eldest sons, Robert, Lord Kerr, later 1st Marquess of Lothian (1636-1703) and Sir William Kerr (b.1638), to be educated in the Netherlands and France from 1651-7. They studied at Leiden and Saumur as well as travelling extensively with their tutor and visiting their grandfather, Lord Ancram, in exile in the Netherlands (*Thomson*, pp.1-24). The 3rd Earl's collection predominated in portraiture of the great and the good, but he also bought a number of fine works of the Dutch school. It is thought that the *Still-life with Glasses* by Claesz. (Catalogue no.13) was probably purchased by him as was probably *An Old Woman and Child saying Grace* by Jacob van Spreeuwen, now at the Museum de Lakenhal, Leiden. The 1st Marquess also collected pictures and a list of 1678 records works bought in Amsterdam, Leiden and Rotterdam as well as Cologne, Venice and Rome (*Pictures for Scotland*, pp.111-12).

Further paintings were later added to those acquired in the early years of the collection, mostly by William Schomberg Robert (1832-70), 8th Marquess of Lothian who was responsible for major refurbishments at Blickling Hall in Norfolk and at Newbattle Abbey, but he was principally interested in works of the Italian School, although he did purchase a work then believed to be by Wouvermans (Newbattle Abbey no.592). However, his brother Schomberg Henry, 9th Marquess of Lothian (1833-1900), temporarily increased the number of Dutch pictures in the family collection. In 1878 a kinswoman, Dame Elizabeth Gomm, left him about 40 paintings on the (unfulfilled) proviso that they might be displayed together in a separate room specifically for them. The *Portrait of a Young Woman in a Feathered Hat* by Willem Drost, now in the Cincinnati Museum of Art, which was probably one of the Gomm paintings, was exhibited by the 9th Marquess at the *RA* 1883 Winter Exhibition (no.261) as by Bol, along with several other of his Dutch paintings (nos 225, 229, 231, 237, 258, 259, 264 and 258). The Gomm pictures were later sold by the 9th Marquess's widow at Christie's, London, on 6 March 1914 (see *Wenley*, p.156).

A group of the Lothian paintings was placed on loan at the National Gallery of Scotland in 1919, and of these, 19 were bequeathed to the Gallery in 1941 by the 11th Marquess. They included works which were listed in the 1720 Newbattle inventory such as a *Still-life* attributed to Pieter Roestraten (noted by Hofstede de Groot) and another *Still-life* attributed to De Heem.

Correspondence of Sir Robert Kerr, First Earl of Ancram, and his son William, Third Earl of Lothian, ed. D. Laing, Edinburgh, 1875; J. M. Gray, 'Notes on the Art Treasures at Newbattle Abbey, Midlothian', *Scottish Leader*, 1887; *HdG 1893*, pp.214-18; *Scots Peerage*, vol.5, pp.452-87; *Waterhouse Notebooks*, vol.29, pp.37-8, vol.30, pp.104-20, pp.206-14; *Pictures for Scotland*, pp.111-14; *Thomson*; *Blickling Hall, Norfolk*, National Trust guidebook, 1984; *Holmes*, p.320; *Border Story : The Name and House of Kerr at Monteviot, Jedburgh, Scotland*, unattributed, Kelso, 1990; *Wenley*.

DAVID LAING

The son of an Edinburgh bookseller, Laing (1793-1878) was a partner in the family business from 1821, until becoming librarian to the Writers to the Signet in 1837. An antiquarian and friend of Sir Walter Scott, Laing's interests were primarily in Scottish history and literature and he edited the letters of Sir Robert Kerr and his son, the 3rd EARL OF LOTHIAN. However, Laing's search for manuscripts, books and papers led him to travel extensively in Britain and abroad where he bought many prints and drawings as well. He went to Europe in 1816, when he visited Paris, and in 1819 he travelled to Denmark and Sweden.

Laing's drawings were bequeathed to the Royal Scottish Academy (where he was an honorary Professor of Ancient

History), and many of these were subsequently transferred to the National Gallery of Scotland in 1910. A further 1500 drawings were generously placed on extended loan in 1966 and 1974. It is for his drawings that Laing is of interest in the context of Dutch art in Scotland and he owned works by Rembrandt, Saenredam, Breenbergh, Cuyp and Lievens. An idea of the extent of this collection can be gained from Keith Andrews's 1984 catalogue of 924 Netherlandish drawings at the National Gallery of Scotland, of which 739 drawings were formerly owned by Laing.

No catalogue of Laing's pictures or any record of where they were purchased has been found in his papers. Although his 'Testamentary Bequests' to the National Gallery of Scotland did not specifically mention any paintings from the Dutch school, it was stated that there were to be included 'two additional paintings by the Old Masters suitable for the Gallery to be selected at the discretion of the Keeper or Director, or by any two persons to be named by the board of Trustees'. The pictures chosen were Avercamp's *Winter Landscape* (Catalogue no.1) and Runciman's *Flight into Egypt*.

David Laing Papers, University of Edinburgh Library; G. Goudie, *David Laing: A Memoir of his Life and Literary Work*, Edinburgh, 1913; D. Murray, *David Laing, Antiquary and Bibliographer*, Glasgow, 1915; *Pictures for Scotland*, pp.67-8; K. Andrews, *Old Master Drawings from the David Laing Bequest*, exhibition catalogue, National Gallery of Scotland, Edinburgh, 1976.

THE MARQUESSES OF LINLITHGOW

See THE EARLS OF HOPETOUN

THE EARLS OF MANSFIELD

The title of Mansfield came to the Murrays in 1776, when William (1705-93), brother of the 6th Viscount Stormont and renowned Chief Justice, was created 1st Earl of Mansfield in Nottingham and was later made 1st Earl of Mansfield in Middlesex in 1792. However, the family's roots are rather more firmly in Scotland than the Mansfield title suggests. Sir David Murray of Gospetrie, who was made 1st Lord Scone and Viscount Stormont, was granted Scone Palace in 1604. It was at Scone that Charles II was first crowned in 1651, and the palace has remained in the Murray's ownership for nearly 400 years.

William, 1st Earl of Mansfield, bought Kenwood House (then called Caen Wood), in Middlesex from John, 3rd EARL OF BUTE, and lived there from 1754 until his death. (The house had previously been owned by the 2nd DUKE OF ARGYLL, the uncle of Lord Bute.) Like Lord Bute at Luton Hoo, the Earl of Mansfield also employed his compatriots, the architects Robert and James Adam, to remodel his house, the first designs for Kenwood being made in 1764. A review of the house in *The Morning Herald* in 1781 noted 'the pictures are almost all family pictures, and those in a stile far from the best' (Bryant, *op. cit.* p.62). The 3rd Earl (1777-1840) bought Wilkie's *The Village Politicians* (still in the Mansfield collection, see L. M. Errington, *Tribute to Wilkie*, National Gallery of Scotland, 1985, no.20), a picture which owes much to the influence of Teniers, whose *Dromedaries* hangs at Scone Palace. It seems that not all the paintings were destined for Kenwood even though this was then the family's prime residence. Bryant notes that a Castiglione (now in the National Gallery of Ireland) was bought in 1800 by the 3rd Earl who chose to hang it at Scone (*ibid.*, p.66). The earliest inventory at Kenwood dates from 1831 and it is not known which paintings remained in Scotland but those at Kenwood were returned when the family sold Kenwood in 1925 (Catalogue no.28).

Scots Peerage, vol.6, pp.186-214; *Waterhouse Notebooks*, vol. 32, pp.79-83; *Holmes*, p.322; *Scone Palace. The Home of the Earls of Mansfield*, unattributed, guidebook, 1989; J. Bryant *The Iveagh Bequest, Kenwood*, London Historic Houses Museums Trust (English Heritage), 1990, pp.58-67; *Gow*, p.31.

THE EARLS OF MAR

See also THE EARLS OF KELLIE

The family home of the Earls of Mar was Alloa House in Clackmannanshire. When the 10th Earl of Kellie died without issue in 1829, John Miller Francis Erskine, 9th Earl of Mar, claimed the Earldom of Kellie on 23 March 1830, as the only surviving collateral male heir and became 11th Earl of Kellie in 1834. Kellie Castle was taken on long lease by the Lorimer family, who later owned it from 1948 until 1970 when it was made over to the National Trust for Scotland. It is difficult to ascertain exactly which paintings formerly belonged to the Earls of Kellie before being inherited by the Earls of Mar and which works were originally in the Mar collection in their own right. It is not known when the Salomon van Ruysdael (Catalogue no.64) came into the collection, but there were other Dutch pictures, including an *Italianate Landscape* attributed to Berchem (sold Sotheby's, London, 17 June 1959, lot 1, as D. van Beyen), a *Landscape with Ruins* attributed to A. van Croos (sold Sotheby's, London, 17 June 1959, lot 3) which hung at Alloa House. At the Sotheby's sale on 17 June 1959 was also a panel (lot 13), optimistically attributed to Pieter Lastman, of *Joseph tending his Flock* and a *Moonlight Scene*, and a picture attributed to Van der Neer (lot 15).

Alexander, Earl of Crawford and Balcarres, *The Earldom of Mar*, 2 vols, Edinburgh, 1882; *Scots Peerage*, vol.5, pp.590-636; H. A. Doubleday, *The Mar Case 1866-1885*, London, 1936; The Rt Hon. the Earl of Mar and Kellie sales, Sotheby's, London, 17 June 1959 and 22 June, 1960; Dr Hew Lorimer, *Kellie Castle and Garden*, National Trust for Scotland guidebook, Edinburgh, 1985; *Holmes*, p.299.

THE RT HON. WILLIAM MCEWAN

McEwan (1827-1913) was MP for Edinburgh Central District and Chairman of McEwan's brewery which is still in the city. He founded the brewery at Fountainbridge in 1856 from where he built up a large domestic business and overseas export trade. He was on the General Committee of the fund-raising Fine Art Loan Exhibition at the Corporation Galleries in Glasgow in 1878, along with JOHN BELL, Thomas Coats, and JOHN GRAHAM-GILBERT. McEwan married Helen, daughter of Thomas Anderson, and they had one child, Margaret, later the Hon. Mrs Ronald Greville, DBE. In later life McEwan went to live at his daughter's house at Polesden Lacey in Surrey, purchased in 1906. He died there and is buried nearby in the parish church of Great Bookham. The Hon. Mrs Greville bequeathed Polesden Lacey and its collection to the National Trust in 1942 as a memorial to her father. McEwan's taste for Dutch painting can clearly be seen in nine of the 12 works known to have been inherited by his daughter (Public Collections, Polesden Lacey). The earliest acquisitions appear to have been five works purchased in 1893 from a Mr Lesser, of which four had been in H. Bingham Mildmay's sale on 24 June at Christie's, London, in the same year. He continued to buy one or two works a year until 1895. However, McEwan's most important purchases were not made for himself but for his country. Determined that the National Gallery of Scotland should be able to display paintings by great Dutch masters, he provided the money for the purchase in 1883 of Frans Hals's *Dutch Gentleman* and *Dutch Lady* (Catalogue nos 20 and 21) and also ensured the acquisition in 1892 of the Gallery's only Rembrandt, *A Woman in Bed* (Catalogue no.50).

Pictures for Scotland, pp.83-4; F. St J. Gore, *Catalogue of the Paintings at Polesden Lacey*, National Trust guidebook, 1976; *Polesden Lacey*, National Trust guidebook, 1985.

ARCHIBALD MCLELLAN

The son of a coachbuilder in Glasgow, whose business he joined, McLellan (1797-1854) was also a bailie, keenly involved in Glasgow's municipal affairs and a member of the council for over 30 years. He was a friend of Sir David Wilkie and Sir Francis Chantrey and was greatly interested in painting, amassing a large and wide ranging collection. He was one of the directors of an exhibition to which he also lent, the 'Glasgow exhibition of pictures by the Old Masters and a selection of the works of Modern Masters under the direction of the Glasgow Dilettanti Society' of 1843 (an annotated copy of the catalogue is in the Getty Museum Library). McLellan also attended the first meetings in 1851 to promote the founding of the Fine Arts Institute in Glasgow, which was later realised 1860-1. In 1853, he made a Deed of Bequest to the citizens of Glasgow 'for all time coming' which stated that his collection, formed over a period of 30 years, should be left to the city and 'form the foundation for a more extensive and complete Collection', in keeping with his belief that the study of art was 'eminently conducive to the elevation and refinement of all classes, as well as intimately connected with the manufacturing and mercantile prosperity of this community' (*Glasgow Catalogue*, p.7). He had commissioned the architect James Smith to design a series of galleries to display the collection on a site purchased on Sauchiehall Street, and the first plans were made in 1851. However, before building was completed, McLellan died in 1854 at his house, Murdoch Castle, Stirlingshire. Outstanding debts prevented the straightforward execution of his Deed of Bequest, made only the previous year, but Glasgow Corporation was persuaded to buy his paintings for £15,000 to prevent their dispersal, as well as the rooms which were to house them, now the McLellan Galleries, but then known as the Corporation Galleries. McLellan's paintings therefore formed the basis of Glasgow's collection which was particularly rich in Dutch and Flemish paintings, with over 130 now listed in the *Glasgow Catalogue* (p.166). He owned Jacob van Ruisdael's *Egmond aan Zee* (Catalogue no.57), but little is known about his sources of acquisition. (The Mitchell Library, Glasgow, has a miniature portrait of McLellan, painted in 1834 by Edward Robinson.)

Glasgow Herald, 27 October 1854; *Waagen*, vol.3, pp.286-91; *Waagen 1857*, pp.457-62; J. Maclehose, *Memoirs and Portraits of One Hundred Glasgow Men*, Glasgow, 1886, vol.2; E. Pinnington *The Art Collection of the Corporation of Glasgow*, Glasgow, 1898, pp.9-10; E. Gallie, 'Archibald McLellan', *The Scottish Art Review*, vol.5, no.1, 1954, pp.7-12; *DNB*, pp.652-3; *Glasgow Catalogue*, pp.7-8; R. Marks, *Burrell : Portrait of a Collector*, 2nd edn, Glasgow, 1988, p.62; E. Williamson, A. Riches and M. Higgs, *The Buildings of Scotland. Glasgow*, London, 1990, pp.242, 277.

H. A. J. MUNRO OF NOVAR

Hugh Andrew Johnstone Munro (1819-78), known as Munro of Novar, was born in Elgin. He became a fellow of Trinity College, Cambridge, and was appointed the University's first Professor of Latin in 1869. Waagen relates that Munro started collecting before 1835. The catalogue made in 1865 shows that Dutch and Flemish paintings were only a small part of Munro's collection, but to gain an idea of its range, it is worth noting that 219 Dutch and Flemish pictures were listed, with roughly similar numbers of Italian and Spanish works, French and German pictures, and a larger number of British paintings. In addition were a number of English watercolours and his famous collection of drawings by J. M. W. Turner, of whom Munro was a close friend and executor. Amongst the Dutch pictures were 19 Ruisdaels, 26 Steens and 13 works by W. van de Velde. Given the high quality of many of the paintings that Munro is known to have owned, the attributions should not be entirely dismissed, despite the startling numbers of examples catalogued.

Amongst pictures that can now be traced is Rembrandt's *Lucretia* (National Gallery of Art, Washington DC), which was mentioned by Waagen (no.34 in the 1865 catalogue). Jan Steen's *The Effects of Intemperance* (National Gallery, London) also appears in the 1865 catalogue (no.207, from 'Mr Beckford's Gallery'), and was sold at an auction of Munro's pictures in London, 6 April 1878, lot 105. Munro also probably owned De Hooch's *Young Couple with a Dog* (Metropolitan Museum of Art, New York) which appears in the 1865 catalogue as no.313, 'A woman standing to right; Man seated in centre coaxing Dog...21½ in. high by 25 wide'. He also owned *Verdonck* by Frans Hals (Catalogue no. 22) as well as the *Madonna of Novar* by Giulio Romano, both now in the National Gallery of Scotland.

After Munro's death the collection was displayed at his house in Hamilton Place in Picadilly, but it was moved to the 'Pantechnicon' where it remained until the sales at Christie's in 1878 (Redford, *op.cit.*, pp.270-1). The sales understandably excited a considerable amount of interest and it was thought that some 1500 came to see the pictures, reflected in the number of catalogue sales. Unfortunately Munro kept no records of his paintings, as was reported in *The Times*, 8 April 1878 (*ibid.*, p.271), and little is known of how this extensive collection was formed. A list of the prices gained at the second sale appeared in *The Times*, 10 June 1878 (*ibid.*, pp.273-7).

Waagen, vol.2, pp.131-42; W. Frost and H. Reeve, *A Complete Catalogue of the Paintings, Water-Colour Drawings, Drawings, and Prints, in the Collection of the late Hugh Andrew Johnstone Munro, Esq., of Novar, at the time of his death deposited in his House, No.6, Hamilton Place, London, with some additional Paintings at Novar*, private publication, 1865; sale of Munro's paintings at Christies, London, 6 April 1878 (mainly modern paintings), 1 June 1878 (153 Old Master paintings); *Irving*, p.372; G. Redford, *Art Sales*, London, 1888, vol.1, pp.270-80 (on notices of 'The Novar Collection').

ROBERT NAPIER

Born in Dumbarton, the son of a blacksmith, Napier (1791-1876) managed to get employment in Robert Stevenson's workshop, where Stevenson's 'Rocket' was built. Napier's talent lay in developing the steam engine for use in ships and it was in the development of marine engineering that he earned both fame and money, building advanced models for many nations (including the Dutch) in the 1850s. Napier lived at West Shandon, Gareloch, Dunbartonshire, and much of his wealth was spent in acquisitions, subsequently known as the 'Shandon collection'. Napier's purchases included British, European and oriental porcelain (as well as Delftware), 'Ancient and Modern' paintings, watercolours, silver, glass and bronzes, sculpture, watches, clocks, enamels and decorative furniture. The superb *View over Flat Country* by Philips Koninck (now in the Ashmolean Museum, Oxford) was one of the works he owned until his death. (Ercole de Roberti's *Wife of Hasdrubal* in the National Gallery of Art, Washington DC, and Bonifacio Veronese's *Holy Family with St Elizabeth and John the Baptist* in Los Angeles County Museum of Art also belonged to him.) Napier sent a number of his paintings to the Art Treasures exhibition held at Manchester in 1857: Rembrandt's *Portrait of a Young Man in a Turban* (no.673), and Dou's *A Dead Rabbit* (no.908), as well as 10 other works by Dutch and Flemish masters. A decade later he was appointed a Royal Commissioner at the great Paris exhibition in 1867. Napier's property was sold at Christie's, London, the year after his death and realised £49,778, his 305 pictures being sold on 13 and 14 April 1877, lots 348-653.

J. C. Robinson, *Catalogue of the works of Art forming the Collection of Robert Napier, of West Shandon, Dunbartonshire*, privately published, 1865; sales of Napier's collection at Christie's, London, 11-20 April, 14-18 May, 4-7 and 11-12 June, 1877; *Irving*, p.385; G. Redford, *Art Sales*, London, 1888, vol.1, p.251; *DNB*, pp.74-5; *Holmes*, p.324.

MRS NISBET HAMILTON OGILVY OF BIEL

The Nisbet Hamilton Ogilvy collection at the Mansion House of Biel in East Lothian included a wide range of pictures from different schools which had been purchased by succesive generations. The earliest collector seems to have been William Nisbet of Dirleton who acquired Saftleven's *Christ Preaching from a Boat* (National Gallery of Scotland, no.1508) and who was painted by Allan Ramsay in 1750. His son William Hamilton Nisbet (1747-1822) was a keen collector of Italian paintings after his Grand Tour in 1776, buying various paintings from the Mattei collection in Rome. Nisbet married Mary, daughter of Sir Robert Manners, in 1777 and it was their only child, Mary Nisbet, who was particularly interested in works of the Dutch school. (She was painted by Gérard *c.*1804, when married to Thomas, 7th Earl of Elgin, but the marriage was dissolved by Act of Parliament in 1808.) She lent four Dutch pictures to the Royal Institution in 1826: Van de Velde's *Shipping Piece* (no.12), *The Larder* by Frans Mieris the younger (no.40), a *Landscape* by Hobbema (no.40) and a Calraet then given to Cuyp (no.45). The last two are now in the National Gallery of Scotland (nos 1506 and 1493). She bought the four portraits by Jan de Bray (Catalogue nos 5-8). Her daughter by her marriage to Lord Elgin was Lady Mary Bruce (1801-83) who married Robert Adam Dundas in 1828. He later changed his surname to Christopher, then to Nisbet-Hamilton. He was MP for Lincolnshire, Chancellor of the Duchy of Lancaster and a Privy Councillor (d.1877). A still-life attributed to De Heem at the National Gallery of Scotland (no.1505) was his purchase and perhaps also the family group by Maes

(Catalogue no.31). It seems that Paul Bril's *Fantastic Landscape* was acquired by his wife three years after her husband's death. The National Gallery of Scotland received this and 27 other paintings in 1921 from the legacy of their daughter, Mrs Nisbet Hamilton Ogilvy who died on 25 June 1920. A typescript list made on 20 September 1920 of the collection at Biel and Archerfield shows that there were 50 paintings, excluding portraits, of which 25 were Dutch seventeenth-century works.

Ogilvy manuscripts, Scottish Record Office (GD 205 Portfolio 18); National Gallery of Scotland Bequest files; *Pictures for Scotland*, pp.109-10.

WILLIAM B. PATERSON

A dealer rather than a collector, Paterson (sometimes also spelt 'Patterson'), had premises in 33 Renfrew Street, Glasgow, which he advertised often in the Glasgow exhibition catalogues, and also in 5 Old Bond Street, London, where, in partnership with Forbes, he opened a gallery in May 1900. (The partnership was dissolved after a short while and Paterson's name appears alone after this.) Patersons interests encompassed not only paintings and in 1901 he lent furniture, bronzes and glass to decorate the Royal Reception Rooms at the Glasgow International Exhibition, as did his potential clients, WILLIAM BURRELL, WILLIAM BEATTIE and ARTHUR SANDERSON. One of Paterson's best clients in Scotland was W. A. COATS for whose collection he also did a valuation for probate and arranged its sale.

(Portraits of Paterson and his wife were exhibited at the Royal Scottish Academy in 1932, nos 476 and 477.)

ARTHUR SANDERSON

Arthur Sanderson lived in 25 Learmonth Terrace, Edinburgh, designed for him by William Scott Morton (1840-1903). The photographs of the interiors of the house in 'A Northern Home', *The Art Journal,* 1897, show lavishly decorated and expensively furnished rooms, complemented by Sanderson's collection of pictures (see fig.11).

Sanderson bought examples from many different schools, though his Dutch collection was sufficiently important to be visited by Hofstede de Groot in 1893. He mentioned works by Jacob van Ruisdael, Dirck Santvoort, C. van Ceulen and two paintings then attributed to Rembrandt (though De Groot pronounced the portrait of a seated woman to be by Jacob Backer). Although the collection was dispersed, some of Sanderson's pictures can be traced. He owned a *Bust of an Old Woman,* formerly ascribed to Rembrandt, which is now in Essen (*Rembrandt Corpus,* vol.1, no.C42), while the *Portrait of a Man* (perhaps portraying Michiel van de Wael), attributed to Frans Hals, is now in the Taft Museum, Cincinnati. An *Old Woman in an Armchair* (that mentioned by De Groot) was included in the Altman bequest to the Metropolitan Museum of Art, New York (no.14. 40.603) as one of Sanderson's Rembrandts but it has been rejected by the *Rembrandt Corpus* (vol.3, C112). Sanderson also owned Gerard ter Borch's *The Card Players* (Los Angeles County Museum of Art) which he exhibited at the Burlington Fine Arts Club, London, in 1900 (no.4). The Santvoort listed by De Groot is now in Auckland City Art Gallery, New Zealand. Sanderson lent some furniture and bronzes to decorate the West Room of the Royal Reception Rooms in the Glasgow International Exhibition of 1901 as well as a number of pictures.

(A photograph of Sanderson appeared in the October issue of *The Connoisseur* in 1901.)

Sales of Sanderson's collection were held: Christie's, London, 3 July 1908 (lots 1-109) and 6 May 1910 (lots 103-26), Knight Frank and Rutley, London, 14-16 June 1911 and 23 May 1913; *HdG 1893*, pp.211-13; C. Monkhouse, 'A Northern Home', *The Art Journal,* 1897, pp.5-9, 34-7, 78-82, 134-8, 210-13, 271-4 (with further photographs of interiors in Learmonth Terrace on pp.258, 260, 304, 305); Gow, pp.126-7 including some reproduced photographs from *The Art Journal, op. cit.*

THOMAS SIVRIGHT

Thomas Sivright of Meggetland and Southouse was a founding director of the Royal Institution in 1819 and was renowned for his extensive and eclectic collections which were sold after his death, at auction in Edinburgh by C. B. Tait at his 'Great Room' at 11 Hanover Street on 1 February 1836. The sale continued over 'Sixteen following lawful days'. Sivright's collection was formed over a period of nearly 30 years and his pictures were described in the sale catalogue as 'long well known to the amateurs of Scotland', with 'fine and undoubted specimens of the pencils of Paul Veronese, Rembrandt, Cuyp and Wynants, with delicious Bits by Ruysdael, Vander Neer, Both and various other masters of lesser note'. A drawing of Rembrandt's *Night Watch* (lot 2798), Cuyp's *View on the Coast of Holland* (lot 2917) and a Wijnants (lot 2860) were illustrated in the catalogue in etchings by W. Geikie, as well a *Self-portrait* given to Karel Dujardin (lot 2907) which was engraved by R. Bell.

INA J. SMILLIE

In January 1963 Miss Ina J. Smillie presented 29 paintings to the University of Glasgow in memory of her father, Andrew Young Smillie, and her fiancé, Captain E. Eric, who was killed in the Second World War. The collection predominates in seventeenth-century Dutch and Flemish painting (24 pictures), although nothing is known about how or from where these works were acquired. A range of artists is represented including J. de Bray, Van Delen, Leemans, Maes and Wouverman with works attributed to S. van Hoogstraten, J. van Huchtenburgh and Van Bloemen as well as a number of anonymous works, complementing the Dutch paintings of Dr William Hunter in the Hunterian Art Gallery, Glasgow, where both collections now hang.

The library of the National Gallery of Scotland has Andrew Smillie's copy of ARTHUR KAY's book, *Treasure Trove in Art,* 1939, which is inscribed 'Andr. J. Smillie, 4 Doune Road, Glasgow'.

H. Miles, *The Smillie Collection,* exhibition catalogue, The University of Glasgow, 1963; *Glasgow University's Pictures.*

JAMES STUART OF DUNEARN

James Stuart (1775-1849) was the eldest son of Charles Stuart of Dunearn, in Fife. He was educated at Edinburgh High School and Edinburgh University, later becoming a writer to the signet in 1798. A deputy lieutenant and JP, he was also a Whig supporter whose enthusiasm earned him Tory dislike. A political row led to a dual with Sir Alexander Boswell whom Stuart shot (*DNB*, pp.91-2). He was acquitted of murder in 1822 but became bankrupt in 1828 and was forced to sell his collection to pay his creditors. He left the country for America on 16 July 1828 (where he remained until 1831, later settling in London where he became editor of *The Courier* and was appointed Inspector of Factories by Lord Melbourne). The auction of pictures 'belonging to the sequestrated estate of James Stuart' was held at Stuart's Edinburgh house, 20 Moray Place, organised by Mansfield and Davidson on 9-11 February 1829. An annotated copy of the catalogue in the Victoria and Albert Museum notes that the total raised was £2808 12s 6d. There were about 60 Dutch pictures in the sale, including works by Cuyp, Ter Borch and Rembrandt. Some of these paintings had been acquired by James Stuart, such as lot 120, Hobbema's *Avenue at Middelharnis* (National Gallery, London (fig.9)) which he seems to have bought from Charles Galli in 1826. However, the catalogue noted that many of the pictures put up for sale had 'long been in the possesion of Mr. Stuart's family'. James was certainly not the only collector in the family for the library of the National Gallery, London, has an annotated catalogue of an auction held from 24 July to 12 August 1786 of *Capital Paintings by the First Masters collected by the late Alexander Stuart Esq. of Dunearn. Now on exhibition at the Large Rooms, Royal Exchange, Edinburgh* (privately published). Apart from a handful of Italian, French and British pictures, the sale of 283 lots consisted almost entirely of Dutch and Flemish paintings with examples by Hals, Lievens, Ostade, Van Goyen, Rembrandt, Roestraten, Molenaer and Rembrandt (as well as one Gouw Ferguson). The annotator wrote that the sale realised £2302 1s 6d and commented: 'Such was the very low state of the Arts at Edinburgh'.

THE DUKES OF SUTHERLAND

The title of 1st Duke of Sutherland was bestowed in 1833 upon Earl Gower, 2nd Marquis of Stafford, shortly before his death six months later at Dunrobin Castle in Scotland. Earl Gower (1785-1833) was the son of the 1st Marquis of Stafford (d.1803) and Lady Louisa Egerton, the sister of Francis Egerton, 3rd Duke of Bridgewater. Earl Gower together with his uncle, the Duke of Bridgewater (1736-1803), and his brother-in-law, the Earl of Carlisle (married to Earl Gower's sister Margaret), formed a 'family triumvirate' which put up money to purchase the important Italian and French paintings from the collection of the Duke of Orléans, sold in London in 1798. Unlike LORD KINNAIRD, who had purchased the Duke of Orléans's Dutch and Flemish pictures (with Hammersley and Morland), the Duke of Bridgewater, Earl Gower and the Earl of Carlisle kept many of their purchases from the Orléans collection. The share-out apportioned about five-eighths of the paintings to the Duke of Bridgewater, two-eighths to Earl Gower and one-eighth to the Earl of Carlisle. The Duke of Bridgewater also owned other pictures, including Dutch paintings, and displayed his collection of some 300 works in a large gallery at his London residence, Cleveland House, which looked on to St James's Square. The Duke of Bridgewater had no children but his nephew, Earl Gower, and wife Elizabeth (the richest heiress in Britain and Countess of Sutherland in her own right) had two surviving sons. The eldest was George Granville Leveson Gower (1786-1868), and the younger was Francis Leveson Gower (1800-57). Because the first born, George, would inherit the titles of 2nd Duke of Sutherland and 3rd Marquis of Stafford, the Duke of Bridgewater decided to entail all his property to the younger son, Francis, on the understanding that he took the (Bridgewater) name of Egerton, and also that the boy's father, Earl Gower, would have a life interest in the Duke of Bridgewater's property.

At the duke's death in 1803, Earl Gower added most of his own collection of pictures to those of the Duke of Bridgewater in the gallery at Cleveland House. A new gallery was added by Charles Heathcote Tathem, and the collection, then renamed 'The Stafford Gallery', was open to the public for one afternoon a week for three months in the summer. In 1818 William Young Ottley wrote his four-volume catalogue of the collection.

At Earl Gower's death in 1833, his younger son Francis Egerton (formerly Leveson Gower), duly inherited his great-uncle's property and pictures, and was made 1st Lord Ellesmere in 1846. He employed the architect Sir Charles Barry to rebuild parts of Cleveland House (renamed Bridgewater House in 1847) and added to the pictures which his great-uncle had purchased, particularly with Dutch and Flemish paintings. In 1944, these pictures came by descent to John, 5th Earl of Ellesmere, who placed some outstanding works on loan at the National Gallery of Scotland in 1946 (for example, Catalogue nos 4, 18, 24, 52 and 68). The 5th Earl of Ellesmere became 6th Duke of Sutherland in 1963 when the 5th Duke of Sutherland died without issue, and the pictures at the National Gallery of Scotland have become known as 'the Duke of Sutherland Loan'.

George Granville Leveson Gower, who became 2nd Duke of Sutherland and 3rd Marquis of Stafford on his father's death in 1833, inherited all of the Stafford estates and the Sutherland estates (including Dunrobin Castle which came from his mother's family). This included Stafford House (now Lancaster House) which had been bought in 1827, and which the 2nd Duke refurbished and enlarged from 1833-41. He seems to have inherited most of his father's collection which he hung at Stafford House, including Dutch paintings such as De Hooch's *The Bedroom* (now at the National Gallery of Art, Washington DC), which had been bought on 13 May 1826 at Christie's, London (lot 14), and also perhaps a Van Beyeren now in the Ashmolean Museum, Oxford (no.A533). He also owned Gerrit Honthorst's *Christ before the High Priest* (National Gallery, London), which was in the collection by 1844. Much of the collection was later dispersed by the 4th Duke who sold Stafford House in 1912. He also sold pictures, for example at Christie's, London, 11 July 1913. His son, the 5th Duke of Sutherland (1888-1963), died without issue and the 6th Dukedom of Sutherland reverted back to the Ellesmeres in 1963. (The Earldom of Sutherland, however, can be inherited through the female line and the 5th Duke of Sutherland's niece inherited the title Countess of Sutherland in her own right, as well as Dunrobin Castle.)

Duke of Sutherland, *A Catalogue of Pictures at Cleveland House*, unattributed, London, 1806; J. Britton, *Catalogue Raisonné of the pictures belonging to ... the Marquis of Stafford in the Gallery of Cleveland House*, London, 1808; W. Y. Ottley, *Collection of Pictures of the ...Marquis of Stafford in London*, 4 vols, London, 1818; *Catalogue of the pictures in the gallery of Stafford House (being the property of the Duke of Sutherland)*, unattributed, London 1883; *Bridgewater House Catalogues*, 1851, 1903, 1926; *Waterhouse Notebooks*, vol.6, p.110, vols 31-2, pp.112-15, vol.66, pp.13-20; Mrs Steuart Erskine, 'The Bridgewater and Ellesmere Collections in Bridgewater House', *The Connoisseur*, May 1903, pp.2-10; *Scots Peerage*, vol.8, pp.318-65; J. Cornforth, 'London's Lost Galleries. Private collections in the early nineteenth century', *Country Life*, 13 June 1968, pp.1566-8; *Pictures for Scotland*, pp.122-7.

THE EARLS OF WEMYSS AND MARCH

Sir John Wemyss of Wemyss was created a baronet of Nova Scotia in 1625, being made Lord Wemyss of Elcho in 1628, and Earl of Wemyss in 1633. The title of Wemyss was taken from the shire of that name in Fife (with which the family had connections through the Macduff Earls of Fife), although the family is first recorded as being landholders at Penshiel in Lammermuir in the thirteenth century. It was not until the eighteenth century that the Wemyss's settled in East Lothian. (The succession of the Earls was somewhat complicated and there is some confusion in the numbering, which here, however, follows that in the *Scots Peerage*.) In 1720 James, the 4th Earl, eloped with the daughter of Colonel Francis Charteris of Amisfield near Haddington. The couple's second son Francis (1723-1808) inherited his grandfather the Colonel's large fortune and lands (including Amisfield House and a number of paintings) on condition that he took the surname of Charteris. Francis's elder brother died in 1787 with no surviving children so Francis also inherited the title of 5th Earl of Wemyss while his younger brother James took on the Wemyss estates in Fife. (James's descendants are Wemyss of Wemyss.) Francis had been educated at Eton until 1739 after which he spent time travelling until 1744, when he returned to Scotland, marrying the following year. He was the most important collector of Dutch art in the family, and commissioned Robert Adam to design Gosford House (at first called Wemyss House). The estate, with a seventeenth-century house (Old Gosford House) at Longniddry, had been purchased in 1781, but Adam's building was unfinished at his death in 1792. Before the completion of Gosford House in 1800, Francis's pictures were kept at Amisfield House, where a remarkably complete manuscript catalogue of pictures with accurate measurements was made in 1771. An incomplete manuscript list was later made in 1810 of paintings at 'Wemyss House' (Gosford House). Dutch pictures were also purchased by Francis Charteris (1772-1853), 8th Earl, who, for example, bought a fine W. van de Velde the younger, *Calm. A States Yacht*, in 1835 (*Treasure Houses 1985*, no.73). About 70 works from the Wemyss collection (including works from many different schools) were exhibited in 1870 at the South Kensington Museum by Lord Elcho, later the 10th Earl, noted in *The Art Journal*, 1870, p.304. (See also Catalogue nos 9, 43, 58, 61, 62 and 63.)

Manuscript lists of pictures at Amisfield House transcribed in *The Transactions of the Antiquarian Society of Scotland*, Edinburgh, 1792, vol.1, pp.77-84.; *HdG 1893*, pp.218-21; *Scots Peerage*, vol.8, pp.475-518; *Waterhouse Notebooks*, vol.31, pp.154-7, vol.32, pp.158-60; *Pictures from Gosford; Holmes*, Amisfield p.299, Gosford House p.312.

Index of Public Collections

This is a guide list of some of the Dutch seventeenth-century paintings with a Scottish provenance which are now in public collections outside Scotland. The list is arranged alphabetically by country. (The source of information, usually general catalogues, is mentioned at the end of each collection's list of pictures.) Only relevant owners are listed and names in SMALL CAPTIALS indicate entries in the Collectors Index. All Christie's and Sotheby's sales are in London unless otherwise stated.

For a list of Dutch paintings in Scottish public collections, see *Birmingham 1989*: Aberdeen p.274, Dundee p.277, Edinburgh pp.277-8, Glasgow pp.278-9, Kilmarnock p.280, Perth p.284, Stirling p.285, The Binns, West Lothian p.287, Brodick Castle, Arran p.287, Crathes Castle, Aberdeenshire p.287, Culzean Castle, Ayrshire p.287, Falkland Palace, Fife, p.287, Fyvie Castle, Aberdeenshire p.287, Hill of Tarvit, Fife p.287 and Leith Hall, Aberdeenshire p.287.

CANADA

Montreal: Montreal Museum of Art

- Jan van de Cappelle, *Dutch River Scene* (no.281), presented by Lord Strathcona, 1927.
- Aert van der Neer, *Moonlight River Scene* (no.1115), with A. G. Grimond of Dundee until sold at Christie's, 25 May 1903.
- Rembrandt, *Portrait of a Young Woman* (no.1006), with DUKE OF HAMILTON before 1836, sold at Hamilton Palace sale 1882, lot 67.

(Source: J. Steegman, *Montreal Museum of Fine Arts Catalogue of Paintings, Montreal*, 1960)

ENGLAND

Anglesey Abbey, Cambridgeshire: The National Trust

- Aelbert Cuyp, *The Baptism of the Eunuch*, in the collection of SIR HUGH HUME CAMPBELL by 1857 when mentioned in *Waagen 1857*, p.441.

(Source: Getty Provenance Index)

London: The National Gallery

- Ferdinand Bol, *Portrait of a Young Lady with Fan* (no.5656), possibly with Robert Philips of The Park, Prestwick, Strathclyde, before being owned by his son, Robert Needham Philips, who died in 1890. Bequeathed to the National Gallery in 1946 by Miss A. M. Philips, Robert Needham's daughter.
- Gerard ter Borch, *Portrait of Hermanna van der Cruis* (no.4596), owned by Hugh Duncan Baillie (who died in 1856), sold at Christie's, 15 May 1858, lot 39.
- Abraham van Calraet (attributed to), *A Boy holding a Grey Horse* (no.2548), with the Earl of Dunmore at Dunmore Park, Stirling, by 1857 and in his sale at London, 13 May 1870, lot 21, where bought in. No longer in the collection by 1878.
- Aelbert Cuyp, *River Landscape with Horsemen and Peasants* (no.6522), with the MARQUESSES OF BUTE from 1764-1989 (Catalogue no.16).
- Gerrit Dou, *Anna and the Blind Tobit* (no.4189), with JOHN BELL until sold at his Glasgow sale, 1-5 February 1881, lot 357. Bought by Sir Renny Watson of Braco Castle, Perthshire, from whose relatives purchased by the Gallery in 1926.
- Willem Claesz. Heda, *Pewter and Silver Vessels and a Crab* (no.1469), in the collection of ARTHUR KAY by 1893. Given to Henry Pfungst who presented it to the Gallery in 1896.
- Meindert Hobbema, *The Avenue, Middelharnis* (no.830), brought to Edinburgh by CHARLES GALLI where exhibited in 1826. Bought by JAMES STUART OF DUNEARN and sold it at his sale, Edinburgh, 9-11 February 1829, lot 120.
- Gerrit van Honthorst, *Christ before the High Priest* (no.3679), purchased by the 2nd DUKE OF SUTHERLAND in or shortly after July 1840. With the 4th Duke by inheritance until sold at Christie's, 11 July 1913, lot 108.
- Jan Lievens, *A Landscape with Tobias and the Angel* (no.72), possibly in DUKE OF ARGYLL sale, London 25-6 May 1798, lot 136.
- Jan Lingelbach, *Peasants loading a Hay Cart* (no.837), in the MARQUESS OF BUTE sale, London, 7-8 June 1822, lot 53.
- Nicolaes Maes, *Portrait of Jan de Reus* (no.2581), in sale of SIR HUGH HUME CAMPBELL, Christie's, 16 June 1894, lot 41.
- Jan van Os, *Dutch Vessels in Calm Water* (no.1462), presented by ARTHUR KAY in 1895.
- Adriaen van Ostade, *A Peasant courting an Elderly Woman* (no.2542), acquired by John Campbell, 2nd MARQUESS OF BREADALBANE (d.1862), sometime after May 1848, and inherited by his sister. At her death in 1878, inherited by her daughter, MRS ROBERT BAILLIE-HAMILTON, who sold it as 'from the collection of the late Marquis of Breadalbane' at Christie's, 5 June 1886, lot 43.
- Jacob Pynas, *Mountain Landscape with Narcissus* (no.6460), with ARTHUR KAY by 1936 until his sale at Christie's, 8-9 April 1943, lot 117.
- Rembrandt, *Bust of a Bearded Man in a Cap* (no.190), with the DUKE OF ARGYLL at Inverary Castle before 1781 (engraved by T. Watson [d.1781] as in the 'Collection of the Duke of Argyle') until the Duke's sale in London, 25-6 May 1798, lot 104.

- Rembrandt *Saskia van Uylenburgh in Arcadian Costume* (no.4930), in the collection of the DUKES OF BUCCLEUCH (Catalogue no.49).
- Rembrandt (attributed to), *Portrait of Margaretha de Geer* (no.5282), inherited from Lady Wantage by the EARL OF CRAWFORD AND BALCARRES in 1920 and sold by him in 1941 to the NACF which presented the work to the Gallery.
- Rembrandt (imitator of), *A Study of an Elderly Man in a Cap* (no.2539), perhaps in the collection of the DUKE OF SUTHERLAND until possibly sold in 1846 by the duchess.
- Pieter Saenredam, *Interior of the Buurkerk at Utrecht* (no.1896), brought to Edinburgh by CHARLES GALLI and exhibited there in 1826. By 1886 owned by Alexander Allan, Edinburgh, until his sale, Edinburgh, 11 January 1896, lot 39, to WILLIAM B. PATERSON. It was bought from Paterson by ARTHUR KAY, perhaps in the same year (certainly by 1899), who presented it to the Gallery in 1902.
- Pieter Saenredam, *Interior of the Grote Kerk at Haarlem* (no.2531), with ARTHUR KAY, but later sold by Revon, Lintz and others at Amsterdam, 27 April 1909, lot 143.
- Jan Steen, *An Interior with a Man offering an Oyster to a Woman* (no.2559), with SIR HUGH HUME CAMPBELL by 1856 until sold at his sale, London, 16 June 1894, lot 49.
- Jan Steen, *The Effects of Intemperance* (no.6442), in the sale of H. A. J. MUNRO OF NOVAR, London, 6 April 1878, lot 105.
- Jan Wijnants, *Landscape with Woman Driving Sheep through a Ruined Archway* (no.2532), acquired after April 1857 by SIR HUGH HUME CAMPBELL and sold at his sale, London, 16 June 1894, lot 52.

(Source: *MacLaren and Brown)*

London: The Wallace Collection

- Jan Both, *Landscape with a Drinking-Pool* (no.P24), in the collection of Colonel Hugh Duncan Baillie of Redcastle, Tarradale, until his sale Christie's, 15 May 1858, lot 31.
- Gerrit Dou (studio), *A Hermit at Prayer* (no.P177), bought by LORD KINNAIRD at Christie's, 26 April 1806, lot 25, and later acquired by the 3rd Marquess of Hertford (d. 1842)

(Source: J. Ingamells, *The Wallace Collection Catalogue of Pictures IV: Dutch and Flemish*, London, 1992)

Oxford: The Ashmolean Museum

- Philips Koninck, *A View over Flat Country* (no.A719), with ROBERT NAPIER of Glasgow until his death, sold 1877, later acquired by JOHN BELL of Glasgow who sold it in 1881.
- Joachim Wtewael, *Adoration of the Shepherds* (no.A770), with LORD KINNAIRD until 1946 (Catalogue no.76).
- Abraham van Beyeren, *Still-life with a Lobster* (no.A533), owned by the 1ST DUKE OF SUTHERLAND at Dunrobin Castle (sold after his death in 1833).

(Source: Gallery files)

Polesden Lacey, Surrey: The National Trust

- Ludolf Bakhuizen, *A Yacht and Fishing Boats* (no.45), purchased after 1893 by the Rt Hon. WILLIAM MCEWAN.
- Gerard Ter Borch, *A Dancing Couple* (no.50), formerly in the collection of 2nd Marquis of Stafford (later 1ST DUKE OF SUTHERLAND) by whom bought at Christie's on 26 April 1806, lot 11, and by inheritance to the Dukes of Sutherland until at least 1854. Purchased in 1896 by the Rt Hon. WILLIAM MCEWAN.
- Aelbert Cuyp, *A Landscape with Herdsman and Bull* (no.36), in the MARQUESS OF BUTE sale, Christie's, 8 June 1822, lot 76.
- Aelbert Cuyp (after), *The Maas in Winter* (no.34), purchased in 1894 by the Rt Hon. WILLIAM MCEWAN.
- Cesar van Everdingen, *A Boy with Sheep* (no.43), in the collection of the 2ND MARQUESS OF BREADALBANE and by descent to MRS ROBERT BAILLIE HAMILTON.
- Pieter de Hooch, *The Golf Players* (no.44), in the collection of SIR HUGH HUME CAMPBELL by 1861, by whom sold in 1894. Purchased in 1894 by the Rt Hon. WILLIAM MCEWAN.
- Aert van der Neer, *A Town on a Frozen River* (no.30), purchased in 1893 by the Rt Hon. WILLIAM MCEWAN.
- Adriaen van Ostade, *Peasants before a Fire* (no.49), purchased in 1893 by the Rt Hon. WILLIAM MCEWAN (Catalogue no.42).
- Isack van Ostade, *A Village Inn* (no.32), purchased in 1893 by the Rt Hon. WILLIAM MCEWAN.
- Jacob Ruisdael, *The Zuider Zee Coast* (no.53), purchased in 1893 by the Rt Hon. WILLIAM MCEWAN.
- Salomon Ruysdael, *A River Scene* (no.31), purchased in 1893 by the Rt Hon. WILLIAM MCEWAN.

(Source: St J. Gore, *Catalogue of the Paintings at Polesden Lacey*, National Trust guidebook, Plaistow, 1976)

IRELAND

National Gallery of Ireland, Dublin

- Nicolaes Berchem, *A Stag Hunt* (no.245), with the MARQUESS OF BREADALBANE until sold at Christie's, 5 June 1886, lot 45.
- Jacob van Ruisdael (after), *A Stormy Sea* (no.916), after 1856 with H. A. J. MUNRO OF NOVAR, until his sale, Christie's, 1 June 1878, lot 99.
- Jan Wijnants, *Wooded Landscape with a River* (no.508), owned by SIR HUGH HUME CAMPBELL by 1856 but elsewhere by 1886 (Catalogue no 74).
- Domenicus van Wijnen, *Temptation of St Anthony* (no.527), presented by ARTHUR KAY in 1901 (Catalogue no.75).

(Source: H. Potterton, *Dutch seventeenth and eighteenth century paintings in the National Gallery of Ireland*, Dublin, 1986)

THE NETHERLANDS

Amsterdam: The Rijksmuseum

- Abraham Beerstraten, *Sea Battle* (no.A3737), from the collection of Robert Baird, Lennoxlove, Haddington, probably sold in 1949.
- Govaert Flinck, *Hera Hiding* (no.A1282), with DUKES OF HAMILTON at Hamilton Palace until sold, Christie's 17-19 June 1882, lot 1049.
- Meindert Hobbema, *A Watermill* (no.C144), in Allan collection, Edinburgh, after 1831 (certainly 1835) but listed elsewhere by 1885.
- Pieter de Hooch, *Women beside a Linen Chest* (no.C1191), unknown Scottish collection sometime after 1794 but listed elsewhere by 1833.
- Cornelis de Man, *The Whale-oil Factory on Jan Mayen Island* (no.A2355), with 4th DUKE OF SUTHERLAND until sold London, 8 February 1908, lot 66.
- Rembrandt, *Self-portrait as the Apostle Paul* (no.A4050), with LORD KINNAIRD from 1809 until sold in 1936 (Catalogue no.54).
- Rembrandt, *Portrait of a Young Woman* (no.A4057), probably purchased by Thomas, 7th EARL OF ELGIN (1766-1841) and thence by descent until sold to Duveen by 1932.
- Rembrandt, *Musical Allegory* (no.A4674), collection of F. Cripps, Scotland, until sold, Christie's, 18 November 1936, lot 155.
- Rembrandt, *Self-portrait* (no.A4691), Dr Alexander Patterson, Glasgow; James E. Mackay, Glasgow; Mary A. Winter, Bearsden, Dunbartonshire, until sold at Sotheby's, 27 May 1959, lot 135.
- Rembrandt, *Portrait of Haesje van Cleyburg* (no.A4833), with LORD KINNAIRD until sold in 1985.

(Source: Gallery files)

Dordrecht: Dordrecht Museum

- Aelbert Cuyp, *Landscape* (no.DM/987/645), probably purchased by the 3rd Duke of Bridgewater and by inheritance to the 6th DUKE OF SUTHERLAND until sold at Christie's, 2 July 1976, lot 81.

(Source: information from A. Chong)

Leiden: Stedelijk Museum 'De Lakenhal'

- Jacob van Spreeuwen, *An Old Woman and Child saying Grace* (no.1116), probably acquired in the 1650s or 1660s by the 3rd EARL OF LOTHIAN (Newbattle Abbey, no.328) as by F. Spreu, *The Grace before the Meat.* It first appears in an inventory of *c.*1788 but left the collection before 1962 (Source: information via C. Vogelaar from R. Wenley)

Rotterdam: Boymans van-Beuningen Museum

- Aelbert Cuyp, *The Milkmaid,* purchased by Lord Francis Egerton, by descent to the 6th DUKE OF SUTHERLAND until sold at Christie's, 2 July 1976, lot 80. (Source: information from A. Chong)
- Rembrandt, *Titus at his Desk,* formerly in the collection of the EARL OF CRAWFORD AND BALCARRES until sold in 1940 (Catalogue no.51).

Utrecht: Centraal Museum

- C. Poelenburgh, *The Flight into Egypt* (no. 8391), in the collection of the MARQUESSES OF BUTE until sold to C. Benedict in Paris; Vitale Bloch, The Hague; purchased by the museum in 1940.

(Source: Gallery files)

NEW ZEALAND

Auckland: Auckland City Art Gallery

- Dirck van Santvoort, *Portrait of a Lady with a Fan,* in the collection of ARTHUR SANDERSON until sold by Knight Frank and Rutley, 14-16 June 1911, lot 607.

(Source: *Old and New Zeeland,* exhibition catalogue, Auckland City Art Gallery, 1992)

SOUTH AFRICA

Cape Town: The Michaelis Collection, The Old Town House, Greenmarket Square

- Willem van Aelst, *A Vase of Flowers,* formerly in the collection of ARTHUR KAY.
- Abraham van Beyeren, *Fish on a Table,* formerly in the collection of ARTHUR KAY.
- Abraham van Beyeren, *Fruit and Still-life,* formerly in the collection of ARTHUR KAY.

(Source: T. M. Wood, *The Michaelis Gift to the Union of South Africa, illustrated catalogue of Flemish and Dutch Paintings,* London, 1913; A. Kay, *Treasure Trove in Art,* Edinburgh and London, 1939)

UNITED STATES

Allentown, Pennsylvania: Allentown Art Museum

- Jan Steen, *Soo de Ouden Songen* (no.61. 60.6, [Kress collection, K21851]), formerly in the collection of 27th EARL OF CRAWFORD AND BALCARRES by whom sold in 1926.

(Source: Kress catalogues)

Boston, Massachusetts: Boston Museum of Fine Arts

- Jacob Adriaensz. Bellevois, *Ships in a Storm* (no.07.499), sold on 31 May 1907, lot 136 (as Bakhuizen), from the collection of Edward Balfour (d. 1927), Balbirnie House, Fife.
- Melchior de Hondecoeter, *Barnyard Fowl and Peacocks* (no.07.501), sold on 31 May 1907, lot 138, from the collection of Edward Balfour (d. 1927), Balbirnie House, Fife.
- Jan van Goyen, *River Landscape with Ferry and Church* (no.07.502), sold on 31 May 1907, lot 139, from the collection of Edward Balfour (d. 1927), Balbirnie House, Fife.
- Jan Molenaer, *Peasants Carousing* (no.07.500), sold on 31 May 1907, lot 56, from the collection of Edward Balfour (d. 1927), Balbirnie House, Fife.
- Rembrandt, *The Artist in his Studio* (no.38.1838), in the collection of the Earls of Morton at Dalmahoy, Kirknewton, Midlothian, sometime after 1773 and sold at Christie's, 27 April 1850, lot 70.

Cincinnati: Cincinnati Museum of Art

- Abraham Bloemart and studio, *The Liberation of St Peter* (no.1983.142), with SIR ARCHIBALD CAMPBELL by 1854 and by descent to Sir Ilay Campbell by 1947, by whom sold in 1974.
- Willem Drost, *Portrait of a Young Woman in a Feathered Hat* (no.1954.21), at Newbattle Abbey, Midlothian, home of the MARQUESSES OF LOTHIAN, sometime after 1828 and certainly from 1875-83.

(Source: M. A. Scott, *Dutch, Flemish, and German Paintings in the Cincinnati Museum of Arts,* Cincinnati, 1987)

Cincinnati: The Taft Museum

- Frans Hals, *Portrait of a Man* (no.1931.450), owned by ARTHUR SANDERSON by 1893 (when seen by Hofstede de Groot) until 1906.

(Source: *Slive*)

Columbia: Columbia Museum

- Nicolaes Maes, *Portrait of a Lady* (no.62.37.17 [K1134]), in collection of WILLIAM BEATTIE of Glasgow, sold at Christie's, 18 July 1924.

(Source: Kress catalogues)

Detroit: The Detroit Institute of Arts

- Frans Hals, *Portrait of Hendrick Swalmius* (no.49.347), owned by Mrs Broun Lindsay of Colstoun near Haddington, East Lothian until 1934.

(Source: *Slive*)

Detroit: The Edsel Ford Collection

- Frans Hals *Young Man in a Plumed Hat* (*Slive,* unaccepted) was in the collection of W. A. COATS until sold to dealer Lawrie and Co., London, 1908.

(Source: *Slive*)

Los Angeles: Los Angeles County Museum of Art

- Gerard Ter Borch, *The Card Players* (no.44.2.7), with ARTHUR SANDERSON by 1900, when exhibited at the Burlington Fine Arts Club, London (no.4), until 1903, when exhibited by Lawrie and Co. (no.19).
- Pieter Saenredam, *North Aisle of the Mariakerk* (Carter collection), with W. A. COATS until exhibited for sale at the Royal Society of British Artists, London, January 1927, no.175 (see Catalogue no.67).

(Source: Getty Provenance Index)

Malibu: The J. Paul Getty Museum

- Cesar van Everdingen, *Vertumnus and Pomona* (no.75.PA.64), in the collection of W. A. COATS by 1904 (when it appears in his catalogue), until sold Christie's, 10 June 1927, lot 103.
- Pieter Lastman *The Resurrection* (no.87.PB.116), *c.*1910, private collection, Scotland, until sold in 1987 to Malcolm Waddingham from whom bought by the Getty Museum the same year.
- Jacob van Ruisdael, *Landscape with Wheatfield* (83.PA.278). Until 1983 in a private collection, Scotland, previously with Thomas Baring in 1846.

(Source: Museum files)

Minneapolis: The Minneapolis Institute of Arts

- Philips Wouverman, *Peasants by an Inn* (no.81.107), with R. BAILLIE HAMILTON in 1881 (noted by *HdG,* no.1020, as in London).

(Source: *Dutch Paintings from America 1990*)

New York: The Metropolitan Museum of Art

- Frans Hals, *Paulus Vershcuur* (no.26.101.11), perhaps owned by Lord Glenesk, Scotland.
- Pieter de Hooch, *A Young Couple with a Dog* (no.14.40.613), probably owned by H. A. J. MUNRO OF NOVAR, his sale, London, 16 July 1878, no.313.
- Jan van Goyen (style of), *River Scene with a Gothic Village Church* (no.65.181.11), bought from Robert Hutcheson of Glasgow by JOHN BELL until his sale at Christie's, 24 June 1881, lot 623.
- Nicolaes Maes, *Young Girl Peeling Apples* (no.14.40.612 Altman collection), with 2nd DUKE OF SUTHERLAND.after 1828 and sold to G. Morant in 1846.
- Rembrandt (copy after), *Portrait of a Young Man* (no.15.30.1), with ROBERT NAPIER by 1865 when included in his catalogue, no.407 (de-accessioned and sold at Parke-Burnet, New York, 17 June 1982).
- Rembrandt (copy after), *Portrait of a Young Woman* (no.15.30.2), with ROBERT NAPIER by 1865 when included in his catalogue, no.408 (de-accessioned and sold at Parke-Burnet, New York, 17 June 1982).
- Rembrandt (style of), *Old Woman in an Armchair* (no.14. 40.603), with ARTHUR SANDERSON until *c.*1906.

(Source: Gallery files)

New York: Frick Collection

- Hendrick van der Burgh (attributed), *Drinkers before the Fireplace* (no.18.1.78), after 1846 with ROBERT NAPIER until his sale, 13 April 1877, lot 475.

(Source: Getty Provenance Index)

Philadelphia: The John G. Johnson Collection, Philadelphia Museum of Art

- Jan Steen, *The Doctor's Visit* (no.510), bought at the Crawford sale at Christie's, 26 April 1806, lot 13, by Charles, 8th LORD KINNAIRD, but elsewhere by 6 April 1876 when sold at Christie's, lot 370.

(Source: *Dutch Paintings in America 1990)*

Saint Louis, Missouri: Saint Louis Art Museum

- Jacob van Ruisdael, *Landscape with Waterfall* (no.44:1974), Fesch sale, Rome, 17 March 1845, lot 208, bought by George James Dennistoun, Edinburgh, but sold before his death in 1855.

(Source: Getty Provenance Index)

Toledo, Ohio: Toledo Museum of Art

- Aelbert Cuyp, *The Riding Lesson,* (no. 1960.2), with EARL OF HOPETOUN AND MARQUESS OF LINLITHGOW until *c.*1909 (Catalogue no.15).
- Meindert Hobbema, *The Water Mill* (no.67.157), inherited by the EARL OF CRAWFORD AND BALCARRES in 1920 from Lady Wantage and sold in 1936.

(Source: Gallery files)

Washington DC: National Gallery of Art

- Pieter de Hooch, *The Box Bed* (no.1942.9.33), purchased at the Radstock sale, London, 1826 by the 1st DUKE OF SUTHERLAND and by descent to the 2nd Duke in 1833 and sold by the Duchess of Sutherland in 1846 (*Dutch Paintings from America 1990,* no.35).
- Jan Davidsz. de Heem, *Vase of Flowers,* (no.1961.6.1.), formerly in the collection of McIntosh of Bridge of Allan.
- Rembrandt, *Self-Portrait* (no.1937.1.72), inherited from the Duke of Montagu by the wife of the 3rd DUKE OF BUCCLEUCH from 1790 and thence by descent until sold in 1928 (Catalogue no.53).
- Rembrandt, *Lucretia* (no.1937.1.76), with H. A. J. MUNRO OF NOVAR by 1854.
- Jacob van Ruisdael, *Forest Scene* (no.1942.9.80) with SIR HUGH HUME CAMPBELL by 1857 (and possibly exhibited by him at the British Institution in 1855, no.64), until his sale at Christie's, 16 June 1894.

(Source: Gallery files)

Bibilography & Abbreviations

Agnews: R. Kingszett, *Dutch and Flemish Pictures from Scottish Collections*, exhibition catalogue, Agnew and Sons Ltd, London, 1978

Amsterdam 1898: Rembrandt: schilderijen bijeengebracht ter gelegenheid van de inhulding van Hare Majesteit Koningen Wilhelmina, Stedelijk Museum, Amsterdam, 1898

Amsterdam 1932: Rembrandt tentoonstelling ter plechtige herdenking van het 300-jarig bestaan der Universiteit van Amsterdam, Rijksmuseum, Amsterdam, 1932

Amsterdam 1969: Rembrandt 1669/1969, Rijksmuseum, Amsterdam, 1969

Amsterdam and Rotterdam: Rembrandt.tentoonstelling ..., Rijksmuseum, Amsterdam; Boymans-van Beuningen Museum, Rotterdam, 1956

Andrews: K. Andrews, *Catalogue of Netherlandish Drawings in the National Gallery of Scotland,* 2vols, Edinburgh, 1985

Barker: N. Barker, 'The Lives and Collections of Alexander William, 25th Earl of Crawford and 8th Earl of Balcarres, and James Ludovic, 26th Earl of Crawford and 9th Earl of Balcarres', *Bibliotheca Lindesiana*, printed by B. Quaritch for presentation to the Roxburghe Club, London, 1977

Bethnal Green 1882-3: J. P. Richter, *Catalogue of the Collection of Paintings Lent for Exhibition by The Marquis of Bute K. T.,* Bethnal Green Museum, London, 1883 (catalogue printed after opening of the exhibition)

Birmingham 1989: Dutch Painting in the Seventeenth Century: Images of a Golden Age in British Collections, exhibition catalogue (ed. C. Wright), Birmingham City Museums and Art Gallery, 1989-90

Bridgewater House Catalogue 1851: Catalogue of the Bridgewater collection of pictures, belonging to the Earl of Ellesmere, at Bridgewater House, Cleveland Square, St James's (unattributed), 7th edn, London, 1851

Bridgewater House Catalogue 1903. L. Cust, *The Bridgewater Gallery: one hundred & twenty of the most noted paintings at Bridgewater House*, London, 1903

Bridgewater House Catalogue 1926: Catalogue of the Collection of Pictures and Statuary of the Right Honourable John Francis Granville Scrope, Earl of Ellesmere, at Bridgewater House, Cleveland Square, St James's, London (unattributed), London, 1926

DNB: The Compact Edition of the Dictionary of National Biography, 2 vols, Oxford, 1975

Dutch Paintings from America 1990: Great Dutch Paintings from America, exhibition catalogue (ed. B. Broos), The Mauritshuis, The Hague, 1990-1; The Fine Arts Museums of San Francisco, 1991

Edinburgh 1883: Works of Old Masters and Scottish National Portraits, loan exhibition, organised by the Board of Manufactures, Royal Scottish Academy, Edinburgh, 1883

Edinburgh 1945: A Selection of Pictures from the Bridgewater House Collection, National Gallery of Scotland, Edinburgh, 1945.

Edinburgh 1949: E. K. Waterhouse, *Dutch and Flemish Paintings from the Collection of the Marquess of Bute*, exhibition catalogue (arranged in conjunction with the Scottish Committee of the Arts Council of Great Britain), National Gallery of Scotland, Edinburgh, 1949

Edinburgh 1950: An Exhibition of Paintings by Rembrandt, arranged by the Arts Council of Great Britain for the Edinburgh Festival Society, National Gallery of Scotland, Edinburgh, 1950

Edinburgh 1984: Dutch Church Painters, Saenredam's 'Great Church' in Context, exhibition catalogue (ed. H. Macandrew), National Gallery of Scotland, Edinburgh, 1984

Edinburgh 1991: Saved for Scotland: Works of Art Acquired with the Help of the National Art Collections Fund, National Gallery of Scotland, Edinburgh, 1991

Edinburgh University Catalogue 1909: Catalogue of Portraits and Busts of Benefactors, Principals, Professors and Others and of the Torrie Collection of Paintings and Bronzes. The property of the University of Edinburgh, Edinburgh, 1909

Farington: The Diaries of Joseph Farington, 1747-1821 (vols 1-6, eds K. Garlick and A. Macintyre, vols 7-16, ed. K. Cave), New Haven and London, 1978-84

Gerson: H. Gerson, *Rembrandt Paintings*, Amsterdam, 1968

Glasgow 1884: J. P. Richter, *The Bute Collection of Pictures*, exhibition at the Corporation Galleries (revised version of *Bethnal Green 1882-3* catalogue), Glasgow, 1884

Glasgow Catalogue: H. Miles, *Dutch and Flemish, Netherlandish and German Paintings in Glasgow Art Gallery and Museum*, 2 vols, Glasgow, 1961

Glasgow University's Pictures: Glasgow University's Pictures, A Selection of Paintings, Drawings, Prints and Other Works from the Hunterian Museum, University of Glasgow, exhibition catalogue (ed. A. McLaren Young), P. and D. Colnaghi, London, 1973

Gow: Ian Gow, *The Scottish Interior*, Edinburgh, 1992

Grimm: Claus Grimm, *Frans Hals: Entwicklung, Werkanalyse, Gesamtkatalog*, Berlin, 1972

Haak: B. Haak, *The Golden Age, Dutch Painting of the Seventeenth Century*, London, 1984

Hals 1989-90: Frans Hals exhibition catalogue (ed. S Slive), National Gallery of Art, Washington DC; Royal Academy of Arts, London; Frans Halsmuseum, Haarlem, 1989-90

Harwood: L. B. Harwood, *Adam Pynacker (c.1620-1673)*, Aetas Aurea Monographs on Dutch and Flemish Painting, VII, Doornspijk, 1988

HdG 1893: C. Hofstede de Groot, 'Hollandsche Kunst in Schotland', *Oud Holland,* 1893, XI.3 (Part 1), pp.129-48, and 4 (Part 2), pp.211-28 (Kraus reprint, Nendeln, 1976)

HdG: C. Hofstede de Groot, *Catalogue Raisonné of the works of the most eminent Dutch Painters of the seventeenth century,* 10 vols, London, 1907-28

Holloway: J. Holloway, *Patrons and Painters: Art in Scotland 1650-1760,* exhibition catalogue, Scottish National Portrait Gallery, Edinburgh, 1989

Holmes: M. Holmes, *The Country House Described: an Index to the Country Houses of Great Britain and Ireland,* Victoria and Albert Museum, London, 1986

Irving: J. Irving, *The Book of Scotsmen, Eminent for Achievements in Arms and Arts, Church and State, Law, Legislation, and Literature, Commerce, Science, Travel, and Philanthropy,* Paisley, 1881

MacLaren and Brown: N. MacLaren, text revised and expanded by C. Brown, *National Gallery Catalogues, The Dutch School 1600-1900,* 2 vols, London, 1991

Manchester 1857: Catalogue of the Art Treasures of the United Kingdom, Collected at Manchester in 1857 (exhibition held at Old Trafford, Manchester), London, 1857

Manchester 1957: Art Treasures Centenary, European Old Masters, exhibition catalogue, Manchester City Art Gallery, 1957

Masters of Dutch Genre Painting: Masters of Seventeenth-Century Dutch Genre Painting, exhibition catalogue (ed. P. C. Sutton), Philadelphia Museum of Art; Gemäldegalerie, Staatliche Museen Preussischer Kulturbesitz, Berlin; Royal Academy of Arts, London, 1984

Masters of Dutch Landscape: Masters of 17th-Century Dutch Landscape Painting, exhibition catalogue (ed. P. C. Sutton), Rijksmuseum, Amsterdam; Boston Museum of Fine Arts; Philadelphia Museum of Art, 1987-8

Mercury: The Hoogsteder-Naumann Mercury Journal (ed. A. Blankert), Zwolle

NACF: National Art Collections Fund

NHMF: National Heritage Memorial Fund

Pictures for Scotland: C. Thompson, *Pictures for Scotland. The National Gallery of Scotland and its collection: a study of the changing attitude to painting since the 1820's,* Edinburgh, 1972

Pictures from Gosford House: Pictures from Gosford House lent by the Earl of Wemyss and March, exhibition catalogue (arranged in conjunction with the Scottish Committee of the Arts Council of Great Britain), National Gallery of Scotland, Edinburgh, 1957

RA: Royal Academy of Arts, London

RA 1899: Winter Exhibition: Works by Rembrandt, Royal Academy of Arts, London, 1899

RA 1929: Exhibition of Dutch Art 1450-1900, Royal Academy of Arts, London, 1929

RA 1938: Exhibition of 17th Century Art in Europe, Royal Academy of Arts, London, 1938

RA 1952-3: Dutch Pictures 1450-1750, Winter exhibition catalogue, Royal Academy of Arts, London, 1952-3

RCAHMS: Royal Commission on the Ancient and Historical Monuments of Scotland

Redford: G. Redford, *Art Sales; a History of Sales of Pictures and other Works of Art,* 2 vols, London 1888

Reiss: S. Reiss, *Aelbert Cuyp,* London, 1975

Rembrandt 1991: Rembrandt, The Master and his Workshop, exhibition catalogue, Altes Museum, Berlin; Rijksmuseum, Amsterdam; National Gallery, London, 1991-2

Rembrandt 1991 Drawings and Etchings: Rembrandt, The Master and his Workshop, Drawings and Etchings, exhibition catalogue, Altes Museum, Berlin; Rijksmuseum, Amsterdam; National Gallery, London, 1991-2

Rembrandt Corpus: J. Bruyn, S. H. Levie, P. J. J. van Thiel and E. van de Wetering, *A Corpus of Rembrandt Paintings,* vol I–, The Hague, Boston and London, 1982– (Stichting Foundation Rembrandt Research Project); vol.1, 1625-31 (1982), vol.2, 1631-34 (1986), vol.3, 1635-42 (1989)

Richter: J.P. Richter *Catalogue of the Collection of the Marquess of Bute,* London, 1884

RKD: Rijksbureau voor Kunsthistorische Documentatie, The Hague

Rosenberg: J. Rosenberg, *Jacob van Ruisdael,* Berlin, 1928

Rotterdam 1991: Perpectives: Saenredam and the architectural painters of the 17th century (eds J. Giltaij and G. Jansen), Museum Boymans-van Beuningen, Rotterdam, 1991

RSA: Royal Scottish Academy, Edinburgh

Ruisdael 1981: S. Slive, *Jacob van Ruisdael,* exhibition catalogue, The Mauritshuis, The Hague; Fogg Art Museum, Cambridge, Mass., 1981-2

Scots Peerage: The Scots Peerage founded on Wood's edition of Sir Robert Douglas's Peerage of Scotland containing an Historical and Genealogical Account of the Nobility of that Kingdom, 9 vols (ed. Sir James Balfour Paul, Lord Lyon King of Arms), Edinburgh, 1905

Slive: S. Slive, *Frans Hals,* 3 vols, New York and London, 1970-4

Smith: J. Smith, *A Catalogue Raisonné of the Works of the Most Eminent Dutch, Flemish and French Painters,* London, 1834

Stafford Gallery Catalogue 1808: J. Britton, *Catalogue Raisonné of the Pictures belonging to the most honourable the Marquis of Stafford in the Gallery of Cleveland House,* London, 1808

Stafford Gallery Catalogue 1818: W. Y. Ottley, *Engravings of the Collection of Pictures of the Most Noble the Marquis of Stafford in London,* 4 vols, London, 1818

Stechow: W. Stechow *Salomon van Ruysdael, eine Einführung in seine Kunst,* Berlin, 1975

Sumowski: W. Sumowski, *Gemälde der Rembrandt Schüler,* 5 vols, Landau, 1983-90

Sutton: P. Sutton, *Pieter de Hooch,* Oxford, 1980

The Torrie Collection: The Torrie Collection, an Exhibition to mark the Quartercentenary of the University of Edinburgh, (ed. D. Macmillan), The Talbot Rice Arts Centre, Edinburgh, 1983

Thomson: D. Thomson, *A Virtuous and Noble Education,* exhibition catalogue, Scottish National Portrait Gallery, Edinburgh, 1971

Treasure Houses 1985: The Treasure Houses of Great Britain, Five Hundred Years of Private Patronage and Art Collecting, exhibition catalogue (ed. G. Jackson-Stops), National Gallery of Art, Washington DC, 1985

Tümpel: C. Tümpel, *Rembrandt,* Amsterdam, 1986

Waagen: G. Waagen, *Treasures of Art in Great Britain,* 3 vols, London, 1854

Waagen 1857: G. Waagen, *Galleries and Cabinets of Art in Great Britain,* 1857, supplementary volume to *Treasures of Art in Great Britain*

Walford: E. J. Walford, *Jacob Ruisdael and the Perception of Landscape,* New Haven and London, 1991

Wantage Catalogue: A Catalogue of Pictures forming the collection of Lord and Lady Wantage at 2 Carlton Gardens, Lockinge House, Berks and Overstone Park and Ardington House, London, 1905

Waterhouse Notebooks: E. K. Waterhouse's unpublished notebooks in the Library of the J. Paul Getty Museum at Wilshire Boulevard, Santa Monica, California

Wenley: R. M. G. Wenley, *The Lothian Picture Collection, History and Context,* unpublished M. Litt. thesis submitted to the University of St Andrews, May 1990

White: C. White, *The Dutch Paintings in the Collection of Her Majesty the Queen,* Cambridge, 1982

INDEX OF FIGURE ILLUSTRATIONS

PHOTOGRAPHIC CREDITS

AIC Photographic Services: Catalogue nos 3, 12, 27, 28, 33, 34, 38, 45, 60, 61, 62, 73

Bulloz: fig.49

B. Keiser: fig.46

Newbery Photographers: fig.35

Antonia Reeve: Catalogue nos 4, 9, 10, 13, 14, 17, 32, 35, 36, 43, 52;
fig. nos 3, 11, 36, 45,

Joe Rock: Catalogue nos 19, 40, 44, 56, 70

Tom Scott: fig.8

Rodney Todd White & Son: fig.35

Royal Commission on the Ancient and Historical Monuments of Scotland:
fig. nos 24, 25, 26, 27, 28, 29, 31, 33